“Israel Shamir dares to speak the t … Monster
Mendacity. His essays wound the … swim-
ming away from perfidious power … n Haifa
to Havana.”

—Prof. Julio Pino

“Israel Shamir is the most incredible man I ever met. Next to Israel Shamir, Norman Finkelstein and his *Holocaust Industry* is a tale for children. Reading him, one believes for a moment that St. Paul was right when he said there is no defence against the truth. The history of David and Goliath would not suffice to illustrate the combat of Israel Shamir . . . It makes one think of an ant tackling the largest monsters having ever traversed the surface of the Earth.”

—Manfred-Christian Stricker
Strasbourg

Flowers of Galilee

The Collected Essays of Israel Shamir

Flowers of Galilee

The Collected Essays of Israel Shamir

Israel Shamir

A Dandelion Books Publication
www.dandelionbooks.net
Tempe, Arizona

A Dandelion Books Publication
Dandelion Books, LLC
Tempe, Arizona

Library of Congress Cataloging-in-Publication Data

Shamir, Israel
Flowers of galilee: the collected essays of israel shamir

Library of Congress Catalog Card Number 2003116003
ISBN 1-893302-78-4

Front cover painting by Suleiman Mansour [Jerusalem] and front cover design by Husni Radwan [Ramallah]; back cover and book design by Amnet Systems Private Ltd. www.amnet-systems.com.

Dandelion Books, LLC
www.dandelionbooks.net

Preface

Make no mistake: were Shamir's articles read only for the qualities they share with other fine political comment, they would be invaluable.

Shamir's capacities for rigorous analysis, for dredging up neglected, uncomfortable facts, for getting to the scene of the action and observing it with clear eyes, take a back seat to none. Some have discovered this to their cost: he is a formidable polemicist as well.

Yet these are not the qualities that make Shamir's thinking and writing uniquely precious. It is rather his almost personal relationship to literature, history, and geography that makes one feel, reading his essays, a sense of revelation.

This manifests itself in several ways. First, people are never cardboard cutouts for Shamir: Palestinian, Norwegian, Malaysian, he takes them seriously. They are not idiots; they are not pathetic victims; they are not specimens. Their opinions, and their ways of looking at the world, matter to him. Shamir seems incapable of condescension.

Second, Shamir sees beauty in the land of Palestine; he loves it deeply. No one evokes its landscape and history as he does. Through his eyes the stubborn, bitter resistance of the Palestinians is more than understood; it is felt.

Third, Shamir is open but not an exhibitionist. He will speak of his feelings and his personal experiences, but he does not ask for our attention, our admiration, or our sympathy. He is courteous; he does not impose on his readers, but he gives us the tools to understand what he feels as he experiences the history through which he lives.

Fourth, his mind discovers illumination throughout our historical and cultural evolution. Like the people he meets on his journeys, the writers and thinkers of the past are very real to him, so he can see the world through their eyes: Only Shamir, for example, could speak of "a Palestinian Rob Roy." (And how typically modest, for Shamir to make so little of his own courage while praising a Palestinian sniper.) For his readers, there is some comfort in this. This world has not, after all, outgrown its artistic heritage. Through Shamir, it speaks to us, not from on high, but from across the table.

Finally, Shamir does not rest with self-satisfied moral condemnation. He is as keen to understand the criminal as the crime: "Sharon and his people are held together by a perverse form of love for the land. It is perverse because they imagine it is possible to love Palestine without Palestinians. But Palestine is not a dead object, it is a live country and Palestinians are her soul." In this and many other passages, we sense almost an informed pity for those whose narrow-mindedness complements their cruelty, and this helps to prevent us from sinking to their level.

Some of Shamir's work is speculative in the very best and most honorable sense of the word. Shamir does not engage in wishful thinking, nor does he speculate where hard work would make more progress. On the contrary, he insists on recognizing that hard work can take us only so far, and that we need to go further, to explore possibilities without which we can have no direction, nor any hope to sustain us. We have to imagine, not only a future, but a present we cannot see. For him religion is not a crutch, but the home of a steady compassion and integrity which humans can emulate, but to which they can scarcely aspire. Literature, history and even economics display, each in their own way, the human soul, and therefore a key to understanding human beings in their most prosaic and pedestrian adventures.

And Shamir's approach works: you may sometimes come away from his writings unconvinced, but rarely uninspired. Shamir writes, not to glorify himself, but to support us in our best impulses. Even when we disagree, we are pushed to new and better ideas than we had before.

I do not know Shamir personally, but I suspect he likes to break taboos. He insists on going after truth wherever he can find it, whether it is in the most respectable journalistic sources or the *Protocols of the Elders of Zion*. Many are understandably appalled at this practice; they see Shamir as a renegade, taking his place among the 'holocaust revisionists' and the traditional anti-semites. What they do not see is that, while traditional anti-semites use stories such as the *Protocols* to condemn an entire people, Shamir uses them to condemn a Jewish Elite, in whom he sees a moneyed clique as dangerous to other Jews as to gentiles. More important, they do not see, or forget, how joyously, even lovingly Shamir takes pride in the courageous Jews who resist Israeli crimes. Even among his opponents, Shamir sees humanity as well as guilt, in Jew and gentile alike. His real enemy is no race or creed, but mean-spiritedness. Thus Shamir has said that, while Barak is an "arrogant and unpleasant man," Sharon is a soldier, far more likely to sit down and share a plate of hummus with his Palestinian foes.

Of Shamir it can be truly said, as it is falsely said of so many, that he hates the crime, not the criminal. It is in this ability to prize humanity, through all the twists and turns of bitter experience and sharp dispute, that Shamir teaches by example his most valuable lesson.

—Prof Michael Neumann,
Trent University

Contents

Introduction

The essays collected in this book were written during the years 2001–2002, in the old Palestinian port-town of Jaffa, on the shore of the Eastern Mediterranean, during the Second Intifada, or Intifada al-Aqsa, but they are not limited to events in Palestine. The war in the Holy Land is presented as the centre-stage of the world-wide struggle of ideas, against a backdrop of such momentous modern developments as the growing influence of American Jewry ("the Rise of the Jews"), the decline of the Left, the ascent of Globalisation, the first steps of the anti-Globalisation movement, and the outbreak of World War Three with America against the Third World. It is a daring attempt to tie together various political, theological, military and social threads, and to formulate fresh concepts that provide people with new tools for analysis and action. While seeking the Liberation of Palestine, the author pursues another, broader goal as well: that of the Liberation of Public Discourse.

These essays attempt to prove the inherent connection between two liberation movements: The Liberation of Palestine can be achieved by the victory of the world's exquisite mosaic over the creeping grey of Globalisation, by the victory of the Spirit over Mammon, by the democratisation of public discourse, by the elimination of the wealth gap, and in the dialectic unity of Left and Right. But it could happen the other way around: if and when Palestine becomes free, discourse will be liberated, and to boot, Globalisation will be defeated and incomes equalised. In these essays Palestine is perceived as a model of the world. There are forces at work here that strive to eliminate its native population, to destroy its churches and mosques, to ruin its nature. But there are opposing forces as well, material as well as spiritual, new and old, and they attract the best men and women into the fray of the battle for Palestine.

It is a story of love as well. I (let's leave this neutral 'author' aside) am deeply in love with the Holy Land, its meagre streams and olive trees, and with its people, the native and adoptive Palestinians. This land is still able to connect Man and Spirit by virtue of its ancient shrines and unique nature. The fall of the Holy Land would create a point of no return for mankind and signify Man's total enslavement by the forces of domination. Our victory will set the world free.

Israel Shamir
Jaffa

Why I Support the Return of Palestinians

Palestine is not a dead object. It is a living country. Palestinians are her soul. Palestine is what Palestinians are re-creating in real time, in the same way that France is what the French created and re-create every day. It is a vast confusion of mind to presume that one can love France and abhor the French. What kind of France would there be without a French soul? Only silly tourists from rich countries, pestered by beggars, prefer to stay in reclusive posh hotels where they can enjoy the country without encountering the natives. It is like loving a beautiful lady but hating her character. To love a country and wish away her inhabitants is a kind of necrophiliac's romance.

The late Russian thinker Lev Gumilev described a country as the symbiosis of its people and landscape. Palestine and the Palestinians are inseparable. The peasants and their olives and springs of water, and the domes of their ancestral sepulchres on the hill-tops, need and complement one another. The Palestinians are not an obscure, mean folk. They created the Star of Ghassul, composed the Bible, built the temples of Jerusalem and Mount Grizim, the palaces of Jericho and Samaria, the churches of the Holy Sepulchre and Nativity, the mosques of Haram a-Sharif, the harbours of Caesarea and Akka, the castles of Monfort and Belvoir. They walked with Jesus, defeated Napoleon and bravely fought at Karameh [the legendary 1968 battle at a refugee camp in Jordan, where Al-Fattah repulsed an Israeli attack]. In their veins the blood of Aegean warriors, Bene Israel, David's heroes, the first Apostles of Christ and the Companions of the Prophet, Arab riders, Norman Crusaders and Turkmen chieftains blend in unique composition. Its spark is not quenched: the poetry of Mahmud Darwish, the wisdom of the late Edward Said, the perfect olive oil, the fervour of prayers and the valiant courage of Intifada prove that.

Without the Palestinians, Palestine dies. Her rivers run poisoned water, the sources dry out, the hills and valleys are disfigured, her fields are worked by imported Chinese while her sons are imprisoned in a ghetto. The idea of a separate Jewish state has collapsed. During the last ten years the mad policies of the Israeli government imported over a million Romanians, Russians and Ukrainians, and Thai and African labourers. Some of them claim Jewish descent: Peruvian tribes, Indians from Assam and endless refugees from the Soviet Union have moved in. Now the Jewish Agency plans to import a Lembda tribe from South Africa in order to ensure the Jewish character of the state. Paradoxically, those who still hold true to the Jewish traditions are isolated in the Jewish state, as was the late Dr. Yeshayahu Leibovich, or imprisoned like the Moroccan Jewish Rabbi Arie Der'i.

Fantasy about a Jewish ingathering has collided with reality. We must end the delusion. Let the sons and daughters of Palestine come back and rebuild Suba and Kakun, Jaffa and Akka. Instead of consecrating the Green Line, let us erase it and live together, the children of Palestine, of the first settlers, of the Moroccans and Russians.

We should live in one state, and not only because of the blatant failure of Oslo. The very idea of partition is wrong. We can follow the example of New Zealand where European incomers live together with the native Maori; the example of Mandela's South Africa; the example of the Caribbean where children of Spanish settlers, African slaves and native Amerindians, have blended into a beautiful new race. Let us tear up our Declarations of false Independence and write a new one of mutual dependence and love.

Part I

The State of Mind

I

The steep slopes of Wadi Keziv in Western Galilee are walled by squat local oaks and thorny bush. On the streambed, oleanders and cypresses look into shallow ponds formed by its springs. I like this secluded canyon. On hot summer days, one can hide in a deep and intricate cave and laze in its cool, clear waters, waiting for deer and hoping for a nymph. On cooler days, you can climb up a steep spur that rises from the depths of the gorge. It is called *Qurain*, the 'Horn' in Arabic, hence the Arab name of the valley, Wadi Qurain. Astride the spur, the Crusader castle of Monfort raises its donjon high and gazes towards the distant Mediterranean Sea.

This place stores many memories. The 12th century Zionists, Teutonic knights of St. Mary, fortified the castle on the spur and called it *Starkenberg*, the Mount of Strength. The name and the remote location didn't help: they were defeated by Baibars, the Arab paragon of valour, who allowed them to depart with their weapons and honour for Acre.

The stony path leading to the spring was the meeting-place of the enchanting characters of *Arabesques*, an exquisite novel by the Palestinian writer Anton Shammas. Shammas, a native of nearby Fassuta, is probably the only non-Jew in the world who writes his novels and poems in Israeli Hebrew.

Farther west, the brook of Keziv flows into the sea at the ruins of az-Ziv, the Christian village destroyed by the Jews in 1948. In this village, in the long-gone 1920s, a local Palestinian girl was visited by another local Palestinian woman, the Virgin. In other words, it is a typical place in the unusual land of Palestine.

These days you can roam the canyon all by yourself. It is as empty of people as the rest of the countryside. The land of Palestine is in trouble, the deepest trouble since the black nights of 1948. People do not venture down here anymore, leaving the canyon to its lean and wiry wild boar. Walking downstream I spotted a few of these gracious animals, so different from their domesticated cousins. It was only outside the gorge, on the plain of Acre, that I came upon a human presence. A few Thai or Chinese peasants were working the fields of a local kibbutz. A middle-aged kibbutznik sat in the shadow, overseeing their work. I joined him for a smoke and a drink of cold water.

He was the epitome of a good Israeli: large, sunburned, with a friendly smile, bushy moustache and brisk talk. Fifty years ago, he, or rather his predecessor, a fighter with the Jewish Storm Troopers, the Palmach, seized the lands of az-Ziv and expelled its peasants to Lebanon. Thirty years ago, he worked the stolen land with his own hands. Now, he oversees the Thais working this land. Very soon, he told me, he will go to New York to visit his son, a web designer. While he is away, some Russians from Maalot town will be hired by the kibbutz to oversee the Asian workers. Not many Jews are interested in working the land, or even in overseeing Thais working it, he said. The kibbutz hopes to get a building permit, build housing and sell the real estate. It is a valuable site, near Naharia and Acre, and it will fetch a premium price despite the crisis, he said.

I shook hands and bid farewell to him, to the sweaty Thais, to the green fields, to the Mountains of Lebanon to the north which conceal the refugee camps where the original inhabitants of as-Ziv dwell, and to the Galilee Mountains to the east which hold the Russian town of Maalot, where I woke up this morning.

II

Maalot is a brand new town for the brand new citizens brought to Israel after the collapse of the Soviet Union from Kharkov and Minsk, Riga and Bukhara. There are not many young people, but plenty of babushkas, elderly Russian ladies. I asked for the City Hall in Hebrew, but I might have spoken Chinese with the same effect. Maalot speaks Russian, reads Russian newspapers, watches Russian TV and eats Russian pork sausage with Russian beer. What made these ordinary Russians seek the light of Zion?

In Russia, as in the US, there are probably at least 20 million people entitled to become Israeli citizens. One does not have to be Jewish. If your daughter from a first marriage was married to an adopted grandchild of a Jew, you can go to Israel with your new family. The former Soviet republics are in dire straits: their workers get no salary for months, so many families send their old folk away to Israel, where they get a few thousand dollars upon arrival, a small pension and public housing, if they are lucky.

The majority of arrivals have had no exposure to Judaism or Jewish culture in Russia, nor are they interested in it. Their Israeli ID cards bear the inscription 'ethnic origin and religion uncertain'. They are not considered 'real Jews' and their dead are buried beyond the fence, on a special plot for those of "dubious origin." After the dreadful explosion in the Dolfi discothèque it created a visible problem: the religious undertakers refused to bury the dead Russian girls in a Jewish cemetery, even as the Israeli government was bombing Palestinians "to avenge Jewish blood."

In the blessed air of the Holy Land many of them look for spiritual and religious revival. Judaism attracts but a few, while others turn to the Church for comfort. It is a risky enterprise: by Israeli law they can be deported for their belief in Christ. They gather and pray away from prying eyes, but on holidays they throng the Holy Sepulchre of Jerusalem, the Nativity Church of Bethlehem, St. George of Lydda and St. Peter of Jaffa.

In 1991, when Russia's future was exceedingly opaque, Israel received a great infusion of young blood from there. Israel-supporters in the US media carried out a two-pronged campaign: they warned of forthcoming pogroms, and also promoted the idea of a beautiful, easy life for immigrants in the US. Whole issues of *Newsweek* and *Time* concentrated on the neo-Nazi Pamyat group and rampant anti-Semitism. At the time, as a reporter for *Haaretz* from Moscow, I interviewed Pamyat leaders. I found this sinister organisation to number about as many members as the Flat Earth Society. Still, a nice Russian Jewish film-maker and his wife came to our countryside house to arrange for protection in case of a pogrom. I tried to calm them down, but I could not fight the mighty media machine alone. Ten years later, I met a Russian Jewish lady writer in Jerusalem who told me she had initiated the rumour of pogroms herself.

"You Israelis should erect a monument to me," she said.

"Certainly," said I. "Any particular reason?"

"I brought you a million Russians: I announced on *Moscow Echo* radio that there will be a pogrom."

I hadn't the heart to disabuse her: her announcements would have had no effect if Israel's American friends hadn't amplified them. Anyway, the frightened and seduced Russians rushed for visas to the American embassy, and at that moment Israel requested the US stop granting them visas. The US gates were closed, and this mass of people on the move was forced to go to Israel.

They had a hard time, for the Israeli elite subjected them to the unique Israeli method of "de-development," (as one might call it), a method already tried out on Oriental Jews and Palestinians. The Israeli media described them as a bunch of criminals and prostitutes; they were required to sign contracts and promises in Hebrew which they did not understand; their specialists were set to sweeping streets or picking oranges. Their rate of divorce skyrocketed; and their children were pushed into drugs. In 1991, Israel ceased to employ the Palestinians from the occupied territories, and the former elite of Russia was expected to take their place in low-paid menial jobs. But sheer mass allowed the Russians to create their own state-within-state, complete with its own media, shops, and mutual assistance. The Russians survived, and figured out the game. The clever ones went back to Moscow, the adventurous left for the US, the peaceable ones departed for Canada. Since then, Israel has been getting mainly old folks, single mothers, and the desperately unemployed.

The Russians are a nice, hard-working but confused community. They hardly understand where they have landed, and incessantly try to compare their situation with that in Baku or Tashkent. Perusal of Russian newspapers shows people at a loss. One writer demands that Palestinians be castrated in order to solve the demographic crisis. Another blames everything on religious Jews, describing them as "blood-sucking parasites." A third accuses the Oriental Jews of failing to live up to his expectations. They are being taught a brief version of the modern Jewish faith and its single commandment: "Thou shalt hate Arabs."

Now Prime Minister Ariel Sharon intends to import another million "Russian Jews." It is possible: if the American Jewish friends of Israel will put a harder squeeze on Ukraine, ten million Ukrainians may suddenly recover their "Jewish roots."

There are dozens of townships like Maalot, apparently produced by cloning. Why else would they be so similar, nay, identical? It is built in a beautiful place, a short walk to the Wadi Keziv, of which townspeople have never heard. Even their children, after ten years in Maalot, do not venture into the surrounding countryside. They spend their time around a pub in the centre of Maalot, dreaming of much better pubs in Haifa.

III

But that was yesterday. I hitched a ride to Nahariya, and from there, I took a train homewards to Jaffa. The train carried a few Africans, probably illegal immigrants judging by their shy demeanour. A Romanian building-team was gulping beer and burping loudly. They were imported from their impoverished East European land to build the houses for elderly Russian immigrants. In Israel like in California, the Jews do not want to take construction jobs.

A Jewish Israeli lawyer in black yarmulke leafed through papers in his semi-opened briefcase. A group of Moroccans discussed the closure of the Acre steel plant and their slim chances of finding other work. The crisis is deepening, one of them said. It is as bad as in 1966. An Israeli soldier, blond and armed, talked Ukrainian with its fricative aitches to his corpulent girlfriend. Under her admiring gaze he expanded upon his own heroic fight against multitudes of Arab terrorists.

I recalled myself at his age: a young paratrooper pleased with my red boots and Uzi sub-machinegun. I was in training not far away from the places we were passing now, in the remote hollow of Marj Sannur, embraced by mountains from all sides. It was early spring, a time when the highlands of Palestine are as beautiful as any place in the Mediterranean. Sometimes I recognize its lovely features in the bare hills around Les Baux de Provence, or in the olive-studded descent from Delphi to the sea, as one imagines spotting one's beloved in a crowd of strangers. A snow-white thick fog covers Sannur valley in the early mornings, turning every day into a White Christmas. As the fog lifts, green grass glitters under the blossoming almond trees on the rise. Chilly February winds blow their pinkish petals, and they flutter about like snowflakes, covering the stony ground.

Through the wire fence of the army camp I saw a peasant tilling his olive trees. He was my father's age, a broad-shouldered, strong, suntanned man wearing white head gear. I lowered my gun and greeted him; he replied with a greeting and put down his tools. We sat down on either side of the fence. I took out cigarettes and he gingerly picked one from the packet with his calloused hand. We spoke of olive oil and of thyme, the main local products, of the holy tomb of Sheikh Ali on the hilltop, of a spring of water in the valley. On my day off I changed into civilian clothes and went to his village. I was invited for a cup of strong Arab coffee with a cardamom seed a-float. Neighbours came to greet me, the stranger, and we carried on an interminable Eastern conversation, asking in turns whether one is content with one's life, children, and work. Apparently, they were pleased with their hard but satisfying peasant lives. For them, Israelis were just another set of foreigners, come in the wake of the Jordanians, British, Turks, Crusaders, and Romans. They harboured no hate, and displayed just an ordinary casual curiosity about a stranger. My host's wife served greenish olive oil, punchy thyme and freshly baked village bread, a common Palestinian meal.

We walked to the nearby well. Lukewarm pure water poured out of an opening in an elaborate centuries-old masonry bearing an Arabic dedication. Beyond the masonry, a hundred-yard tunnel, work of my host's ancestors, was cut into the face of the cliff. Palestinian springs need permanent attention; they quickly silt up unless their water course is cleaned regularly. It was the job of his son Elias to take care of the spring, but he is in an Israeli jail now, he observed matter-of-factly. Elias had brought home a Communist newspaper, somebody informed the authorities, and they offered him a choice, exile or jail. Palestinians can be detained without a trial: it is called 'administrative detention'. Formally, it is limited to six months, but it can be extended as often as the military want. Elias preferred jail in his homeland to exile.

Envy is an ill feeling, but I envied him, this Elias from Sannur. I envied his place in this serene landscape, and his devotion to it. Why wasn't I born in this house near the cool spring, beside the vineyard, on this goat-trodden slope? Why have I found myself locked up in an urban ghetto "for Jews only"? I am entitled to live in a similar village in Greece or Provence, but not in Palestine. And that is not because of Palestinian lack of hospitality; they would not mind my buying or renting a place in this village. But the Jewish state would not allow me, or any 'Jew' to live in a Palestinian village. A Jew may reside only in a segregated settlement "for Jews," where a Palestinian can come only as a menial worker. Outside, a Jew must go armed. A tourist from abroad can wander in Palestinian areas freely, but the Jewish state jails an Israeli Jew who goes there, unless he is participating in some armed intrusion.

History has come full circle: by locking Palestinians out we locked ourselves in. The very idea of Jewish emancipation was to get out of the ghetto, and now we have forced ourselves back into it. We really do not deserve this. We Israelis are less 'Jewish' than anybody you know. Quite a few people have demanded that we be described as 'Israeli' or 'Hebrew' in the identity cards we have to carry at all times. But the High Court has forbidden this: we have to have "Ethnicity: Jew" stamped into our documents.

Our fate was forced upon us as it was upon the Young Frankenstein of Mel Brooks. In this horror spoof, Dr. Frederick Frankenstein (Gene Wilder), the American professor, descendant of the Monster's creator, inherits his ancestral castle in werewolf-bountiful Transylvania. He is a rational modern American, but the locals expect him to continue the unpleasant traditions of the infamous Frankensteins. He tries to fight his fate, insists on being called American way, 'Fronk-en-steen', but the loyal family servants stubbornly stick to 'Frank-en-schtain'.

Unwittingly, the brilliant Jewish film-maker created the fable of the Jewish state reborn. The founders wanted to begin their lives anew, to become 'Israelis', another of the tribes of Palestine. They dropped Jewish names, dropped the Jewish language, dropped the synagogue and Talmud, and learned to work the land and use the gun. They were joined by many people who never knew their way to a synagogue in the first place. But the Jewish fate descended upon them all and returned them to the ghetto.

And then we began to fulfil the predictions of our enemies. We treat non-Jews as animals, assassinate their leaders, kill their children by the hundreds, forbid them freedom of movement and worship, refuse them employment and confiscate their land. We shoot at churches and besiege mosques. We launder stolen cash for crooks from Peru or France, export torture tools to Latin American dictators, provide refuge for Miami mafia dons. We squeeze American, German, Swiss and Polish coffers. We have the highest rate of interest, four times that of the US, and the biggest social gap in the advanced countries. In short, we fulfill every expectation of an anti-Semite. We even elected a professional goy-killer for the Prime Minister.

The train rolled through Nathania, and I thought of the hundreds of thousands, maybe millions of Americans, Jews and Christian Zionists, who lobby, pray, support and pay . . . no, not for the Jewish state, built as they imagine on the ruins of Palestine. That would be bad enough. But the reality is worse. I thought of the millions of Palestinians, rotting in refugee camps and jails, dispossessed, expelled—victims not of Jewish greed for land, as they imagine, but of something worse: of a ghost.

IV

The Jewish state is a virtual state that is quickly losing all remaining connection to reality. This ghost of a state kills people and collects money in America; it continues some nefarious existence, like the legal term, 'estate of the deceased'. Its fields are worked by imported guest-workers, guarded by imported Russians and Ethiopians, explained away by the Israeli professors who forever lecture in American universities, and by brave generals on the lookout for a big kickback from American weapon-makers. Unemployment grows daily, vital services are on strike; the tourist industry has collapsed months ago. Hotels are boarded up and other branches of the national economy are close to collapse. Israelis buy flats in Florida and Prague, while houses in Israel go begging for buyers. Sharon's desire to punish the Palestinians has the sting of punishing one's own left hand. Palestinians and Israelis are intertwined and integrated, and their separation kills the economy of both.

From far away America, Israel looks like a giant nuclear state, the great ally of the United States, a Jewish state that is a source of pride for American Jews. A visitor leaves our shores with a strong feeling of our identity and prosperity. Only we, permanent residents, know that it is a cardboard sham. Israel is collapsing. Its active citizens emigrate in despair, even as the generals complete the destruction of the country. A cruel fate befalls the native Palestinians: a ghost kills them, that spiritless body that walks the corridors of Congress and the deserts of the Middle East in a zombie-trance.

For the sake of this spectre, important American Jews squeeze pennies from their employees and countrymen, cut down on pensions to the old and on assistance for children, reduce the health and education budgets, dry up help to Africa and Latin America, build improbable coalitions with notorious racists of the ilk of Pat Robertson and Jerry Falwell, demand the destruction of Iraq, bless the bombing of Afghani refugees, keep Afro-Americans in their ghettos, undermine their host society and make enemies for themselves and for America. These deeds would be vile enough even if they accomplished something of value to someone, but they are worse because they are useless.

The Zionist experiment has practically collapsed. It can run for many years to come on life-support, brain-dead and vegetating. It can kill some people, maybe even start the next world war. But it cannot come to life.

The Jewish state of Israel is a state of mind, a projection of the American Jewish mind. The worries and problems it articulates are American Jewish problems. For Israeli 'Jews' there is no need for segregation, war, or subjugation of natives. We eat no bagels with lox, speak no Yiddish, read no Saul Bellow or Sholem Aleichem, and avoid synagogues. We prefer Arab food and Greek music. My neighbourhood has seven pork butchers to a kosher one. Forty per cent of Tel Aviv weddings are performed outside the Jewish framework: young Israelis prefer to go to Cyprus to get married, just to avoid contact with Rabbis. Tel Aviv is the gay capital of the Middle East, though according to Jewish law, gays should be exterminated. Sometimes I wish our great supporters, American Jews, would give us a stern and sober look and walk away in disgust. It is just a case of mistaken identity. We are not what they think we are. We need their protection against the Gentiles as much as fish needs a pair of waterproof boots.

V

I reach my home in Jaffa the Maritime, a dilapidated town of crumbling pink mansions built by Arab nobles and traders. My neighbours are out: the imam has gone to his small mosque, the Moroccan family next door is busy fixing old cars in the garage, the Armenian guide has taken his guests to Jerusalem. Another neighbour, a Russian painter, comes to borrow a lump of sugar. We live together, one of the few desegregated communities, in a small sliver of the land between the road and the sea, a remainder of Jaffa of old.

Salinger's Esme would love this place of squalor. Bulldozers of the Jewish state have torn down every second house and given the town its jagged look. They have also dumped building waste on the seashore, in preparation for big real estate development. They intended to build another Maalot here, but the Intifada tension upset their plans for "Judaising" Jaffa. It has remained semi-ruined and unkempt, for local people are not permitted to repair their houses.

Still, it is a good place, reminiscent of Durrell's *Alexandria Quartet*. Drug dealers' big Cadillacs cruise its unpaved streets; kids in long galabie dresses play at the corner; the bells of St. Anthony Catholic church blend with those of St. George Orthodox church and with the call of the muezzin from the nearby Ajami mosque; fishermen carry their catch to the seashore restaurants for the diners from Tel Aviv; Palestinian women crack seeds and chat outside their homes; the smell of fresh falafel comes from market stalls; ten stray cats stare down a king-size rat; the French ambassador returns to his residence; a film crew shoots a Beirut scene.

Jaffa was once called the Bride of the East, and it competed with its neighbours, Beirut and Alexandria. Surrounded by fragrant orange groves, this city of one hundred thousand inhabitants boasted the first cinema in the Levant, and housed the headquarters of European companies. Americans and Germans built their red-roofed houses on its outskirts, and in 1909, the East European Zionist Jews established Tel Aviv farther to the north.

On an evil day in November 1947, the UN, under heavy pressure from the United States government, decided to divide the land we shared. It was not necessary, not even asked for. The religious Jews were against it; enlightened Jews from Germany, such as Buber and Magnus, were against it. Palestinians were against it. We could live together as brothers, and eventually create a new nation, uniting Jewish fervour and Palestinian love of the land. But American Jewish organisations supported Ben Gurion and Golda Meyer, advocates of partition. Expectedly, it did not work out well.

Three-fifths of Palestine was given over to the Jewish rule, and two-fifths was supposed to remain Palestinian. Even in the new Jewish state, the native Palestinians were a majority. Jaffa was supposed to remain Palestinian. It was a rough deal for Palestinians, but the new Israeli leaders thought it not rough enough. They besieged and shelled Jaffa, till its population shrank to five thousand out of the pre-war population of one hundred thousand. The rest escaped to Gaza and Lebanon, to the refugee camps where they live to this very day.

The mansions and palaces of Jaffa were repopulated by Arab refugees from the destroyed villages in the hinterland and by Bulgarians, a nice Balkan folk, imported to fill the vacuum. A small part of the city was gentrified and became the Old Jaffa, a neat and exclusive museum piece, the preferred abode of kitsch painters and antique dealers. Our Jaffa remained a lingering memory of One Palestine, Complete, the Paradise Lost. It attracted a few artists, who moved into the ruined mansions, and lived alongside the local Palestinians, sharing their hopes and sorrows.

Before the Intifada, a refugee from a Gaza camp would come to visit his lost home. It was a horrible situation, for present dwellers and for the true owners, since the owners are not allowed to return. My neighbour, a nice Bulgarian lady made a noble attempt to return her house to the expelled Palestinian family, but the government did not permit it. It is hard to repay a loan, people say: you take somebody else's money, but return your own cash. You borrow for a while, but return for good. It is even harder to return stolen goods. Still, sooner or later it has to be done. There was a good opportunity for solving the problem in 1967, when Palestine was reunited.

Many good people see the Six Day War as the "mother of all the troubles." Without it, Jews and Palestinians would have been able to live separately, they say. But separate states will not bring the refugees back from Gaza into their homes in Jaffa, and I think it would be wonderful to see their return happening. Besides, I think it is better for us to live together—we are rather complementary types, and person-to-person manage together very well. That is why I do not mind the 1967 conquest *per se* (as distinct from the occupation military regime). We could return the refugees, settle old quarrels and live together in equality, children of Palestine and newcomers. We would not be an exclusive Jewish state, but we would be happy and content people.

There was once an illusion of a choice: a Jewish state, or a democratic state. We chose neither, for we disenfranchised natives and disdained democracy, and our Jewishness is, at best, a virtual idea. If American Jews did not bribe Israelis on a large scale, we would just forget about the Diaspora and dissolve into the hospitable Middle East as another of its tribes. If they continue to bankroll us, we shall oblige them with a small show of Jewishness.

We are master-sellers of illusion, and as long as there are buyers, we shall provide the goods. In 1946 a group of dedicated men from all over the world came to Palestine under the aegis of the UN. They were sent to prepare the ground for the partition of the land. Among other places, they visited the southernmost kibbutz, Revivim in the arid Negev. There, they came upon a wonderful flowerbed of roses, anemones, and violets adorning the front of the kibbutz office. In their report, the members of the delegation expressed their amazement and declared: "Jews make the desert bloom, let them have the Negev."

As they left, the kibbutz youngsters went out and pulled the now-withering flowers out of the sand. They had bought them fresh that same morning in the Jaffa market and planted them as a stage-prop for the UN visit. They had learned the trick from the Tel Aviv municipal employees, who had rammed trees into the sand next to their Mayor's house to make a favourable impression on Winston Churchill. This small show had the Negev with its two hundred thousand Palestinians transferred to the Jewish state. Most of the natives were expelled across the newly drawn border, to the camps of Gaza or Jordan. It was cruel and useless: even now, fifty years later, the Negev south of Beersheba has a smaller population than in 1948.

VI

To replace the Palestinians, Mossad persuaded the Jewish communities of North Africa to leave their homeland for Israel. The North African Jews are a fine but broken people. They became worried for their future, as the French began to withdraw from North Africa. Only the strongest personalities made the right choice and remained with their people: Moroccans, Tunisians, Algerians and Libyans. They had no reason to regret it: now they are ministers and advisers to kings. Others, seduced by the great charm of French civilisation, rejected the phantom of the Jewish state and moved to France. They gave the world Jacques Derrida and Albert Memmi.

Those who moved to Israel supply 75% of its jail population. Their income is a fraction of that of European Jews. Their scientists and writers have little chance of tenure in Israeli universities. Their self-esteem is exceedingly low. It is no shame to be a Moroccan, the Israelis say, and quickly add that it is no great honour either.

The North Africans were brought in, sprayed with DDT lice-killer and placed in refugee camps that soon became the towns of Netivot, Dimona and Yerucham. They are still there, in the stark desert outpost towns full of unemployment and misery, drawing social benefits and nursing a deep dislike of the Ashkenazi Jews who lounge in Tel Aviv's cafes. Some Oriental Jews came to the conclusion that the Holocaust was a fit punishment for the hated AshkeNazi, as they spell it. Israel is probably the only place on earth where you are liable to hear, "It's a pity you didn't burn in Auschwitz." Even the great

Sephardic luminary Rabbi Obadiah Joseph recently explained the Holocaust in terms of the European Jews' sins.

A somewhat confusing slogan, "AshkeNazis to Auschwitz," adorned my Russian friend's Jerusalem house for quite a while. He complained to police but received no response. The lowest positions in the police force are occupied mainly by Oriental Jews, and they have no time for Russians' complaints. They were once in the position of the Russians, but they have been de-developed even more thoroughly.

Whenever an Oriental Jew moves upwards, the system arranges his downfall. Popular Oriental politicians who could possibly threaten the Ashkenazi elite's dominance find themselves in jail. Arye Der'i, a brilliant Moroccan minister who brought his party from none to seventeen seats in the 120-strong parliament, is still in jail after a ten-year-long police surveillance produced some doubtful charges against him. His predecessor Aharon Abu Hatzera, son of a Moroccan Jewish sainted Rabbi and minister, was sent to jail for financial irregularities that are quite ordinary in our Middle Eastern country. Powerful Iraqi Jewish publisher Ofer Nimrodi spent over a year in prison before his trial, but was quickly released afterwards, when the charges against him collapsed. Yitzhak Mordecai, a Kurdish Minister of Defence with an eye on the Prime Minister's post, was set up as a sexual abuser. The Moroccan Professor and Minister Shlomo Ben Ami was made a fall-guy for Sharon's infamous Progress to Temple Mount.

While the Oriental Jews are unhappy, the kibbutz is not managing too well either. Ari Shavit of *Haaretz* published a beautiful reportage on Negba, the famous and well-established kibbutz in the Negev. It has been a long time since that kibbutz was able to celebrate the birth of a child. The kibbutzim Negba and Ruhama have become old folks' homes, their youth long gone to Los Angeles.

Thus the conjuring tricks of Revivim, the conquest of Negev, the expulsion of the Palestinians and the destruction of the Moroccan Jewish community succeeded separately, but ultimately failed altogether. It could be expected: evil and immoral deeds cannot bear good fruit. Zionist leaders dreamed of making Palestine as Jewish as England is English. They failed. Palestine is as Jewish as Jamaica is English.

We children of Jews have a great luxury of choice. An Italian is an Italian; Italian is his language, his culture, his faith, his tradition, his art and his landscapes. He cannot be separated from Dante and Giotto, from Tuscan villages and Madonna, from pasta and Venice. Being a Jew is a matter of choice. An Italian Jew can become an Italian. An American Jew can be just an American. Not many descendants of Jews practice our old religion; even fewer speak Hebrew or other Jewish languages. The majority have parted with the traditional Jewish ways of making a living.

Personal choice remains in the hands of each individual. A rich and powerful American of Jewish origin may feel about his Jewishness as he feels about any other hobby. Maybe he collects stamps, or plays golf, but he probably would not create a Philatelist State on the ruins of Monaco (this Principality prints beautiful stamps), or endow his golf club with the newest F-16. If American Jews would forget about us for ten years, we would sort out our problems and reach a new natural equilibrium in Palestine. If they have too much money and desire to influence, let them spend it on improving the lot of their Afro-American neighbours.

They actually did it before the advent of Zionism. A Chicago businessman Julius Rosenwald, the owner of Sears, Roebuck and Co., supported schooling for Afro-Americans in the 1920s to the tune of $2 million a year. (A Zionist emissary complained: "It's hard for us to accept the idea that one of ours gives his money to backward niggers.") This tradition could be restored. It is said, charity begins at home, and their home is America.

The land of Palestine is being ruined now, in front of our very eyes. Its beautiful old villages are bombed to oblivion; churches are emptied of their flocks; olive trees are uprooted. Such ruin has not befallen the land since the Assyrian invasion 2700 years ago. Nothing can comfort us in the face of this great destruction. Certainly, the people responsible for it—whether Israeli killers or their American supporters—will be damned forever.

Still, a wry irony of history will remain as a footnote in the books: the Jewish leadership committed these crimes in vain, and failed to achieve its purpose. Even if the last Palestinian were to be crucified on the hill of Golgotha, even that would not breathe life into the virtual Jewish state of Israel.

Olives of Aboud

[Written in June 2001, as Israeli forces began mass destruction of olive trees in Palestinian territories.]

As the CIA-brokered cease fire went into effect, I received an anxious call from the village of Aboud, on the western slopes of the Samarian Hills. The village was raided by the army, and two men were shot. Today I went there, to see the village and to feel the cease fire.

Aboud is surrounded by the new Jewish settlements from all sides. A brand new Jewish road leads to the area. It forks off to Aboud some three miles away from the village, and there the road is blocked by cyclopean heaps of earth. We tried our luck at the other end, with the same result. Eventually we found a narrow dirt track the peasants broke through this morning, and drove in.

Aboud is one of the prettiest Palestinian villages, strongly reminiscent of Tuscany. Its time-mellowed stone houses grow on the gentle hills. Vines climb up their balconies, leafy fig trees shade its streets. The prosperity of this well-established village is seen in the spaciousness of the mansions, in the meticulously clean roads. The old men sit on the stone beaches in a small and shady walled enclosure, like the aldermen of Ithaca gathered by young Telemachus. That is the biblical 'gate of the city', or a *diwan*. Kids bring them coffee and fresh fruits. Local people are not the refugees of Gaza and Deheisheh; here, as in a time warp, one can see the Holy Land as it should and could be.

Three millennia-old Aboud received the faith of Christ from Christ himself, says the local tradition, and there is the church ready to prove it, one of the oldest on earth, built in the days of Constantine in the 4th century, or maybe even older, as some archaeologists claim. The church is a dainty thing, carefully restored and well taken care of. The Byzantine capitals of its columns bear the image of cross and palm branches. They recently discovered a plaque in old Aramaic script immured in the southern wall of the church.

Aboud has more than one church: there is a Catholic, a Greek Orthodox and an American-built Church of God. There is also a new mosque, as Christians and Muslims of the Holy Land live together in great harmony. On December 17th all of them, the Muslims and the Christians, go to venerate the village patron saint, St. Barbara. She was a local girl who fell in love with a young Christian and was baptized. It happened in the rough days of Roman emperor Diocletian, and she was martyred in the persecutions. The restored oldest Byzantine church of

St. Barbara is still seen on a hill a mile away from the village. At the foot of the hill, there is her burial cave, and there the peasants light their candles and ask their wishes to be fulfilled.

It is a good place to understand the complete lunacy of the prevailing Jewish view of Palestine as the 'land without people' sparsely inhabited by the Arab nomad latecomers. Archaeologists have proven that this village was never destroyed or abandoned since the time immemorial, and our eyes agree with it. Age-old olive trees cover the hills, confirming the deep roots of Aboud and providing it with olive oil, its main staple food and source of livelihood.

Just outside a village, two giant American-built Caterpillar bulldozers were slowly devouring the olive trees. They were huge, covered on every side by armour plates. Like moving fortresses, they seemed impregnable, towering above the landscape like the mechanical monsters of the Evil Empire attacking Ewocks in *Star Wars*.

The peasants stood on the heaps of earth blocking the entrance to the village and watched the machines destroying their livelihood. They could not walk towards them, as they were not allowed to leave their village, their prison. A tent and a few soldiers with a machine gun were perched on the hill above the entrance to keep the people in. Last night, on Sabbath eve, they opened fire on the villagers who ventured out, and wounded two men. The rest ran back in to safety. Then the army went in, driving through the village in their jeeps, met by the stones of the kids. The Jewish settlers and soldiers sprayed windows and roofs with their bullets and drove away, apparently feeling their Shabbat duty fulfilled.

I crossed the line of siege and approached an Israeli officer in a jeep, a wide American Hummer, who oversaw the devastation. "Why do you do this?" I asked. "Don't you know there is a cease fire?"

"Tell it to Arik (Sharon)," he replied. "We are just following orders." But he and the other soldiers, and the bulldozer drivers were not despondent about these orders. These age-old trees meant nothing to them, as the village and two millennia old Church, and the people meant nothing to them. Just something to be devoured and destroyed.

Palestine never was the deserted land the first Zionists claimed they found at their arrival. But it will become one, unless we stop these machines.

The Green Rain of Yassouf

Most soothing, tender and sensual to the touch, picking olives is akin to telling beads. Oriental men wear 'mesbaha' beads of wood or stone on their wrist, reminding of prayer and calming down frayed nerves, but olives are much better: they are alive. Olives are tender but not fragile, like peasant girls, and picking them has a touch of comfort: nothing can go wrong. Olives detach from the branch without fear and remorse, smoothly enter the palm and roll down into the safety of the ground sheets stretched to catch them.

It is harvest time, and every tree on the terraced slope is attended. Whole families are out, under the trees and up on ladders, forming a vast pane suitable for Pieter Bruegel the Elder's brush. We pick olives together with the Hafez family, five or six of us; standing below the thick branches of the broad stretched-out craggy old tree, fingering this live rosary of our lady, the sweet land of Palestine. Hair of ripe Minnesota corn, sky-blue eyes—unexpected for a stranger, but not unusual features in these places—laughing lips, seven-and-a-half-year old Rowan, young daughter of sturdy shrewd Hafez, climbed to the treetop, and the olives she picks fall down on our hands, shoulders and heads like green rain. Before going to the next tree, we lift the edges of the sheets and the dense stream of olives fills the bag. A light grey foal grazes nearby, gathering strength for his turn: he will carry the bags into the village above the valley.

We pick olives in Yassouf, a blissfully obscure village in the highlands. Its tall and spacious houses, built of soft and light stone, witness its old prosperity, created by the relentless toil; broad staircases lead to the flat roofs, where they lounge warm summer evenings and enjoy the breeze from the distant Mediterranean. There are plenty of pomegranate trees, and in a thousand year-old description of Palestine, by a contemporary of William the Conqueror, the village of Yassouf is mentioned for abundance of pomegranates and for wisdom of a learned sheikh al-Yassoufi who made himself a name in remote Damascus.

It is paradise, or not too far from it. We arrived yesterday at the village, built on the ridge between two valleys. Above the village, a hilltop retains the old sanctuary, *bema*, one of the high places where ancestors of Hafez and Rowan witnessed the miraculous communion of celestial and earthly forces. The villagers often go there, to seek spiritual comfort, as did their forefathers, the people of the small principality of Israel: we are in the Holy Land, and for its people, a daily miracle of faith goes hand in hand with the daily portion of toil. The kings of the Bible tried to ban these local bema places and monopolise the faith in the centralised, easy-to-tax-and-control temple, but ordinary people preferred their local sanctuaries for daily worship. The peasants preserved the two-tier structure of local and universal faith, similar to the fusion of Shinto and Buddhism in Japan. They are religious but not fanatical. They do not wear the Islamic garb; women do not cover their pretty faces. These two aspects, local and universal, survived millennia and blended together. The temple became the gorgeous Umayyad Mosque of al Aqsa, and on the high place of Yassouf, people pray to its God.

These are venerable old trees; they have heard many an oath and seen many a secret in their long lives. A miraculous shallow well that never runs dry even in the hottest July, but rests in rainy winter; a holy tomb which probably changed names many times since the days immemorial, and now is called Sheikh Abu Zarad. There are ruins from the first days of Yassouf, well over four thousand years ago, and since then the village has not been deserted. In the biblical heydays, it belonged to Joseph, the strongest of the tribes of Israel. When Jerusalem fell under the sway of the Jews, these lands and these people retained their own Israelite identity, and eventually accepted Christ. The domed shrine at the top still calls for prayer. In February, the hilltop turns white with almond blossoms; now it is fresh and green, and affords a superb view of the rolling hills of Samaria.

But we came too late for the view from the hilltop, as sun sets early in the autumn. Instead, in the dusk we went down to the village spring, the throbbing heart of the village. Water quietly gushed from the opening in the rock, flew into the covered tunnel and poured out to give life to the gardens. We sat under the fig trees, and they spread their broad trefoil leaves like Japanese Noh dancers raise their fans, in one incessant gracious movement. In the moonlight, between the leaves, giant black butterflies took wing: they are bats, dwellers of the nearby caves, emerging in the dark to drink water and feast on the fruits

Usually, a talk at the spring flows freely and joyously like its water. There is no better place to sit and chat with the villagers about the harvest, the good old days, the children, and the last essay of Edward Said reprinted in the local paper. The farmers are not boors: some of them have travelled the big world, from Basra to San Francisco; others attended a small university branch in the vicinity. Their political education was completed in an Israeli jail, an almost unavoidable stage in the upbringing of a young man in our land. Their Hebrew, acquired there, or through long work in the Israeli building industry, is fluent and idiomatic, and they are keen to practice it with a friendly Israeli.

But now our hosts were gloomy, and worries did not move away from their sad eyes. Even at the dinner, as we feasted on rice with nuts and yogurt, they were rather pensive. We knew the reason: a new dread had nested on the bare hilltop and spread its webbed wings over the village. The army had confiscated the lands of Yassouf for military purposes, and transferred the site to the settlers.

They built a concrete prefab monster entwined by barbed wire, interspersed with guard towers, and appropriated the name of the nearby Apple spring. The settlement was not willing to stay put on the land stolen a decade ago from the people of Yassouf, but kept encroaching on the entire countryside, throwing out its metastases onto surrounding hills, eating up the olive groves and vineyards.

The farmers did not dare to go to their own fields, for the settlers were harsh men with guns, quick to draw. They shot at the villagers, often kidnapped and tortured them, set fire to their fields. They had to keep the farmers away for five years, and after that, according to the Ottoman law they found in the old books, the fallow land would revert to the state. To the Jewish state. The state would then give the land to the Jewish settlers. Meanwhile, they tried to starve the farmers.

The village was cut off from the world by trenches and mounds of earth six feet high. Even small unpaved roads, barely suitable for a four-wheel drive, were truncated by the army. The village became an island. The British ambassador to Tel Aviv recently said that Israel had turned Palestine into one huge detention camp. He was wrong: instead of one camp, they created a New Gulag Archipelago of Palestine. The Nobel-winning author of *Gulag*, Alexander Solzhenitsyn, claimed that the original Russian Gulag was designed and managed by Jews; his claim was questioned and denied by Jewish organisations. But there is no doubt who designed the Gulag of Palestine. Cars cannot leave or enter the island of Yassouf, and visitors are forced to leave their cars before crossing on foot. The nearest city, Nablous, or Neapolis of old, is eight miles distant, but four hours' drive and many humiliating checkpoints away. It took us ages to reach Yassouf, as we drove through numerous checkpoints and roadblocks, and we had to abandon our car half a mile away from the village, stopped by an insurmountable siege dam.

On the way, devastation was everywhere: the olives on both sides were torched or uprooted, as if this venerable tree was the foremost enemy of the Jews. And in a way it was: olives are the chief provider and intercessor for the Palestinians. Their main meal consists of flat oven-baked bread and olive oil, spiced by thyme and enlivened by a bunch of grapes. Their kings and priests of old were anointed with its oil. The sacraments of the church, a precious gift of Palestine to mankind, are but consecration of olive. In baptism, the Palestinians are anointed before the full immersion, and their skins retain the soft suppleness of olive oil. Oil is used for the rites of wedlock, and for the last rites, confirming the inseparable bond of the people and their land. The famed explorer of the Qumran scrolls, John Allegro, ruined his reputation by penning a heretical book identifying Jesus Christ with the hallucinogenic mushroom. If and when I shall decide to follow him, I shall compare the Olive Tree of Virgin Oil and Our Lady the Virgin, the supreme mediatrix of Palestine.

As long as there are olives, the peasants of Palestine are invincible, and that is why their adversaries turned their rage against the trees. They cut them whenever they could. In the last years, eighteen thousand beautiful olives, old giants and young saplings, were uprooted. The settlers stopped the farmers from harvesting, ambushed them on the way home and robbed them. We, the International and Israeli friends of Palestine, came, like Seven Samurai in the old Kurosawa film, to help the peasants pick their olives and protect them from the robbers.

Of the many good things one can do on our good Earth, helping Palestinians is the best and most pleasant one I know of. Kibbutz can't compete with it. Young kibbutzniks are usually boring and aloof, while old kibbutzniks are, well, old. In kibbutz, you have the company of other foreigners, or none. Palestinians are so friendly, so open, so ready to talk to you. The Internationals bask in their friendliness, live in enchanted villages, see the warm blue sky over the incomparable landscape of Palestinian hills, and enjoy the fabulous hospitality of the peasants. And if occasionally they are shot at by the settlers or the army, it is just a small price for all the fun, an additional divertissement, courtesy of the IDF. That is, after all, why the Samurai are needed.

The people who help Palestinians are different from kibbutz volunteers. They are more heterogeneous, from a 19-year-old Uppsala student to a Brighton housewife, from a Georgia Reverend to a Boston teacher, from a French farmer to an Italian MP. They are united by their feelings of compassion, of natural justice, and, yes, by their daring. They work in the shadow of Israeli tanks, and protect the olives and men with their own bodies. The harvest in the Samarian mountains is a joy but not for timid souls. We were to experience its rough side without further delay.

We were picking olives, filling the bags with the green gold, when suddenly a Jeep drove down the stony ruddy road and screeched to a halt near us, raising a cloud of dust; behind it was a bigger vehicle, an army troop carrier full of soldiers. A single man jumped out of the jeep, aiming an automatic rifle M-16 straight at the child on the tree.

"Go away, you bloody Arabs," he yelled in Brooklynese. He lifted a rock and hurled it into the nearest group of workers. A farmer, who could not turn away, was hit and nursed his hand.

"Come one step closer and I'll shoot!" he shouted when Laurie tried to talk to him. He was large, unkempt, ferocious, intentionally working himself into a high degree of hysteria.

"Don't even touch the olives!" he screamed at the peasants.

From around the road bend, three men appeared running. They seemed like nothing you ever saw. To their shaven foreheads, black boxes were strapped by narrow black belts; black belts crisscrossed their bare arms. Jews put on the phylacteries, as this setup is called, for a morning prayer, but on these young men they looked like the amulets of a warlike tribe. They wore dark trousers and dark tee shirts; white shawls with black stripes flew behind their backs. Their rifles were pointed at us. They looked possessed by some strange demon, these young men in Jewish ritual dress and with their ideas from the Book of Joshua. I was not astonished when one of them pulled out a long curved blade. The scene reminded me of the recent movie, *The Time Machine*, with the sudden appearance of ferocious Morlocks and their onslaught on bucolic Eloi.

They pushed the women and cursed the men, their eyes burning with hate. Timid peasants, the Palestinians recoiled. A Samurai unarmed, I tried to reason with the attackers.

"Let the farmers harvest their olives," I beseeched. "It is their trees, it is their life. Be good neighbours to them!"

"Go away, you Arab-lover," hissed one of them. "You support our enemies. It is our land. It is the land of the Jews; the Goyim do not belong here."

In more peaceful circumstances, I would laugh: these disturbed young men from New York wished to expel the proper and rightful descendents of the people of Israel from their ancestral land. Never mind the incredible silliness of a two-thousand-year-old claim in the country where five years of absence voids all claims. Never mind that their 'Jewish' ancestors probably hiked from the Eurasian steppe and never saw Palestine. Never mind that even the Jews of old never lived and hardly visited the land of Israel, between Bethel, Carmel and Jezreel. Soon the Romanian guest workers from Bucharest may expel the people of Florence, claiming direct descent from ancient Rome. But their rifles were no laughing stock.

"Why do you burn olives, are the olives your enemies, too?"

"Yes, the olives of our enemy are our enemies. And you are our enemies, too!" he shrieked. "Anti-Semites!"

This word works magic with the Americans. Whenever an American is called an 'anti-Semite', he is supposed to prostrate on the ground, and swear eternal love and fealty to the Jewish people. I know it because daily I receive letters from people who were called 'anti-Semites' for their support of Palestine and they could not cope with it. I provide them with psychological first aid: after being punished for anti-Soviet activity, and condemned for anti-American opinions, an anti-Nomian lover of anti-Quity, I take the anti-Semitic label in my stride. Nowadays, if one is not called an anti-S, this means one is clearly in the wrong, sandwiched between Sharon and Soros.

Like 'Arab-lover', or 'Nigger-lover', an 'anti-Semite' is a label that smears its user by association. It is often used by the settlers, by Foxman the spymaster, Kahane the racist, Mort Zuckermann the *USA Today* owner, Conrad Black the husband of Barbara Amiel, Sharon the mass murderer, Richard Perle the warmonger, Tom Friedman the shyster, Shylock the loan-shark and Elie Wiesel the pay-as-you-cry holocaust weepy. It was used against T.S. Elliot and Dostoyevsky, Genet and Hamsun, St. John and Yeats, Marx and Woody Allen, and it is a much better company to be in. Still, our Americans hesitated for a moment, our good Israelis began to explain their position, but it was a good English girl from Manchester, Jennifer, who proved the superiority of Brits and saved the day by a brusque "fuck you."

The barrel of M-16 rifle made a curve and pointed at her. The soldiers looked at the goings on with interest. I turned to them.

"Stop them! They're aiming their guns at us!"

"They haven't shot you, yet," answered the sergeant.

The soldiers would not intervene as long as the Morlocks had their way, but the moment we engaged them, the awesome armed might of the Jewish state will be visited upon us. The Morlocks knew it too: they smashed a camera of Dave's, pushed Angie, poured insults at the girls, and threw stones.

"Won't you stop them?" I appealed to the soldiers.

"Sorry, pal. Only police may deal with them," replied the officer. "But we can arrest YOU, if you insist."

The army takes care of the Palestinians, and the police state will be visited upon us—this simple ruse is one of the more inspired inventions of the Jewish genius. Probably they borrowed it from the European settlements in China, where they had different police forces and different sets of law for Europeans and for Chinese. That is why the Morlocks may do what they want. The Palestinians were visibly upset: they are not fighters, but farmers with women and children harvesting their olives; they did not come there to die. Not yet, anyway. The settlers kill the villagers for sport or for fun, with and without provocation. For the last week, they murdered a few men who dared to harvest their own olives. If the villagers would defend themselves, would just dare to raise their hands at a Jew, they would be all slaughtered and their village wiped out. But the olives had to be harvested, and the stand-off continued.

"All the troubles are caused by the bloody settlers," called out Uri, a good Israeli, who kept off the settler thugs to the right of me. "Without them, we would live peacefully. We would visit Yassouf with passports, like tourists. It is them, the settlers."

Indeed, it was easy, almost obligatory to hate the vicious young men, who destroyed crops and starved villages. This particular settlement is known as a bulwark of the Kahanist or Judeo-Nazi creed, as the late Professor Leibovich called it. They celebrated the assassination of Prime Minister Rabin; they worshipped Baruch Goldstein, the mass murderer from Brooklyn; they published the banned book of Rabbi Alba that openly proclaims the religious duty of the Jew to exterminate Gentiles. They were so evil it required no effort to hate them and to agree with Uri.

But as I looked at the blank faces of the soldiers, a memory came back from the days of my childhood. The hoodlums do not go around robbing strangers: they would send forth a little kid to relieve you of the burden of your wallet. If you'd push the kid away, they would fall on you like a ton of bricks for molesting the youth. It was quite pointless to hate the small kid since he was sent by the bigger hoods.

These young crackpots were sent by the bigger hoods, too. That is why the soldiers did not bat an eyelid when the settlers attacked the farmers. It was the division of labour: the thugs starved the peasants, the army protected the thugs, and the government endorsed it. While the army guns kept down the Palestinians, the US army kept down Iraq, the only state in the region that might be able to provide the balance of power, and the US diplomats wielded their veto in the Security Council. And beyond them, one could see the biggest hoods that did not care for olives, peasants or soldiers. On one end of the chain of command, there was a crazy Brooklyn settler with an M-16; on the other end, Bronfman and Zuckerman, Sulzberger and Wolfowitz, Foxman and Friedman.

And somewhere between, were we, the Israelis and the American Jews, who duly voted and paid taxes and supported the scheme, because without our support, Wolfowitz would have to conquer Baghdad single-handedly and Bronfman would have to burn the olives himself.

Still, each man and beast has its pest, and we had to deal with our own. The farmers of Yassouf and their international supporters, that's us, stood our ground and did not flinch. Police arrived and consorted with the settlers. In a while, a tall, smiley, cropped-hair liaison officer came down to us.

"You may pick your olives, but work in the bottom of the valley, where the settlers won't see you and get annoyed."

It was a minor victory, a compromise, but it didn't matter. We would harvest olives, that was the bottom line. We rolled down the valley, its slopes reinforced by numerous terraces, and the harvest continued. Down here, the olives were smaller and fewer. For three years, the peasants were prohibited from working their fields, although the olive needs a lot of care. Normally, peasants plough around the trees every year with an old-fashioned plough pulled by a donkey: the terraces are too small for a tractor. Otherwise, winter rains run off the land and fail to reach the roots. The terrace walls need a lot of maintenance, too. But it couldn't be done now, for the farmers prudently avoided taking up their hoes and spades, dangerous weapons in the eyes of their well-armed tormentors.

Again the small streams of green and black olives ran down our hands to the ground sheets. They grow on the same tree, as God made them different, some green and some black, Hussein told us, but they give the same oil. It was God's sign to us humans: we are made different, and it is a good thing, making the world more beautiful and various, if we remember our common humanity.

We laid out our lunch under a big olive tree. Umm Tarik, the only woman in many-coloured national dress, brought big round bread straight from the oven. It was liberally sprinkled with olive oil, as were the balls of white goat cheese. Hassan passed around a zir, a Palestinian amphora full of cool water from the Apple spring. The zir was cold and wet outside, covered with minuscule drops of dew. It is made of porous clay, and it sweats profusely, cooling the drink inside. With years, the pores clog up, and then it can be used to store wine or oil.

"I miss Ramat Gan (a suburb of Tel Aviv)," said Hassan. "Before the trouble, I used to work there, painting houses. It was good work, and my Yemenite employer was a decent man, he treated me as a member of his family. Sometimes I would overnight there, and have an evening stroll in Tel Aviv by the sea. Now for two years I have not left the village."

Everybody had good memories from the days they worked in the big cities in the West of Palestine, and brought some cash back home. It was a mutually convenient arrangement for the newcomers and the peasants, profoundly unequal but bearable. All over the world, farmers and peasants work for a while in the cities when their land does not call them for harvest or planting. For local people, "the Jewish" Tel Aviv and Ramat Gan were no more foreign than "the Arab" Nablous or Jerusalem, as the country is but one unit. Palestine is a small country, and Yassouf is in the very middle of it, thirty miles to the sea, and thirty miles to the Jordan border. The industrial cities of the seaboard were built well before the state of Israel came into being; they were built by the labour of Yassouf's peasants, and they were rightly theirs. Not exclusively theirs, but theirs as well. The arrangement was undone, when the Jews began their land snatch.

"Do you see the settlement?" Hussein asked us. "My father sowed his wheat on that hillside. At first, they took the land, and later, they locked us up in the village. Now we have but little land, and no work."

"The story of the Holy land repeats the story of God's promise," said the Reverend. "Christ said: 'everybody is chosen.' The Jews replied: 'sorry, only we are.' Now, Palestinians say: 'let us live together in this land.' And the Jews reply: 'sorry, it is for us only.'"

"There should be an independent Palestinian state," said Uri, "with its own flag, and a real border. Barak cheated everybody, as he intended to split your lands into few bits and pieces. We should go back to '67 borders, and then things will be fine."

"Do you know how the Talmud rules on partition?" I asked. "Two men found a shawl, and each one said, 'it is mine.' They came to a judge, and the judge asked them, "How should I divide the shawl?" The first one said, 'divide it 50-50, equally.' The second one said, 'no, it is all mine.' The judge said, 'there is no disagreement about one half of the shawl, both agree it should belong to the second man. I shall divide the remaining half of the shawl equally, so the first man, the seeker of justice, will have one fourth, while the second man, the egoist, will have three quarters.' That is the Jewish approach. Maybe Palestinians should learn it, too."

Kamal added some broken twigs into the small fire to make coffee. He was an elder man, respected by the village, an important man in the local politics and beyond. In 1967, a young man of 20, he parted with his newborn daughter for he was sentenced by the Jews to forty years of prison for his belonging to the Resistance. He emerged from the eternal shade of Ramleh Gaol when his daughter was twenty-one.

"We also have a story of dividing a find," said Kamal. "It is the story of a woman who found a child and brought him up. Then another woman came in, the natural mother of the child, and demanded him back. They came to be judged by Sheikh Abu Zarad, and the sheikh said: 'I shall cut the child into two halves, and give each of you one half.' One woman said, 'good, let us split the child.' But another woman said: 'I won't agree to carve up my child.' And the sheikh awarded the child to the second woman, as she was the real mother."

My cheeks were burning with shame. Kamal did not tell me anything new, but, trying to wisecrack, I forgot the true wisdom of Solomon's judgement, and he, a real descendent of Bible heroes, reminded me of it. The Palestinians, like the true mother, did not agree to partition. History proved they were right: Palestine can't be divided. The peasants need the industrial cities to work between the seasons and to sell their oil; they need the seashore of the Mediterranean, splashing a few miles away from their home, they need the wholeness of the land as one needs two hands and two eyes.

The settlers were not monsters, but thoroughly misled men. Like me, they read too much of the Babylonian Talmud, too little of the Palestinian Bible. They felt the incredibly strong pull of the land, and it attracted them to the hills of Samaria. They were looking for union with the enchanted land of Palestine, and they loved it with the weird love of necrophiliacs. They were ready to kill the land in order to possess it. They did not understand the local ways, and earned their living by collecting money in America. Instead of hatred, I felt sorry for the settlers. They had a unique chance to make peace with their neighbours, and with the land, and they blew it. By ruining the land, they prepare their new exile with their own hands. The true mother will have the child, and therefore the Palestinian victory is inevitable, for the judgement of Solomon is but a parable of Divine judgement.

"But where are the good Jews?" the reader hastens to enquire. "For the balance, for the political correctness, for our comfort, please show us some good Jews! There are not only settlers, but Peace Now and other movements friendly to Palestinians."

Yes, there is a difference between the brutal settlers and their supporters, on one side, and the liberal Israelis, traditional Labour voters, on another side. The Jewish chauvinists want Palestine without Palestinians. They would import Chinese to work the fields and Russians to guard the Chinese. They were an obviously repelling lot.

The liberal Israelis could envisage a sort of common future, where Palestinians could leave their watched-over Bantustans and come to work in Tel Aviv equipped with a working permit, to be harassed by police, to work without social security, below minimal wage, underpaid by their employers. The idea of brotherly equality, not of some heavenly sort, but of ordinary fair play towards the native son of the land was as foreign to them as to the settlers.

They would give them a flag and an anthem, but take away their land and their way of life.

Both kinds of Israelis were united in their rejection of Palestine. They sang of a "new dress of concrete and asphalt for the old Land of Israel." The liberals dreamed of creating a high-tech sliver of America, and did not need the hills of Samaria. The chauvinists wanted to erase the very memory of Palestine, and re-create the kingdom of hate and vengeance.

And few, very few of us understood that we have been given a rare chance to learn from the Palestinians. With our East European arrogance, we came to teach and change them, but we should learn and change ourselves. It was not enough to help them; we, the conquerors, have to adjust to the superior civilisation of the conquered. It was done before us: the victorious Vikings adjusted to the ways of England and France, Russia and Sicily; the triumphant Greeks of Alexander became Egyptians and Syrians, Imperial Manchu became Chinese. It has to be done for our sakes as well, since otherwise we are doomed to re-create a ghetto for us and a ghetto for them.

Take an ant and he will build an anthill. Take a Jew and he will create a ghetto. Take a Palestinian . . . Well, my friend Musa invited his old father from a Samarian village to his new home in Vermont, and his old father began to build terraces to plant olives.

The Palestinians can't imagine themselves without the land and its unique way of life. Thousands of years ago, after the Great Mycenaean Drought was over, their ancestors formed a symbiosis with the olive, and the vine, and the donkey, and the small mountain springs, and their shrines on the hilltops. This single complex of the landscape, the people and the Divine spirit was the great achievement of Palestinians, and they carried it through centuries and preserved it to this very day. If they are undermined, mankind will lose its anchors and crash on the rocks of history. We were much privileged that they accepted our small help.

In the evening, we trekked back to the village, to the spacious mansion of Hussein. It would not seem out of place in Cannes or Sonoma. On its great balcony, we sat in the straw chairs made by the Beidan villagers. The friendly but dignified cats of Hussein jumped on our laps, while his shy daughters brought in sweet mint tea. Folks came in to chat with the strangers as they are wont to do in the remote villages. Small kerosene lamps stood on the tables and banisters: the Israeli overlords refused to connect the village to the electric grid. Even that was good, for we watched the full moon of October slowly floating in the darkening skies and shining on the terraced hills, and on the roofs, and on the dull armour of a Merkaba tank on the hillside, his guns trained on the village, and on the silent ancient knurled olives of Yassoof.

Ode to Farris
or
The Return of the Knight

[This was written in the summer of 2001, in an attempt to create a different image of the Palestinian struggle: to awaken admiration instead of pity.]

Nobody is allowed to enter or leave the Gaza Strip. It is surrounded by barbed wire, its gates are locked, and even with the proper documents one cannot visit this largest high-security prison on earth, home to over one million Palestinians. The Israeli army, once a fabled fighting force, has become a mere prison guard. The IDF's tactics were formulated back in the 1930s: "You do not have to kill a million: kill the best, and the rest will be cowered." This method was first deployed by the British with the help of their Jewish allies during the Palestinian uprising of 1936. Since then, thousands of the best sons and daughters of this land, the potential elite of the Palestinians, have been exterminated. Once again, the Israeli army is being used to implement the same master-plan of "cooling the restive natives" by routinely shooting potential rebels.

Their job is easy: the strongest and biggest army in the Middle East, a major nuclear power, has all the weapons in the world, while the jailed Palestinians have only stones and light guns. Recently, the Israelis intercepted a boatload of weapons on its way to Gaza. The Army boasted of a major victory, but expressed "concern." They have reason for concern. Since 1973, the Israeli army has rarely had to worry about return-fire. The Jewish soldiers have become used to soft jobs. They prefer to shoot unarmed kids.

Gaza is a sci-fi reality, reminiscent of some *Prison Planet* B-movie, its barbed wire fence guards a secret: the unbroken will of its people. It is a B-movie set, but its men and women are first grade.

This secret message came out of Palestine embodied in a thirteen-year-old boy, Farris Ode. He was the youthful Palestinian David we saw confronting the Jewish Goliath on the outskirts of Gaza in the immortal photo by AP photographer Laurent Rebours. Farris the Fearless threw his stones at the armoured monster with the grace of St. George, the beloved saint of Palestine. He confronted the enemy with the nonchalance of a village boy chasing away a

David and Goliath

ferocious dog. The picture was taken on the 29th of October, and a few days later, on the 8th of November, a Jewish sniper murdered him in cold blood.

He leaves behind a picture of a hero, a poster to be placed next to Che Guevara's, a name to be spoken in the same breath with the name of Gavroche, the brave rebel kid from the barricades of Paris in Victor Hugo's novel, *Les Misérables,* a symbol of the unvanquished, irreducible human spirit. He emerged from a different time, a time when heroism was not a dirty word, when men went to war ready to fight and die for a noble cause. Symbolically, his first name means 'Knight', and his surname, 'the Return of'. His image truly evoked the idea of the return of the gallant knights of yore. This spirit is totally foreign to cheap commercial hedonism, the main ideology of our days, abundantly supplied by American pop-culture. Farris's legacy is a sign of the failure of Israel's master plan. This young rebel was born under Israeli military occupation and he died defying the soldiers of the IDF.

This message of hope was not immediately understood by friends of Palestine, for we have become accustomed to the idea of Palestinian suffering and martyrdom. In our writing, we unconsciously copycat the somewhat effeminate approach of presenting 'our side' as unfortunate victims deserving of compassion and pity. The last thing we should feel towards the Palestinians is pity. Admiration, love, solidarity, hero-worship, even envy, but not pity. If you pity them, you might as well pity the three hundred warriors of King Leonidas who fell defending Thermopylae, or the Russian soldiers who stopped Guderian's tanks with their bodies, or even Gary Cooper in *High Noon*. Heroes should not be pitied: they are an uplifting example for us.

At first, we failed to correctly place the image of Farris. The narrative of suffering called for a picture of a crouching Muhammad Dorra, dying in front of our eyes, a child-companion to the little naked Vietnamese girl running out of the fiery hell of napalm.

The image of the Knight Who Came Back, Farris Ode belongs to a different set of icons: that of a hero. Its place is next to that of the Marines on Iwo Jima, or in a church next to his countryman, St. George. After all, the warrior-saint was martyred and buried in the Palestinian soil, not far from Farris, in the crypt of the old Byzantine church in Lydda.

The adversaries of the Palestinians understood this reality better than their supporters. The American Jewish-dominated press spared no effort to erase the memory of Farris, as they surely do not want heroic passions being spread around. MSNBC.com ran a silly contest for the most important Picture of the Year that offered a choice between Dorrah the Martyr and some dog pictures. (They always give you a choice, and it is always the wrong one, whatever you choose.) The dogs were promoted by the Israeli consul in LA and voted for by many Israeli supporters, while the partisans of Palestine rose to vote for Dorrah. The really important picture, the icon of Farris, was not offered to the public.

But that was not enough. The *Washington Post* sent its own correspondent in Palestine, Lee Hockstader, to debunk the fallen boy's memory. This AIPAC-run rag could depend on Hockstader. His reports should be studied in schools of journalism, in a course on disinformation. When the Israeli army tanks and gun-ships blasted defenceless Bethlehem, Hockstader wrote: "In the Biblical (he would not mention 'Nativity', would he?) town of Bethlehem, Israeli soldiers and Palestinians fought with tanks, missiles, helicopters, machineguns and stones."[1] I suspect that Hockstader's history of WWII would narrate a tale where the US and Japan fought with nuclear bombs.

Hockstader duly justified Israeli raids on a civilian population with lines such as: "Israeli army spokesmen say that the raids are limited and essentially defensive. But the Israeli government takes a broader view, noting that the raids give local military commanders flexibility against an elusive enemy." He takes "a broader view" of Israeli actions, but the Palestinians in his reports are just mad terrorists: "The Palestinians have been threatening to exact a price for what they regard as a war of aggression. A representative of the Islamic Resistance Movement known as Hamas, called for further suicide bombings and mortar fire against Israel."

A fellow Hockstader-watcher, Francois Smith, wrote on the Web: "I am offended that this guy thinks I'm dumb enough to believe him. Watch out for Lee Hockstader. I think he has an agenda."

Well, he certainly has: the agenda of enforcing Jewish supremacy and smearing Palestinians. Debunking Farris fits this agenda perfectly. Hockstader went to Gaza and reported that Farris was a bad boy who did not obey his mommy and daddy, that he played truant at school, that he was an 'adolescent daredevil', who actually wanted to be killed, and a merciful Jewish sniper just fulfilled his wish. Hockstader missed nothing: the kid was shot while lifting a stone, and therefore had to be killed; his posthumous fame was 'the hullabaloo over his death'; and anyway, his mother received "a $10,000 check from President Saddam Hussein of Iraq."

Hockstader had played it safe. If he had dared to infer that the settler parents of the killed infant in Hebron wished their child dead, or just mentioned a fat check her parents received from the hands of the butcher of Sabra and Shatila, if he would refer to the Israeli reaction as 'hullabaloo',—Hockstader would not have made it out of Israel alive, and Katherine Graham, the *Washington Post*'s owner, would be repenting his deed to her last day.

Jews have successfully intimidated their enemies, and not only by the magic of words. Lord Moyne, British Minister of State in the Middle East, dozens of British soldiers and officers and hundreds of Palestinian leaders were assassinated by Jews in their drive for supremacy in the Holy Land in the 1940s, until the terrorized Brits sailed away from Haifa Bay on May 15, 1948. Even today, two peace activists and men of the cloth in San Francisco, a Catholic priest Labib Kobti and a Jewish Rabbi Michael Lerner, receive death threats from Jewish terrorist groups—and take them very seriously.

The Palestinians are rather peaceful peasants and city folk. They know how to tend olives and vines, how to make a *zir*, a jar that keeps water cool even in the hottest *hamsin*. Their beautiful stone masonry adorns every corner of Palestine. They write poetry and venerate their holy tombs. They are not warriors, certainly not killers. With astonishment and disbelief they stare in the mirror of a Jewish-dominated press and see their faces obscured by a bloody terrorist's mask. Nevertheless, these peasants are able to give us all a lesson in heroism, whenever an enemy tries to snatch their land. Palestinians proved their valour many centuries ago, in the legendary days of Judges, when their ancestors battled the overseas invader.

In the 1930s, a fervent Russian Jewish nationalist and founder of Sharon's political party, Vladimir Zeev Jabotinsky wrote (in his native Russian) a historical novel, *Samson*, elaborating on the Bible story of the suicide bomber who killed three thousand men and women (*Judges*, 18:27) and died with the enemies. A few years ago, this novel was published in Israel in a modern Hebrew translation, and a *Davar* newspaper reviewer noted an interesting aberration.

For Jabotinsky, the Brits were the modern Philistines, while the Israelites became the Jews. But for a modern Israeli reader, the novel reads as a glorification of the Palestinian fight against Israeli rule. The highly civilized Philistines with their superior military technology, invaders from overseas, hedonistic dwellers of the Coastal Plain and belligerent intruders in the Highlands reminded the reviewer of modern Israeli Jews. While Samson's people, Banu Israel, the natives of the Highlands, certain of their deep roots, confident of the inevitable victory of their attachment to the soil over the military might of the invader, reminded him of modern Palestinian Highlanders.

It makes sense, as the Palestinians are the true descendants of Biblical Israel, of the indigenous people who accepted Christ and remained in the Holy Land forever, while those who rejected Christ were doomed to wander until they see the error of their ways. The Israelis know it. In the genetic labs of Tel Aviv, the researchers of the 'Jewish DNA' proudly parade every result that tenuously confirms the blood-relation of Jews and Palestinians. They know that our Jewish claim to the proud sobriquet of Israel is at least dubious. Like Richard III, we seized the title and the crown, and, like Richard III, we feel insecure while the legitimate heirs are still alive. That is the psychological explanation of our inexplicably cruel treatment of the native Palestinians.

The Israelis want to be Palestinians. We adopted their cuisine and serve their falafel and hummus as our own ethnic food. We adopted the native cactus, *sabra*, growing at the site of their ruined villages, as the name of our local-born sons and daughters. Our modern Hebrew language came to life with hundreds of Palestinian words. We just need to ask their forgiveness, embrace them as long lost brothers and learn from them. That is the one ray of hope coming out of the present darkness.

As modern Israeli archaeological studies have made clear, three thousand years ago the Highland tribes (the B'nai Israel of the Bible) eventually achieved a *modus vivendi* with the Coastal 'people of the sea', and together, these sons of Samson and Delilah became the progenitors of the Bible bards, of Christ's apostles and of modern Palestinians. The advanced Philistine technology and the Highlanders' love of our parched land combined to achieve the spiritual miracle of ancient Palestine. It is not impossible, and it is highly desirable, that history will repeat itself, and the glorious image of young Farris fighting the tank will blend with images of King David and St. George in the minds and schoolbooks of our Palestinian children.

Notes

1. WP 3.4.01.

The Battle for Palestine

The main road of the Palestinian Highlands from Nablous to Jerusalem runs through Wadi Haramiyeh, a narrow defile in the Samaria Mountains. From time to time, its olive-grown walls recede and leave space for a village, tiny En Sinya, a neat and charming cluster of spacious homes, or splendid Sinjil, named after Raymond de Saint-Gilles, the Count of Toulouse, its liege lord and Crusader. This is the heartland of Palestine, where every stone keeps memories of old battles and skirmishes. I love this area: in Sinjil I was taken for a foreign-born son of local folks who emigrated to America in the 1940s. In En Sinya an old peasant told me of "his friend Moshe Sharet," a Palestinian Jew and an Israeli Minister of State who was brought up in the village years before the Zionist segregation. I drank water from the small spring of En al-Haramiyeh, guarded by a ruined Ottoman Khan, near yet another ruin, King Baldwin's Tower, that stands watch over the southern entrance of the defile. Its relief makes it a likely place for brigands' ambush, and indeed 'Wadi Haramiyeh' means just that, the Valley of Brigands.

On March 3, a Palestinian Rob Roy armed with an old, WWII—vintage carbine, successfully laid low the whole troup of heavily-armed Jews, soldiers and settlers. One after another, he shot the soldiers and their officers, and escaped unharmed. In one stroke, he erased the overblown myth of Israeli military valor. Never again will the supporters of Israel sneer at Arab courage, never again will they tell stories of shoes dropped in Sinai and the Six Day War. He repeated the feat of Karameh and returned the honour to the Palestinians.

He also provided a healthy alternative to the morbid attraction of suicide bombers, and not too soon. For a long time I wanted to persuade my Palestinian brothers and sisters to desist from this madness, for I loathed to be seen as an ideological tool of Zionism. I understand the motives of the *shaheeds* (martyrs), I salute their courage, but I deeply regret their deeds. They are inefficient, and blind. It is highly probable[2] that some suicide cells are thoroughly infiltrated by Israeli counter-intelligence: too often their living bombs explode in the wrong places, at the wrong time, against the wrong targets. Their deeds are used by the Israeli propaganda machine to full advantage. Their death is a terrible loss to mankind. They sacrifice themselves as the son of Abraham brought himself to be sacrificed, but merciful God replaced his sacrifice with a ram.

The marksman offered a different route to glory, one that does not lead through the Valley of Death. A full story of the Battle at Haramiyeh Pass should be sung by bards, and taught by guerrilla-fighters all over the world. One against ten, the Lone Ranger hit the most hated symbol of Jewish rule in Palestine, a checkpoint, where bored, overfed, sadistic Israeli soldiers daily humiliate, beat and often murder the local people.

Just a day before the battle, the soldiers committed probably the most revolting and cowardly act of cruelty. A Palestinian woman about to give birth came to the checkpoint, accompanied by her husband. The soldiers let her through and then opened fire. Her husband was killed; the pregnant woman was wounded and gave birth in the hospital. The soldiers were not reprimanded, but the Army "expressed regrets" to the survivors.

The Israeli Army's main concern is to keep the local population vulnerable and unable to defend itself. The IDF soldiers are accustomed to killing unarmed civilians. Their preferred victims are children; their weapon of choice, a long-range high-velocity sharp-shooter rifle. Their idea of entertainment was witnessed by an expert on "the dark side of the [Israel Defence] Force," the former chief of the *New York Times* Middle East bureau, Chris Hedges: the soldiers pour abuse at the children of the refugee camp and shoot and maim them as they approach the deadly trap.[3]

Still, the shooting of the pregnant woman was a deed as fateful as the Biblical slaughter of the Levite's concubine. The Lord God of Palestine noticed the plight of His sons. The evil deeds of Zionist soldiers had to be punished. The curse promised by the Lord to the misbehaving children of Israel (Deut. 28) fell on their heads. Whatever will be discovered by the military commission of enquiry, this is the most likely explanation of the event. He Who gave victory to the young shepherd David against Goliath granted victory to the lone warrior in Wadi Haramiyeh.

The surprise attack on the checkpoint dealt a deadly blow to the psychotic Israeli superiority complex. Cowards and sadists are unable to cope with defeat: they respond with homicidal rage. That is why the Army began an all-out assault on Palestinian towns and villages. As I write, soldiers shoot at ambulances that try to remove the wounded civilians. The US jets with Israeli pilots bomb a school for the blind in Gaza. Crack troops of the Golani division accompanied by tanks storm the Tul Karem refugee camps. Some Israeli strategists would like to repeat the massacre of Sabra and Shatila, the previous feat of General Sharon. They dug out a Waffen-SS commander's memoir on reducing the Warsaw ghetto, for the Wehrmacht suffered extremely low casualties in 1943.[4]

Brazen Sharon has surpassed Hitler: the German dictator carefully avoided giving the public orders to kill Jews, while the Jewish ruler unabashedly called for the killing of the Palestinians on prime-time television. Many Germans were disgusted by the Nazis, "crossed the lines" and served in the Allied armies against the Third Reich, while the Jews still hesitate to break the bond of false loyalty to their Third Malkuth. Israelis of conscience refuse to participate directly in the ethnic cleansing. It is a very good thing but it is not enough. We should follow the example of Ernst Thaelmann and Joe Slovo, cross the lines, and join the Palestinian fighters on the barricades of Gaza and Tul Karem. In the British daily, the *Guardian*,[5] Jonathan Freedland called the Israeli protesters 'heroes'. I reserve this title for the marksman from the Brigands' Defile.

Notes

2. See my article, "Doubt and Certainty."
3. It was published in *Harpers* magazine, October 2001, http://www.harpers.org/online/gaza_diary/?pg=1.
4. *Haaretz*, 27.1.02.
5. *Guardian*, 6.3.02.

The City of the Moon

An arch is homage to the moon, as it is formed by two mirroring crescents. Full moon produces the perfectly round barrel vault favoured by the Romans; the pointed Muslim arches are formed by waxing seventh-day crescents. In Nablous, there are arches for every day of the lunar month, even upturned arches composed of waning moons. A diligent student of architecture could compose a conclusive History of the Arch in this ancient Palestinian city.

In the Kasbah, an archway flows into archway, creating enfilades, and fading in the dim shadows. Near the Salahie Mosque, underground passages form a wind rose of the nautical charts. My gaze sinks in the black pupil of an opening, and stumbles upon arches like shutter blades in the camera aperture. Nablous is a molehill; generations of crafty dwarves could burrow the long winding tunnels under the solid stone houses of the Old City, connecting its bazaars, mosques and churches.

Hussein leads through the tunnels, finding his way in their clew. Claustrophobic in any other place, in Nablous they protect and envelop like a mother's embrace. They hide us from watchful eyes and night visors of the snipers nesting on the Mount of Curse. We have to cross a square, a well-proportionate Italianate square with a cosy children's playground. We cling to the walls of the squat colonial building. We are not afraid of narrow and confined tunnels; it is the open spaces we dread.

Bullets shriek in the air, and hit an unseen wall. A machinegun replies, and soon, a night orchestra of volleys and flares shakes the mountain air. The city has been besieged for half a year, since April, and the Jews sporadically shoot at its dwellers. The walls on the square are bejewelled with bright coloured portraits of the slain: a five-year-old boy, or a young girl next to a moustachioed sturdy warrior. The golden dome of the Rock, the Palestinian epitome of perfect harmony, shines behind their heads, crowning the martyrs with glory. In Nablous one is never alone: eyes of the snipers and eyes of the martyrs follow one everywhere.

A strange feeling of being a prey came to me. I remembered the first time being shot at, in the grey and yellow barren hills above the Suez—Cairo highway. Egyptian artillery opened fire on us, a company of young paratroops who just had landed in the desert. The falling shells raised clouds of sand and dust, the earth shook of impact very near us, just like it did at the last winter war games, when the supporting artillery miscalculated and almost covered us by its salvos. "What are you doing, silly artillerists," thought I, "we are here, you are shooting at us! If you keep like this, you will hit us!" And then I realized it was no mistake. We weren't at winter manoeuvres, but at real war, and the artillery aimed at us in order to kill.

We sneaked into a modern building and walked up to the second floor by the broad staircase, to the Internet Café. It was full: many young boys and girls dared the snipers' fire and came to this place of refuge and escape. Some of them were fighters; they used the relative lull in shooting, laid down their AK guns on top of the monitor and chatted online with their pen pals from California and Bahrain, Stockholm and Damascus.

I key in a message from Nablous into an Israeli forum and receive a speedy reply from a David Silver in Tel Aviv. "I do not pity them. I have no sorrow for them. I would drive ALL of THEM out to hell. With their children, girls, maidens, women, grannies, with their simple-minded belief in their lies, with their beastly cunning, with their patience and despair, their laughter, their tears, their food, their pride and heroism, their revenge, their working force. OUT! Their fathers, husbands and grandfathers are bloody murderers, admirers of murderers, scoundrels, thieves, cowards and pathological liars. After the expulsion, they can seek our friendship, though I wouldn't build on it." So much for "inherent Jewish pity and sweet obstinacy against violence," as Jean-Paul Sartre wrote in 1945.

An Italian espresso machine flashed green and red lights, working out its steam. The war in the modern city has an incongruous touch: computers are connected to the world net, faxes throw out sheets of neatly printed news, the bakery opens between the shelling spells, a cousin arrives from Kentucky, and young fighters prepare their home lessons for tomorrow's exam at the local university.

It was hard to comprehend that just across the valley there were boys of the same age sent down here from small seacoast towns to reduce Nablous. But it was the reality. A heavy boom shook the house and the monitors blinked and went off. It was a home-made mine, said a young fighter. No, it was 81 mm mortar, said his friend. They rushed down the staircase and out, and we followed them into the starry night. Israelis often send their reconnaissance forces into the city in these hours. They enter the houses, round up men and take them to their torture cellars. To extract information, they say, but there is another purpose: a man tortured, like a girl raped, is a broken and subdued creature. Over one hundred thousand Palestinians and uncounted Lebanese were tortured by Israelis, probably the planetary record. The fighters are on the streets to stop the torturers, or at least to make them pay.

The odds are absurdly disproportionate: the second or third strongest army in the world backed by its only superpower, against these young men and girls. If Israelis really want to, they break into the Old City anytime, night or day. In

Bulldoser

bloody April 2002, over one hundred men and women were slaughtered in Nablous. A whole family of eight found its death when the tanks and armoured bulldozers crushed their home at the edge of the city on their heads. Another house was bombed by F16, and the municipality with great difficulty extracted the dead bodies of two old spinsters from beneath the rubble.

But the city is alive. As shelling and shooting stops, the citizens go out from their homes into uncertainty of the markets, disregarding the curfew. Sellers roll out their vegetable stalls, fragrance of spices perfumes the air, old women from nearby villages sneak in and sell their olive oil and crushed olives, for we are in the heart of the olive country. The mosques are full, though they provide no safe refuge: Israelis do not mind shooting at mosques and churches. A small Catholic chapel was ruined in April; an Orthodox church of St. Demetrius was miraculously saved from a missile hit that devastated the street in front of it. The oldest mosque of the city, the Green al-Hadr Mosque, had its wall crushed by a tank in April, but it has been repaired since then.

The speediness of repairs is amazing. The moment an Israeli tank leaves the rubbles, municipality teams come in. They remove the bodies of dead and wounded and start to fix the house. Still, Israelis destroy faster than Naboulsies are able to repair. The chain tracks of Israeli tanks smashed the ceramic flooring of bazaars and demolished the new water supply system. The signs of fresh devastation melt into the old ruins laid low by the 1927 earthquake, and of an even older one in the second century BC, when the Jews razed to the ground the predecessor of Nablous, ancient Shechem. (Its four-thousand-years-old Cyclopean walls still stand at the edge of Balata refugee camp just outside the city.)

But the city did not die. The Jewish rule in Palestine was bloody, cruel but rather short-lived. The country was conquered by the Jewish invader in the second half of the second century BC, its cities were ruined, and the native population expelled, enslaved or turned into 'second-grade native Jews' as in Galilee. High taxation, genocide and apartheid were rampant even then. Sixty years later Pompey the Great landed on its shores and liberated the Palestinians from the Jewish yoke.

After the Roman army subdued the rebellious Jews, the retired Roman soldiers married pretty local women and rebuilt the city they named Neapolis, or Nablous. It is still reminiscent of its Italian namesake, Neapolis or Naples, with its relentless continuity of styles and fiery temper of citizens. Its houses grow like trees, displaying the smooth transition of its historic periods. The Roman foundation smoothly gives way to the Byzantine first floor, transforms into an Abbasid structure, shifts to become a Crusader town house and ends with the last repair done in May after the latest Israeli bombardment; a perfect amalgam of time and space.

Such is the house of Hussein. The vault of the cellar was probably done by a local mason in the days of Titus Flavius; while the roof was fixed up just recently. We stand on the roof and see in front of us the huge dark shape of the Mount of Curse with its Israeli military base. A yellow halo of floodlights stands above its barbed wire perimeter, and engines of tanks roar like dragons waiting for their signal to fly down and devour the city. On the street below, a group of fighters brandish their Tommy-guns. On the other side of the valley, the Mount of Blessing rises up to the unseen church of the Holy Virgin and the site of the Samarian temple. Flares dim the starlight and we duck as a heavy machinegun begins to comb the city.

Joseph Revisited

[This essay was written in Nablous, in February 2001, after the battle for the Tomb of Joseph.]

I

It is not easy to visit Joseph these days. Roadblocks manned by nervous Israeli soldiers have surrounded his city of Nablous; trenches or heaps of earth block the smallest entrances and exits. On a normal morning, commuters pour in from nearby villages for work or shopping. Now they do so at their own peril, and the local citizens venture out of their homes at the risk of their lives, for the soldiers shoot without warning. Still, one can sneak with daring and caution, into the old capital of Samaria on foot.

The city rests like the sachet of myrrh between the twin breasts of Mt. Ebal and Mt. Gerizim. Nablous is Neapolis of old, founded by Titus Flavius in the heyday of the Roman Empire. The Roman traditions have not died in this Palestinian San Francisco with its lavish Turkish baths. It is also famous for its fragrant olive soap, spicy *kubbeh* soup, and the hardy spirit of its inhabitants. They fielded a strong guerrilla force against Napoleon, rebelled against Egyptian invaders, and kept the Jewish settlers at bay. During the last uprising, Nablous gained renown as Jabal an-Nar, the Mount of Fire. Israelis rarely dared to enter the narrow streets of its old city. Today, this defiant ancient city is the home of the fearless Tanzim fighters.

I came here to visit one of the most charming shrines of the Holy Land, the Tomb of Joseph, the hero of Bible and Koran stories. A local lad, he 'made it' in Egypt and was brought back by Banu Israel to be buried in his ancestral home. The locals have venerated the tomb, as they have the numerous shrines and tombs that adorn the hilltops and crossroads of Palestine. The shrines have deep roots in the Palestinian soul; they predate all modern faiths, have survived all religious reforms, and still are able to turn Man to God.

One needs to take their names with a grain of salt, as they change with the passage of time. There are a dozen tombs for Sheikh Ali, and even Joshua bin Nun has quite a few. Other tombs have multiple names, like the cave on Mount Olives, called the Tomb of Pelagia by Christians, Rabia al-Adawiya by Moslems and Hulda by Jews. Although some orthodox Moslem, Christian and Jewish clerics object to venerating shrines, the common people still come to seek union with the Divine, or beseech favours, glory and harvest for men, children and love for women. The tomb of Joseph is no exception. It is a simple domed building, recently refurbished, standing next to the ancient mound of Shechem. On any given day, Palestinian peasant women in black dresses with rich embroidery can be seen paying their respects at the tomb of the chaste lover, whose long eyelashes reduced the fortress of Zuleika's heart.

A few months ago, Joseph's tomb was all over the news. The people of Nablous fought well-armed Israeli soldiers over the remains of their ancestor Joseph, as the Achaeans fought the Trojans for the body of Patrocles. Some two score Palestinians died there, the Israelis lost one mercenary and a few were wounded. Pictures of the gun battle were transmitted around the globe, as fire-fights raged, ambulances raced to hospitals and morgues, and heavy machinegun bursts tore at stones and flesh. The virtual reality of TV screens accompanied by the voices of the experts presented the ultimate proof of Arab hate for Jewish holy places.

The tale of the despoiled Tomb remained in the news for a long time. An important Muslim divine from Russia was angry enough to write an open letter to the Palestinians, condemning the sacrilege. Major international newspapers unleashed harsh editorials on the subject. A visiting Martian would have presumed that the main desire of Palestinians is to go about desecrating holy Jewish monuments. For those who did not get it the first 108 times, the *New York Times* repeated the story last week.

That was just one time too many for me. This well circulated Jewish American newspaper always stirs the suspicious side of my brain. I recall their reports on the impending Jewish pogroms in Moscow in 1990 that somehow never materialized but sent one million Russian Jews to Israel. I remember their reports on the 90,000 victims of the Timisoara 'massacre' in Romania that turned out to be exaggerated a thousand-fold. (The reports led to the summary execution of the president Ceausescu and his wife.) I remember how the *New York Times* fulminated against the Cuban military assistance to Namibia that broke the spine of South African apartheid. Knowing the Palestinians, who had worshipped at the shrine for uncounted generations, I had difficulty believing they would destroy it.

II

What I found at the site of Joseph's resting place was like a replay of the old Jewish joke: "Is it true that Cohen won a million in the state lottery? Yes, it is true, but it was only ten dollars, in a poker game, and he actually lost it." Instead of the expected ruins, the tomb shone in its pristine beauty. No traces of war could be seen. The Nablous municipality hired the best masons, brought in Italian experts and restored the tomb to its original state. They removed the barbed wire, the machinegun positions, the armoured vehicles, the soldiers' scrubby mess hall, the guard slots. An Israeli-built military base vanished, to be replaced by the resurrected holy tomb. It was a joy to revisit Joseph, as my previous visit, a month before the uprising, had been quite disconcerting.

Then I visited Nablous in the company of two tourists, a Christian and a Jew. We visited the Samaritan synagogue, drank water from Jacob's Well in the church, looked into the Green Mosque and decided to pay our respects to Joseph. An old Palestinian policeman, who had cut out his teeth in the British army, allowed us to approach the tomb but warned us that we wouldn't be let in. He was right. Young Russian boys in Israeli army fatigues, helmets and rifles popped out and told us that in order to enter the tomb one has to go to the army HQ out of town, submit to a security check and interrogation, then come back on the armoured bus. We moved on to more accessible sites.

For generations, the Tomb of Joseph was cherished and attended by the people of Nablous, but it was seized by the Israelis in 1975. The infamous Oslo accords left it as an armed Israeli enclave in the heart of the Palestinian city. It became the Yeshiva of a Cabbalist sect led by Rabbi Yitzhak Ginzburg. His name may ring a bell. He stated in an interview with *Jewish Week* that a Jew is entitled to cut off the liver of a Gentile in order to save his own life, as the life of a Jew is incomparably more precious than the life of a Gentile. He was asked by the interviewer to soften his message, but he remained adamant. Many Israeli papers reproduced this interview, for the name 'Ginzburg' was fairly well known.

A year earlier, Ginzburg's disciples made a sortie to a neighbouring Palestinian village, and a sect member murdered a thirteen-year-old girl. He was arrested and brought to trial. Ginzburg was called as a witness for the defence, and under oath proclaimed that a Jew should not be tried for killing a Gentile, as the commandment, "Thou shall not murder" refers only to Jews. Killing a Gentile is, at worst, a misdemeanour, said he, as "one can not compare the blood of Jews and the blood of Gentiles." Uncomfortable though that is, he had voiced the standard interpretation of *Halachah*, the Jewish Law.

In his *Cultural History of the Jews*, Zvi Howard Adelman[6] quotes Ginzburg and some of his colleagues. One of his fellow-Cabbalists, Rabbi Israel Ariel, wrote in 1982 at the time of the Sabra and Shatila massacre, "Beirut is part of the Land of Israel . . . Our leaders should have entered Lebanon and Beirut without hesitation, and killed every one of them. Not a memory should have remained."

Adelman concludes, "Many Jews, especially religious Jews today in Israel and their supporters abroad continue to adhere to the traditional Jewish ethics that other Jews would like to ignore or explain away."

Certainly, many people who consider themselves 'Jews' are not aware of somewhat dubious religious traditions and morals of our ancestors. These traditions are not dead; though they were dormant for many years, they have come back to life. The late Hebrew University Professor, Israel Shahak, wrote a compelling short tract on this subject, "Three Thousand Years of Jewish Tradition," and brought out the hard facts that we modern Jews did not know.

Ginzburg and his sect are more popular among American Jews than in Israel; but we share the responsibility. The Israeli government subsidized Ginzburg, and forced the Palestinians to accept this enclave of hatred in the heart of Nablous. American Jews supported Ginzburg, Israeli Jews fought to protect his cannibalistic sect. In this minor rehearsal for the forthcoming confrontation over Jerusalem's Holy Places, twenty young Palestinians paid with their lives for their right to worship at the Tomb, and I am certain, Joseph son of Jacob fought on the Palestinian side to rid his tomb of the cannibals.

III

Now, as before 1975, local folk and tourists, Moslems, Samaritans, Jews, Christians and freethinkers can visit the place freely (if they can sneak by Israeli checkpoints and escape Israeli sharpshooters). Visitors can put a flower on the gravestone of a favourite hero of the Bible, the Koran prophet, the lover of Ferdowsi's poem and Saadi verses, the truth-seeker of the Sufi revelation of Jami. Joseph has come back to the people who always venerated him. You are free to visit him, but please leave your tanks behind.

Palestinians fought the army base, not the holy place. The holy places of Jerusalem, Bethlehem and Hebron will be safe in Palestinian hands, as they have been for uncounted generations. Without the local veneration, none would have survived. Please remember this when the problem of Jerusalem comes forth.

This latest saga of the events surrounding Joseph's tomb is just one more proof that the American mass media is an unreliable source. This great nation, the formidable superpower, gets its knowledge and navigates its course in the sea of world politics by using a Mickey Mouse telescope. If the media lords misled you on the issue of Palestine, why do you think they are honest about any other matter? Perhaps the suffering of the Palestinians should help the Europeans and Americans to notice the reefs ahoy their own ship.

Notes

6. Available on the website of The Department for Jewish Zionist Education. The full quote:

> "Many Jews, especially religious Jews today in Israel and their supporters abroad continue to adhere to traditional Jewish ethics that other Jews would like to ignore or explain away. For example, Rabbi Yitzhak Ginzburg of Joseph's Tomb in Nablous/Shechem, after several of his students were remanded on suspicion of

murdering a teenage Arab girl: 'Jewish blood is not the same as the blood of a goy.' Rabbi Ido Elba: 'According to the Torah, we are in a situation of *pikuah nefesh* [saving a life] in time of war, and in such a situation one may kill any Gentile.' Rabbi Yisrael Ariel wrote in 1982 that 'Beirut is part of the Land of Israel . . . our leaders should have entered Lebanon and Beirut without hesitation, and killed every single one of them. Not a memory should have remained.'" It is usually yeshiva students who chant "Death to the Arabs" on CNN. The stealing and corruption by religious leaders that has recently been documented in trials in Israel and abroad continues to raise the question of the relationship between Judaism and ethics.

Cornerstone of Violence

[This essay was written in August 2001.]

I

As F-16's again bomb cities of Palestine, and young men again sacrifice their lives and the lives of others, Martin Indyk, writing in the *New York Times*, proclaims that the "Violence is worsening."[7] The BBC and CNN join in, like a Greek chorus, echoing Indyk with their reports of "Violence in Palestine." Bush from his Olympus issues another plea to "break the cycle of Violence." This faceless and causeless 'Violence' should probably be capitalized, as the 'Wrath' in the first line of the *Iliad*.

This eternal poem begins with a call to "sing the Wrath of Achilles." In Homer's world, 'Wrath' (or 'Fury', 'War', 'Love', 'Hope') is "condition personified." Nowadays, we tend to see "an angry Achilles" or "a violent husband" rather than Wrath or Violence *per se* unless the abuser is the Jewish state, in which case, we revert to the Homeric concept of Violence as 'independent being', and forget that violence is a nasty human behaviour. People seriously discuss how to "deal with" Violence in order to bring Peace.

In the real world, Violence is not like weather. Somebody does it, and we can usually identify the violent factor. So it was, when the "Mitchell process" was invoked and the daily quota of killed slowly began to crawl down, Jewish fundamentalists laid the cornerstone of the Third Temple, and the army followed it up with a wave of assassinations in Nablous and Ramallah. Sharon's assassins did not stop their murdering spree until a suicide bomber obliged by responding.

That was no coincidence. The Jewish elites, in Israel and in America, want the Palestinian uprising to go on. They want not peace, but low intensity conflict. A war with Palestinians allows the Israeli leaders to keep their heterogeneous communities together, away from each other's throat. What is more important, the war allows the Jewish leaders around the world to continue their arduous task of reviving World Jewry, a medieval run-down construct. That is why it makes no sense to speak against 'Violence' and for 'Peace'. As long as the supremacist Jewish state exists, it will ensure violence and avoid peace.

The recent assassinations also had the intent of covering up the cornerstone provocation under a heap of corpses. The meaning of this obscure ceremony was further obscured by the mainstream media, and all references to it mysteriously vaporised. For instance, Reuters reported on August 3, 2001: "Israeli police stormed the Temple Mount, revered by Muslims as al-Haram al-Sharif, after Palestinians threw stones at Jews worshipping at the Western Wall below."

II

Why, all of a sudden, did Palestinians begin to stone Jews? The cornerstone story was omitted, and the average American or European was left with the impression that the "wild" Muslims attacked peaceful worshipping Jews just out of spite. On this count, the unanimity of the English-language media was horrifying. The BBC, once more objective than American networks, closed the gap. They also reported of "Israeli soldiers who entered the mosques responding to the Muslim stone throwers," moving a reference to the cornerstone to the end of the item. It now appears that the airing of the BBC documentary on Sharon was a singular act of courage that will not be repeated soon.

As for the American networks, their coverage continues to be consistent. They market the Israeli line without hesitation. That is why we shall revisit the details of the strange, already forgotten story of the cornerstone. This was not your average Israeli provocation. It brought to mind the black magic incantations of *Pulsa diNura*, the cabbalistic formula used on the Prime Minister, Yitzhak Rabin. In 1995, the Israeli media covered a gathering of important Cabbalists who invoked evil spirits and beseeched them to extinguish the Prime Minister's life. Soon afterwards, Rabin was assassinated by a Jewish religious fanatic. An organizer of the *Pulsa diNura* ceremony was tried by Israeli court of law and sent to jail for incitement to murder. You do not have to believe in black magic in order to understand the logic of the judge.

In order to comprehend the idea of the cornerstone laying, imagine: you wake up one beautiful Sunday morning in your suburban home, have your coffee and proceed to your church. There you encounter a commotion. In front of the church, a band of men, well protected by armed soldiers and police, are busy installing a huge billboard saying: "On this place, a synagogue will be erected in 2001." In the background, there is the roar of bulldozer engines and the amplified voice of a Rabbi blessing the new synagogue. You would probably feel as hysterical as the hero of the *Hitchhiker's Guide to the Galaxy*. Supplant your parish church by St. Peter or the Holy Sepulchre, and you will understand the feelings of Jerusalemites.

Though the Temple Mount Loyalists, the group that performed this magic ceremony, is tiny and hardly mainstream, one can't say that about the body that gave them the green light. Overruling police objections, the Supreme Court, the highest Jewish legal authority, permitted them to do their act on an auspicious date, the Ninth day of the Moon month of Ab, with its mystic meaning. All the might of the Jewish state, including thousands of policemen and soldiers, was mobilized to allow the ceremony to take place. That is why one can compare the pithy Loyalist band with the sharp thin end of the dental pick in the dentist's hand, pushing deep inside the tooth to check whether the nerve is dead.

The results of this painful examination were unambiguous. The nerve was apparently alive, and the quick mobilization of the Palestinians forced the Jews to re-route the Loyalists' procession. The ceremony took place outside the Old City, a little earlier than planned. It lasted for a few minutes, and the stone was returned to its usual place, in the deep protective shadow of the US Consulate. This push of the pick caused sharp pain and the predictable response of the Jerusalemites; and afterwards, the vicious attack of the police on the believers in the mosque—well described by the young American girl, Rebecca Elswitt.[8] What was the reason for all the trouble? Why did the Palestinian kids dare to confront the Border Police, famous for their brutality? Why is the cornerstone so important?

III

Many Jews and their Christian-Zionist allies believe that the precious beauty of Haram al-Sharif, the Seventh century mosques of Jerusalem should be destroyed and on its ruins, a Jewish temple should be erected. Not for the purpose of prayer, as traditional Judaism forbids any meddling with the Mountain of the Lord. Mystically inclined Jews believe this act will make Jewish domination of the world total and irreversible. This belief is not the exclusive domain of kooks and freaks, nor even of Zionists only, but rather a widespread conviction.

Mainstream media of the West usually presents the conflict in terms of Muslims vs. Jews. But the conflict as seen by these Jews, is Jews vs. Gentiles, or "Jacob" against "Edom." In their mind, the Temple Mount is a magic Ring of Power, one they should assume when the time is right. As the Ring in Tolkien's *Lord of the Rings* (the British professor was a very learned man), it should bring forth the Messiah.

For the Jewish mystics, the Messiah of Jews is not the Christian Messiah, a gentle Jesus with a message for all mankind. The Messiah of Jews would forever enslave the Nations of the earth and make the Chosen People the masters of the universe. Their Messiah, Lord Enslaver of the Nations of Earth, is called 'Antichrist' by Church fathers who were well aware of the Jewish doctrine.

As millennia digits jump from 1 to 2 on the meter of our Cosmic Cabby, apocalyptic thoughts come into many heads. This is not the first time some Jews have dreamed of world domination and of the eternal kingdom of the

Antichrist. Only now, they have in their possession nuclear weapons, the latest jets and battleships, huge wealth, the blind support of the US, tens of millions of willing 'Christian Zionist' slaves, and a broad web of tame and docile international media.

Ten years ago, a leading Israeli journalist, Nahum Barnea, wrote in *Yediot Aharonot*: "Jewish influence on the American foreign policy grew enormously in the 1970s and 1980s. Owing to this influence, Israel became a top recipient of American foreign aid. But this influence has also generated myths. This myth brings us to the *Protocols of the Elders of Zion*, a book which claimed that the Jews rule over the world. The situation is filled with irony. For decades the Jews tried hard to refute the myth of the *Protocols*, treating it as a morbid manifestation of anti-Semitism. Now the Jews turn the very same myth to their advantage. Some even believe it."

Israel Shahak commented: "The ruling Likud party (let alone the extreme right-wing) genuinely believes in the myth (of Jewish domination of the world and of enslavement of Gentiles)." However, these observations should be corrected.

The Jews have a polemic tradition to exaggerate claims of their opponents and make their refutation an easier task. Nobody thinks the Jews rule over the world: it is too daunting a job. The question is, whether the Jews possess the global-size domination drive. Would they *like* to rule the world? Well, some would, while others quietly go along with them.

The leading Israeli daily, *Haaretz* reported that Sharon, like Barak before him, sneaks out to visit the wizards of Cabbala for advice. It is all quite fashionable: Cabbala schools, courses and shops have drawn their net over the Jewish state. The Holy Land would turn into a Waste Land, according to their guidelines. This is not a matter of chance. The Cabbala is ascribed to the First Century mystic Simeon b. Yohai, whose best known maxim reads, "Smash the head of the best of snakes, kill the best of Gentiles."[9]

This archaic model of domination, genocide and enslavement calls for archaic religious content. Many Israelis sense the re-emergence of the ancient spirit of hate and dominance. The weekend supplement of *Haaretz* published a short fiction story. It featured an American president who tried to disobey the orders of the Cabbalists and was removed by his subordinates. The Jews are destined to rule the world, preached Rabbi Leichtman, a leading Cabbalist, in a long article printed in *Vesti*, a Russian-Israeli paper. In the chat rooms of the Israeli Internet one can find more heady stuff. They quote an old poem by Uri Zvi Greenberg, a late Hebrew poet, who called for the extermination of the Gentiles. Greenberg did not limit himself to Palestinians, like the late Menachem Begin, nor only to Arabs, like the highest spiritual authority in Israel, Rabbi Obadiah Joseph. The extermination of Edom, a traditional code-word for European and American Gentiles, appears as a plausible option in the feverish minds of Cabbala followers.

IV

This feeling spills into the Jewish Diaspora. In the heart of the US, in Atlanta, there was a recent debate in the Jewish Community Centre in the presence of the Israeli Consul, a Jewish businessman, a prominent Atlanta rabbi and a *New York Times* reporter. An observer wrote to me, "I was struck mostly by the comments of the rabbi. While claiming to be a non-Zionist, he declared (we have him on tape) that the ultimate reason for creating Israel, as he sees it, is to become the world's controller of power and wealth. Jews will eventually overthrow world governments and be assigned positions to lead the world. This, he felt, will occur in a short number of years."

At the other end of the world, in Russia, a Jewish follower of Sharon's own ultra-Nationalist Jabotinsky movement, 'Eliezer Dacevich-Voronel', who described himself as a University Professor, composed a poem: "We, the Chosen Ones, are united by hatred to the slave tribes that rose, dethroned our ancestors and rejected our God. Once you knew of your place in the world: 'a swine must stay in its sty'. You revolted, and forced us to serve you, but now your end is nigh. We are your masters. You are our slaves. This is God's design. Soon our sun will rise again, and the slaves will not dare to look at it. And then, the Lord of My People will appear in Heaven, while we, the dozen of dozen thousands (i.e., 144,000) of Chosen Ones will sit in the great amphitheatre and watch the miserable columns of souls crawling into their paradise. By God's will, we shall name it Auschwitz."

They speak even of genetically re-constructing the King Antichrist. The brilliant maverick, Dr. Avi Ben Abraham, seems to be the man behind the project. This unusual man recently returned to Israel after some years in California, where he worked on a Star Trek-like Deep Freeze project for very wealthy Jews. Loaded with money, Ben Abraham built a palace in Caesarea on the seashore of the Mediterranean, some fifty km north of Tel Aviv, and contacted the Italian genetic expert, Dr. Severino Antinori. Ben Abraham, who received his doctor of medicine degree at the unheard-of age of 18, hinted at his plans in an interview with *Haaretz*. A few days ago, his project received some benign attention from the *New York Daily News*, the newspaper of Mortimer Zuckerman, a Jewish supremacist billionaire and the head of the Conference of Jewish American Organisations.

The men of hate and vengeance are ready to seize the magic ring of power, the Temple Mount, to enforce and perpetuate the rule of the Antichrist. But it can not be done by brute force, due to a medieval prohibition, *Issur Homah*. A premature action could backfire. A Jewish religious leader from Brooklyn, Lubavitcher Rebbe, was considered by his disciples a potential Messiah, and that is why he never ever came to the Holy Land. He did not feel himself ready for the trial of forces. Meanwhile, the children of Palestine keep these religious fanatics at bay. Sharon and his band of mad believers try their hand by snatching the Orient House, a Husseini mansion in Jerusalem. If this is allowed to quietly pass, it will make for one more step to the Ring of Power.

V

The soul-searching Russian writer, Eugene Zamyatin, composed a short fable of Gospel quality. It is a story of a man who decided to build a temple, but had no money. He waylaid a merchant on the highway, tortured him to death, extracted a lot of cash and built the temple. He invited a Bishop and many priests and ordinary folks, but in a short time they left the church: the place stank of murder. One can not build a temple on the blood of innocents. An elder contemporary of Zamyatin, a Jewish thinker from Odessa, the 'spiritual Zionist' Ahad HaAm, put it in simple and beautiful words: "If this be the Messiah, I do not wish to see His coming."

Notes

7. 8.8.01.
8. Rebecca Elsewit, see App 1.
9. In the *Mechilta* it says, "*tov shebagoyim harog*," "kill the best among the gentiles" (14:7; cf. Soferim ch. 15:10).

The Baron's Braid

[This essay was written in February 2002 and is included here because of its subject, the Temple Mount.]

I

Beautiful as ever, spring came to Palestine. It is a lovely time, when the pale fire of almond blossom lights the mountain valleys, the grass is brilliant green (soon it will be sun-scorched), the sky is blue and soft and without its harsh summer glare, and plump white sheep crawl the hills. The Creator of Spring is apparently unconcerned with the human doings, or He knows better.

In the sixteenth month of the Intifada, the ease of Israeli intrusions into the autonomous areas makes transparent the legal fiction of a Palestinian quasi-state. Friends of Palestine were worried that the Palestinian Autonomy will become an Arab Bantustan in the Greater Israel. We can rest assured: the Autonomy is not up to being a Bantustan. It is a big-game reserve. Probably Sharon and his Minister of Tourism, the settler Beni Elon, consider that it will attract adventurous tourists to Israel, who will prefer it to South Africa or Kenya. [This prediction was realised, and now "American Jews in Israel offer 'terror tourism' package in West Bank," an Associated Press headline recently reported. Ed]

Edward Herman[10] of Znet wrote of an approaching 'final solution' for the Palestinians along the lines of German 'final solution' for the Jews. The same thought occurred to the IDF. Our generals have learned from the German suppression of the Warsaw Ghetto rebellion, *Haaretz* reported.[11] They are excited by the extremely low casualties the Wehrmacht suffered in Warsaw in 1943, and hope to repeat their feat if and when they crush the remainder of the Autonomy.

On the other hand, there are more signs of civil disobedience and Israeli officers' refusal to implement 'the final solution'. I went to the demonstration at the Tel Aviv Museum, and found many wonderful young men and girls there, standing next to old peace fighters. It was a real peace camp, without quote marks. They applauded a message from Arafat, and supported the refusing officers. Peace Now, a Labour-affiliated movement, didn't join: its members feel uncomfortable with any refusal to obey army orders. It is never easy to refuse orders, though the IDF is tolerant of dissent. The rebels will be discharged from the commanding positions at worst, not court-marshalled. Their refusal to serve in the Palestinian territories is a blow for the Israeli war machine, though hundreds of other soldiers and officers expressed their desire to fill the vacated place at checkpoints and snipers' nests. The rebels have made an important first step by deciding to stay away from evil.

The Tel Aviv weekly *Ha-Ir* published brief (less than 100 words each) explanations by the soldiers of why they decided to refuse orders. It is grim reading, replete with accounts of checkpoint mistreatment, torture and starvation of the Palestinians. The murder of children, an integral feature of the Jewish state, occupies a prominent place in this table of horrors. The anti-Semites of old claimed Jews murder Christian children. This revolting bloody myth was shattered and destroyed in Israel. We murder Muslim children as easily as Christian ones, without prejudice. Even Ami Ayalon, tough, lean, bald, mean ex-Head of the dreaded State Security Service, wondered aloud why so few Israeli soldiers refuse to kill children.

I am a notch less jubilant than I should be, as Israelis have a wonderful capacity for using protest in their own interests. For instance, after the Sabra and Shatila massacre there was a giant demonstration, by a few hundred thousand Israelis. But it was utilised to make Israelis feel good. For the following seventeen years the torture centre, al Hiyam in South Lebanon remained operative, and occupation of the South was over only recently. Sharon, the butcher of Sabra and Shatila, was elected Prime Minister. There is a danger that the brave act of the officers will be used to promote good feeling among Israel supporters, rather than to change things. An Israeli friend of Palestine, Henry Lowe wrote, "In America, right-wing apologists for colonialist Israel are already using the reservists' statement to say: "See, only in Israel can this happen. This is a clear indication that Israel is a democracy, while the Arabs are . . ." Moreover, their insistence on the sacred character of the Green Line is at least somewhat naïve.

How now, Israel and Palestine? What will happen next?

II

Sharon could try to push on with the Final Solution—the creation of a Palestinians-free Palestine. Until now he had hoped the Palestinians would run away from their unbearable living conditions. Relatively wealthy and well-connected people do emigrate, distancing themselves until better days come. But the Jews leave much faster. Young Israelis move abroad to study and do not come back. A gifted musician, Adi Schmidt, my friend's son, announced his intention to leave for good and performed his farewell concert in Tel Aviv. The shekel has entered the free-fall zone, and investments have zeroed. That is why the government has to take bold steps.

They would love to provoke a civil war among Palestinians. More pressure in connection with this-or-that action of militias, meetings with select PNA ministers, demands for the arrest and surrender of activists—these are the strategies intent upon causing it. But unexpectedly, the Palestinians do not rush into self-destruction.

Failing a Palestinian civil war, Sharon has other means for provoking the Palestinians and Israel's neighbours, and for cleansing the land of its Goy inhabitants in the aftermath of the provocation. He can break into Al Aqsa Mosque, the beautiful complex built by the Umayyad Caliphs in the Seventh Century; the naked nerve of Palestine. In 1996, Bibi Netanyahu opened a tunnel near the Mosque and caused 96 deaths in the ensuring uproar. Sharon's own violation of the Mosque 16 months ago launched the Intifada. Recently Sharon obtained the useful recommendation of the Shabak to open the Mosque for Jewish worship.

In normal circumstances, non-Muslims are allowed to visit al-Aqsa. Its broad and shady courts, the supreme harmony of Qubbet as-Sahra, the Dome of the Rock, and the spacious naves of the main building of the mosque make it a perfect place for a pleasant stroll, rest and contemplation. Millions of tourists and tens of millions of believers used to come here. But since a long time, the Israeli government has been preventing Muslims from coming to the place where the Prophet, peace upon him, prayed with other prophets. A Jerusalem Muslim has to be over forty years of age to pass the Israeli police blocks on his way to prayer. A Muslim from Gaza or Ramallah can not come hitherto pray at all. The mosque leaders do not want to see strangers in their home, while their sons are not permitted to enter.

Parts of the Mosque grounds are already confiscated by the Jews. The broad square at front of the Western Wall was the site of a picturesque Mughrabi neighbourhood. It also belonged to the mosque, but after the Israeli conquest of Jerusalem in 1967, it was razed. Some of its dwellers remained buried under the ruins; such was the haste of the conquerors to eliminate the Palestinian presence. The Western Wall is a part of the Mosque grounds, too. According to an age-old tradition, confirmed by the British authorities, the Wall belongs to the Mosque, though the Jews are entitled to pray at it. After 1967, it was confiscated, along with the Southern Wall.

The Jewish nationalist right wing dreams to erect the Jewish temple on the ruins of the mosque. They believe the mountain has magic qualities, and once in Jewish possession it would forever enshrine Jewish supremacy over the Christian and Muslim world.[12] The Jewish temple will overshadow the Holy Sepulchre, as well. For them, takeover of the mosque is not just a means of provoking more violence, but an end in itself.

This opinion is shared by the 'Christian Zionists', an American religious group which effectively denies the New Testament, rejects the Eucharist and the Virgin and believes in the eternal chosenness of the Jews. The Christian Zionists consider it their duty to serve Jews by hastening the big war. As the rise of such a sect at the end of time was prophesied by the Church fathers, their opponents call them 'The Church of the Antichrist'. The US President George W. Bush and some of his advisers are extremely close to this church of "Armageddon wishers." They will oblige the Jews and threaten Israel's neighbours, Iran and Iraq with nuclear destruction, while Israel takes over the mosques.

If the takeover passes peacefully, Sharon will inscribe his name next to that of King Herod, the builder of the previous Jewish temple. If it causes big disturbances, Sharon will be able to kill and expel the Palestinians. If it causes a big war, the Armageddon-wishers will be well pleased.

III

There is a contingency plan for the less starry-eyed. Sober if devious Zionists considered the election of Sharon just a certain stage in the realization of the Oslo strategy. The Palestinians rejected Barak's proposal of an "independent Palestinian state," i.e., a chain of Bantustans without the refugees' return, without Jerusalem, without its own borders and without hope. But they have suffered so much since then, and lost many of their best men and women.

A Jewish folk-tale tells of a man who felt miserable in his small and crowded house. His Rabbi advised him to take in his goat. The man came a week later in tears, as now it was truly impossible to move in the house. The Rabbi allowed him to remove the goat, and he became a contented and happy citizen.

Sharon is the goat of this fable. When he is removed, the Jewish media of the US will praise our great humanism. Europeans will bless us for our benevolence. The nice guys who refused to serve in the territories will become heroes. The place of bloody Sharon will be taken by his not-less-bloody Minister of Defence Fuad Ben Eliezer, by Avrum Burg, or a general from the granaries of the Labour Party. The army will withdraw from Nablous and Ramallah. Happy Palestinians will agree to the Oslo plan in Barak's interpretation minus the end-of-conflict declaration. They will return into their enclaves, into the slow strangulation of the Barak days. They will have to forget about their confiscated lands and houses, about al Aqsa mosque, about Jerusalem.

The Israeli right-wing and its allies in AIPAC will present it as an American betrayal, to be quoted next to General Eisenhower's orders of 1956. The independence of the US administration from the Jewish lobby will be confirmed. The painful events of the Intifada and its end will be presented as victory of Good over Evil. They will not mention that the Zionist Good and the Zionist Evil sat around the same table and planned it together. But for an objective observer it would mean something different. Again, for the nth time, the 'bad cop' will have passed his softened Palestinian victim into the tender paws of the 'good cop'.

Yes, the soldiers and the officers who refused to participate in the oppression are very good guys and they did a good deed. But I am worried that it will be used to promote good feeling among Israel's supporters, and to legitimize the very structure of apartheid. Their brave words are used to support the 'unilateral separation', a code word for fencing the Palestinians into one big well-guarded zone.

One can't change the paradigm of the Jewish state, the paradigm of oppression and apartheid, from within. A character of Raspe's book, *Baron Munchausen* (familiarised by Terry Gilliam's movie) extracted himself and his horse from a deep bog by pulling up his braid. If you believe this tall story, you may believe that the good guys can change Israeli Jewish society from within, without their joining forces with Palestinians.

A much better solution was offered by the Jewish Orthodox congregation of Neturei Karta, the sons of the pre-Zionist Jewish community of the Holy Land. They were mistreated almost as much as other native sons of Palestine, mainly for their steadfast refusal to participate in Zionist atrocities. These wise men in big black hats, like my Uncle from Tiberias, a peaceful and pious Rabbi, remind me that the Jews once lived like good neighbours with the Palestinians. In an impassioned call, they say that the crux of the problem is the very existence of the 'Jewish' state. The only realistic hope for a lasting peace is that the United Nations will assist in the dismantling of the Israeli state and return the land to Gentile auspices.

Once, Stalin jokingly asked how many battalions the Pope could field. Nevertheless, a Pope saw the Soviet Union dismantled. Neturei Karta Jews have no battalions, but I think they will see the state of Israel dismantled and a new Palestine, a country of all its sons and daughters, take its place.

Notes

10. http://www.zmag.org/sustainers/content/2002-02/11herman.cfm.
11. 27.1.02.
12. See my article "The Cornerstone of Violence."

The Invasion

I

This week, we learned the full measure of despair and humiliation. Our protests and petitions, emails and demonstrations turned out to be as powerful as charms and curses against tanks. Politically correct or outrageous, witty or rude, friends of equality in Palestine were out-gunned. The US President acclaimed "Israeli right to self-defence"; the BBC and CNN found a formula "in response"; and Sharon's troops invaded Palestinian towns. They effectively eliminated Palestinian self-rule and carried out intensive searches, mass arrests, and cold-blooded executions. In Bethlehem, a peaceful demonstration of European non-violent protesters was machine-gunned by the invaders. Local people speak of dozens of murdered Palestinians, shot point-blank. Israel and the US, long managed by a single set of men, block the UN and the international organisations, while preparing Part Two of their operation, the invasion of Gaza.

It is a difficult time, but not as bleak as our enemies would like us to think. The suborned Western media reported on "fighting between Palestinians and Israelis." But, as a matter of fact, Israeli soldiers met with little resistance. Why did the fabulously brave Palestinian fighters not give the invading Jews a fight?

One answer is obvious, and it was offered by the Israeli journalist and peace activist, Uri Avneri. The disparity of force is too big for the poorly equipped Palestinians to take on the third strongest army in the world that is backed up by its tame Juggernaut, the US. But there is another reason Avneri did not mention: for Palestinians, the Palestinian National Authority (PNA) hasn't become the national symbol worth defending and dying for. Life under the PNA has been remained life under Jewish rule.

It is not the right time to dwell on the PNA's faults, already well described by Robert Fisk and many others. I shall quote only Muna Hamzeh from Deheisheh refugee camp, who wrote:

> Since Arafat and his authority took control of Zone A in Bethlehem in December 1995, this is what he has used "funds" for in Bethlehem: to build a new police station with a new jail; new headquarters for his Preventive Security forces; new headquarters for his intelligence; new presidential headquarters for Arafat and his VIP guests; and a personal helicopter pad built on Jabal Anton, a small hilltop overlooking

> Deheisheh and the only natural extension for the camp, where Arafat would have been better off building a playground for the refugee camp's children. This is what Arafat built in Bethlehem. ("Holocaust Revisited," 12.3.02)

Muna Hamze exaggerates: Bethlehem received a fresh facelift, its roads were paved, Manger square refurbished, new hotels opened and quality of life improved in the years of PNA administrative control. Still she expressed the gut feeling of many of her countrymen, from Professor Said to the refugees in Deheisheh, deeply dissatisfied with the PNA. Whether they tried to deliver the goods to the ultimate ruler, Israel, or to the squeezed population, they aren't popular. The PNA was established by the Israelis in order to police the Palestinian population. It was not established to improve Palestinians' lives. **I doubt it has the capacity to do much more than it did.**

In the unfolding Palestinian holocaust, the PNA was forced to play the morally ambiguous, nay, impossible, part of the *Judenrat*, the Jewish Authority established by Germans in the ghetto and camps of occupied Europe. Germans had as little desire as Israelis to police and administrate their alien subjects. They preferred to give them a limited self-rule in internal affairs. Some enlightened Nazis were ready to arrange a separate Jewish state within the framework of the Third Reich, somewhat along the lines of Sharon's vision of the Palestinian state. They actually did it around Lublin, an area of Poland with a big Jewish population. It had a few names: Lublinland, Jewishland, Judenland, Jewish Reserve, and Jewish Autonomous Area.

After the war, many books and plays were produced about the activities of this Jewish Authority. Jews were unhappy with their own Judenrat. They considered it "corrupt," "attentive to the demands of the enemy," and other allegations so familiar to us today. But the Judenrat could not have achieved more than it did. Nor could the PNA. Palestinians did not receive a *bout de soufflé*; second wind; they were and remain subjects of the Jewish apartheid state, within or without the PNA.

Sharon's invasion buried forever the screwy idea of Palestinian self-rule ('independence') on a small slice of Palestine. It was basically the Nazi idea of Lublinland transferred to Ramallah by the Jewish pseudo-Left. The idea of democracy in all of Palestine, the liquidation of apartheid, has again come to the forefront. Do not look back with nostalgia to the days of the PNA; look forward with hope to tomorrow's free and democratic Palestine, from the River to the Sea.

II

Muna Hamze called her essay "Holocaust Revisited." The holocaust image has been invoked by Jose Saramago, the Portuguese Nobel Prize winning writer who compared the besieged Ramallah with the Warsaw Ghetto. Saramago, who just yesterday was glorified by the Jewish press because of his unorthodox treatment of Jesus, became the object of massive attack. Among the attackers were the leading lights of the Israeli Jewish pseudo-Left, Ari Shavit and Tom Segev.

Tom Segev mobilized his pen to the service of the Jewish state:

> Saramago declared that Israel's actions in the territories are comparable to the crimes that were perpetrated at Auschwitz and Buchenwald. That sounds more like something he read on the inside of the door of a public lavatory than something he wrote in his books. What he said was harmful to the cause it was supposed to serve, so he also emerged from the episode looking stupid.

Somehow I have tired of hearing this well-meaning mantra, ***harmful to the cause***, from the Jewish 'Left-wing' advisers to Palestinians, from Tom Friedman and Tom Segev. I do not believe they wish this cause to succeed. And now, the practical difference between the Jewish 'soft Left' and 'hard Right' has become cosmetic. The following lines were written by the 'leftist' Ari Shavit, but they could be written by 'extreme Rightist' Barbara Amiel, Conrad Black's wife and a friend of Sharon and Pinochet:

> The things Jose Saramago said on Monday in Ramallah were not clear criticism of the occupation. They were an ugly incitement against the Jews. They were not merely foolish, nor only a statement of groundless historical fact. They were a form of bloodletting. For if Ramallah is Auschwitz—and that's the parallel Saramago drew—then Israel is the Third Reich. It deserves extinction. Maybe not all its citizens should be killed, but its sovereign institutions should be smashed. And if Ramallah is Auschwitz, then Tel Aviv is Dresden. Burning it would not be a war crime.

Professor Alan Stoleroff answered him well:

> Once again there is an attempt by a Left-wing Israeli to face the cold facts of the ongoing crimes against humanity and war crimes committed by the Israeli occupation. If Saramago's words, or my own Jewish words, had compared the encirclement and the blockades to the Warsaw ghetto, would you react the same way? Didn't it come out in Israeli papers that an Israeli general had urged the study of Nazi tactics at Warsaw in order to put down the Intifada? Didn't Israeli soldiers stamp serial numbers on detained Palestinians? Don't 40% of Israeli Jews respond positively to survey questions when asked if they favour

> transfer of the Arabs? And the carpet bombing of Dresden WAS itself a war crime.
>
> If Shavit insists, I am ready to oblige: Israel, this Jewish apartheid state, deserves to disappear. Its sovereign institutions indeed should be dismantled. And its supporters elsewhere turn themselves into participants in war crimes, and into combatants at their own peril. They would not be allowed to claim their neutrality. The chasm is not an ethnic or religious one, as proven by Jerry Levin of Alabama.

Jerry Levin, the CNN Bureau Chief in Beirut who was held hostage by the Hizballah in 1984–85, is working these days with CPT (Christian Peacemaker Teams) to protect defenceless Palestinian children, women and men from settler rage and violence. He calls to mind "Adam Shapiro, who is Jewish, is a member of the International Solidarity movement, and works in Ramallah." One should add marvellous Jennifer Loewenstein, whose report from Gaza is now on Palestine networks, and other friends of equality elsewhere. These people of differing opinions together with their friends take on the Left-Right block of Jewish supremacists.

Convoy to Bethlehem

[This was written after an Israeli incursion into Bethlehem in October 2001.]

A new Audi car, squashed like an empty cigarette box in the ashtray of a nervous chain-smoker, greeted us at the entrance to Bethlehem. Other cars were flattened into thin sheets of glass and steel. Israeli tank crews, like all vicious punks, love to smash cars and dustbins. Little kids crouched on the corner intent on their game with spent cartridges, making the most of a sudden lull in the fighting. Bethlehem was quiet, for the first time since Saturday, October 20, when Israeli Merkaba tanks rolled into the City of Christ to implement Sharon's pet project, the re-occupation of Palestine.

It was quiet when a new force entered the area: the Christians of Jerusalem had come to relieve their besieged neighbour. It was a wondrous sight, reminiscent of the Crusades, when the Solidarity Convoy led by the bishops and clergy of all denominations—Catholic, Orthodox and Muslim—came carrying crosses and banners and broke the strangling ring of the Israeli blockade to move along the heavily damaged streets towards the Church of the Nativity. Unlike the Bush 'Crusade' to Afghanistan, this Crusade was felicitously met by Christians and Muslims alike, as there is no dispute between these inter-twined communities. We passed the burnt-out Paradise Hotel (it had received a direct hit), the double-bent electric pillars, the pictures of young boys and girls killed by Israeli sharpshooters, and the local people came out of their shelters to join the procession.

Israeli tanks left the main streets and crawled away into their lairs, like dragons disturbed at prey. On the way I met so many old friends, local shopkeepers and guides. They were quite despondent: As things are, with this war going on, they said, there are no tourists, no income, and no hope. Jerusalem and Bethlehem stand together or fall together. Bethlehem is but a suburb of Jerusalem. I used to come here so often with my tourists and pilgrims, to this bourgeois city of spacious villas, king-size souvenir shops, grand Greco-Palestinian families, neat nuns, tourist crowds and many expatriates, to pay homage to the Church of the Nativity, that great Justinian edifice, the oldest extant building of Palestine.

The plaza in front of the church, Manger square, was full of local people using the chance to see some sunlight after days behind shutters. Last Sunday, an Israeli sharpshooter had killed a local sixteen-year-old choir boy, Johnny Thaljieh, at the church doorstep, and now his soft face was looking out of a

Israel Shamir in Ramallah

hastily printed poster. This square was rebuilt in the Italianate style by the PNA just two years ago, before the Millennium festivities, and no longer looked as it did in the days of Israeli direct rule, when it was an incongruous parking-lot for the Border Police jeeps and tourist buses.

In the church, among the priests and laity, I saw a tall American with a proud upper lip, long curly hair and exotic head gear. It was Rabbi Jeremy Milgrom, of Rabbis for Human Rights. "I thought I was the only Jew here," he said. "I am sure thousands of Israelis would come if they were aware of the situation."

It is true, Israeli TV, docile as Stalin's media, had downplayed the invasion and had broadcast only peaceful pictures of friendly tanks on quiet streets. Still, on the previous night Jerusalem had hosted a big Jewish rally calling for the expulsion of all non-Jews from the Holy Land. Israeli TV reported on Friday night, just before the invasion, that two-thirds of Israeli Jews support this Final Solution. However, every one of us has his freedom of choice, and Rabbi Milgrom chose a Judaism one can live with. I was mightily pleased to see him: God knows, this Sodom needs a few just men.

The interior of the church bore the pockmarks of bullets: Israeli tank crews trained their heavy turret machine-guns on the cradle of Christ. It reminded me of William Dalrymple's "splendid, effective and impressive" book, as the *Financial Times* called it, *From the Holy Mountain*,[13] in which he writes of "a wave of attacks on Church property in Israel. A Jerusalem church, a Baptist chapel and a Christian bookshop had been burned to the ground; there were attempts to arson the Anglican churches in West Jerusalem and Ramleh and two churches in Acre. The Protestant cemetery on Mt. Zion was desecrated no fewer than eight times."

He could have added the story of Daniel Koren, an Israeli soldier whose bullets pulverised the images of Christ and the Virgin in the church of St. Anthony in Jaffa. Dalrymple mentions the deeds of the Jewish 'Mayor' of Jerusalem, Ehud Olmert, who destroyed the newly discovered Christian monasteries and churches in Jerusalem in order to obliterate the very memory of a Christian presence in the Holy Land—the same Mayor Olmert who demolished three more Palestinian homes on the morning we walked the streets of Bethlehem.

In the Grotto of the Nativity, a few candles burned and a Palestinian family quietly prayed by the Star, as their ancestors had done since the days of Sharon's cruel predecessor, King Herod the Great.

It is no strange coincidence that this invasion began while the US Air Force was laying Afghani cities low. Apparently, Sharon's government had decided to utilise the US-Afghani operation to divert attention from the conquest of Palestine. The thief sees in any calamity just another opportunity to steal. While our eyes are attracted to the deserts beyond the Oxus River, while America is scared silly by white powder in an envelope, while humanitarian agencies groan under the masses of starving Afghanis, while the Anglo-American fleet blocks possible Iraqi or Syrian relief, the Israelis grab the remainder of Palestine and eradicate the memory of Christ from His native land.

The opposite reading is also possible. Some Israeli involvement in 9/11 appears to be proven beyond reasonable doubt. Israeli supporters in the US pushed hard for the war in Afghanistan and elsewhere. Could it be that the Towers collapsed and cities were bombed in order to provide Sharon with the once-in-a-lifetime opportunity of a Final Solution?

Sharon's men in the American mass media gave him support by raising the current wave of Arab-bashing and general racist chant. "Osama Bin Laden's shifty, oily, Semitic features leer from every news bulletin, in a barely concealed appeal to the American viewers' racism. Dr. Joseph Goebbels could not have done it better," the British historian David Irving wrote from America. He should know: he is a biographer of Goebbels.

President Bush demanded immediate Israeli withdrawal. He did it *sotto voce*, saving his harsh "there will be no discussion" line for the Afghanis. We shall see whose will prevails, and whether the President's charter goes as far as Israel, whether his bark could be backed by a bite. In P. G. Wodehouse's hilarious novel, *A Damsel in Distress*, there is a wonderful line fully applicable to President Bush:

> Your argument seems to be without a flaw. But what then? We applaud the Man of Logic, but what of the Man of Action? What are you going to do about it?

After our visit to the great church, our procession moved to Beth Jalla, a sister city of Bethlehem. Beth Jalla's two hospitals had been shelled, and ten people were killed by indiscriminate Israeli fire. The bereaved families stood in the church yard, clutching portraits of their dead and receiving condolences. Especially touching was the stunning beauty of Rania Elias, a twenty-year-old girl killed in her own bedroom by an Israeli shell. She had sat for her portrait in a white wedding dress, the dress she was buried in.

Beth Jalla is grim but defiant. On its streets stood young men with AK machineguns. *C'est le Tanzim*, the people's militia, explained a Coptic priest to his Maronite fellows. Dashing Tanzim boys in their berets reminded me of Fidel's young *barbudos*, as if the Palestinian revolution had gained its second breath. As the convoy moved out, the tanks moved in, and the chatter of small arms echoed over the twin cities.

A big, dark-skinned Oriental Jewish taxi driver picked me up at the checkpoint. The massive steering wheel of his Mercedes turned like a toy in his huge hands. He looked like a twin of the giant Tanzim guerrilla I saw fifteen minutes and five hundred yards away, in the Aida refugee camp. "I lived all my life with Arabs," he said. "My wife tells me I am an Arab in my heart. We should live together. As things are, with this war going on, there are no tourists, no income, and no hope. Jerusalem and Bethlehem stand together or fall together."

Yes, despite the official brainwashing, on both sides of the Divide, there is a tacit understanding: the Holy Land can't be divided; it has to be tended jointly by all of us as equals. There is enough room to pray, to play, to grow olive trees, write software and guide tourists. Tanks must go, together with the artificial border between Israel and Palestine.

Notes

13. Publisher: HarperCollins Publishers, 1997, www.fireandwater.com, ISBN 0 00 6547745.

The Last Action Heroes

The East celebrated Easter in May this year, a long time after the West. There was little of the festive spirit, for the Nativity Church of Bethlehem had been besieged for a month. Starved priests and laity had lain in the grotto where the Virgin gave birth to Christ; bodies of policemen slain by Israeli sharp-shooters were piled under the golden *Tree of Jesse* mosaic. From time to time, the attackers propelled flares to the wooden roof of the basilica and watched the weakened by long fast defenders putting the fires out. But Easter brought its miracle, and it was called ISM.

What is ISM? For the reply, go a few hundred yards away from the church, on the broad terrace overlooking the gentle descent of the hills towards the Dead Sea, above the road's double bend. There is a small Byzantine sanctuary adjacent to a water cistern. The Eastern wind blew a layer of desert-dust over its floor mosaics, and proverbial thorns broke through their red crosses. It has an aquatic character like many shrines of the Holy Land and it is called *Bir Daoud* (David's Well), in memory of a legendary exploit.

Once, the conquering army from the cities of the plain declared War on Terror and sealed this hilly village in an effort to catch a local man, the Palestinian terrorist leader Daoud, who had attacked the conquerors' settlements. But his companions, a motley band of men, challenged the invaders' order. They dared the road checks, defied security measures, sneaked into the village, and, against enormous odds, brought a draught of water from the Bethlehem village well to Daoud, or King David, as we call him now.

Millennia passed by, and this exploit was repeated by the new version of King David's companions, the International Solidarity Movement, or ISM, as the land of Palestine became the scene of the most dramatic confrontation and international involvement for decades, if not centuries. Young European and American men and women, who were born too late to join the International Brigades in Republican Spain in 1936, joined the ISM and came to the green hills of Bethlehem and Hebron. They came in a troublesome time: Israeli leaders had carefully laid a plan to expel and exterminate Palestinians and create a country as Jewish as Germany was Aryan. The ISM volunteers derailed this plan by their very presence and saved the local peasants from destruction and expulsion. They live dangerously, playing a cat-and-mouse game with Israeli *mechaslim* ('exterminators'), dodging snipers' bullets, staying in defenceless villages with the peasants. If King David is too far for you, think of them as the Last Action Heroes, of Schwarzenegger fame.

Though some of them have Jewish parents, they rejected the separatist "for Jews only" frameworks perpetuated by Peacenik Zionists. They stand for equality, for the "International Association of Good People," as Isaac Babel would say. They came from the land of Folke Bernadotte, and the land of Abe Lincoln, and the land of T.E. Lawrence. Some of the ISM volunteers saw action in the protests of Seattle, Gothenburg and Genoa, confronting the two-headed dragon of Globalisation and Zionism. Others came to the Holy Land in April 2002, just in time for Israel's Easter Offensive, as Sharon's willing executioners demolished houses, uprooted olive trees, deported thousands of Palestinians into concentration camps, slaughtered hundreds of men, women and children in the Jenin refugee camp and Nablous. When Israel's Juggernaut rolled into Bethlehem, over two hundred local people sought refuge in the church.

The tradition of refuge actually precedes Christianity and was known to mankind from the dawn of civilisation. Churches always provided the place of refuge, and Victor Hugo's *Hunchback of Notre Dame* supplies immediate reference. In Latin America, persecuted people, illegal immigrants and labour leaders were often saved by hiding in churches, while during WWII many thousands of Jews found refuge in Christian churches and monasteries. That is why the people of Bethlehem believed they would be safe behind the thick walls of the oldest church in Christendom.

The Nativity church of Bethlehem was built in AD 325, one of the first three grand Christian edifices of the Holy Land, and the only survivor. Its turbulent history was, on a balance, a rather lucky one: the invading Persians refused the orders of their Jewish commissars to destroy it in AD 614, and the Saracens refused similar orders of Hakim, the mad Caliph of Egypt, in AD 1009, while on both occasions its sister church, the Holy Sepulchre of Jerusalem, was burned and destroyed. In AD 1099, Tancred, the future Prince of Galilee, received at Latrun, thirty miles of hostile territory away, the reports of enemy plans to destroy the Nativity, and he rode through the night at the head of his knights to relieve it.

Crusader-Kings of Jerusalem chose to be crowned in the Nativity, and kings of England and France sent their precious gifts to its see. In AD 1145, the most beautiful mosaic adorned its walls, still showing the Tree of Jesse, and the Tree of Life, and Doubting Thomas touching the wounds of Christ Resurrected. In 1932, the British uncovered a gorgeous Fourth Century floor mosaic, and in AD 2000, Yasser Arafat rebuilt the Manger Square in front of the basilica. The church had been adored by millions throughout the centuries, and that is why people believed they would remain safe in its protection.

But the Jews do not care for sanctity of churches. Granted, there are differences of opinion: Zionist disciples of Rabbi Kook, the main religious denomination in Israel, believe all churches must be destroyed soon, and even before the mosques. For them, the eradication of Christianity is a more important task than the elimination of Palestinians. Their traditionalist opponents think there

Bethlehem Gate

is no rush, and it should be done by the Jewish Messiah of Vengeance, when he arrives. Secular Jews just do not care. That is why the Jewish army had no mental difficulty about surrounding the church or about maintaining the cruellest siege of its long history.

Forty monks and priests remained on duty in the church, together with 200 refugees. For a month, the Israelis did not allow food or water to be brought to the besieged. As in the medieval sieges, people starved and died, after trying to survive on rainwater boiled with lemon leaves and grass. Stench of corpses and of infected wounds filled the old church.

State-of-the-art cameras assisted sharp-shooters who hung outside and shot at every moving figure. Even before the siege, they shot dead a choir boy Johnny, and as I write it, on Easter Saturday May 4, they murdered a lay churchman on duty.

They did it with impunity, as they had allies in the media of the West. The Danish fairy tale writer, Hans Christian Andersen, wrote of the Snow Queen's magic mirror that distorts reality and changes beautiful things into ugly ones, and vice versa. In the magic mirror of CNN, this oldest church became "a place where some Christians believe Jesus was born." The refugees were described as 'terrorists'. The monks and priests became 'hostages' in the magic mirror of the Snow Queen. Cries of the besieged would not come through the Israeli-managed western media.

In this dark hour, ISM rode in. As the Holy Land had prepared for Good Friday (the majority of Palestinian Christians belongs to the Greek Orthodox Church of Jerusalem), two dozen volunteers divided into two groups: One of them staged a diversion in the best tradition of Alistair McLean's *Guns of Navarone*. While Israeli soldiers momentarily taken aback by their foolhardy bravery proceeded to capture them, the second group rushed forward and entered the gates of the church. They brought with them some food and water to the starving beleaguered refugees, something to look forward to for Easter Sunday. Probably the history books will call their breakthrough 'the Easter Rescue'.

When Zionism is laid to rest, the names of these daring men and women will be carved on the walls of the church. In the sacristy, next to the sword of Godfrey de Bouillon, the Defender of the Holy Sepulchre (the leader of the First Crusade refused the crown, but accepted the title) will be the baseball hats and sneakers of the Defenders of the Nativity.

Those who got into the church, to share hunger and danger of the siege: Alistair Hillman (UK), Allan Lindgaard (Denmark), Erik Algers (Sweden), Jacqueline Soohen (Canada) Kristen Schurr (USA), Larry Hales (USA), Mary Kelly (Ireland), Nauman Zaidi (USA), Stefan Coster (Sweden), and Robert O'Neill (USA).

Those who sacrificed their freedom, created diversion and were jailed: Jeff Kingham (USA), Jo Harrison (UK), Johannes Wahlstrom (Sweden), James Hanna (USA), Kate Thomas (UK), Marcia Tubbs (UK), John Caruso (USA), Nathan Musselman (USA), Nathan Mauger (USA), Trevor Baumgartner (USA), Thomas Kootsoukos (USA), Ida Fasten (Sweden), Huwaida Arraf (USA).

The diversionary group was arrested for the dreadful crime of bringing food to the starving refugees in the Church at Easter: At first, the men were separated from women and taken to jail in the illegal Jewish settlement of Etzion. The women were sent to Jerusalem, then brought before the court, where they were sentenced to be deported. On the way to the jail transport, the English girls jumped off and escaped their guards. One of them was caught by an Israeli civilian who did not hesitate to pull a knife on a girl. The other two are on the run, together with the Swedish girl Ida.

They showed what real civil disobedience is, and how a non-violent and humanitarian action can make a difference even in the brutal circumstances of the Israeli occupation. At the time of writing the men are still in jail in occupied Hebron, in the hands of its fanatical settlers.

Though they committed no offence in the territory of Israel, they have been sentenced to be deported and forbidden to enter Israel for ten years. One hopes the apartheid 'state of Israel' will not last that long. Their sentence proved that for Israelis, 'Palestinian territories' are just a legal fiction to be applied or discarded whenever needed. We could do the same and demand equality for all, Jew and Gentile alike, in the whole of Palestine.

As a professional journalist, I regret that this tense drama of siege, breakthrough, diversion, relief, salvation, arrest, escape and confrontation at Easter in the shadow of the great church, the best stuff there is, did not reach the mass audience of Europe and America, that it was not broadcasted by all TV stations and reprinted by all newspapers.

But the regret does not diminish my joy, as one of the kids who broke the siege was my own son.

Hills of Judea

A small radical organisation named Taayush organised a convoy to deliver food and water to the besieged peasants of Yatta. I went there with some 200 Israelis, Jews and Palestinians, and found a grim and disturbing picture. But first, a few words about the place.

Yatta is a Palestinian equivalent of Calabria: harsh bare hills, rocky slopes, rare small springs of water, meagre grass, a land of shepherds and their flocks. That is the biblical Judea proper, the home country of King David. Here he lived as an outlaw before he became a king, and the places named Carmel, Yatta, Maon are mentioned in the Bible. Local peasants have not changed much since these days. They still live the same way and walk the same flocks. They build no houses, but live in caves, big spacious airy caves, with enough room for their sheep. These caves remind us of the cave in nearby Bethlehem, where Jesus was born. They collect rainwater, and dig wells to store it. They are handsome folk, tall, with wonderful white teeth and friendly smiles. They preserved a local dialect and even some biblical traditions that disappeared elsewhere.

The Jews prefer a Zionist legend, that our ancestors were expelled from these places, and the country was repopulated by Arab nomads. Legends are very good, but archaeology proves the opposite. The peasants of Southern Judea never moved from their places, never studied Talmud, never spoke Yiddish or Ladino. They were and remained shepherds. Some romantic Romanians say they are the only real descendants of Romans and modern Italians are newcomers. It is the Italians' good luck that the Romanians are not as strong and insistent as Jews.

The peasants of South Yatta had no such good luck. The state of Israel confiscated their land, dynamited their caves, brought bulldozers and ruined wells. Jews from Brooklyn and Russia took over the hilltops and built a few settlements of stone villas with red roofs. They also brought hundreds of Thai and Chinese to work for them. They drilled the hills for water, and the tiny local springs dried up.

Now the cave dwellers stay on the bare hills. Whenever they put up tents, the Jewish Army destroys them. We came there and met these peasants. They showed us their ruins. It is not an easy thing to destroy caves and wells, but it can be done with modern technique. With enough dynamite, you can throw people of the caves further into the Stone Age. What we saw explained the American attraction to Israel.

Israel/Palestine is the model of the world Americans want to achieve. It has peasants and their flocks dying of thirst, and on the hilltop, there are villas and a swimming pool for the Chosen folk. It has a huge army, and it has many labourers without any rights. In order to turn all the world into Palestine, they began World War III against the Third World.

While we spoke with the peasants, an army jeep drove by. "We came to protect you," said the officer.

"We do not need protection," the activists replied.

"You will get it anyway. We do not allow the Jews and the Arabs to be together without our presence," he insisted, like an old-fashioned duenna in a *commedia del arte.*

Eventually we drove back. "It is a beautiful land," a girl said, "and we could live so well together." She was right. Palestine is beautiful, and we could live here together very well on one condition. We must have equal rights. Jews and non-Jews should have the same protection of the law, right to vote, and even more important—right to drink water. It sounds very radical. But the events in Palestine mean so much because there is a magic connection between the Holy Land and the world. *If we make here the world of equality, equality will come everywhere.*

But meanwhile, the world goes in the opposite direction. Soon, America will bomb Iraq and Afghanistan and millions of refugees will run into Europe. The European way of life will be destroyed. Rich people will remain in their small settlements with armed perimeters and the army will dynamite the wells. Probably, that is one of the goals of the American New World Order, that looks too similar to the old idea of revenge.

On the way home, the car radio brought us the words of President Bush. He compared Muslims to Nazis. Just a few years ago, his father compared Communists to Nazis. Apparently, Americans can have only two ideologies on the Earth: one, neo-liberalism, the faith of *vae victis*, and another, Zionism.

PART II

Galilee Flowers

[This essay was written in the spring 2001, and it was meant to undermine the 'Judeo-Christian' myth of the US fancy, to help believing Christians understand the real relationship of Jewish and Christian narratives.]

When in 1543 the typhoon-blown Portuguese schooners approached the shores of Japan, the astonished sailors could not believe their eyes: on a warm spring day, the tropical "island ahoy" was buried under snow. They were witness to one of the real Seven Wonders of the World, the flowers of *sakura*, the wild cherry of Japan. As soon as the benevolent heaven bestows this seasonal gift upon earth, the Japanese forget their wives and kids, their duties, employers and bills; they just sit under the trees, drink sake wine and write poems, short and sharp as daggers.

That is why, these days, leaving behind our man-made troubles, I sit under the white cloud of a tree and watch the beautiful white and pink blossoms of the almond trees that cover the hills of Galilee. These lovely blossoms are our version of the Japanese *sakura*, and a chance to indulge in the custom of flower viewing. A honey aroma wafts through the air; the skies are crystal blue. Yellow daisies dance on the lush green grass at the base of these almond wonders, interspersed by violet cyclamen and red anemones. The glorious backdrop is provided by the huge snow mass of Jabal al Sheikh (Mt Hermon). Palestine is a sister to Japan. These two hilly lands are home to stubborn mountain folk, devoted to their customs and ways.

For all the similarities in the landscape, there are differences. The hill we sit on, all white like Jaffa sea surf, is the ruin of a village. If we were in Japan it would be alive and humming. The village of Birim has been dead for fifty years. It is beautiful even in death, like Ophelia floating down the stream in the pre-Raphaelite painting of Millais. It was not ruined by war. Its Christian inhabitants were expelled from their houses well after the 1948 war. They were told to leave for a week or two, for 'security' reasons. They had no option but to believe the Israeli officers and move out. Their village was dynamited, their church surrounded by barbed wire. They went to the Israeli Supreme Court, they went to the government, commissions were appointed and petitions signed. Nothing helped. For fifty years since then, they have lived in the nearby villages, and on Sundays they return to worship in their church. Their lands were seized by their Jewish neighbours, but they still bring their dead to be buried in the church graveyard, under the sign of the cross.

Until the arrival of the Israeli army, this ruined village with its orphaned church was the home of the rural Christians of Birim who for centuries of Moslem rule lived in peace with their Moslem neighbours of Nebi Yosha and with the old Sephardi Jewish community of nearby Safed. This Guernica of Galilee undermines the "Clash of Civilizations" myth of a "Judeo-Christian" civilization opposing a "monstrous" Islam. Among followers of Samuel Huntington's myth, one can find a friend of Marc Rich and a newly minted New York citizen, W. J. Clinton, and a friend of A. Sharon, G. W. Bush.

The problems of the Middle East are ugly enough without the current Moslem-bashing. The pro-Israeli pundits of the *New York Times* quote the blood-curdling verses on Jihad and re-tell the old traditions of religious wars and persecutions to 'prove' Islam's cruelty and intolerance. An upper-class Jewish lady, Barbara Amiel, who happens to be the wife and guiding light of the Pinochet-worshipping media-mogul Conrad Black, writes *sotto voce* about 'exclusivist' Islam and Jewish 'moderation'. In order to incite hatred, Israel's lobby works all the ropes. Before the rise of Israel, Arab sheiks were depicted as romantic heroes in movies starring Rudolf Valentino. Nowadays, the pro-Israel producers of Hollywood turn out propaganda films of ill-shaven Moslem terrorists with the subtlety of Edward D. Wood, Jr. This new prejudice is amplified a hundredfold by the Christian Zionist Congress, claiming "protection for Christians of Palestine from the Moslem (?!) persecution." These people obviously have not walked among the ruins of Birim.

Another email drops into my laptop, this time from Gaza. An American lady, Alison Weir from San Francisco, evades Israeli bullets, comforts the scared Palestinian kids, and writes:

> The problem is when you know the truth, it is far too cruel, far too diametrically opposite to what we used to think and what everyone still thinks to express. The lie is too big, the repression too complete, the Palestinians' lives too horrible to write about reasonably.

Well, Alison is right. We face a huge lie, an anti-Moslem blood libel, and it is time to stop it. I do not think the problems of the Middle East are directly related to religion. But if the supporters of Israel want to wake up the sleeping ghost of religious intolerance to incite Christians against Moslems, let us audit their balance.

If these Christian Zionists care for Christ, not only for Zion, let them learn what Jews and Moslems feel towards Christ. Rami Rozen expressed the Jewish tradition in a long feature in a major Israeli newspaper, *Haaretz*:[14]

> Jews feel towards Jesus today what they felt in 4 CE or in the Middle Ages . . . It is not fear, it is hatred and contempt. For centuries, Jews

> concealed from Christians their hate for Jesus, and this tradition continues even now.

"He [Jesus Christ] is revolting and repulsive," intervened an important modern religious Jewish thinker. This "repulsion passed from the observant Jews to the general Israeli public," Rozen replied.

On Christmas Eve, according to a feature in the Jerusalem local paper, *Kol Ha-Ir*,[15] Hassids customarily do not read holy books, as it could save Jesus from eternal punishment (the Talmud teaches that Jesus boils in hell).[16] This custom was dying out, but Hassids of Habad, fervent nationalists, brought it back to life. I still remember old Jews spitting while passing by a church and cursing the dead while passing by a Christian cemetery. Last year in Jerusalem a Jew decided to refresh the tradition. He spat at a Holy Cross being carried in procession in a city street. Police saved him from consequent trouble, but the court fined him $50, despite his claim that he had been fulfilling his religious duty.

Last year the biggest Israeli tabloid, *Yedioth Aharonoth*, re-printed in its library the Jewish anti-Gospel, *Toledoth Eshu*, compiled in the Middle Ages. It is the third recent reprint, including one in a newspaper. If the Gospel is the book of love, *Toledoth* is the book of hate for Christ. The hero of the book is Judas. He captures Jesus by polluting his purity. According to *Toledoth*, the conception of Christ was in sin, the miracles of Jesus were witchcraft, his resurrection but a trick.

Writing on the Passion of Jesus, Joseph Dan, Professor of Jewish mysticism at the Hebrew University in Jerusalem, stated:

> The modern Jewish apologists, hesitantly adopted by the church, preferred to put the blame on the Romans. But the medieval Jew did not wish to pass the buck. He tried to prove that Jesus had to be killed, and he was proud of killing Him. The Jews hated and despised Christ and Christians.

Prof. Dan added that there is little place to doubt that the Jewish enemies of Jesus caused his execution. Even today, Jews in Israel refer to Jesus by the demeaning word 'Yeshu' (instead of 'Yeshua') meaning 'perish his name'. There is an ongoing argument about whether His name was turned into a swear word, or other way around. In a similar pun, the Gospel is called 'Avon Gilaion', the booklet of Sin. These are the endearing feelings towards Christ of the friends of Christian Zionists.

What about Moslems? The Moslems venerate Christ. He is called 'The Word of God', 'Logos', 'Messiah', 'Christ', 'the Prophet' and is considered a Messenger of God, along with Abraham, Moses and Muhammad. Many chapters of the Koran tell the story of Christ, his virgin birth and his persecution by Jews.

His saintly mother is admired, and the Immaculate Conception is one of the tenets of Islam. The name of Christ glorifies the golden edifice of Haram al-Sharif. According to the Moslem faith, it was there that the founder of Islam met Jesus, and they prayed together. The Hadith, the Moslem tradition, says in the name of the prophet: "We do not forbid you to believe in Christ; we order you to." Moslems identify their prophet Muhammad with Paracletes the Helper (Jn 14:16) whose coming was predicted by Jesus. They venerate places associated with the life of Jesus: the place of Ascension, the Tomb of Lazarus and the Nativity are adjacent to a mosque and perfectly accessible by Christians.

Although Moslems (and many Protestants) do not consider that Jesus is God, they proclaim him to be the Messiah, the Anointed one, the Paradise Dweller. This religious idea, familiar to Nestorians and other early churches but rejected by mainstream Christianity, opened the gates for those Jews who could not part with the notion of strict monotheism. That is why many Palestinian Jews and Christians of the Seventh Century accepted Islam and became Palestinian Moslems. They remained in their villages; they did not depart for Poland or England; they did not learn Yiddish; they did not study the Talmud, but they continued to shepherd their flocks and plant almond trees. They remained faithful to their land and to the great idea of the fraternity of man.

In the south of Hebron, in the ruins of Susiah, one can see how in the course of two centuries a synagogue slowly evolved into a mosque as the population of nearby caves abandoned the exclusionary faith of the Babylonian wizards and adopted Islam. These shepherds still live there, in the same caves. In the last year, the Israeli army has twice tried to expel them to provide more room for new settlers from Brooklyn.

Why, in this season of blossoming almond trees, do I brood on the sensitive subject of Jewish and Moslem attitudes towards Christ? Because one has to stop the mills of hatred operated by Israel's supporters. Because the 'Judeo-Christian' code-language is being used to justify the barbed wire around Birim's Church and the tanks around Bethlehem. Because there is a duty to remove an obstacle from the path of the blind.

Modern Jews are still haunted by a Christ Complex. Whether we confess or deny it, this special feeling—call it subconscious hostility to Christ—still remains with Jews, even the most liberal ones. Compare it with the Electra and Oedipus complex. We do not have sex with our mothers and daughters, and we do not normally demolish churches. Still these suppressed feelings influence our behaviour.

The majority of Christian Zionists are simple, misled souls, people of good intentions but little knowledge. They think they "support Jews," but they promote the Christ-hating spirit among the Jews. It was not in vain that a hero of the Zionist Bible, *Exodus* by Leon Uris, kept a poster in his room saying "We crucified Christ." It was not in vain that an Israeli soldier on the roadblock of

Bethlehem told me yesterday, "We starve the beasts," referring to the native Christians of the city of the Nativity. It is not for nothing that the Gospel was burned at the stake in Israel, that anti-Gospel literature is widely spread; that new immigrant Jews embracing Christianity are persecuted and deported; that every preacher of the Christian faith in Israel can be sent to jail according to new anti-Christian laws; that Israeli archaeologists raze the Christian holy sites and memories off the face of the Holy Land.

To the leaders of the Christian Zionists, who surely know these facts, but lead their innocent flock on the path of the Anti-Christ, I say:

> Whoever causes one of these little ones who believe in Christ to sin, it would be better for him to have a large millstone tied round his neck and be drowned in the deep sea. (Mt 18:6).

To my Jewish brothers I say: the opinions of medieval Jews do not bind us. Every Jew can decide for himself, whether to pray for the destruction of the Gentiles or to share the blessing of the Holy Land with the villagers of Birim and Bethlehem. Within the Jewish people, there always were spiritual descendants of the prophets who wished to bring peace and blessing to all the children of Adam. As true as this almond blossom, in you the prophecy will be fulfilled: "All the nations of the earth will bless you." (Deut. 7).

Notes

14. 28.1.94.
15. 14.12.93.
16. Gittin, 56b–57a.

Mamilla Pool

I

Things move really fast nowadays. Just yesterday we hardly dared to call the Israeli policy of official discrimination against Palestinians by the harsh word 'apartheid'. Today, as Sharon's tanks and missiles pound defenceless cities and villages, the word barely suffices. It has become an unjustified insult to the white supremacists of South Africa. They, after all, did not use gun-ships and tanks against the natives; they did not lay siege to Soweto. They did not deny the humanity of their *kaffirs*. The Jewish supremacists made it one better. They have returned us, as if by magic wand, to the world of Joshua and Saul.

As the search for the right word continues, the courageous Robert Fisk proposes calling the events in Palestine a 'civil war'. If this is civil war, the slaughter of a lamb is a bullfight. The disparity of forces is just too large. No, Virginia, it is not 'civil war', it is creeping genocide.

This is the point in our saga, where the good Jewish guy is supposed to take out his hanky and exclaim: "How could we, eternal victims of persecutions, commit such crimes!" Well, do not hold your breath waiting for this line. It happened before and it can happen again.

Jews are not more bloodthirsty than the rest of mankind. But the mad idea of being the Chosen ones, the idea of supremacy, whether of race or religion, is the moving force behind genocides. If you believe God chose your people to rule the world, if you think others but subhuman, you will be punished by the same God whose name you took in vain. Instead of a gentle frog, he would turn you into a murderous maniac.

When the Japanese got a whiff of this malady in the 1930s, they raped Nanking and ate the liver of their prisoners. Germans, obsessed by the Aryan superiority complex, filled Babi Yar with corpses. As thoughtful readers of *Joshua* and *Judges*, the father pilgrim-founders of the United States tried on the 'Chosen' crown and succeeded in nearly exterminating the Native American peoples.

The Jewish chosen-ness led to genocide time and again. Outside of Jerusalem's Jaffa gate (Bab al-Halil), there was once a small neighbourhood called Mamilla, destroyed by real-estate developers just a few years ago. In its place they created a monstrous 'village' for the super-rich, abutting the plush Hilton Hotel. A bit farther away there is the old Mamilla cemetery of the Arab nobles and the Mamilla Pool, a water reservoir dug by Pontius Pilate. During the development works, the workers came upon a burial cave holding hundreds of sculls and bones. It was adorned by a cross and the legend: "God alone knows their names." The *Biblical Archaeology Review*, published by the Jewish American Herschel Shanks, printed a long feature[17] by the Israeli archaeologist Ronny Reich on this discovery.

The dead were laid to their eternal rest in AD 614, the most dreadful year in the history of Palestine until the Twentieth Century. The Scottish scholar Adam Smith, wrote in his *Historical Geography of Palestine*: "Until now, the terrible devastation of 614 is visible in the land, it could not be healed."

By 614 Palestine was a part of the Roman successor state, the Byzantine Empire. It was a prosperous, predominantly Christian land of well-developed agriculture, of harnessed water systems and carefully laid terraces. Pilgrims came in flocks to the Holy places. The Constantine-built edifices of the Ascension on the Mount of Olives and of the Holy Sepulchre were among the man-made wonders of the world. The Judean wilderness was enlivened by eighty monasteries, where precious manuscripts were collected and prayers offered. The Fathers of the church, St. Jerome of Bethlehem and Origen and Eusebius of Caesarea, were still a living memory. One of the best Palestinian writers, on a par with the Minor Prophets, blessed John Moschos, just completed his *Spiritual Meadow*.

There was also a small, wealthy Jewish community living in their midst, mainly in Tiberias on the shores of the Sea of Galilee. Their scholars had just completed their version of the Talmud, the codification of their faith, Rabbinic Judaism; but for instruction they deferred to the prevailing Jewish community in Persian Babylonia.

II

In 614 local Palestinian Jews allied with their Babylonian co-religionists and assisted the Persians in their conquest of the Holy Land. Twenty-six thousand Jews participated in the onslaught. In the aftermath of the Persian victory, the Jews perpetrated a massive holocaust of Palestine's Christians. They burned the churches and the monasteries, killed monks and priests, burned books. The beautiful basilica of Fishes and Loaves in Tabgha, the Ascension on the Mount of Olives, St. Stephen opposite Damascus Gate and the Hagia Sion on Mt. Zion are just at the top of the list of perished edifices. Indeed, very few churches survived the onslaught. The Great Laura of St. Sabas, tucked away in the bottomless Ravine of Fire (Wadi an-Nar) was saved by its remote location and steep crags. The Church of the Nativity miraculously survived: when Jews commanded its destruction, the Persians balked. They perceived the Magi mosaic above the lintel as the portrait of Persian kings.

This devastation was not the worst crime. When Jerusalem surrendered to the Persians, thousands of local Christians became prisoners of war and were herded to the Mamilla Pool area. The Israeli archaeologist Ronny Reich writes:

> They were probably sold to the highest bidder. According to some sources, the Christian captives at Mamilla Pond were bought by Jews and were then slain on the spot.

The Oxford Professor Henry Hart Milman's *History of the Jews* describes it in stronger terms:

> It had come at length, the long-expected hour of triumph and vengeance; and the Jews did not neglect the opportunity. They washed away the profanation of the holy city in Christian blood. The Persians are said to have sold the miserable captives for money. The vengeance of the Jews was stronger than their avarice; not only did they not scruple to sacrifice their treasures in the purchase of these devoted bondsmen, they put to death all they had purchased at a lavish price. It was a rumour of the time that 90,000 perished.

An eyewitness to the massacre, Strategius of St. Sabas, was more vivid:

> Thereupon the vile Jews . . . rejoiced exceedingly, because they detested the Christians, and they conceived an evil plan. As of old they bought the Lord from the Jews with silver, so they purchased Christians out of the reservoir . . . How many souls were slain in the reservoir of Mamilla! How many perished of hunger and thirst! How many priests and monks were massacred by the sword! How many maidens, refusing their abominable outrages, were given over to death by the enemy! How many parents perished on top of their children! How many of the people were brought up by the Jews and butchered, and became confessors of Christ! Who can count the multitude of the corpses of those who were massacred in Jerusalem!

Strategius estimated the victims of the holocaust at 66,000.

In plain prose, the Jews ransomed the Christians from the hands of the Persian soldiers for good money to slaughter them at Mamilla Pool, "and it ran with blood." Jews massacred between 60,000 and 90,000 Palestinian Christians in Jerusalem alone, almost 1.5 million in today's values (the total earth's population was, according to the *Encyclopaedia Britannica* about 300 million, twenty times smaller than today). A few days later, the Persian military understood the magnitude of the massacre and stopped the Jews.

III

To his credit, the Israeli archaeologist Ronny Reich does not try to shift the blame for the massacres onto the Persians, as it is usually done nowadays. He admits that "the Persian Empire was not based on religious principles and was indeed inclined to religious tolerance." This good man is clearly unsuitable to write for the *Washington Post*. That paper's correspondent in Israel would have had no trouble describing the massacre as "retaliatory strike by the Jews who suffered under Christian rule."

The holocaust of the Christian Palestinians in year 614 is well documented and you will find it described in older books. It has been censored out of modern guides and history books. Elliott Horowitz described, in his brilliant expose of the Jewish apologia[18] how almost all Jewish historians suppressed the facts and re-wrote history. The cover-up continues even now. Recent Israeli publications attach the blame to the Persians, as they push the responsibility for the Sabra and Shatila massacre onto the Lebanese Maronites. Horowitz writes:

> Raul Hilberg, in *The Destruction of the European Jews*, asserted that "preventive attack, armed resistance, and revenge are almost completely absent in two thousand years of Jewish ghetto history." Avi Yona, a leading Israeli historian, Leon Polyakov, author of *History of Anti-Semitism* (published at the expense of Marc Rich, the thief - ISH) and many others glossed over the holocaust of 614, kept silent or denied it completely. Benzion Dinur, a former director of the Holocaust Museum Yad va-Shem, told his readers euphemistically, in language that might have offended him if used with regard to Jews, that "recalcitrant Christians were firmly held in check."

As a rule, Jewish historical and ideological writing is notoriously unreliable and apologetic, Horowitz shows. Granted, "not all Jews," *vide* Horowitz, Finkelstein and other wonderful men, but they would be the first to agree with the truth of the above. The feeling of self-righteousness and perpetual victimhood reinforced by a tendentious, distorted historical narrative is a source of mental dysfunction, an obsession common to many modern Jews. This obsession intoxicates Jews and gives them unusual strength in promoting their own distorted narrative. In a way, this massive distortion of reality turns Jews into victorious berserks of ideological struggle. Still, while being a successful strategy, it is a mental disease, a danger to the souls of Jews and to the lives of others.

The Jews are not unique. Germans were intoxicated by the injustice of Versailles, and Adolf Hitler gave voice to the ill. Eric Margolis of the *Toronto*

Sun[19] wrote about Armenians inflamed by the story of their holocaust. They massacred thousands of their peaceful Azeri neighbours in the 1990s, and uprooted 800,000 native non-Armenians. "It's time to recognize all the world's horrors," Margolis concludes. It is time to recognise the danger of inflammatory and one-sided narrative, I would add. The same system of tendentious reality-distorting narrative was deployed by the Jewish activists of militant feminism, communism, psychoanalysis, neo-conservatism, neo-liberalism, Zionism and a plethora of smaller movements as the means to enrage and intoxicate supporters for the ideological struggle.

As a result, we live in a psychotic, sick world. Our main communication system, the media, aggravates the malady, and leads us to our perdition. It is necessary to promote balanced, alternative discourse in order to return to the common sense. Since the Jews have become so prominent in the modern world, Jewish lopsided discourse has to be deconstructed and the crown of martyrdom carefully removed.

The tragic events of 614 should be returned into historical narrative, for it will help the Jews to heal their paranoid delusion. Without this knowledge one cannot understand the provisions of the treaty between the Jerusalemites and Caliph Omar ibn Khattab, concluded in the year 638. In the Sulh al Quds, as this treaty of capitulation is called, Patriarch Sofronius demanded, and the powerful Arab ruler concurred to protect the people of Jerusalem from the ferocity of the Jews.

The genocide of the AD 614 was the most horrible, but not the only genocide wreaked by Jews in those troubled years. Though the biblical story of the Canaan conquest by Joshua is just a story, it influenced Jewish souls. The Sixth Century was an era of strong Jewish influence, and it had more than its fair share of genocide.

Just a few years before 614, in 610, the Jews of Antioch massacred Christians. The Jewish historian Graetz wrote:

> [The Jews] fell upon their Christian neighbours and retaliated for the injuries which they had suffered; they killed all that fell into their hands, and threw their bodies into the fire, as the Christians had done to them a century before. The Patriarch Anastasius, an object of special hate, was shamefully abused by them, and his body dragged through the streets before he was put to death.

For Graetz, as for IDF spokesmen, Jews always kill "in retaliation." This dogma was not invented by CNN and Sharon: it is deeply rooted in the Jewish psyche as the ultimate defence. This historian (like other Jewish historians) did not care to mention that:

> The Jews of Antioch disembowelled the great Patriarch Anastasius, forced him to eat his own intestines; they hurled his genitals into his face.[20]

IV

After the Arab conquest, a majority of Palestinian Jews accepted the message of the Messenger, as did the majority of Palestinian Christians, albeit for somewhat different reasons. For local Christians, Islam was a sort of Nestorian Christianity without icons, without Constantinople's interference and without Greeks. (The Greek domination of the Palestinian church remains a problem for the local Christians to this very day.)

For ordinary local Jews, Islam was the return to the faith of Abraham and Moses. They had not been able to follow the intricacies of the new Babylonian faith anyway. The majority of them became Muslims and blended into the Palestinian population.

V

Modern Jews do not have to feel guilty for the misdeeds of Jews long gone. No son is responsible for the sins of his father. Israel could have turned this mass grave with its Byzantine chapel and mosaics into a small and poignant memorial reminding its citizens of a horrible page in the history of the land and of the dangers of genocidal supremacy. Instead, the Israeli authorities preferred to demolish the tomb and create an underground parking-lot in its place. That did not cause a murmur.

The guardians of the Jewish conscience, Amos Oz and others, have objected to the destruction of ancient remains. No, not of the tomb at Mamilla. They ran a petition against the keepers of the Haram al-Sharif mosque complex for digging a ten-inch trench to lay a new pipe. It did not matter to them that in an op-ed in *Haaretz*, the leading Israeli archaeologist denied any relevance of the mosque-works to science. They still described it as "a barbaric act of Muslims aimed at the obliteration of the Jewish heritage of Jerusalem." Among the signatories I found, to my amazement and sorrow, the name of Ronny Reich. One thought he might have told those who obliterated the vestiges of the Jewish heritage at Mamilla Pool.

Censored history creates a distorted picture of reality. Recognition of the past is a necessary step on the way to sanity. The Germans and the Japanese have recognized the crimes of their fathers, have come to grips with their moral failings and have emerged as humbler, less boastful folks, akin to the rest of the human race. We Jews have so far failed to exorcise the haughty spirit of the Chosen-ness, and find ourselves in a dire predicament.

That is why the idea of supremacy is still with us, still calling for genocide. In 1982, Amos Oz[21] met an Israeli who shared with the writer his dream of becoming a Jewish Hitler to the Palestinians. Persistent rumours identify the potential Hitler as Ariel Sharon. Whether it is true or not, slowly this dream is becoming a reality.

The *Haaretz* published an ad on its front page,[22] a *fatwa*, signed by a group of Rabbis. The Rabbis proclaimed the theological identification of Ishmael (the Arabs) with the Amalek. 'Amalek' is mentioned in the Bible as the name of a tribe that caused trouble for the Children of Israel. In this story the God of Israel commands His people to exterminate the Amalek tribe completely, including its livestock. King Saul botched the job: he exterminated them all right, but failed to kill nubile, unwed maidens. This 'failure' cost him his crown. The obligation to exterminate the people of Amalek is still counted among the tenets of the Jewish faith, though for centuries nobody identified a living nation with the accursed tribe.

There was one exclusion, which shows how dangerous the ruling is. At the end of WWII, some Jews, including the late Prime Minister Menachem Begin, identified the Germans with Amalek. Indeed, a Jewish religious socialist and a fighter against Nazis, Abba Kovner, hatched a plot in 1945 to poison the water-supply system of German cities and to kill "six million Germans." He obtained poison from the future President of Israel, Efraim Katzir. Katzir, supposedly, thought Kovner intended to poison "only" a few thousand German POWs. The plan mercifully flopped when Kovner was stopped by British officials in a European port. This story was published last year in Israel in a biography of Kovner written by Prof Dina Porat, head of the Anti-Semitism Research Centre at Tel Aviv University.[23]

In plain English, the Rabbis' *fatwa* means: our religious duty is to kill all Arabs, including women and babies and their livestock to the last cat. The liberal *Haaretz*, whose editor and owner are sufficiently versed to understand the *fatwa*, did not hesitate to place the ad. Some Palestinian activists recently criticized me for associating with the Russian weekly *Zavtra* and for quoting the American weekly *Spotlight*. I wonder why they have not condemned me for writing in *Haaretz*? *Zavtra* and *Spotlight* have never published a call to genocide, after all.

It would be unfair to single out *Haaretz*. Another prominent Jewish newspaper, the *Washington Post*, published an equally passionate call to genocide by Charles Krauthammer.[24] This adept of King Saul cannot rely upon his audience's knowledge of the Bible, so he refers to General Powell's slaughter of routed Iraqi troops at the end of the Gulf war. He quotes Colin Powell saying of the Iraqi army: "First we're going to cut it off, then we're going to kill it." For Krauthammer with his carefully chosen quotes, multitudes of slain Arabs do not qualify for the human pronoun 'them'. They are an 'it'. In the last stage of the Gulf War, immense numbers of retreating and disarmed Iraqis were slaughtered in cold blood by the US Air Force, their bodies buried by bulldozers in the desert sand in huge and nameless mass graves. The number of victims of this hecatomb is estimated from one hundred thousand to half a million. God alone knows their names.

Krauthammer wants to repeat this feat in Palestine. 'It' is already cut off, divided by the Israeli army into seventy pieces. Now it is ready for the great kill. "Kill it!" he calls with great passion. He must be worried that the Persians will again stop the bloodbath before the Mamilla Pool fills up. His worries are our hopes.

Notes

17. BAR, 1996, v 22 No 2.
18. "The Vengeance of the Jews Was Stronger Than Their Avarice": Modern Historians and the Persian Conquest of Jerusalem in 614, published in *Jewish Social Studies*, Volume 4, Number 2 (Indiana University).
19. 22.04.2001.
20. Horowitz, ibid.
21. *Here and there in the Land of Israel*, Amos Oz.
22. 21 November, 2000.
23. *Haaretz*, 28 April 2001.
24. *Washington Post*, 20 Apr 2001.

April is the Cruellest Month

[Written for the April 9, 2001 commemoration of the Deir Yassin massacre.]

On a beautiful spring day, when the skies of the Holy Land are a tender blue and the grass is a verdant green, air-conditioned buses ferry tourists from the City of the Plain to the City in the Mountains. A small distance past the halfway point, just beyond the reconstructed Ottoman inn of Bab al-Wad, the Gate of the Valley, the bus drives past the red-painted skeletons of armoured vehicles. This is where the tour guides make their routine pitch: "These vehicles are in memory of the heroic break-through of Jews relieving the blockade of Jerusalem imposed by the aggression of nine Arab states." The number of Arab states varies with the mood of the guides and how they size up their audience.

The battle for the road to Jerusalem was a high point of the 1948 Civil war in Palestine, and it ended with the Zionist Jews of the Plain capturing the prosperous West End of Jerusalem with the white stone mansions of the Arab nobles and the German, Greek and Armenian merchants. In the course of these battles they also subdued the neutral, non-Zionist Jewish neighbourhoods. Zionists expelled the Gentiles in a massive sweep of ethnic cleansing and contained the local Jews in the ghetto. In order to achieve this feat, on their way to the city they razed Palestinian villages to the ground.

The rusted junk is barely an adequate backdrop for the standard Israeli narration, and it would not qualify for a realistic film production. It is a staged scene that lacks the authentic look that movie directors require. The story of the blockade and aggression is a theatre play, not a cinema script. It is an encore performance for tourist indoctrination on the non-stop trip to the Wailing Wall and the Holocaust Museum.

The war for this road was over in April 1948, weeks before Israel declared its independence on the fifteenth of May, before the hapless rag-tag units of Arab neighbours entered Palestine and saved what remained of the native population. As T.S. Elliot observed, April is the cruellest month. And so it was that fateful April when the Palestinians were doomed to start a journey to five decades of exile. Its apotheosis was reached near the entrance to Jerusalem, where the Sacharov gardens lead to a cemetery, to a lunatic asylum and to Deir Yassin.

Death has many names. The Czechs call it Lidice, the French word is Oradur, in Vietnamese they use My Lai. For every Palestinian it is Deir Yassin. On the night of the ninth of April 1948, the Jewish terrorist groups Etzel and Lehi attacked the peaceful village and massacred its men, women and children. I do not want to repeat the gory tale of sliced off ears, gutted bellies, raped women, torched men, bodies dumped in stone quarries or the triumphal parade of the murderers. Existentially, all massacres are alike, from Babi Yar to Chain Saw Gang to Deir Yassin. Yet, the Deir Yassin massacre is special for three reasons.

One: it is well documented and witnessed. Other Jewish fighters from the Hagana and Palmach, Jewish Scouts, Red Cross representatives and the British police of Jerusalem left complete records of the event. It was just one of many massacres of Palestinians by the Jews during the war of 1948, but none received as much attention. This is probably due to the fact that Jerusalem, the seat of the British Mandate in Palestine, was just around the corner.

Two: Deir Yassin massacre had dire consequences beyond its own tragic fate. The horror of the massacre triggered the mass flight from nearby Palestinian villages and gave the Jews full control of the western approaches to Jerusalem. The flight was a prudent and rational choice for the civilian population. As I write this, my TV glares with the image of Macedonian peasants fleeing a war zone. My mother's family escaped from burning Minsk on June 22, 1941, and survived. My father's family remained and perished. After the war my parents could return like other war refugees. The Palestinians, however, have not been allowed to come back, to this very day.

Three: the careers of the murderers. The commanders of the Etzel and Lehi gangs, Menahem Begin and Yitzhak Shamir, eventually became Israeli prime ministers. None of them expressed any remorse, and Menahem Begin lived the last days of his life in the house with a panoramic view of Deir Yassin. No Nuremberg judges, no vengeance, no penitence, just a path of roses all the way to a Nobel Peace prize. Menahem Begin was proud of the operation, and in his letter to the killers he congratulated them for fulfilling their national duty. "You are creators of Israel's history," he wrote. Yitzhak Shamir was also pleased that it helped to achieve his dream: to expel the *nochrim* (non-Jews) from the Jewish state.

The field commander of the operation, Judah Lapidot, also had quite a career. His superior, Menahem Begin, appointed him to run the campaign for the right of Russian Jews to immigrate to Israel. He called for compassion and family reunion; he orchestrated the demonstrations in New York and London with that memorable slogan, "Let My People Go." If you supported the right of Russian Jews to immigrate to Israel, maybe you have come across this man. By then the blood stains of Deir Yassin had presumably washed off his hands. For the political indoctrination of Russian immigrants he even published a Russian-language 'version' of "Oh Jerusalem," a best-seller by Lapierre and Collins, expurgating the story of Deir Yassin.

But there is yet another reason why this event was historically significant. Deir Yassin demonstrated the full scope of Zionist tactics. After the mass murder became known, the Jewish leadership blamed . . . the Arabs. David Ben Gurion, the first Prime Minister of Israel, announced that the Arab rogue gangs had perpetrated it. When this version collapsed, the Jewish leaders began the damage-control procedures. They sent an apology to Emir Abdallah. Ben Gurion publicly distanced himself and his government from the bloody massacre, saying it stained the name of every honest Jew and that it was the work of dissident terrorists. His public relations techniques remain a source of pride for the good-hearted pro-Zionist 'liberals' abroad.

"What a horrible, dreadful story," a humanist Jew told me when I drove him by the remaining houses of Deir Yassin, then added, "But Ben Gurion condemned the terrorists, and they were duly punished."

"Yes," I responded. "They were duly punished and promoted to the highest government posts."

Just three days after the massacre, the terrorist gangs were incorporated into the emerging Israeli army, the commanders received high positions, and a general amnesty forgave their crimes. The same pattern, an initial denial followed by apologies and a final act of clemency and promotion, was applied after the first historically verifiable atrocity committed by Prime Minister Sharon. It was at the Palestinian village of Qibya, where Sharon's unit dynamited houses with their inhabitants and massacred some sixty men, women and children. After the murders became public, Prime Minister Ben Gurion at first blamed rogue Arab gangs. When that did not wash, he blamed Arab Jews, who, he said, being Arabs by their mentality, committed the unauthorized wild raid of vengeance and killed the peasants. For Sharon, it was the usual path of roses all the way to the post of Prime Minister. It sometimes appears that to become the Prime Minister of Israel it helps to have a massacre to your name.

The same pattern was repeated after the massacre of Kafr Kasem, where Israeli troops lined up the local peasants and machine-gunned them down. When the denial failed, and Communist MPs disclosed the gory details, the perpetrators were court-martialled and sentenced to long prison terms. They were out before the end of the year, while the commander of the murderers became the head of Israel Bonds. If you ever purchased Israeli Bonds, you may have met him. I am certain he had washed the blood off his hands by the time he shook yours.

Now, with the passing of fifty years, the Jewish establishment has decided to, once again, take a stab at Deir Yassin revisionism. The Zionist Organization of America pioneered the art of denying history and published, at the expense of American taxpayer, a booklet called *Deir Yassin: History of a Lie*. The ZOA revisionists have utilized all the methods of their adversaries, the 'Holocaust deniers': they discount the eye-witness accounts of the survivors, the Red Cross, the British police, Jewish Scouts and other Jewish observers who were present at the scene of massacre. They discount even Ben Gurion's apology, since after all, the commanders of these gangs became in turn prime ministers of the Jewish state. For the ZOA, only the testimony of the murderers has any validity. That is, if the murderers are Jews.

Still, there are righteous people, and probably because of them the Almighty does not wipe us off the face of the earth. There is an organization called Deir Yassin Remembered, which fights all attempts to erase the memory. They publish books, organize meetings, and they are working on a project to build a memorial at the scene of the massacre, so the innocent victims will have this last comfort, their names and the memory saved forever (Isa 56:5). It will have to do, until the surviving sons of Deir Yassin and neighbouring villages return from their refugee camps to the land of their fathers.

Not Another Peace Plan

It is warm in the low hills bordering the plain. Purple-dark *turmus*, lupines, a favourite flower of March, run along the dirt track from the refugee camp to a nearby quarry. The place is swarming with soldiers assisting security men in the selection job. Men are separated from their womenfolk. They are handcuffed by mass-produced plastic handcuffs, standard black sacks on their heads. They are taken to the quarry, beaten, some are shot, and some are tortured. Their houses were demolished by huge Caterpillar machines. It is another morning of ethnic cleansing in Palestine, and one hundred and seventy victims are claimed in a week.

In another world, twenty miles away, Israelis fight with heavy road traffic. It is another day of shopping and entertainment. In the Qiriya government buildings, politicians and officials discuss the Saudi Peace plan. HRH Prince Abdullah proposed to Israel full acceptance of the Arab world in exchange for full withdrawal from territories occupied in 1967. Israeli responses show the true difference between opposing streams of Israeli public opinion.

Brutal Sharon and his right-wing followers flatly reject the proposal. They do not give a damn about Arab recognition.

Liberal Peres of the Labour Party replies as follows: Yes, we gladly accept the Saudi Peace plan. It is a great plan, and the Prince's offer to recognise and accept Israel is a wonderful thing. Surely we won't give up the lands or withdraw, but the plan is good.

In the *quid pro quo* trade, the Jewish 'Left' is for the quid. Quo can wait, as it has waited for the last fifty years. The Israeli Right is not all that much interested even in playing the game of 'peace process'.

The purpose of this game is to calm the frayed nerves of contemporaries, who witness an unpleasant thing, the Palestinian Holocaust. It is hard to live without hope, and that is why fertile minds invent new proposals, new frameworks and discussion tables. While the proposals are being discussed, the Holocaust goes on. Palestine is destroyed, Palestinians murdered and tortured, and it is still the first stage of the new an-Nakba. In today's (12.03.2002) *Haaretz*,[25] Amnon Barzilai reports on the new opinion poll carried out by the Jaffe Institute for Strategic Studies. According to it, 46% of Jews in Israel support mass deportation (transfer) of the Palestinians. If the question is asked in a more 'soft' form, the support for the Final Solution raises to 60%.

Nazis never openly declared their intention to massacre Jews and Gypsies: they called for 'deportation' and 'transfer'. Even in 1938, these ideas did not have the wholehearted support in Nazi Germany that they have now in the Jewish state.

But what is the Jewish state? Is it Israel, the small sliver of land in the Middle East? How would it be able to bend the will of Europeans and Americans? The Jewish historian, Solomon Lurie, author of the fundamental study of anti-Semitism in antiquity, spoke of a "non-territorial Jewish nation-state." Now this powerful non-territorial state stretching from New York to Moscow accepted the Nazi doctrine as its policy, and genocide as its praxis. A good example is provided by the Jewish American law professor from Harvard, Alan Dershowitz, who writes in Sir Conrad Black's *Jerusalem Post*:[26]

> The first act of [Palestinian] terrorism should result in the destruction of a small village which has been used as a base for terrorist operations. The residents would be given 24 hours to leave, and then troops will come in and bulldoze all of the buildings.

That was the standard practice of Nazi troops in occupied Europe. Since Dershowitz and others of that ilk were teaching a generation of American students, while Black and his comrades-in-arms were busy promoting this agenda, it is not strange that the US gives its full support to the Israeli war machine. Rumours of the impending US attack on Iraq and Saudi Arabia were designed to freeze the neighbouring Arab nations in a state of horrified expectation.

Apparently they succeeded. The Saudi Prince Abdullah probably understands as well as anybody in the Middle East that any 'peace proposal' will be utilised by Zionists in order to stall the talks and continue with their homicidal plans. But he apparently felt his first duty was to his people, to the Saudis, threatened by the Damocles' Sword of the US Air Force. There is not a slight chance for this or other peace plan, be it Zinni, Tenet, or Mitchell plan. In 1970–72 a whole set of peace proposals were produced by Jarring and other statesmen. Israel used the time to beef up its Bar-Lev line along the Suez, meanwhile stalling or rejecting the proposals. The pattern repeated itself after Madrid and Oslo.

Their murderous plans are laid out. The media they control stifles reporting and discussion of the Palestinian Holocaust. The US Armed Forces provide them with total protection. Their hand can not be stayed. Not by ritual peace proposals, anyway.

Instead of this waste of words, HRH Prince Abdullah and other leaders should move their country's currency deposits from the dollar to the Euro and gold. Non-Islamic interest-taking banking must be outlawed as another form of loan sharking. We can do the same, and add a full scale boycott of newspapers and professors supporting the genocide in Palestine.

Mankind still has a chance to save Palestinians and be saved. Dershowitz, Black and Co. should be treated as accessories to Sharon's war crimes, and the Jewish state must be deNazified, as thoroughly as Germany was after 1945.

Notes

25. http://www.haaretz.co.il/hasen/pages/ShArt.jhtml?itemNo=140196&contrassID=2&subContrassID=1&sbSubContrassID=0.
26. http://www.jpost.com/Editions/2002/03/11/Opinion/Opinion.44919.html.

PART III

The Failed Test

[My very first English-language essay: it was published on the Web in January 2001, and appeared on hundreds of sites and in a score of languages. It was misunderstood by many readers for a rhetoric piece, but for me it was a painful recognition: the traditional Jewish discourse was based on a lie.]

I

Among the colourful revellers on Allenby Street, in a crowded restaurant on a merry-making Tel Aviv night, a vision came to me, a vision of an angel in battle-dress writing three words on a wall: "Mene, Tekel Ufarsin." My Angel-English dictionary prompts a translation: "You were tested and you failed."

These are the darkest days for the people of Israel. They are dark because ours and our fathers' lamentations and protests against injustice have turned out to be about as genuine as a three-dollar bill.

In 1968, a young Jewish Russian kid, I scrawled "Hands off Czechoslovakia" on the walls of my native Russian city. The beautiful deep voice of a Jewish Russian poet Alexander Galitch still resonates in my ears: "Citizens, our Motherland is in danger, our tanks are on foreign soil!" Some Russian Jews demonstrated on Red Square against the invasion and were beaten up by the police. We protested against Russian tanks in Budapest and Prague and Kabul as Russian citizens who valued honour above loyalty, humankind above kinship. At the same time Jewish American kids were demonstrating against their country's intervention in Vietnam, and Jewish boys and girls in Europe were struggling against racism. Years passed by, and now our Jewish tanks are on foreign soil.

Our Jewish army murders civilians, demolishes houses, and imposes sieges on hungry villages. Our crimes are on a par with the Russian crimes committed in Chechnya and Afghanistan and the American crimes in Vietnam. Surely Israeli intellectuals are demonstrating *en masse* on our equivalent of Pennsylvania Avenue or Trafalgar Square, and American Jews are raising their voices against the American-armed killers of Palestinians—and surely the Russian Jews are going to speak up for the human rights of the enslaved Gentiles of the Holy Land? No fear! Our literati are busy indeed as they exalt the courage of our Jewish soldiers, venerate the steady hand of our Jewish snipers, glorify the immense humanity of the Jewish folk who could pulverize all the Gentiles of Palestine but kindly limit themselves to a few dozen wounded and maimed a day.

My grandfather in the Pale of Settlement railed against the restrictions on the free movement of Jews in the Russian Empire. In our generation, Anatoly Sharansky became a symbol of struggle for human rights. Yet in our own country, the Gentiles are fenced into reservations and concentration camps that make the Pale—pale in comparison.

A Palestinian cannot go to the next village without the Jewish *Ausweis*; he is forever checked by our Checkists. He can only dream of the sea washing the shores of his ancestral home—we don't let Palestinians pollute the Jewish purity of our beaches.

For years, Jews have protested against discrimination in employment and education. Yet in our own Jewish state we created a system of total national discrimination. In our state-owned Electric Company, among thirteen thousand employees there are six Gentiles (0.05%).

Gentiles form forty percent of the population between the Jordan River and the Mediterranean, but only one-in-four has the right to vote. There are no Gentiles in the Israeli Supreme Court, in the Air Force, in the secret services. There is not even one Gentile on the board of the main Israeli oh-so-liberal newspaper, *Haaretz*.

II

In light of these events, the complaints of the Diaspora Jews deserve to be revisited. We didn't really fight for human rights, but for the rights of Jews. We struggled for freedom of movement and freedom of choice—but only for Jews. We spoke of universal suffrage, but we meant the right of Jews to vote. We do not mind invasion and occupation so long as we are doing the invading and occupying.

The sight of a child raising hands before a machine-gun toting thug grieves us only if it is a Jewish child. The Gentile kid can be shot at with impunity. Apparently, when the Jewish poet Bialik wrote: "The Devil did not invent a fit punishment for the murder of a child," he actually meant "a Jewish child." When the scenes of pogrom horrified him, he was horrified that the violence was directed against Jews. Otherwise, there is nothing wrong with pogroms *per se*. Several weeks ago, the Jews of Upper Nazareth mounted a pogrom against the Gentiles of Nazareth, but no *pogromchik* was brought to justice. The Israeli Police helped out by murdering some of the pogrom victims. Worse still, the pogroms of Ramallah and Beth Jallah were carried out with helicopter gunships and tanks.

Tsarist Russia, 'the Empire of pogroms', was much hated by our grandfathers and eventually destroyed by them. Still, all the 19th century Jewish pogroms in Russia caused fewer casualties than we murder in a matter of weeks. The most horrible pogrom of Kishinev claimed forty-five dead and six hundred wounded. Over the last three months, four hundred Palestinians have been killed and many thousands wounded. After a pogrom in Tsarist Russia, all Russian writers and intelligentsia condemned the perpetrators. In the Jewish state, barely a few dozen gathered to demonstrate in Tel Aviv, while the Hebrew Writers Union has endorsed the pogrom against Gentiles.

In 1991, the majority of Russian Jews took the stand against communism and raised the banner of private property. Apparently, they actually meant Jewish private property, since we confiscate Gentile property with the greatest of ease.

Take a stroll through the best areas of Jerusalem, wander through Talbieh, Old Katamon, the Greek and German Colonies, and admire the marvellous palaces. They belonged to Gentiles—Germans, Armenians, Greeks, British, Russians, and Palestinians—Christian and Moslem. All of them were confiscated and bestowed upon Jews. Just in the last few weeks, hundreds of acres of Gentile property were confiscated and scores of Gentile houses seized or demolished.

Right before his arrest, the Russian Jewish media-lord Gusinsky came to Israel and sang his fervent support for the Jewish state. At the same time, he was demanding that the West assist him in his fight with the Russian authorities, which had seized his TV station. His support of Israel proves that Mr. Gusinsky does not object to confiscation; he is just against confiscation of Jewish property. He is against Jews being arrested; the Gentiles can rot forever in the prisons of the Jewish state.

In no time at all, we have succeeded in undermining the long-term achievements of Jews in the struggle for democracy, human rights and equality. What exactly did we abhor about the German Nazis? Their racism? Our own racism is no less widespread and is potentially as virulent. The Russian language newspaper *Direct Speech*, published in Jerusalem, asked hundreds of Russian Jews about their feelings towards the Palestinians. Typical answers were: "I would kill all Arabs," "All Arabs should be eliminated," "Arabs must be expelled," and "An Arab is an Arab. They all have to be eliminated." I am not sure that a street poll of Berlin in 1938 would have produced more damning results, as the Nazi idea of the Final Solution did not emerge until 1941.

III

Apparently, we Jews fought racism while it was someone else's racism. We were against death squads and the *Sonderkommando* as long as they acted against us. Our own killers, our Jewish Sondercommando, are the objects of our tender admiration. The Jewish state is the only place in the world possessing official death squads that embrace a policy of assassination and the practice of medieval torture. No cause for alarm, my dear Jewish readers; we only torture and assassinate Gentiles.

We were against ghettos while we were confined in a ghetto. Now the most liberal Israeli peace-plan calls for the creation of a few Gentile ghetto girt by barbed wire and surrounded by Jewish tanks and Jewish-owned factories where *Arbeit macht* the Gentiles *frei*. We shall give the ghetto their independence, but not before we remove all their sources of income and sustenance.

Israelis are brainwashed from kindergarten; they are taught that they belong to the Chosen People, who are *Über Alles*. They are indoctrinated in the belief that the Gentiles are not fully human, and therefore they can be killed and their land expropriated at will. After all, Israel fulfilled at least one UN resolution: the one that called Zionism a form of racism.

What upsets me is that the internationalist upbringing in the Soviet Union, which we Russian Jews received, could not withstand the poisonous Zionist propaganda of Jewish superiority. What I regret most is the moral collapse of my own Russian community in the Holy Land.

The angel wrote his fiery words, prophets called upon the people to repent, and we still have a choice. We can choose the way of Nineveh and repent, return the stolen property, give full equality to Gentiles, stop discrimination and murder, and hope to be forgiven by God, if not for our sake, then for the sake of our cats and dogs. Or we can persist in our evil ways, as did the people of Sodom, and wait for the flood of fire and burning sulphur to rain down from the angry heavens of Palestine.

Rape of Dulcinea

[This piece was written as a response to a long article by Elie Wiesel,[27] an American Jewish Holocaust activist and a Nobel Peace Prize winner, in January 2001.]

I

The touching words of Elie Wiesel painted a beautiful portrait of the Jewish people, yearning, loving and praying for Jerusalem over the centuries and cherishing its name from generation to generation.

This potent image reminded me, an Israeli writer from Jaffa, of something familiar yet elusive. I finally made the connection by revisiting my well-thumbed volume of *Don Quixote*. Wiesel's evocative article is so wonderfully reminiscent of the immortal love of the Knight of Sad Visage for his belle Dulcinea de Toboso. Don Quixote travelled all over Spain proclaiming her name. He performed formidable feats, defeated giants, who turned out to be windmills, brought justice to the oppressed, all for the sake of his beloved. When he decided that his achievements made him worthy, he sent his arms-bearer, Sancho Panza, to his Dame with a message of adoration.

Now I find myself in the somewhat embarrassing position of Sancho Panza. I have to inform my master, Don Wiesel Quixote, that his Dulcinea is well. She is happily married, has a bunch of kids, and she is quite busy with laundry and other domestic chores. While he fought brigands and restored governors, somebody else took care of his beloved, fed her, provided her with food, made love to her, made her a mother and grandmother. Do not rush, dear knight, to Toboso, lest it break your heart.

Elie, the Jerusalem that you write of so movingly is not now and never has been desolate. She has lived happily across the centuries in the embrace of another people, the Palestinians of Jerusalem, who have taken good care of her. They made her the beautiful city she is, adorned her with a magnificent piece of jewellery, the Golden Dome of Haram al Sharif, built her houses with pointed arches and wide porches and planted cypresses and palm trees.

They do not mind if the knight-errant visits their beloved city on his way from New York to Saragosa. But be reasonable, old man. Stay within the frame of the story and within the bounds of common decency. Don Quixote did not drive his jeep into Toboso to rape his old flame. OK, you loved her, and thought about her, but it does not give you the right to kill her children, bulldoze her rose garden and put your boots on her dining room table. All your words just prove that you confuse your desires with reality. You ask why the Palestinians want Jerusalem? Because she belongs to them, because they live there and it is their hometown. Granted, you dreamed about her in your remote Transylvania. So did many people around the world. She is so wonderful and certainly worth dreaming about.

II

Many people have adored this city across the ages. Swedish farmers left their villages and moved there to build the lovely American Colony together with the Vesters, a devout Christian family from Chicago. You can read about it in the works of Selma Lagerlof, another Nobel Prize winner. On the slopes of the Mount of Olives, the Russians built the dainty church of Mary Magdalene. Ethiopians erected their Resurrection monastery amid the ruins left by the Crusaders.

The British died for her and left as their architectural legacy the St. George Cathedral and St. Andrew's. The Germans built the lovely German Colony and nursed the city's sick in the Schneller Hospital. My devout great-grandfather moved into the protection of her thick walls in the 1870s from a Lithuanian Jewish village and threw his lot in with the hospitable Jerusalemites. He found his eternal rest until the day of Resurrection on the slopes of the Mount of Olives. None of them thought to rape their Dulcinea. They just left bouquets of architectural flowers as testament of their adoration.

Those who love Jerusalem are legion. It is disingenuous of Elie Wiesel to reduce the struggle for this city to a tug-of-war between Muslims and Jews. It is a question of coveting property versus having the deed of ownership. The resolution of this case should be based on the Tenth Commandment that our fathers observed. They knew that veneration does not amount to the right of ownership. Millions of Protestants venerate the Catholic-owned Gethsemane Garden, but it does not transfer the garden into their hands. Millions of Catholics visit the Tomb of Mary, but it still belongs to the Eastern Church. For generations, the Moslems have come to kneel at the birthplace of Jesus in Bethlehem, but the church remains Christian.

III

What water did to the Gremlins in Spielberg's movies, Zionism has inflicted on the jolly Jewish folk of Eastern Europe. It caused them to carry out an ethnic cleansing of Gentiles in West Jerusalem, to convert the Schneller hospital and church into a military base and to build a Holiday Inn on top of the venerated shrine of Sheik Bader. The Jewish State forbids the Christians of Bethlehem to pray in the Holy Sepulchre and bans Moslems below the age of forty from attending Friday prayers at the Aqsa Mosque. This is the rape of the Holy City you profess to love.

In order to justify this rape, you invoke the names of King Solomon and Jeremiah, quote the Koran and the Bible. Let me tell you a Jewish Hassidic tale, one you might have heard in your childhood. A Jewish midrash, a legend, mentions that Abraham had a daughter. A simple-minded Hassid asked his Rabbi why Abraham did not wed his daughter and his son Isaac. The Rabbi responded that Abraham did not want to marry a real son to a legendary daughter.

Legends are the stuff that dreams are made of. Some are charming, some are horrible, and none is valid as a land deed or as a political platform. Elie, you certainly would not like to lose your private home in New York because of a few verses written in the Book of Mormon. This game is rather irrelevant, but I will play one more round with you for the entertainment of the crowd. As every archaeologist will tell you, King Solomon and his temple belong to the fantasy realm of Abraham's daughter. Moreover, not that it matters, but the name 'Jerusalem' does not occur even once in the Jewish Holy Book, the Torah.

Do you want to play some more games? I'll show you more. The Jews are not even mentioned in the Jewish Bible. Get that thick book off of your shelf and check it. None of the great and legendary men you named, from King David to the prophets, were called 'the Jews'. This ethnonym appears for the first and only time in the Bible in the Persian story of the very late Book of Esther. The self-identification of the Jews with the tribes of Israel and with the heroes of the Bible is as valid as the story of Rome being founded by the Trojan prince Aeneas. If the modern Turks, who call themselves 'the descendants of Troy' would conquer Rome, dynamite Borromini's baroque masterpieces and expel her inhabitants in order to re-establish the legacy of Aeneas, they would just be repeating the folly of the Zionists.

IV

Our ancestors, the humble East European folk of Yids, whose language was Yiddish, had a tradition of adorning themselves with the impressive heraldic lions of Biblical heroes. Their claim of descent from these legends was as valid as the claims of Thomas Hardy's ambitious farmer girl Tess. But even the fictional Tess did not conspire to evict the lords from their castle and claim the manor for herself.

Once, walking with the Christian pilgrims to the great Church of the Holy Sepulchre, I was stopped by a Hassidic Jew. He inquired whether my companions were Jews, and, receiving a negative reply, exclaimed in amazement: "What are these *Goyim* (Gentiles) looking for in the Holy City?" He had never heard of the Passion of Jesus Christ, whose name he used as a swear word. I am equally amazed that a Jewish professor from Boston University is as ignorant as the simple-minded Hassidic Jew. Jerusalem is holy to billions of believers: Catholic, Protestant, and Eastern Christians, Sunni and Shia Moslems, to thousands of Hassidic and Sephardi Jews. Still, as a city, Jerusalem is not different from any other place in the world; she belongs to her citizens.

Twenty more years of Zionist control of this ancient city will turn her into another Newark and forever ruin her charm. Jerusalem needs to be restored to its inhabitants. The seized properties in Talbieh and Lifta, Katamon and Malcha should be returned to their owners. Professor Wiesel, respect Gentile property rights as you would like Gentiles to respect your right to your lovely house. The holy sites of Jerusalem are regulated by the 150-year-old international statute (Status Quo) that should not be tampered with. The last attempt to touch it caused the siege of Sevastopol and the charge of the Light Brigade at Balaclava. The next attempt could cause a nuclear war.

Notes

27. It was written as a response to a long article by Elie Wiesel, "Jerusalem in My Heart," *New York Times*, 1/25/2001.

A Tale of Two States

[This piece was written in January 2001 in response to an article by an Israeli peace activist, Uri Avneri. It has become a basis for the anti-apartheid movement as an answer to the bankruptcy of the traditional approach to the Jewish-Palestinian problem with its demand to stop the occupation.]

I

A few weeks before the eruption of the second Palestinian *intifadah*, I wandered over to Cinemateque square, a middle-class Tel Aviv neighbourhood. In the cool breeze of the late afternoon a few dozen retirees with their families were having a nice outing. The old ladies knitted while kids drew flags on big sheets of paper. This peaceful gathering was the commemoration by the Israeli peace camp of the seventh anniversary of the Oslo accords. The keynote speaker was Uri Avneri.

This handsome man with a noble head of white hair invoked, as he always does, his vision of two states co-existing in the Holy Land, an independent Palestine next to the Jewish state. Every word sounded right, but it was as exciting as yesterday's news, as entertaining as a re-run of an old TV serial. Not surprisingly, there were no young activists, as the traditional peace camp no longer attracts new, dynamic blood. Mr. Avneri is recycling the same tired speech over the Net these days, calling for the two-states solution.

Please don't misunderstand me. Uri Avneri is a man of good intentions, a brave supporter of Palestinian rights, an activist doing more than his share and an efficient organizer. It's just that his political agenda is as dead as a dodo bird.

Let us face the hard facts on the ground: the idea of two states in Palestine is, and has always been, a bluff. After being partitioned for only nineteen years, Palestine has been united for thirty-three years. No Israeli or Palestinian under the age of forty even remembers the 'partition years' between 1948–1967. It is a period of time that Mr. Avneri latches onto as some kind of Paradise Lost. No Israeli politician, including the late lamented Mr. Rabin, has ever seriously considered relinquishing any part of historical Palestine. The endless negotiations have been a sideshow designed to mollify the public. Thirty years ago, the Israeli singer Arik Einstein was assuring us that "The talks will be resumed soon." They are still singing the same old song.

In the meantime, behind the smoke screen of 'temporary military occupation', the hard-nosed Israeli leadership has confiscated Palestinian fields and houses to make room for Jewish settlements, and imprisoned and killed thousands of Palestinians. A succession of leftist and rightist Israeli regimes perpetuated this legal fiction in order to deny the civic rights of the conquered population. It was a brilliant idea, worthy of the Jewish genius: to carry on negotiations forever while giving lip service to the idea of two states.

Honesty forces me to tell my Palestinian and Israeli friends: you've been duped. Our wise men played a cruel game with you, teasing you with empty promises like the stale old 'tale of two states' narrated by Mr. Avneri. There have always been only two paths for the Palestinians to emerge from serfdom. One is to beat Israel; the second is to join it. The third option, of a new partition, is just an illusion: a juicy but unreachable carrot dangled in front of the donkey.

If I were a fan of conspiracy theories I could well imagine that these good people of the Israeli peace movement intentionally supplied this left leg to our shaky apartheid structure. By continually re-painting the [old armistice] Green Line, they have endorsed the non-citizen status of the Palestinians in their own land. By calling some lands 'occupied territories' they have exempted themselves from the need to battle against the exclusion of Palestinians from the country's political life. By combating the annexation of the territories they have helped to concoct the fraud of independent Palestinian Bantustans.

But the idea of such a conspiracy is just too mind-boggling. I do not think Mr. Avneri and the peace camp received their briefings in the offices of the Shabak.[28] They were just too keen to believe that the Israeli generals would conclude a fair peace with the Palestinians.

Even a kid watching James Bond movies eventually understands that the hero won't be eaten by crocodiles and won't die in the flames, and that there is no reason for expecting these eventualities. There is even less reason for expecting that an Israeli government will sign a just peace with the Palestinians. They will always deploy an exit-strategy in the 'peace process'.

II

Exactly what sort of 'peace' might Israel offer? In an article published in that popular keeper of the Zionist faith, the *New York Times* [15/12/2000], a good American Jew named Richard Bernstein recommended to President-elect Bush a recent book by another pundit of that ilk, Robert Kaplan. He disclosed the real Israeli peace plan:

> For decades I have heard that there would be either a Greater Israel, or a Palestinian state. It turns out there will be both: a Palestinian mini-state,

without control over its skies or main highways, situated within a dynamic Israel that will continue to attract workers from across the border, making it the stabilizing force of Greater Syria.

Thank you, kind Bernstein and gentle Kaplan, for clarifying that Israel and its American Zionist allies intend to keep the Palestinians forever locked in reservations and competing with their brethren from Jordan and Syria for work from their Jewish masters. That is the peace that Israeli doves have been cooing about.

Should it work, perhaps the US could adopt the idea and grant independence to the Afro-Hispanic US population, with a capital in the South Bronx. The new state could consist of five hundred enclaves circled by super-highways and miles of reinforced concrete walls, and could contain all the US's non-whites. If that be peace, I choose war.

The more I think about it, the less inclined I become to giving the peace camp the benefit of the doubt as to their intentions. Too often, they use that pesky phrase, 'the Jewish state'. It's easy enough to understand why: Zionism came of age in the years of the crude biological racism that was part-and-parcel of the ideologies promoted by Weininger, Nordau, Chamberlain and Hitler. Zionists believe that a person belongs to a nation by virtue of blood. For them, a Jew is always and forever a Jew, thus the notion 'two states for two nations'. The peace movement is, first and foremost, still about preserving a 'Jewish state'. The second of these two states, the remainder of Palestine, is just an incidental by-product of the process.

III

A 'bi-national state' is a misnomer, too. There are no two nations, Jews and Arabs, as they want us to believe. Rather, there are a number of communities: the Moroccans of Ramle, the Russians of Ashdod, the software wiz-kids of Hertzliya Pituah, the millionaires of Caesarea, the settlers of Tapuah, the scholars of Mea Shearim, the Ethiopians of Ophakim. These, and the no-less-diverse native Palestinian communities could form the beautiful mosaic of the Holy Land. These communities constitute two nations only in the imagination of the Zionist establishment, the pre-'48 settlers and their aging children. This 'First Israel' has good reason for clinging onto this fantasy, as this minority still monopolizes power over the other communities and retains all its perks.

No outsider has ever succeeded in getting anywhere close to the centre of power. There is hardly a Russian (20% of the electorate) or a Moroccan (30%) in an independent position of power and influence in Israel. When an Oriental Jew was elected to the ceremonial post of President, the 'First Israel' went into mourning.

An unfortunate problem for the dominant elite is that they have run out of talent and ideas. They took exclusivity to its extreme and turned respect for the military into idolatry. The farce of General Sharon battling for power with General Barak, and the ancient murderer of Kana, Shimon Peres, as the Great White Hope, is surely adequate proof of the bankruptcy of the 'First Israel'. The Zionist idea has collapsed; only blood and war keep the Golem in motion.

IV

Behind the smoke of racist realities and illusions we already live in a united Palestine. The Green line exists only in our minds, while the sea of apartheid splashes on both sides of it. It is in our common interest to abolish the fiction completely and establish equality before the law for everybody in all of Palestine (Israel), from the Jordan River to the Mediterranean Sea. Then we can enjoy one law for both the native son of the land and the newcomer, as the Bible commands us: the same law for the kibbutznik of Afikim and for the fellah of Yatta.

It could have happened years ago if the Israeli left had not nurtured the illusions of partition. Jerusalem is a suitable case to consider. The Palestinian population of the city—one-third of United Jerusalem—is entitled to participate in the municipal elections and can send their deputies to the City Council. But they accepted the silly advice of the Israeli peace camp and boycotted the elections in order to sustain the Green Line. It was a ruinous decision, and one they should re-think. Remember that Israel would not be able to demolish houses in Jerusalem; the Palestinians of East Jerusalem would live better if they could participate in elections. Their vote would remove Ehud Olmert, the racist and elected-by-Jews-only 'Mayor' of Jerusalem, and good riddance. Even for this purpose alone we should ask Palestinians to vote.

Without the Green Line, the horrors of occupation would have ended long ago, in the same fashion that military rule in Palestinian Galilee was ended in 1966. The 40% of the Knesset Members elected by Palestinians would have been able to cancel all discriminatory laws, including the Law of Absentee Property and the present Law of Citizenship.

In a representative state, the return of Palestinian refugees does not have to be traumatic. If the refugees from Deheishe were to return to Sataf and Suba, it would be a short ten-mile relocation. If the peasants of Deir Yassin come back to their ancient homes, nobody will suffer. The peasants of Sheich Munis will have to settle for hefty compensation, at the expense of Tel Aviv University, which is built on their land. Maybe they will use their compensation money to build new houses next to the university, or just buy flats in Ramat Aviv Gimel. We can borrow a leaf from the Polish book of law: Poland restored the property to Jewish refugees, but did not permit the expulsion of the current tenants.

The removal of the Green line will actually be good for all of us, even for the settlers. They should be able to remain and live in safety and security like equals in our commonwealth. Without the army to enforce their superiority, they will have to either mend their evil ways and become good neighbours, or go back to Brooklyn.

So how do we get to the Promised Land? We're already there! Historical Palestine is unified, but apartheid is not dismantled yet. We already have one state, but we have no democracy. Stop the empty rhetoric of occupation and two states. We need no tricks, no 'creative solutions', just good old universal suffrage, the 'One Man, One Vote' principle. We demanded it for our grandfathers in Eastern Europe. They received it from the Gentiles one-hundred-and-fifty years ago; it is the right time to pass this most basic of rights to the Palestinian natives of this land.

Dreams of Israeli withdrawal will anyway remain dreams: the Israeli establishment will never give up its holdings. But we can utilise its avarice. If it can not give, let it take—and lose its positions of superiority.

It is useless to shout to the drowning moneylender, "*Give me your hand*!" He does not know how to give. Instead, shout: "*Take my hand*!" and he will clutch at it.

This was the advice of the Sufi sage, Haji Nasr ad-Din. We should say, "Annex the territories, but give the Palestinians full equality." It does not mean that the struggle against military occupation is wrong. *Au contraire*, occupation is wrong, as the military rule of Nazareth and Acre in 1948–1966 was wrong. But the way out of it is not partition but absorption and equality.

In 1948, Sir John Glubb, the British commander of the Arab Legion, was forced to cede to the Jewish state the lands of the Triangle containing the villages of Taibe and Umm el Fahm. He insisted on one thing: the peasants should remain and receive full rights in the state of Israel. As a result, we have these rather prosperous communities, and their dwellers do not want to become part of the proposed Palestinian state. It is the best proof that absorption is better than partition.

Notes

28. Israeli Internal Security Service.

Summer Fool, Winter Fool

[This is an essay about the elections of 2001, when Israelis chose Ariel Sharon as their Prime Minister.]

I

Walking along the Tel Aviv seashore promenade, I was approached by a slick blond guy who invited me to visit lady luck. A mixed crowd of tourists and folk from Afula and Dimona had gathered to watch a street artist with nifty hands, three glasses and a ball. "Guess where the ball is and you win a hundred bucks!" he said. I laughed. Did he take me for a country hick? No big city man would try this game, knowing that one can't beat the dealer. The right choice in this game is to refuse to choose.

I am often asked, how it is possible that the Israelis chose Sharon in the elections, and why 40% of Israeli citizens did not vote at all. The election was a sham. It was similar to the Soviet style one-party elections. Of course, the Russians never came up with the brilliant idea of offering their citizens the choice between Brezhnev and Chernenko. The citizens of Israel might well envy Buridan's ass. This silly animal of the medieval allegory could not choose between two identical bales of hay. We had to choose between two equally unappetizing generals, old Arab-fighters, unconvincingly mouthing the word 'peace'. The choice was further trivialised by their declared intent to form a coalition government immediately after the elections.

The victory went to General Sharon, the world-famous symbol of 'cruel Zionism'. His name is connected with the mass murders of civilians in Qibya, Sabra and Shatila, and the siege of Beirut. His "sightseeing" of Haram al-Sharif jump-started the most recent eruption of civil war in Palestine. He is a certified war criminal. Still, I did not rush to save Barak's skin. The choice of Sharon has some advantages for Palestinians.

II

The elections can be seen as just another of the endless 'con' games that plague Israeli politics. It is a good-cop/bad-cop routine on the Palestinians. Labour and Likud are re-enacting a memorable dialogue in the great American novel, *Moby*

Dick. When Ishmael, the hero of Melville's book, seeks a place on a whaler, the mean skipper Bildad offers him a pittance, while his co-owner, captain Peleg, explodes in visible anger: "Why, blast your eyes, Bildad, thou dost not want to swindle this young man! He must have more than that." Then he offers him much less than Ishmael could rightly expect. Well, in our life, Ishmael is not asked; he just has to submit.

Having said that, I will be the first to admit that the two candidates still differ. The Jewish joke tells of two kinds of fools, a summer fool and a winter fool. Whenever the summer fool comes in, you immediately recognize him for a fool. Whenever the winter fool comes in, he removes his great coat, shakes the snow off his fur hat; only then do you realise that he is a fool. Barak is a winter fool. Until he started to shoot, it was possible to retain a few delusions about the man. Sharon is a summer fool. You immediately see him for what he is. There is an advantage in dealing with such a man. His peace-cooing will convince no one.

Barak reminds me of my late spinster aunt Ethel. She refused every suitor, after leading them on and making them promises. For years, we hoped she would do the right thing and get married. Or at least find herself a lover to make up for decades of loneliness. But she could not. We felt pity for whoever happened to be her current suitor, as we watched him crawl painfully home. He should have known better; Aunt Ethel would not surrender even if she wanted, as she was afraid of men.

Ehud Barak was notorious for promising and reneging on his promises. Actually, he did not fulfill a single promise to the Palestinians (or to anybody else, notably the Russian Israelis). For instance, his government decided to free the villages of Anata and Abu Dis. A few days later, he found a reason to keep them under military rule. In the interview given to the *Vesti* newspaper last week, he was invited to name his main achievement. Barak replied: "I revealed to the world the true face of Arafat." We do not need a Prime Minister for this task. Barak changed opinions twice a day, he sent and recalled delegations, he was unreliable. He promised the Russian community to eliminate the religious diktat and failed to do it. Speaking in American terms, you would not buy a new car from him, let alone a used one.

What is worse, Barak does not like Palestinians. This arrogant and unpleasant man refused to invite the Palestinian citizens of Israel, who elected him, into his government. On a personal level, I find it easier to visualize Sharon eating hummus in the company of Palestinian friends, than Barak hiring a Palestinian gardener. He would probably prefer a Thai. The war-crime record of Sharon is not unique. Barak's long list of assassinations would not look good in the Hague, either. We are doomed to live with war criminals. A just court would try not only Sharon and Barak, but the perpetrators of sanctions against the people of Iraq and the Serbia bombing. The murderers of three million Vietnamese still walk free, and probably sit on Capitol Hill. Many Israelis of Sharon's generation were Arab fighters, and quite ruthless ones, too. But they did not look on a Palestinian as a low-life who ought to be contained or exterminated.

III

Like many of my Israeli contemporaries, I did my time in the army. I remember the smell of cordite, jeep flight in the desert, the green sky of night vision, shrieks of shrapnel, the Suez crossing, twin tents, the fellowship of arms. As a young soldier in a crack unit, I was proud of my red boots and paratroopers' wings. I listened with a wistful heart to the stories of the brave deeds of Arik Sharon and Meir Har Zion. (Yes, it was before Sabra and Shatila.) I am not ashamed to admit I cherish them, together with the courage of Karame fighters and that dare-devil Leila Khaled. Soldiers can understand other soldiers. Together we form Palestine.

The elections proved that the majority of Israelis, including those who did not vote, disagree with Barak's notion of separation, call it Hafrada in Hebrew or Apartheid in Afrikaans. The majority does not want the country to be partitioned again, and this idea failed. Nobody in the country below the age of forty remembers the separate existence of 'small Israel'. We have to go forward, not back. That is the way of normalization, not separation.

Whenever the beautiful green Palestine is united, all her communities will bring their best achievements into the common cause of making this special land the best place on earth, as it should be. The Palestinians will contribute their art of growing olives and tending the springs, their peasant love of the land and unbroken spirit of Intifada. Our Israeli contribution won't include Einstein's theory or Wall Street wizardry, as we do not understand it, but the military exploits worthy of Crusaders' glory. In Palestine, we don't need peace. We do not need separation, even on the best of terms. We need love and compassion, and life together. This solution ended Maori wars in New Zealand; it would work here as well. We do not need a de Gaulle in the position of prime minister. We need a de Klerk.

Israeli suppression of Palestinians from 1947 until now was made possible only by the external support of Israel's ill-advised allies. Sharon's grisly past makes the unlimited support of organised American Jewry less likely and more precarious. The watchful presence of international observers, the possibility of the UN intervention unencumbered by a US veto, and the looming presence of a resurrected Iraq will be necessary to concentrate Sharon's mind. He is not the peaceful messiah on the white colt, but he is not worse than Barak.

A military man, Sharon should be offered a choice: unification of the country on the basis of 'one man, one vote', and full rights for all inhabitants of the land, or the Hague tribunal.

[I miscalculated: the support of the US Jews for Sharon was enthusiastic, while the Bush administration stood by him constantly. The US Jews were much stronger and much nastier than I thought. Still, for a while I tried to reason with them.]

PART IV

Kid Sister

I

Just before the *Intifada*, the US Congress adopted a resolution supporting Israel and called upon the Palestinians to accept their fate stoically. Now, four months and four hundred dead later, the Congress has confirmed its position and sent a whole-hearted blessing to General Sharon. You would not get such a result even in the Israeli parliament. That is why a UN commission sent to investigate the war crimes received short shrift: How dare they speak of war crimes? The Mitchell commission also found itself brushed aside last week. In response, US warplanes bombed . . . Iraq (Surely some mistake?).

Innocent outsiders must question how Israel can get off scot-free with war crimes and receive the blessings of the US congress as a bonus. Could it be Divine intervention? The answer is "no." There is another agent to thank for this state of affairs. We Israelis enjoy full immunity, and have no doubt that if and when our government decides to turn the Palestinians into canned meat, the *New York Times* will celebrate its nutritional values. If that is their intent, then they should hasten the process, because with the present blockade the Palestinians are losing weight with every passing day.

All is fine on the Israeli side of the barricades. The Israeli shekel remains strong. Even the celebrated financier, George Soros, knows it would not be healthy to take a position against it. This major backer of Bill and Hillary Clinton was not afraid to bet against the pound and Britain, against the dollar and the American economy. He bought short and declared, "I don't think you can run markets on patriotic principles."[29] However, Israelis are famous for extraordinary solutions, and caution (or, after all, true patriotism?) keeps him away from our shores.

The Tel Aviv stock exchange rallies on the news that Intel has decided to invest a cool five billion dollars in Israel. The beauty of it all is that the siege of the Palestinians and the prosperity of Tel Aviv are maintained at the expense of the American taxpayer and investor. Since 1967 we have received some $170 billion from the people of the US. This money could be used to feed and school all the underprivileged kids of America. It could pay to compensate the descendants of the African slaves and help them out of their hardship. It could save the sick and comfort the miserable; it could turn Africa into a paradise. But it was abducted and shipped to our shores. Every dollar invested by the Israeli lobby into senators and congressmen has been returned a hundred fold, as promised by the Bible.

Apart from the taxpayer's money, the supporters of Israel—business executives—invested billions of dollars that their shareholders entrusted to them. There is no sound business reason behind Intel's investment, or other similar investments: Israel has no pool of qualified workers, they have to be imported like everything else. The risks of investment in our country are great and the profits are meagre. But then they are playing with somebody else's money.

II

Israel's supporters fleece America in a grand way, but they also go after other prey. In England, a Czech Jewish émigré who adopted the name 'Robert Maxwell', stole millions of dollars from the pension funds of his British employees and shipped the money to Israel. He was found dead in suspicious circumstances, but Israel never refunded the stolen goods. In another English scandal, Dame Shirley Porter, daughter of salesman Jack Cohen, the supermarket chain owner and the one-time mayor of the City of Westminster, misappropriated $50 million and presented lavish gifts to Tel Aviv University, built on the ruins of the destroyed Palestinian village of Sheikh Munis. She was found guilty by the British High Court and given a fine of £27 million. As all her property had already been transferred to Israel, the fine remains unpaid. Again, Israel did not return the stolen goods.

Moving on to France: a group of Israeli and local Jewish financiers transferred to Israel some $40 million of public funds and disappeared to Tel Aviv. In a bigger operation, some textile factory owners of Paris transferred many millions to Tel Aviv, and some of them are standing trial. Russian Jew and Israeli citizen Lev Cherny, a great supporter of Yeltsin's democracy, 'privatised' the Russian aluminum industry, which has the biggest reserves in the world. Now the income from that industry flows directly to lovely Savion, the Beverly Hills of Israel, while back in the frozen wastes of Siberia the population has been reduced to poverty. The Swiss and the Germans keep paying umpteen billions of dollars to Israel for the confiscated property of Jews, though Israel has never paid a penny for confiscated property of goyim. The Europeans meekly comply under threat from the toughest of Kray Brothers, the mightiest enforcer of Jewish loans, the US.

Israel's supporters overseas are like a giant Hoover vacuum cleaner, sucking out money and sweat from all over the world. Witness Marc Rich, the thieving billionaire, pardoned by the best supporter of Israel, Bill Clinton. He was a Mossad agent. Remember Fujimori, the thieving ex-president of Peru? Israeli banks helped him to launder the money. Sometimes, the Palestinians and their friends bemoan their inability to build up their own Arab lobby to counteract the Israeli lobby. They miss the most important point. The Israeli lobby should not be just a Palestinian concern, but the concern of all Americans. When oil runs out of a tanker's hull, it should concern the crew and the owners, not only the fish. Israel's supporters swindle all Americans of their money, and antagonize America's potential friends abroad. Many American politicians support the swindle in order to remain in power. For personal political ambitions, they betray the trust of their voters.

John F. Kennedy told Gore Vidal that in 1948 Harry Truman was on the verge of losing the presidential election, but a Zionist supporter brought to him $2 million in cash and saved his skin. It caused America to vote for the creation of the Jewish State. This pattern perpetuates itself. The politicians take bribes, sell pardons, accept 'donations', and help the Israeli lobby rob the people of America.

The actual direct contribution of American Jews to the welfare of Israel is quite small and tax exempt. It would hardly cover the cost of the choppers and missiles to kill Palestinians with, much less support the Israeli life style to which we have become accustomed. But what Israel supporters collect in campaign contributions is enough to bribe politicians and embezzle a good chunk of American money from the US treasury. If such a swindle were hatched by, say, the Libyan lobby, the media would rightly demand that these people be registered as foreign agents of influence. That is where the Israeli lobby cashes in on the solidarity of the many American Jews and right-wing Christian Zionists in the national media.

Ahmed Amr, an independent journalist from Seattle, Washington, has lamented the almost total absence of Arab-Americans in the American media, saying: "Could it be, that like white men can't jump, the Arab-Americans can't write? Could it be that mainly Jewish gentlemen can write?" Well, he should know better. Even Jews who can write but fail to support Israel are also deprived of access to the national mainstream media. Israel's supporters have silenced the voice of Americans who would speak up for the Palestinians, including that of notable Jewish intellectuals like Noam Chomsky. They silenced the 'native' Anglo-Americans' voice, as well. The stock exchange rises and falls, but there is no new Faulkner out of the South, no new Cheever in New England, no new John Barth from Maryland. The Hollywood-made films have degraded into sheer escapism and the production of Arab-hate crap.

III

The enemy of Palestinians and of ordinary Americans, British and French citizens is not 'the Jew' *per se*, as some people tend to think. There are thousands and thousands of wonderful folk of Jewish descent—doctors, artists, rabbis, or unemployed. A lot of them object to Israeli crimes and to AIPAC policies. Some of them are on the front line of the struggle for human rights. Still, the organised majority complies with the demands of the self-proclaimed Jewish leadership.

Hesitating American Jews are in the position of the elder sister in Raymond Chandler's *Big Sleep*, who covers up the crimes of her wild kid sister. Probably you remember it as one of the best American movies of all times, scripted by William Faulkner, directed by Howard Hawks and acted by Humphrey Bogart and Lauren Bacall. As the cover-up continues, the young sister comes to believe she has immunity and keeps up her killing spree. Eventually her crimes endanger the seemingly secure position of the elder sister. It is not a day too early for misguided Lauren to call for Bogart to rein the crazed youth in, before she brings the house down on the heads of her blind supporters.

In spiritual terms, the blind support of Israel has divided the Jews into sheep and goats (Mt 25:32), into sons of saints and sons of Mammon worshippers, the descendants of prophets and of their killers, those who profess unity of mankind and adepts of national exclusivity, those who wait for the Saviour of Man and those who expect the Enslaver of Gentiles. The former ones will make the name of Jews blessed, but those who partake in the starving of poor peasants under Israeli-imposed siege, those who would let them rot in jails, they will certainly bring shame to all of us.

The covenant of Israel's supporters is not an ethnic monolith. It admits Gentiles as well. To enter it is enough to disregard the poor, the weak, and the oppressed. On the other hand, every Jew can opt out of it by rejecting Israeli crimes. There is no biological guilt or virtue. The believing Jews of *Naturei Karta* opted out and supported the Palestinian right to equality. So did *Jews for Justice*, and many others who did not care to join a political group but stood away from evil. Well-meaning French aristocracy rebelled against the Ancient Regime in 1789; they did not wait for the 'national razor' of 1793.

It is in the interest of Americans, Jews and Gentiles alike, to make a start by imposing a full embargo on Israel, like the one imposed on Libya and Iraq. The idea of an exclusive Jewish state is as wrong as the idea of an exclusive Aryan or White State. Palestine/Israel should become a democracy based on the principle of ONE MAN—ONE VOTE. Do not worry for us Israelis and Palestinians. We, the sons of Abraham, can live together. Just cut off supplies to the Generals' Junta, and we shall see the light.

A democratic Israel/Palestine will turn off the Zionist Hoover machine. The long madness of Don Quixote will be over, and he will again be called Don Quexana the Good. The fruits of labour will come to those who need it, not to Israeli generals. Americans will again become welcome guests in the Middle East. Who knows, maybe even the great American cinema will be re-born from its golden ashes.

Notes

29. http://www.newsmax.com/archives/articles/2001/9/23/163013.shtml."Soros: Patriotism Ends at the Stock Market," Wes Vernon, Newsmax.com | September 25, 2001.

New Portnoy's Complaint

I

The Viennese Jewish shrinks decided to dis-invite the American Palestinian Professor Edward Said, who had been called to give a lecture in memory of Sigmund Freud. The Professor had been seen throwing a stone in the direction of the Israeli border. The psychiatrists said it reveals a lot about his subconscious. They would never throw a rock, like the wild Arab from Columbia University; they prefer Sharon's missiles.

I think if this attitude can be taken about Professor Said, it should be taken about others as well. A generation ago, in 1969, Phillip Roth decided to probe the subconscious of his contemporary American Jew. In the novel, *Portnoy's Complaint*, Roth's hero, Alexander Portnoy, lies on the psychiatrist's couch and tells of his inner feelings, domineering mother and adolescent sex. What would a modern Portnoy blabber about on a new (model 2001) couch?

We can find important clues by probing the press. Philip Weiss[30] in the *New York Observer* noted that the Jews are to politics and media what the blacks are to basketball. The leading media powerhouses like the *New York Times* and the *Washington Post* are fully kosher, owned by Jews with a substantial majority of the editorials and the op-eds written by Jews. Their voices are representative of the Jewish American subconscious. With very few exceptions, they are supportive of Israel, its policies towards the Palestinians and its brave ruler, General Sharon.

The situation in our land is well known. The Jews rule supreme. The local non-Jewish inhabitants have but few rights. A large majority of them are disenfranchised. Their property is seized at will and their sources of independent livelihood are destroyed. Their cities are besieged, activists assassinated, women and children starved. They have no access to public media, to welfare; they are not allowed to even go to the beach. None of this is secret. It is freely discussed in the Israeli media.

It would be a gross exaggeration to say that the Jews of Israel hate goys and wish them all gone. To borrow the expression of Conrad Black, the owner of British and Canadian newspapers, it would be "a lie worthy of Goebbels." Israel imports hundreds of thousands of *goys* and *shiksas*: Chinese, Thai, Romanians, Ukrainians, Russians and Africans. In just the last few months, the Israeli Ministry of Labour issued thousands of new permits for guest workers.

The Jews of Israel welcome goys, as long as they have no rights, make no demands and agree to work for minimal wages. At the first sign of trouble, they are taken by force and loaded onto the first plane back home.

That is the country adored by William Safire, Tom Friedman and other self-conscious Jews in the mainstream media. "Tell me what you like, and I'll tell you what you are," goes the Latin adage. The pro-Israel position of the American Jews in the media is a good indication of their subconscious feelings towards the world at large.

Their favourite neo-liberal globalising trend is but a tendency to turn the whole world, excluding the United States, into a Palestine with a small ruling class, a big security machine and voiceless, impoverished natives. But let us give the gentlemen of the press their due. They could be worse. The more vocal part of American Jewry considers them rather soft. The US correspondent of *Haaretz* in Washington, Nitzan Horovitz, writes,[31] "The Israeli lobby in the US (AIPAC) is more intransigent[32] than any government of Israel, including that of Sharon."

It is a Jewish supremacist organisation, according to Yossi Beilin, an Israeli ex-minister who is not much of a liberal himself.

What do they hate in Palestinians? The Palestinians have their roots, they are living in harmony with their environment, they love their villages, they stick to their land, and they can live without Jewish guidance. The Jewish supremacists wish to destroy their society, to confiscate their land and turn them into slaves sweating in Jewish factories. If that is what Portnoy 2001 feels about Palestinians, why would he feel differently about other goys? A good Viennese shrink would pronounce him sick and possibly dangerous to his neighbours. He is as sick as any bigot of the Ku Klux Klan, but much more influential due to his control over the media.

II

What is the source of Portnoy's influence? Why has he changed so much since 1969? Phillip Weiss points to the success of Jews in breaking through barriers, enriching themselves and occupying commanding positions in the establishment. He writes, "I don't claim to know how Jewish the membership of the establishment is. Twenty percent, 50 percent? I'm guessing 30." Even 30% would be sufficient to promote any idea, if the other 70% have no interest in the subject. In many financial companies, a 10% controlling share is as good as total ownership, as the rest is divided among small shareholders.

In the absence of solid statistics for the US, it is instructive to consider the economy of Apartheid-era South Africa. The British weekly *Economist*, hardly a 'hate publication', estimated that the Jews who constituted 0.03% of the population owned sixty percent of that rich country's market capitalization.

All other players, Anglos, Boers, Indians and native Africans competed for the remaining 40%.

The power of money is translated into the rule over minds by the feudal structure of the media. At the peak there are media lords, the proprietors. They delegate authority to their faithful retainers, the chief editors, who in turn choose loyal soldiers. The structure does not stand alone, but links to the financial and trading structures, the main ad-suppliers. The ad-suppliers are more important than the readers. In England, the *Daily Herald*, a newspaper targeted at a working class constituency, went bankrupt. Although it had five times as many readers as *The Times*, it only attracted half the advertising revenues. Advertisements account for approximately 75% of the revenue of an average newspaper. In the case of Radio and TV broadcasters, that figure leaps to almost 100%. It is no wonder that the media is accountable only to its 'paying' patrons, the privileged few who are members of an elite club.

Contrary to conventional wisdom, the media is not the message. The media is not a line of business, either. Lev Chernoi, a Russian-Israeli billionaire who sold his vast media empire to another ex-Israeli tycoon, Mr. Berezovsky, put it concisely in a recent interview: "Media is politics." The media is a means of shaping public consensus, of swaying the consciousness of a nation. There was a time when the readership provided some feedback. Not anymore. Ordinary people still own most of the body parts of America and they are the muscle, but the nerve system and the brain have been taken over by the club of media lords and the managers of finance and trade, a new dominant power in the world. They decide what Americans think. Americans enforce their decision on how we should manage our planet, from the rain forests of the Amazon to the last besieged Palestinian village.

The Club has disposed of the pretence of pluralism in the press. Russian politicians and journalists visiting the US often express amazement at how, in this huge and heterogeneous country, the scope of expressed opinions is so narrow. "You succeeded where the communists failed," is a frequent observation. Indeed, the differences between American newspaper coverage and TV News have all but disappeared. Noam Chomsky recently wrote to me:

> The editors of the *NY Times*, and their brethren, have refused—not "missed," but refused to publish a single word about the sending of unprecedented numbers of military helicopters to Israel. Last week, the latest $5.5 billion deal was struck between the Pentagon and the IDF for more advanced Apaches. They recognize how the (US) population is likely to react. To date, the total coverage of this massive transfer of public funds has been one opinion piece in a newspaper in Raleigh, North Carolina. I've actually attempted to personally contact editors I've known for years. No use. The discipline, and uniformity, are really

impressive. People who thought that Stalin had reached the limits of totalitarianism are quite wrong.

Well, Joseph Stalin had no such compliant media-machine or modern technology at his disposal. Its potential is not yet fully realized, as the three major networks plan to launch one united and unified news programme every night, to spread the message to every house in America. A painter, Diane Harvey, wrote in despair:

> Its main technique is through feeding the public an entire world-view made out of toxic substitutes for information and truth. The 360-degree, surround-sound World Lie most people believe is built and sustained by the non-stop flow of highly purposeful, integrated and carefully directed fabrications. The spirit of truth has departed, an upgraded version of global totalitarianism has been coalescing into a new death-grip on human freedom.[33]

III

Paradoxically, this machine is vulnerable because it is so formidable. The subjugation and destruction of Palestine is but one of its applications. Do not ask for whom the bell tolls, it tolls for you, as no man is an island, said the Elizabethan poet, John Donne, proclaiming the common humanity of Man. These words sent Ernest Hemingway to fight for freedom in Spain in 1936, as freedom is indivisible. We repeated these words in 1968; we should repeat them now. The struggle for freedom in the US and the battle for Palestine are but one war.

Whenever the Almighty sends a malaise, says a Jewish parable, He sends the cure for it. The cure lies in democracy. The media should be returned to the people, taken out of the rich men's hands. Israel/Palestine should be democratised, equal rights provided to Jew and Gentile alike. It would cure Portnoy's New Complaint.

Notes

30. *New York Observer*, 22.01.01.
31. March 16, 2001.
32. In Israeli parlance, the Jewish supremacists are called 'right-wing', while national moderates are called 'left-wing', though this division has no connection to their social positions.
33. http://www.rense.com/general8/harv.htm.

Up to a Point

[An address to the UNESCO conference on Getting the Facts Right in June 2001.]

The media world was well described in the brilliant novel by Evelyn Waugh, *The Scoop*. Though the main plot of the book unfolds in Africa, the relevant scene takes place on Fleet Street, at the office of the *Daily Beast* owner, Lord Copper. The media baron asked his foreign editor from time to time: Is Yokohama the capital of Japan? Does Hong Kong belong to us? The editor had two 'safe' answers. When Lord Copper was right, he said, *Definitely, Lord Copper.* When he was wrong, he said, *Up to a point, Lord Copper*. That is the fork, from **definitely** to **up to a point** of the permissible borders of mainstream media discourse. We journalists are dependent creatures. We would like to be honest and sincere, but we have to think of our mortgages and of our vocation. If we were to step over the borders established by the media owners, we would have to look for a different occupation altogether.

Speaking of Palestine, the borders of permitted discourse are as narrow as the waist of Zuleika Dobson. I would say they coincide with the borders of internal Jewish Israeli mainstream discourse, from Meretz to Sharon. If we compare it with pre-Mandela South Africa, it is similar to the White mainstream discourse, from Nationalist to Progressive, not including the ANC. In my view, this discourse is exclusivist, even supremacist. It is based on sustaining Jewish supremacy in Palestine. It does not offer equality or even a safe future to the local inhabitants. But that is all you are allowed to say. You may support the creation of Palestinian reservations, which puts you firmly in the Israeli 'liberal' camp, or you can back mass expulsion and ethnic cleansing, and you will be called a hardliner or a hawk. These are the firm borders of the discourse. Whoever crosses the borders, and speaks for equality of a Jew and Gentile in the Holy Land, finds himself in the wilderness. His voice will be silenced, maybe for good.

I know this first hand. I live in Jaffa, a town with a mixed population. There are Palestinians, Moroccans, Israeli Ashkenazi Jews and Russians, and we all live together rather harmoniously. But a lot of people who were born in Jaffa live in refugee camps and are forbidden to return just because of their religion or ethnicity. I find it morally impossible that a Jew from New York, Paris or Novosibirsk, like me, can come and live in Jaffa, while a local man, born in Jaffa, may not come back home. I called for the return of the Palestinian refugees and immediately lost my job with *Haaretz*. That is the most liberal Israeli newspaper.

The case of Palestine coverage in the media is special for one reason. We have a peculiar vocabulary, developed for the local coverage. If I kill Ahmad, it would be reported that 'Ahmad was killed by an Israeli'. But if, God forbid, Ahmad would kill me, you would learn that 'a Jew was murdered'.

As in *Dr Jeckyll and Mr Hyde*, an Israeli may kill; but if an Israeli is killed, he turns into a Jew. It is absolutely forbidden to speak about Jewish atrocities and murders. The Jews are forever victims. It often appears that we have three nations in Palestine: Jews, Israelis and Palestinians. Israelis may commit crimes, but it is innocent—always innocent—Jews that are murdered. If you confuse these two words and refer to a murderer as 'a Jew', you will be called an anti-Semite, and probably you will lose your job.

It should not be too complicated to cover our story. It is not even as complicated as other places of world concern. The right of national self-determination inclusive of autonomy or independence isn't an easy right to realize, as Corsicans can tell you. Palestine should be easier to cover: it is not a question of national self determination, but of basic human rights. Kosovo? In Kosovo, Albanians were discriminated against and tormented by Serb authorities, but they always had the technical right to vote, and the Yugoslav government never withdrew their citizenship. They were distant second-class citizens, but still citizens. Kurds in Turkey? They also can vote.

The coverage of Palestine should be easier, but it is not. A journalist may write and speak about marginal problems, like the Jewish settlers beyond the Green Line. But the basic power structure of Jewish dominance in Palestine may not be questioned. We are not permitted to say the Palestinians have no right to vote, no right to move to other parts of their country, and no right to return to their homes in the only country they have ever known.

In my opinion, the source of the media bias in covering the Palestinians is tremendously important, for it speaks volumes about the power structure of the US and Europe. It gives us unique feedback from the obscure world of media lords. And, it goes without saying, that 'establishment' journalists are not given much leeway on reporting on this valuable feedback. They are always too busy writing **'definitely'**.

The reason is obvious. Too many of our media lords subscribe to the notion of Jewish supremacy, and they are spread around the globe. In England, there is Conrad Black: he owns many papers in Canada, the US, and in Israel. In our country, he owns the *Jerusalem Post*. When he bought this paper, he dismissed the staff and hired people of his opinions. He is a right-wing Zionist, a zealous supporter of Jewish supremacy.

In the US, there are too many of them to count. But allow us to mention Mortimer Zuckerman, a media lord and the current head of the Presidents'

Conference of American Jewish Organizations, the big daddy of all Jewish groups in America. He is one of the richest men in America; he made his fortune speculating in real estate and owns the third largest 'serious' American weekly magazine, *US News and World Report*. He also owns the tabloid, the *Daily News*, for New York and New Jersey readers. His newspapers generally advocate the brutal rule of market forces. With one exception: they call for generous annual subsidy of Israel by American tax payers. Two ex-Prime Ministers of Israel, Netanyahu of the war-mongering Likud and Barak of the slightly less hawkish Labour party, supported Zuckerman in his quest for the leadership of the Conference of Presidents of Major Jewish Organizations. This side of the Ku Klux Klan, this association of fifty-two heads of American Jewish organizations is the most bigoted body of men in American politics. *Haaretz* recently reported that Mortimer Zuckerman had dismissed his *shiksa* wife in order to get this coveted chair. As long as he stayed married to a non-Jewish woman, his colleagues, Jewish billionaires, would not trust him. And he is one of the most influential publishers in the US.

On the other end of the planet, in Russia, the TV stations and newspapers also are under the ownership of Israeli citizens. One of them, Vladimir Gusinsky, was forced to part with his TV station. But his extremely pro-Israeli staff was quickly hired by another channel, belonging to another Israeli citizen, Mr. Chernoi. In 1985, he was an accountant living on a salary of $100 a month. Today he is worth $5 billion, owns virtually all the aluminum plants in Russia, and lives in Israel's own Beverly Hills. Currently, he is under investigation for thirty-four murders, money laundering and membership in the Russian mafia. In a recent quip, he was quoted as saying that "the media is not business. The media is politics and influence." He uses his media empire to stifle all criticism of Israel in Russia.

I spoke recently to a young Russian military attaché in one of the Western capitals. He told me: "Your Israeli situation is similar to ours, but we have Chechnya a thousand miles away, while you have it next door."

I asked him: "Do you want to say that Chechens have no right of vote?"

He was amazed. He did not know that the Palestinians have no right to vote. The media of Gusinsky, Chernoi, and Berezovsky, that is of three powerful media lords, all of them Israeli citizens, took care to cultivate his ignorance.

This international group of Jewish media lords, from Washington to Moscow, is not subservient to the interests of Israel. But support of Israel is a part of their agenda. On the top of the list is globalisation and neo-liberalism—what they call 'freedom of market forces'. On political matters, they tend to distrust democracy and personal freedoms and make constant demands for corporate liberties.

Mutual support is also high on their list of priorities. When Gusinsky was under investigation for embezzling funds, the *New York Times* and the *Washington Post*, that is the late Mrs. Kathryn Graham and Mr. Sultzberger, both published virtually identical lead stories and editorials supporting the 'Independent Russian Press'. 'Independent' appears to be a code word for 'Jewish-owned'.

This should be a serious cause for concern. When an Egyptian businessman bought Harrods in London, the newspapers went into a fury. The headlines blared 'our national heritage is being taken away by foreigners'. In Israel, no outsider is allowed to own a newspaper. There was a rich Russian Jew, Gregory Lerner, who tried to buy a newspaper in Israel. He was sent to jail for six years for various mafia-related crimes. It is worth noting that before he made his rush into the media, nobody cared about his offences. An Iraqi Jew took over a newspaper, and very soon he found himself in jail. Because the media is not a business, it is the nerve system of a country.

In my opinion, the case of Palestine is much more important for you, for Europeans and Americans, than just another case of injustice, because it proves that this international group of Jewish media lords has become a mite too powerful. In my experience, Jewish journalists can be as objective as any. Actually, the best coverage of Palestine is done by Jewish journalists, from Susanne Goldenberg of the *Guardian* to Gideon Levy of *Haaretz*. But it is easier to squeeze a camel through a needle's eye than to find an objective media lord. This problem can be solved if newspapers were treated like precious water sources and other all-important public utilities. That is, unless we want to delegate all these newspapers to the murky realm of 'ethnic press', and build from scratch a new network of free press.

Vampire Killers

I

Folk tales about vampires provide readers with various remedies for the calamity of a ghoulish attack. A fistful of graveyard dirt is favoured, garlic is beneficial, and the cross is the most efficient. But these remedies don't always work. In Roman Polansky's hilarious horror comedy, *The Fearless Vampire Killers*, the hero tries to scare off a Jewish vampire with a cross. The Jew looks back at him with a kind understanding smile, straight from *Fiddler on the Roof*, and bares his fangs. The cross does not ward him off. Polansky's work comes to mind as I follow the new wave of Holocaust controversies.

The Revisionist historians (called 'Holocaust deniers' by their adversaries), intended to meet in Beirut to compare their notes on Nazi genocide. The American Jewish establishment, including the Zionist Organization of America and the Anti-Defamation League, demanded a ban on the conference, and the Lebanese government complied with their request.

The ZOA is not against revisionism *per se*. This organization pioneered the art of denying history and published, at the expense of the American taxpayer, a booklet called "Deir Yassin: History of a Lie." Deir Yassin was the peaceful village the Jewish terrorist groups Etzel and Lehi attacked on the ninth of April 1948, and massacred its men, women and children. I do not want to repeat the gory tale of sliced off ears, gutted bellies, raped women, torched men, bodies dumped in stone quarries or the triumphal parade of the murderers. Existentially, all massacres are alike, from Babi Yar to Chain Saw Gang to Deir Yassin.

ZOA revisionists have utilized all the methods of their adversaries, the 'deniers': they discount the eye-witness accounts of the survivors, the Red Cross, the British police, the Jewish Scouts and those of other Jewish observers who were present at the scene of the massacre. They discount even Ben Gurion's apology, since after all, the commanders of these gangs became in their turn prime ministers of the Jewish state. For ZOA, only the testimony of the murderers has any validity. That is, if the murderers are Jews.

If Jews are the victims, these same American Zionist organizations spare no effort in challenging revisionism. This morally dubious position was no doubt of great comfort to those who gathered in Beirut. By their logic, if the Israelis are telling a tall tale about what happened in 1948, perhaps the Jewish memories of the Holocaust are also flawed.

They remind us of successful downgrading of other calamities in our age. Timisoara Massacre in Romania was widely reported by the *New York Times*, the BBC and CNN etc, perpetrated by Ceausescu, and estimated at 90,000 civilians. Ceausescu was summarily executed, friends of the West came to power, but the independent enquiry found that only 96 persons died, one thousand times less than previously estimated. First reports of 9/11 spoke of 60,000 dead, out of them 4,000 Israelis. Now we know there were 3,000 dead, out of them about 40 Jews, twenty times less than all victims and one hundred times less Jewish victims than estimated.

Another downgrading happened after the Kishinev pogrom. At first, the Jewish witnesses and organisations claimed 500 dead, later the number climbed down to 48, ten times less. Modern historians note that in all pogroms of Tsarist Russia, share of Jewish victims was about one-third of the total amount of casualties in the low-intensity Ukrainian peasant warfare against the Jewish bourgeoisie (some even call it "Ukrainian Intifada"). Certainly it is different from the picture we the Jews were taught in school.

The infamous massacre of Jews in 1648 perpetrated by Cossacks of Chmielnicki was estimated at 500,000 Jewish victims, until downgraded by a factor of 10 by the modern Jewish researcher Jonathan Israel.[34] He even denied there was a massacre of Jews; but Jews suffered as much as everybody else in this civil war between the Ukrainians, the Poles and the Jews.

Inspired by these achievements, the Revisionists scored a few hits, and the tales of soap manufactured from human fat, or Wiesel's fiery furnaces were laid to rest, together with more fantastic reports. Revisionists question the actual number of Jewish casualties, as well. It is not an easy issue, as the very definition of 'casualty' is based on interpretation.

A good example of 'victim definition' was provided in last weekend's *Haaretz*. When the Gulf war ended in 1991, there was one reported Israeli casualty of the war. Today, there are officially one hundred Israelis who are recognized as casualties of the Gulf war, and their dependents receive a pension at Iraqi expense. Some of the victims died of stress, some could not remove their gas masks and suffocated. The *Haaretz* article asserted that many more claims were declined by the Israeli authorities.

While assessing the Jewish casualties of WWII, Jewish organisations took the pre-war Jewish population, extracted the post-war numbers and arrived at the number of over five million Jews who died at war. This amount includes the Jewish soldiers, like my uncle who fought at Leningrad and perished in battle. It also includes my elderly grandfather who died of hunger and old age in the Jewish quarter of Stanislawow. It included victims of diseases, typhus and malnutrition. It had to be a large number, for it was a horrible war. For instance, in Byelorussia with its many Jews, every fourth person, Jew or Goy, perished at war.

That is why one should deny the very concept of Jewish holocaust, for it artificially separates the dead Jews from the vast number of their dead compatriots and fellow sufferers. This concept separates my uncle soldier Abraham and his trench buddy Ivan, though they were killed by the same shell. This concept separates my old grandfather from other old people in his city, who died at the same time. It separates my young aunt who was strafed by the Luftwaffe, from her Polish boyfriend. This is the concept of exclusivity, and it should be rejected. It should be rejected as it poisons minds of Jews, infects them with hatred to non-Jews, and with feelings of exclusivity.

But the Revisionists take a different line: they risked their careers and fortunes trying to undermine what they call 'the Myth of the Holocaust'. One can understand the challenge. Nowadays, one may openly doubt the Immaculate Conception or (maybe) challenge some founding myths of Israel. Yet the cult of the Holocaust retains a unique, court-enforced prohibition against any investigation that might cast a doubt on its sacred dogma. Dogmas have a way of attracting critical minds. Still, behind this red *muleta*, the charging bull's horns meet thin air. The arguments about gas chambers and soap production might be challenging, but they are quite irrelevant. Where is the matador?

II

A courageous step was taken by Dr. Norman Finkelstein in his best-selling expose *The Holocaust Industry*. There is, however, an important distinction between Dr. Finkelstein and the Revisionist historians gathered in Beirut. Dr. Finkelstein, a son of holocaust survivors, stayed away from the possibly illegal discussion of facts and concentrated on the ideological construct of the Holocaust cult.

A fat lot of good it did him. A Jewish organization called 'Lawyers without Borders' has already sued him in France. These lawyers were at perfect peace, when the Israeli legal machine pronounced a six-month probationary sentence on a Jewish murderer of a Gentile child. They did not move a finger when a fifteen-year-old girl Suad was placed in solitary confinement, was refused legal aid and was subjected to mental torture. They are visibly absent from Israeli military courts where a single Jewish officer can mete out a long imprisonment sentence to a Gentile civilian on grounds of undisclosed evidence. Apparently, these lawyers are aware of certain borders.

Finkelstein set out to explore the secret of our discreet Jewish charm, a charm that opens American hearts and the coffers of Swiss bankers. His conclusion is that we do it by appealing to European and American guilt feelings.

> The Holocaust cult[35] has proven to be an indispensable ideological weapon. Through its deployment, one of the world's most formidable

> military powers, with a horrendous human rights record, has cast itself as a victim state, and the most successful ethnic group in the US has acquired victim status.

Finkelstein carries out a brilliant analysis of the Holocaust cult, and makes a startling discovery: it is but a shabby construct of a few clichés stitched together by the sorrowful voice of Elie Wiesel in a limo.

Finkelstein is not aware of the magnitude of his discovery, as he still believes that the Holocaust cult is a great concept, second only to the invention of the wheel. It solved the eternal problem of the rich and influential, warding off the envy and hate of the poor and exploited. It allowed Marc Rich and other swindlers to cheat and steal; it allowed the Israeli army to murder children and starve women with impunity. His opinion is shared by many Israelis. Ari Shavit, a well-known *Haaretz* writer, expressed it best in 1996, when the Israeli Army killed over a hundred civilian refugees in Kana, Lebanon: "We may murder with impunity, because the Holocaust museum is on our side." Boaz Evron, Tom Segev and other Israeli writers have articulated the same notion.

One can sum up the thesis of Dr. Finkelstein as follows. The Jews succeeded in squaring the circle and solved the problem that befuddled the aristocracy and the run-o-the-mill millionaires. Namely, they disarmed their opponents by appealing to their compassion and guilt feelings.

III

I admire Dr. Finkelstein for his persistent belief in the good heart of his fellow Man. I trust he also believes in fairies. In my own estimate, compassion and guilt feelings can get you a free bowl of soup. Maybe. Not uncounted billions of dollars. Dr. Finkelstein is not blind. He noticed that the Gypsies, another victim of the Nazis, received next to nothing from a 'compassionate' Germany. The capacity of Americans to feel collective guilt towards their Vietnamese victims (five million killed, one million widows, Coventry-style destruction laced with Agent Orange) was recently expressed by Defence Secretary William Cohen: "There is no place for apology (let alone compensation). A war is a war." Despite having all the facts at his disposal, Dr. Finkelstein grasps his cross and tries to frighten the vampire away.

What is the source of power that fuels the Holocaust Industry? This is no idle or theoretical question. The making of yet another Palestinian tragedy is now in high gear, with the slow strangulation of its cities. Every day, a tree is uprooted, a house is demolished, a child is murdered. In Jerusalem, the Jews celebrated Purim by a pogrom against Gentiles, and it made page six in the local papers. In Hebron, the Kahane boys celebrated Purim at the tomb of the mass murderer Goldstein. This is no time to pussyfoot around.

In *Ulysses*, Bloom expresses the feelings of his creator James Joyce towards the bloody concept of Irish liberation by farting at the epitaph of an Irish freedom fighter. My grandfather, my aunts and uncles died in WWII. But I swear by their memory, if I thought that guilt feelings over the Holocaust cult caused the death of a single Palestinian child, I would turn the Holocaust memorial into a public urinal.

The shabbiness of the Holocaust cult and the ease with which it sucks billions is a solid proof of the real power behind this industry. This power is obscure, unseen, ineffable, but quite real. **It is not a power derived from the Holocaust, but rather, the Holocaust cult is a display of raw muscle by those who wield real power.**

In the new religiosity of the US, sometimes called 'Judeo-Christianity', the Holocaust had superseded the Passion of Christ, while the establishment of the state of Israel replaced the Resurrection, confirming the centrality of Jews in American discourse.

That is why all efforts of the revisionists are doomed. The people who promote the cult can promote anything, for they dominate public discourse. The Holocaust cult is just a small manifestation of their abilities. This power will just smile in the face of Dr. Finkelstein's revelations.

Notes

34. Jonathan Israel, European Jewry, Oxford 1985.
35. Dr Finkelstein distinguishes between 'holocaust', the historical event, and the Holocaust, the ideological construct. I took the liberty to rename it "the Holocaust cult" in the interests of lucidity.

Bankers and Robbers

I

"Swiss Holocaust cash revealed to be myth," announced *The Times* this Saturday (October 13, 2001), thereby lowering the curtain on a bizarre and obnoxious drama of extortion and robbery. It began in 1995, when two important gentlemen, Edgar Bronfman (Chairman of the World Jewish Congress), and Abraham Burg (a rising star of Israeli politics) visited Swiss banks on a humanitarian mission. "You have billions of dollars deposited by Jews before WWII," they said. "We want the moneys repaid immediately, whilst the survivors of the Jewish holocaust are still alive. Let them enjoy the last years of their lives in relative comfort." Bronfman and Burg are men that banks and insurance companies wake up and listen to.

Edgar Bronfman inherited his billions from his father Sam. Sam made his fortune by the illegal trafficking of booze in the US: he blended the stuff in Canada and smuggled it across the lake through his network of gangsters during the Prohibition period. Sam Bronfman made even more money as a loan shark. Shortly before his death, he was asked by a journalist: "What is the greatest invention of mankind?" True to form, he replied, "interest on loans."

Capitals earned by crime and squeezed from debtors can help in politics—in Jewish politics as well, as you do not have to be elected to become an important figure. You can always rent two rooms in an office building and put up the sign of 'World Jewish Association', 'Survivors' Forum', or 'Jewish Liberation Organization', and you are in business. There is no copyright to such titles. Bronfman's World Jewish Congress was exactly such a tiny body with a grand title. Before Bronfman, it had this or that nice Jewish fatherly figure in the chair, such as his predecessor Nahum Goldmann, but it pulled no strings and cut no ice. With the vast capital of Bronfman, it became a power structure.

Avrum (Abraham) Burg, Speaker of the Israeli Knesset (Parliament) and a candidate for leadership of the Israeli Labour, was the son of an important Israeli politician (a leader of the National Religious Party) Dr. Burg , who served all governments of Israel as a Minister for over forty years until his demise. Avrum provided a good soundbyte on the ABC's *Nightline* on August 2, 2001, when he described Palestinians as "people you do not want your daughter to get married to." Avrum needed a sponsor to advance in politics, while Bronfman needed a reliable Israeli partner for his plan.

No bank or insurance company can refuse such important gentlemen. After a short resistance, the Swiss gnomes gave in, and the titular heads of Jews walked away with a large pot of cash. "These Jews want to rob our banks and insurance companies in the name of their holocaust," the Swiss probably fumigated. But they were mistaken.

While this story began as *Elders of Zion Revisited*, its continuation followed the script of *The Sting*. Six years passed by, but almost no money left the benevolent grasp of international commissions created by Bronfman and Burg. Practically nothing was given to the survivors of the Jewish holocaust. The moneys were misappropriated by the same people who had demanded justice for victims. Recently the authoritative *Los Angeles Times*[36] stated:

> An international commission created to resolve Holocaust-era insurance disputes has reportedly spent more than $30 million on salaries, hotel bills and newspaper ads while distributing only $3 million to claimants.

The members of the commission turned it into a high-class travel agency and entertainment spot, the *LA Times* added:

> The documents show that since 1998 the commission has held at least 18 meetings with up to 100 participants at hotels in London, Jerusalem, Rome, Washington and New York.

About the slave labour settlement, the *Independent*[37] reported:

> While the victims of the Holocaust will receive (maybe) between USD 2,500 and USD 7,500, the [Jewish] lawyers who negotiated the settlement will collect fees well in excess of USD1 Million each.

The *Times* reported that the Swiss banks had checked the dormant accounts and found that they did not even belong to the Jewish victims of the Holocaust. They belonged mainly to 'wealthy non-Jewish people who forgot about their money'.

Now, the Swiss didn't pay $1.5 Billion to Bronfman and Burg because they had been convinced by their claims. They paid because they had no choice. Bronfman (together with Marc Rich) was an important supporter of President Bill Clinton, and Clinton did his asking, probably stopping just short of bombing Zurich.

Some parts of the story began to surface in CUNY Professor Norman Finkelstein's best-selling book, *Holocaust Industry* and caused a major controversy. Finkelstein objected to the extortionist methods of the Jewish organisations. They presented him as a liar and an anti-Semite. Now, a year after his book was published, more unexpected and juicy details of sordid dealing are beginning to leak. If their data is confirmed, we will be looking at the greatest robbery ever perpetuated in the Twentieth century.

Apparently, Professor Finkelstein got some things wrong: to the chagrin of the Jew-haters, the victims of the robbery were not only banks and insurance companies, but ordinary folk of Jewish origin. To the embarrassment of Jews, the robbers were the self-appointed Jewish leaders who claim to represent the Jewish people.

II

The man behind this discovery is very different from the New York Professor Finkelstein. Martin Stern is a wealthy British businessman, deeply involved with real estate, Jewish and Zionist causes. He works in London and spends his weekends in his spacious apartment in Jerusalem's Orthodox neighbourhood. He does not miss a single prayer in his *shul*, gives to charities and loves Israel.

His casual meeting with a Swiss banker in Villar, a prestigious resort in the Swiss Alps, started the machinery of holocaust claims. The banker told Stern an interesting small tale. His bank, Union Swisse (USB), computerised its business in 1987 and discovered many accounts dormant since 1939. The bank managers came to the conclusion that some SF 45 million (USD30 Million) of deposits had probably belonged to Jews who died during or after the war.

"We did not want to keep somebody else's money," said the honest Swiss banker. "we called the World Jewish Congress and asked them to help find the heirs to the funds. The Congress replied: 'It is not on our agenda.' " Cold-shouldered, the Swiss transferred the $30 million to the Red Cross.

Martin Stern was touched by the story and told it on Israeli Radio. Two weeks after the broadcast, "coincidentally," Bronfman and Burg knocked on the doors of the Swiss Banking Corporation, demanding the cash. As noted above, they got the money but kept it for their purposes. Martin Stern felt he was involved and he followed the story's development.

He became increasingly worried by the way the Holocaust money was handled. Over and above their own salaries, the Claims Conference spent USD 43 million on food parcels for Russian Jews. Bronfman and Burg did not mention this subject when they went to the Swiss banks and asked them to speed up the payment to survivors, to people who owned the money. Had their agenda changed?

Family circumstances led Stern to a correlated story about an insurance company, the Generali. Before WWII, the Generali was a big Italian insurance business owned by Italian Jews. 'Many insurance companies before WWII were in Jewish hands, as in those days insurance was a small man's bank,' Stern explains. The Generali had big assets in Palestine, as well as in the Balkans and

Italy. Despite the war, Italian fascism and the Holocaust, the Generali retained its Jewish connection. They did not want to follow the example of the Swiss and the Germans and denied all knowledge of the relevant pre-war policies. Stern investigated at his own expense and succeeded in locating the secret storage where the Generali bosses kept the pre-war policies. He found out that the Generali owes huge sums to the heirs of its insured. His discovery forced the Generali to mend its ways and agree to pay, wishing to make amends to its policy holders personally.

III

Now, if the deceased had not been Jews, their heirs would have been free to retrieve the value of their policies from the relevant insurance company or bank. But, as you have been suspecting all along, we Jews are different. We are different because we are more than somewhat naïve. That is why we agreed to have an intermediary—the Jewish leaders—deal with the (largely Gentile) World.

From the 1950s on, Jewish leaders made a fortune as the intermediary, for compensation did not go straight to heirs and survivors but went to the sticky hands of the leaders. Israeli Jews were supposed to receive the compensation and pension via Israeli channels, while European Jews received their money straight from the Goyim. Astonishingly, the survivors who were paid via Jewish hands, always got less, sometimes much less. The Jewish state, Jewish banks and Jewish organisations profited on every transaction, and they did not miss a single trick. When Israel ran high inflation, the pensions of the survivors were always under-indexed. Banks did not transmit the funds on time.

When the Russian Jews arrived in Israel, the Jewish leaders reached an agreement with Germany to provide for the survivors. The lion's share of the funds given by the Germans remained in the hands of Jewish organisations, intermediaries and other dealers.

Whoever relied upon our Jewish brothers was screwed up, as robbing fellow-Jews is a favourite pastime of Jewish crooks, leaders and bankers. A cynical man would say: the very idea of the Jewish People is the best invention of crooks. In the days of our grandfathers it was not working all that well, as the Jews knew: a Jewish crook would cheat a fellow Jew as fast as he would cheat a Goy, and probably faster. But on this occasion we forgot this important notion.

IV

After Martin Stern found the policies, the Generali Insurance agreed to cooperate and pay. But the Israeli and Jewish politicians wanted to remain in the game.

They negotiated a fixed settlement with the Generali on behalf of Jewish policy holders. It was a crazy idea: whether the Jews are a religious or an ethnic group, surely they insured their lives as private persons. Moreover, they did not empower Israeli politicians to represent them. But the politicians negotiated the settlement, received one hundred million dollars, called it The Generali Fund, and began to use it as their own. They forgot the interest of Jewish policy holders, or, probably, they never considered it to be anything but a figure of speech.

By June '01, of 1250 policy information requests the Generali Fund had treated only 72. The policy holders were sent hither and thither, often refused for no reason or received no reply at all. In despair, they turned to the Italians, who promptly paid. This was additional proof that we Jews need Jewish intermediaries as much as fish need boots. During the same time, the Fund trustees made 270 'ex gratia humanitarian payments'. They sent food parcels to Russian Jews, in order to attract them to Israel. I am sure the Generali would have been very happy to feed Russian Jews and to increase their Zionist zeal, but why did the Israeli politicians not invite it to do so while negotiating the settlement?

Martin Stern discovered that the trustees of the GF became frequent fliers to Italy at the expense of the Fund, and when it seemed to be insufficient money, they did not hesitate to ask the Generali for substantial fees. The problem crossed the ocean, and the American claimants discovered that their claims had been 'settled' by the politicians. American Jewish organisations supported their Israeli buddies. An important player in the system was Lawrence Eagleburger, a former US Secretary of State. This great man chairs the commission of Jewish leaders for dealing with Holocaust-related insurance claims and draws a $350,000 annual salary. In Stern's opinion, the insurance settlement money would barely suffice to pay the policy holders. That is why he is horrified by the ease with which Messrs Bronfman and Burg waste the funds on 'other worthy causes'.

V

Although the Jewish organisations gave Swiss and German banks a hard time, they became much more timid when they came upon a Jewish bank. The Bank Leumi of Israel has probably more funds of perished Jews than any Swiss or German bank. You will laugh, but Israeli bankers are not in a rush to return the money. As a matter of fact, they stick to the cash like glue. Before WWII, many European Jews deposited their savings in the Anglo-Palestine Bank, the main Jewish bank of British Palestine, as Bank Leumi was called before 1948. Some of them made deposits, others rented safe deposit boxes. Not only Jews used the bank—its cellars stored vast fortunes of Palestinian Christians and Muslims as well.

Many Palestinians lost their deposits in the great upheaval of 1948. Israeli banks used all ways to block their moneys and let them disappear as inflation soared. But the Jews did not fare better. Apparently, the worst place where a Jew could leave his money for safe keeping was the Bank Leumi, the National Bank of Israel. The Holocaust survivors and the heirs of victims were met with the adamant refusal of Bank Leumi to open up its documentation for inspection.

In course of privatisation, Bank Leumi became partly owned by the Generali. Migdal Insurance, the Generali and the Bank Leumi constitute an intertwined group of businesses and businessmen with dubious records. The same men sit on the boards of these companies, sharing perks and shifting funds around.

Martin Stern discovered that in the 1950s, Bank Leumi staff opened, without external control and supervision, even without writing a protocol, all dormant safe deposit boxes. Their contents were pushed into brown envelopes and stored hidden from the public eye. As a colourful detail, he was told of a trunk that had stood in the offices of the Bank Leumi for years, to the chagrin of typists who tore their stockings on its corners. When the trunk was opened, they found a real treasure, apparently placed for safekeeping by a Coptic church. To date, the trunk has not been returned to the Church.

Martin Stern could not believe such flagrant breach of banking laws was possible. In the course of his struggle in the interests of Holocaust survivors and their heirs, he demanded that the Bank Leumi officials publish the names of safe deposit box owners, whose deposits were removed by the bank. At first, the Director General of the Bank, Galia Maor, denied the bank had opened the boxes. When presented with evidence, she replied sternly, "we found only love letters." I wonder whether such a reply, if given by the Swiss, would be acceptable to the Jewish organisations.

The fate of currency deposits was not different from that of safe deposit boxes, as the Bank Leumi could win both ways. Before WWII, a Mrs. Klausner deposited £170 in the Bank Leumi, an equivalent of USD 25,000 in today's value. When she came to claim her deposit, Bank Leumi offered her NIS 13 [13 New Israeli Shekels], or US $4. In order to avoid future embarrassment, the bank officials began to destroy old documentation.

The tricks of the Bank Leumi attracted the attention of the Israeli press and the Knesset (Parliament), and a parliamentary commission of enquiry was called for. It took six months of intensive negotiations to form the commission, but in its charter there was one conspicuous fault. The survivors demanded to find out the persons responsible for hiding their funds for half a century. This demand was not included in the charter. Even worse, the commission included persons responsible for the present state of things. Zvi Barak was a member of the Bank Leumi management. He sits also in the management of the Generali Fund. He was sent to investigate the Swiss banks and now he is supposed to find out the culprits in his own bank.

Michael Kleiner is an MP for the extreme right Herut party. He wrote to the parliamentary commission of enquiry: "The Bank destroys documents in two different sections, and now there is deep suspicion regarding the Holocaust deposits and especially the brown envelopes of the safe boxes."

Recently Bank Leumi became known for its large-scale cash laundering, when the fortunes stolen by Vladimir Montesinos and his boss Alberto Fujimori, an ex-president of Peru, were traced to the Bank Leumi's office in Switzerland. One cannot understand the word 'laundering' in reference to such a bank, as it would probably dirty a handkerchief laundered in it.

VI

The biggest achievement of the Jewish leaders was recorded in Germany, in 1991, when East Germany joined the German Federal Republic. After 1945, Socialist East Germany did not return property to its German pre-war owners, whether Gentiles or Jews. Their logic was good. East Germans did not subscribe to the notion of the 'Jewish people'. They dealt on equal footing with the German citizens, Jews or not. They thought the Nazi idea of Jewish separateness was laid to rest in 1945. They were wrong. West Germany accepted the feudal concept of Jewry in 1950, when it paid compensation for the Jewish property—not to survivors or their heirs, but to the State of Israel and the Jewish leaders elsewhere. The West Germans did it again in 1991.

For instance, two Germans, Moses and Peter, perished in the war, and left some property in East Germany. The property of Peter the Gentile remained in the hands of the German government until his heir was found. If he had no heirs, the property would remain in the hands of the German people. But the property of Moses the Jew would pass into the hands of Messrs. Bronfman & Burg, the leaders and representatives of the Jewish People, and members of the Conference for Claims. The Germans transferred property that had belonged to their Jewish citizens in the territory of the East Germany, into the hands of the Conference.

(What does it mean—'Jewish property'? Is there 'Gentile property' as well? Why did the Jews who always object to the very concept of Jewry, not object now? Why should compensation for Bernstein's burned-out house go to 'Jewry'? For a lawyer, whatever has property and rights, certainly exists. Jewry exists, for there is 'Jewish property', which goes to Jewry, if the individual Jewish owner is dead.)

The Conference was a fictitious body of 44 men representing nobody. Some of them were sent, for instance, by a grandly named Anglo-Jewish Association, whose total membership is about fifty. Only two persons 'represent' millions of Israeli Jews. This Conference was supposed to find the rightful heirs of Moses, and of other Germans of Jewish origin.

However, the Jewish leaders had a better idea. They knew that many owners would never come to claim their houses anyway, and the property would become theirs. But that was not enough for the greedy bastards. They set a certain date after which they would not consider the claims of heirs. That was a strike worthy of Jewish genius: some thirty billion dollars worth of property became theirs as if by right. From now on, they can take the rightful claims of heirs lightly. And the billions of dollars in rent would accumulate in their accounts.

American Jewish survivors' organisations have begun their fight against the Jewish leaders. They demand that the Conference make public full lists of its assets, that they find the real heirs and give up those assets. They are thinking of suing Germany, Italy and other countries and organisations that for some mysterious reason subscribed to the medieval idea of 'Jewish property'. They say that property could be the property of individual Jews only, and not that of some odd 'Jewish property' residual owner. As this story proved, such ideas are good for the self-proclaimed Jewish leaders for keeping them in the style to which they are accustomed, but for ordinary folks of Jewish origin this is the right time to give up the expensive illusions of Jewish solidarity.

Notes

36. http://www.infobeat.com/cgi-bin/WebObjects/IBFrontEnd.woa/wa/fullStory.
37. *Independent*, 18.06.01, by Mary Dejevsky from Washington.

Fiesta of St. Fermin

I

Recently, travelling in Northern Spain, I came upon the old capital of Navarre. Pamplona was celebrating the *feria* of St. Fermin, and thousands of *aficionados* had crowded the narrow streets leading to the famed bullring. There were also a lot of foreigners earnestly following Hemingway's steps. In the morning, young boys ran the arena with the young bulls, competing in speed and grace. It was an exciting show, awash with adrenaline, but it drew no blood. It was different in the evening hours, when grown men fought mature bulls, ferocious coal-black creatures with sharp horns, moving at the speed of a TGV train, weighing over half a ton each, every ounce of them loaded with the resolve of a bullterrier.

The tribunes above the arena are divided into two differently populated sections. In the *Sombra* section, the upper class sombrely applauds the show. They are the important people, and a matador tries his best to show them his art. In the *Sol*, under the direct rays of the Pyrenean sun, the simple folk made merry by splashing buckets of Sangria, sharing home-cooked food with strangers and singing the chant of St. Fermin. They love the bullfight too, but there is not much action on their side of the ring.

The matador works unbelievably close to the beast, just slightly shifting weight to avoid the deadly horns. If not for the animal's lack of understanding, a man would have a slim chance of surviving a confrontation with a bull. But the bull is fascinated with the red cloth, the *muleta*, that the matador unveils in front of him. Instead of going for the matador, he flies at the cloth. In the end, tired of his labours lost, frustrated by vain assaults on the unvanquished red cloth, the bull stood still, lowered his neck and waited for the merciful steel.

The bullfight is an apt metaphor for the fruitless fight for civil rights in Palestine. The Jewish settlements in the midst of the Palestinian population are like the red cloth. The settlements annoy us, as they ruin the Biblical beauty of the Highlands. They annoy us by their visible injustice, as they are open only to Jews, while a goy can not even enter their limits. They annoy us because they are the reason for separate for-Jews-only roads. They annoy us because of the provocative demeanour of the settlers, who do their worst to humiliate their non-Jewish neighbours. They annoy us because they supplant olive trees with ugly prefabs. So we charge at them, while the matador moves away, and the important people above applaud.

For once, let us direct the rage of the bull away from the distracting and annoying *muleta*. The constant focus on the settlements is a distraction. On any given day, even in Jewish newspapers, in *Haaretz* or the *New York Times*, you can publish a critique of the illegal settlements, provided you stop there. But there is a man behind the red cloth. And there are those who sent him to fight the bull. The matador is the state of Israel. No settlement would exist for even a day, without the Israeli war machine behind it. When the native inhabitants of Hebron are locked for months in their homes, the curfew is imposed by the Israeli army, not by the four hundred Jewish settlers. But there is a man in the Sombra who commands the matador. Israel would not be able to commit its atrocities without support from abroad.

II

Maxim Rodinson, a noted French Marxist and biographer of the Prophet, defined Israel as 'a settler state', a colony. But every settler state has its mother country, the source of external power. French Algeria was manned and supported by France. The US was a settler state, whose mother country was England. What is the external power supporting Israel? What is its mother country? It is not the US, it is the constellation of important Jewish communities and first and foremost, the American Jewish community.

They send money and they organize public support and they influence the policies of the state of Israel. They are visibly more hawkish than even Sharon's Likud. The late unlamented 'Rabbi' Kahane was probably nearest to the hearts of Israel's supporters in America. This phenomenon of overseas Jews posing as 'more Israeli than Israelis', well described by Uri Avneri, exists for a variety of reasons. But I shall limit myself to addressing just one of the causes. The American Jews get no flak from their operations. They sit in the shade and send the matador to fight.

The men who send the Israeli troops to enforce the siege of Hebron and other Palestinian communities, live at ease in New York or Los Angeles, watch TV and put pressure on their congressmen to support the slaughter. These folk have no worries at all. Perhaps it is time to direct some heat their way.

Wars can never end, as long as their chief perpetrators sit in peace. Michael L. Calderon reminded us this week: "The French, Americans, and Afrikaner South Africans did not abandon their exploits in Algeria, Indochina, Namibia and Angola because of a collective "change of heart." Indeed these victories were won on two fronts. One was the front of actual warfare, and peoples of Algeria, Vietnam, Angola and Cuba bore the brunt of it. The second front was the international pressure and domestic protests.

The second front of the war for Palestine should be opened now, and we should know whom to pressure and against whom to protest. In my opinion, the buck stops at the door of self-appointed heads of the organized Jewish communities and media lords, Bronfman, Foxman, Sulzberger, et al. They are nasty and powerful men, and I understand the desire of the friends of Palestine to look for a less formidable adversary, like the Hebron settlers. Alas, that is as unprofitable as looking for a lost coin under the lamp post, just because that is where the light shines. One must look for the coin where one dropped it, even if it is inconvenient.

Confronting the leadership of the American Jewish community has become an urgent necessity. Why has it not been done until now? There is still the irresistible tendency to exonerate them from blame for the tragedy of the Palestinians, and to explain it all by 'American imperialist policies'. Even a great friend of Palestine, Noam Chomsky, whom I admire this side of idol worship, subscribes to this view. In a recent public appearance at MIT, he said that the pro-Israeli policies of the US are not caused by the influence of the Jewish lobby, but by the interests of American elites. *Amicus Plato, magis amica veritas.* I beg to disagree.

His opinion was repeated by many good people, all of them sincere supporters of the Palestinians. Usually they quote *The Fateful Triangle*, a classic work by Noam Chomsky, or express it like good Dr. Gabor Mate. He wrote to me:

> While they, Bronfmans and their colleagues certainly do their share to mislead and confuse the public—Jewish and non-Jewish—even they are small beer (metaphor intended) compared with the real interests U.S. policy serves. It's a question of the strategic interest of the U.S. corporate-state in having an obedient pit bull in the Middle East, with a nuclear capability, sufficiently nervous and aggressive to jump at Arab throats on demand, should the need arise—but also sufficiently dependent so that the leash can be pulled short whenever necessary. As one U.S. State Department official said some years ago, "in Israel we have an unsinkable aircraft carrier in the Middle East."

III

If you look carefully at these arguments, they collapse like a house of cards. American planes do not land on this 'aircraft carrier' even in case of war—they have bases elsewhere, in Saudi Arabia, Turkey, etc. Cyprus was once called 'the unsinkable aircraft carrier', but it was dropped with great ease. The obedience of this pit bull is not much to speak about, as its supply of weapons to China proved. And about Israel's being a dependable ally, there are strong doubts. Some Israeli politicians promote a different alliance, namely with Russia and its immensely rich and powerful Russian Jewish community, as America pulls the leash too much, in their opinion.

Some people explain US policies by 'oil interests'. As it happens, there is no oil in Palestine, bar olive oil. One can not envisage Israeli intervention in Saudi Arabia or Iran for the sake of American oil supplies: that would explode the entire Middle East.

The idea of Israel as a 'local proxy', or a 'local cop on the beat' also stores no water. I do not know of a single American corporate interest that would not be better off by allying with Turkey instead of Israel, for instance. As a Palestinian analyst wrote:

> Turkey would have been a better investment, for example, as a "normal" regional power that can help US policy, without costing half as much. Being Muslim may help as well in having a legitimate claim to "ruling over" the weak Arab countries.

One can add that Turkey was the traditional ruler of the area up to 1917, and it has the biggest and strongest army, totally pro-American and pro-Western. In other words, the concept of Israel as a servile dupe of American imperialism is a non-starter. Edward Herman, who co-authored *Manufacturing Consent* with Chomsky, agrees with this assessment:

> The Jewish lobby here is extremely important. I did have a piece on them directly, and it drew some criticism from several people on the left who argued that the lobby was much less important than US strategic interests in the Middle East. I've always felt that the lobby was at least of equal importance; fortunately for the lobby, the two have been at least reconcilable.

The means of confronting the self-proclaimed Jewish leadership can be direct, creative and non-violent. A good example was set by Berkeley students, the bearers of the tradition of 1968. They built two gates to the campus, one for Jews, another one for non-Jews, in order to give Americans a taste of Israeli 'roads for Jews only'. I can envisage heaps of earth on the driveways of Mr. Bronfman or Mr. Foxman. As good Jews, they certainly observe the rule of Hillel the Elder and do not do unto others whatever they hate themselves. As they support blocking Palestinian driveways, they would probably enjoy the same treatment. By the same rule, as they support illegal settlements, they no doubt will be pleased if some good people were to squat on their private estates.

I think such sit-ins would be fun, and they would attract many good Americans of Jewish ancestry. After all, their fathers protested White supremacy in the South; now the sons can protest Jewish supremacy in Palestine, without having to travel out of town. Instead of a boring demonstration in front of a boring Federal office building, instead of a dangerous show-down with Israeli soldiers on the hills of al-Khadr, the *Not In My Name* people, *Rabbis for Human Rights,* etc. can lead the struggle against the real adversary, back in the good old United States of America. They should do it together with other American activists, including Palestinian exiles.

This experiment will answer the question of the Jewish lobby's influence in the US and on the events in Palestine. I believe it would be very effective if there were real pressure on Mr. Bronfman and his super-rich friends in the Sombra to end their anti-Palestinian belligerence. Maybe they will signal the matador to send the bull back to his cows, instead of to the carver's bench.

[Despite many positive responses, none of the Jewish activists in the US dared to demonstrate against 'their own' community. They demanded from the Americans to demonstrate against corporations and administration with solid Anglo-Saxon names, but weren't ready to take such steps themselves. It caused acute disappointment with their line, and I turned again to the question of Jewish influence in the US.]

Nincompoop

"President Bush should be declared a Distinguished Zionist," quipped Tsahi HaNegbi, an Israeli thug-turned-minister, when the words of the American president ceased to reverberate in the end-of-June heat of Middle East.

"No, Bush should be co-opted into the Likud caucus," parried the Opposition leader, Yossi Sarid. Israeli Labour leader, Shimon Peres, looked sillier than ever, as Bush took away his favourite prop, 'the threat of American intervention'. Peres and Sarid have never advocated Palestinian human rights out of sympathy or common humanity, but rather to hoodwink their supporters in the notoriously nationalistic Israeli electorate: "We would deal with Palestinians and their lands as ruthlessly as [right-wing] Likud, but we treasure our special relations with the US. Americans would not allow it; that is why we are forced to behave like human beings." Now their forced interpretation had collapsed. Americans do not mind. They do not mind anything at all, and now Israel may continue its uninterrupted slide into a fascist nightmare.

With a wry smile, I look through the emails and articles of yesteryear, when Bush, Jr. was elected President. Many right-wing pundits expressed the opinion that the Jews had lost their stranglehold on American policy. "Jews in Bush's Cabinet? Don't Hold Your Breath," lamented Phillip Weiss of the *NY Observer*. Justin Raimondo of *Antiwar.com* was gleefully pleased with what appeared to be a Jewish setback. Just a few months later, they learned that the regained Anglo-Saxon supremacy in the United States was but a mirage. By astutely providing funds for both Republicans and Democrats, for practically all candidates of the left and right, the Jewish leadership is able to influence the choice of the candidates they prefer. Maybe they can't order a specific person for this-or-that position, but they are able to influence the shortlist, so the final choice doesn't matter at all. They know what they want: they prefer nincompoops, people of limited intelligence, competence, willpower and doubtful morality, no matter whether they are called Bush or Gore.

"Choosing a weak ruler" is the name of the game a rising ethnic or religious minority plays, whenever the populace is not yet ready to accept its true rulers. In *Babylon-5* and other SF movies, the aliens prefer a weak-kneed Terran man as their stooge. They learned it from history. In the second half of the first millennium, a large Eurasian state of Khazaria was the subject of a takeover.

Indigenous Khazars were governed and protected by Turkic warrior nobility, headed by their elected Khan, the King. Between the Sixth and Eighth Centuries they received a few waves of Jewish refugees, at first from Sasanid

Persia, later from Abbasid Iraq and Byzantium. Benevolent and tolerant Turkic khans believed they had acquired useful, clever and diligent subjects, but in no time at all, the new arrivals took over Khazaria.

For a while they preserved the façade of traditional aristocratic rule, and enthroned an increasingly weak Khan. In 803, Obadiah the Jew became the real ruler of Khazaria, while Khan the Goy was still shown to people once a year as a proof of legitimacy of Obadiah's power. Eventually, the last Gentile Khan was discarded. The fiction of Khazar rule came to an end, and a Jewish Beg [community leader] openly assumed the power in Khazaria.

It is often claimed that the Jewish rulers caused a mass conversion of Khazars to the Jewish faith. Arthur Koestler, a Jewish novelist, thought that modern East European (Ashkenazi) Jews are the descendents of these Khazar converts,[38] but two leading Russian scientists, an archaeologist Artamonov and a historian Leon Gumilev[39] came to the conclusion that ordinary Khazars were not converted to Judaism. The Jews were the ruling class in Khazaria; they didn't share the Covenant or important positions with outsiders, according to Gumilev. The Khazars became subject to an ethnically and religiously alien rule. They had to pay for the army and police, and for adventurous foreign policy. In the end, they lost their country.

The ruling Jews had it very good but very brief: within a hundred years of their full takeover, the Khazar Empire disintegrated totally. Such set-ups do not last, as they destroy their own power base. Khazars did not mind: they had no share in the Empire's fabulous wealth. They became Tatars, Kazaks and other nations of the steppe. The neighbours did not miss the Empire, as it was prone to genocide and slave trade. The Jews wandered out of the devastated Caspian basin into the deep-freeze of Poland and Lithuania, and dropped out of history for a thousand-year slumber.

The Jews of Khazaria needed a nincompoop for a Khan because their power was far from complete, and only a nincompoop would surrender to their demands. The Middle Eastern speech of Bush proved that this scion of a wealthy and powerful family is like a rabbit caught in the headlights of a car. The countdown for the demise of the American Empire has started.

Notes

38. Arthur Koestler, *The Thirteenth Tribe.*
39. Leon Gumilev, *Russia and the Great Steppe* [in Russian].

Prince Charming

[A talk given at Stanford University, California and at the American University, Cairo. It offers a politically correct way to discuss the Jewish power and its possible repercussions for the US.]

I

"What does he find in her?" jealously gossip the shrills. "Why does he shower her with gifts? What's she got that we haven't?"

She costs him a lot of money and good will, she alienated him from his old buddies, and for a good reason: The murderous little bitch, hers is a brand name for every mean trick. Yet he, usually tight-fisted and penny-pinching, generously cares and stonewalls for her, lays low her enemies and silences her critics. What is the secret behind the peculiar love affair between the Daughter of Zion from the Middle East and the Superpower across the ocean?

These questions tease the mind and call us to explore the source of the great anomaly of our time. Like exploring the source of the Nile in a past century, it requires an ability to look into a lion's eyes with a white hunter's disdain for death and Sherlock Holmes' detective talents.

The current favourite explanation is a vaguely defined "strategic interest of American corporations" sometimes deciphered as the desire of the US weapon industries to sell its wares to Arabs. Others prefer "America's need to have a base," or "the local cop on the beat" in a troubled area. Idealists believe in 'Americans' guilt feelings', in the long shadow of the Jewish holocaust or in 'psychological similarity'. Another prolific school explains the anomaly in terms of oil. Arab oil has to be under American control and who is better to do the job than ferocious Hassidic Jews?

Although this school explains everything in terms of oil, whether it is the war in Afghanistan, the looming American attack on Iraq, tension between India and Pakistan, or trouble in Palestine. They remind me of ancient Greek philosophers who believed in the existence of one basic element of which the world is built:

Thales said, water is the basis of all things.
Anaximenes said, air is the basis of all things.
Heraclites said, all is fire.

It is all pipelines, proclaims a chorus of experts whenever there is a discussion of reasons behind American policies in the Middle East.

It seems quite convincing, until one is reminded of a cheerful line of Afif Safiye, the witty PNA man in London: "Palestine has a lot of oil. Olive oil."

In order to understand the obscure charms of the Daughter of Zion, we should remember that Uncle Sam is not the first lover of this plucky girl. In Bush's predecessors, the British Empire in 1917–1922 and the Soviet Union in 1945–1949, we have a precedent; thus the advantage of full acquaintance with sources and motives. The archive documents were aired, published and analysed by better men; we need only sum up the fruits of their labour to find out "what attracts them."

II

The first Prince Charming to be seduced by her husky voice was British Foreign Secretary Lord Balfour, who promised to turn Palestine into a National Home for the Jews. Britain reneged on promises given to Arabs, seized Palestine, enforced Jewish rule in the land, killed and exiled every unbending Palestinian leader, destroyed the Palestinian economy and trained the future IDF shock troops to deal with the natives. They got preciously little in return. Palestine was an expensive thing to run, and it caused a lot of trouble. Perfide Albion became an object of much dislike in the Middle East. British soldiers and officers were killed by both Palestinians and by not-so-easily placated Zionists.

Traditional explanation for their strange behaviour is identical to that given for the US support. It is again 'imperialism', 'oil', 'strategic value', 'divide and rule' and similar platitudes (minus 'guilt' and holocaust, since it happened well before Hitler). But a neat "collection of the official documents, memoranda and letters of those in power in London and in Palestine" in the decisive years 1917–1922 contains just one reference to the economic value of Palestine as perceived by the British statesmen of the time, "Palestine has no strategic value whatsoever.[40]" There is no 'oil' in the index at all.

In private discussions behind the closed doors of the Whitehall, one can't find even a shred of imperialist desires to divide and rule. Contrariwise, the British leaders "anticipated great trouble from Zionists" (General Allenby). As Lord Cecil succulently put it, "we (the British) are not going to get anything out of [possession of Palestine]." The British did not need Palestine; they would have loved to get rid of the place, but they did not dare. The Palestine Papers put the "imperialist" explanation and 'oil factor' to rest, as possible explanation for the tumultuous affair between the Zionists and the British Empire.

Now, a thoughtful Israeli writer, Tom Segev, has proposed a quite different motive in his best-selling book, *One Palestine, Complete*. Published in English last year, it was acclaimed by the Jewish pundits of America as "thoroughly researched" (*Jewish Week*), "fascinating" (*Hadassah* Magazine), "landmark of information" (*Houston Jewish Herald*); and the great admirer of Sharon, Ron Grossman of the *Chicago Tribune* called it "brilliant . . . an utterly fascinating narrative of the period."

Segev does not mince words. He rejects oil-strategy explanations and in the very beginning of his book, affirms: England did it because its rulers "certainly believed in the great power of World Jewry[41] to influence world events, whether in the US or in revolutionary Russia. The British government had come to the conclusion that it is worth its while to conquer Palestine, to suppress its people and to give it to Zionists: it did this in order to curry favour with World Jewry.

The Prime Minister, Lloyd George "feared Jews," and in his memoirs he explained his momentous decision to support Zionists by his urgent need to form an alliance, "a contract with Jewry," "a highly influential power whose goodwill was worth paying for," in order to win the war.

> The Jews had every intention of determining the outcome of the WWI. They could influence the US to intensify their involvement in the war, and as the real movers behind the Russian revolution, they also controlled Russia's attitude towards Germany. The Jews offered themselves to the highest bidder, and unless Britain would clinch the deal first, the Germans would have bought them.

The astute Lloyd George based his opinion on the reports of British ambassadors, which were unequivocal. "The influence of the Jews is very great," noted his man in Washington. "They are well-organised and especially in the press, in finance, and in politics their influence is considerable." The ambassador in Turkey reported that an international connection with Jews was the real power behind Ataturk's revolution. The Foreign Office Under-Secretary Lord Cecil summed it up thus: "I do not think it is easy to exaggerate the international power of the Jews." The Royal Institute of International Affairs asserted that "the sympathy of Jews was vital to winning the war."

Jews fully shared this vision of united and powerful Jewry, writes Segev. The Postmaster General Herbert Samuel, a Jew and a Zionist, proposed in 1915 to give Palestine to Jews so that "millions of Jews scattered around the world, including the two million in the US, would show lasting gratitude for all generations." (It actually lasted less than twenty years until the beginning of Zionist anti-British terror.) With characteristic British understatement, Samuel wrote, "the goodwill of the whole Jewish race may not be without its value." The Zionist leader Chaim Weizmann "did his best to encourage this impression," says Segev. He "conjured up the myth of Jewish power" and "reinforced British predilection for seeing the Jews everywhere and behind every decisive event."

But the Brits did not bite until 1917, when their military situation became desperate. The Russian Front had been collapsing under the influence of the Bolsheviks, and the Germans had transferred divisions to the Western Front. Britain decided to deal with the Jews so they would push America into a European war.

III

Tom Segev did not discover America, but he has introduced a much-needed rhetoric device, called 'perception'. Wisely, he does not say, "Jews wielded such power that Britain preferred to deal with them and surrender Palestine, sacrificing thousands of British soldiers and millions of Palestinians in the process." Instead, the Israeli writer uses a formula perfectly acceptable even to severe Political Correctness enforcement-officers: not 'Jewish power', but 'the perception of Jewish power'. 'Belief in Jewish power' was the moving factor, akin to 'belief in witchcraft'. His device and its application allow us to continue to deal with our subject peacefully, leaving the adjacent but troublesome question of reality vs. perception to some other time.

A perception is almost as good as the real thing, wrote Mark Twain in his "£1 Million Bill." The American hero of this short story is universally accepted as a millionaire, though he has not a penny to his name, and he still makes millions on the basis of the perception.

The *New York Times* review of Tom Segev's book describes Balfour and other British supporters of Zionists as "acting from anti-Semitic reasons." It is an interesting definition: even devout Christian Zionists fully supportive of the Jewish state are considered 'anti-Semites', if they perceive and refer to the power of the Jews. Before WWII, an anti-Semite was one who considers Jewish power to be a negative phenomenon. After the war, in order to be innocent, one was not even to notice the Jews. That is why an open, no-holds-barred debate of the real extent of Jewish power would not be an easy one, as it is notoriously hard to measure and prove influence, and no newspaper or TV network of the Western world would touch the subject with a barge pole.

Segev further protects himself by attributing to the Brits a silly belief that "the Jews control the world."[42] No sane person, from Lloyd George to Hitler, ever thought so. The world is too big and complex to control. But the Jewish apologists usually attribute this exaggerated claim to their opponents, refute it, and consider the case closed. We shan't fall for this, but keep the case open a bit longer.

Segev does not consider why hard-nosed British politicians and civil servants succumbed to such an illusion, and why they ascribed the "decisive influence" to the Jews and not to West African witch doctors or Chinese Tao masters.

This lacuna is filled by the thick volume by University of California Professor Alfred S. Lindemann, *Esau's Tears,* published by Cambridge University Press.[43]

Lindemann refers to the Russo-Japanese War of 1905, when Jacob H. Schiff, the American financier, blocked the Russian attempt to obtain the bonds they sought on the international markets for financing the war, and provided financial support for Japan, eventually causing the humiliating defeat of Russia. Afterwards, Schiff boasted that "international Jewry is a power after all."[44] Simon Wolf, another important American Jewish leader and confidant of presidents, lectured the Russians:

> The Jews of the world control much of it. There is no use in disguising the fact that in the US, the Jews form an important factor in the formation of the public opinion and in the control of finances . . . they exercise an all-potent and powerful influence.

In 1905, after the Russo-Japanese war, their boasts were accepted as justified. Winston Churchill and Theodore Herzl firmly believed that international Jewry had enormous power in international relations. Professor Lindemann concludes: "They were not wrong in believing that Jews were a power in the world, and a rising one, particularly because of influence they could exercise in the up-and-coming US."

Lindemann concurs that the reason behind the Balfour Declaration was Balfour's and US President Wilson's fear that the Germans might make such a declaration, rally influential Jews to the cause of the Central Powers and put paid to the Anglo-American war effort.[45] That is why the English rushed to outbid other potential buyers of the perceived Jewish influence.

IV

It is well outside the scope of this piece to decide or even discuss whether the Jews actually delivered the goods as promised, or were able to do it—or even whether such Jews existed. It suffices to say that it certainly appears so. America threw its fresh forces into the battlefields of Europe, the tired German armies were defeated, and the Treaty of Versailles sealed the fate of Germany and Palestine. Long-standing traditionally good relations between German Jews and Germans were irrevocably ruined by the perceived alliance of the Jews with Germany's enemy. Eventually, ordinary Jews, ordinary Germans and ordinary Palestinians were made to pay a terrible price for the ambitions of the American Jewish leadership.

The British did not dare to cheat on the Jews after the war, as they were threatened again by possible Jewish desertion, this time to the Russian cause.

Head of British Military Intelligence General MacDonough warned the highest circles of the Empire:

> The most important thing about Palestine is not its topographical relation to Syria or anything else, but that it interests the whole of the Jews all over the world. Zionists tell me that if the Jewish people did not get what they were asking for in Palestine, we should have the whole of Jewry turning Bolsheviks and supporting Bolshevism in all the other countries as they have done in Russia.[46]

Quite recently, the Israeli right-wing, notably Sharon, Lieberman and Netanyahu, repeatedly declared that if the Jewish people don't get what they are asking for in Palestine, they will switch their support to President Putin's Russia. It took a few trips by Israeli ministers to Russia to bolster the American leadership's commitment to support Israel, although 'the Russian alliance' was an empty threat. Now, for the first time in centuries, the Jews have lost their perceived position of power-broker between two powers. Putin's Russia is too weak to threaten America; the radical Left is rather weak and has no identifiable Jews; European Jews have not recovered from WWII. It is the luck (or skill) of Israeli leaders that the US is led by the nincompoop Bush, not by people like President Nixon, or Lord Curzon, the man who said in March 1920:

> The Zionists are after a Jewish state with the Arabs as hewers of wood and drawers of water. That is not my view. I want the Arabs to have a chance and I do not want a Jewish State.[47]

But Nixon was impeached through the efforts of the Jewish-managed *Washington Post*, and Lord Curzon perished in strange circumstances.

As he predicted, the British Empire got very little good out of the deal with the Jews, even in the medium run. British victory over Germany in 1918 was a Pyrrhic one, as it accelerated the decline of the Empire. Many politicians moaned that instead of begging for a Zionist alliance and pushing for victory in 1915–1917, it would have been better to make peace with Germany.

British rule in Palestine gave England no influence, no profits, no strategic advantage. It did not even guarantee them Jewish support, let alone gratitude. Organised mainstream Jewry supported America, Jewish communists supported Russia, and the Jewish right-wing looked towards Mussolini and Hitler for inspiration and assistance. The Zionist militant organisations, Hagana, Irgun and Stern Gang humiliated, terrorised and murdered British soldiers, officials and statesmen. Very soon, the English understood they made a big mistake in entering the deal. They discovered, as many leaders before and after them, including Yasser Arafat, that one needs a very long spoon when eating with the Devil from the same bowl.

V

The love affair between the English Prince Charming and the Daughter of Zion was over, but she did not remain lonely and deserted. The place of the British gentleman was taken by Joseph Stalin. In 1945–1949, the Soviet Union became the strong supporter of the fledging Jewish state. Russia voted for the partition of Palestine, was first to recognise Israel, and was the main supplier of arms to the Zionists (via their Czech satellite), while the West imposed its blockade on the Palestinian side. Eventually, the Russian admirer dumped the girl, like his British predecessor, and returned to support the Palestinian cause. The strange zigzag of Russian policy intrigued politicians and scholars, who offered predictable explanations: 'Stalin's desire for a Middle East foothold', 'Soviet belief in the pro-Communist sympathies of Jews in Palestine', 'Russia's desire to undermine British imperialism', and surely, 'oil', 'expansionism' and 'imperialism'.

All these explanations seem plausible. For us, the Israelis, the favourite one, connected Russia's move with the Israeli Left. In 1948, the fighters of Palmach imitated the Red Army and sang Russian songs; some of them had Russian or Polish Communist backgrounds. Geo-strategists preferred the Russian search for a harbour in the Mediterranean, although political scientists saw it as the struggle between the Russian Bear and the British Lion for influence in the Middle East.

We would not know the right answer, but last year the Foreign Offices of Moscow and Tel Aviv jointly published two heavy (I know, I carried them) volumes of documents pertaining to this period. They contain secret and confidential letters from Stalin and to Stalin, and provide full insight into the Second Lover's Tale.

"Yes, our support of a Zionist state is a complete break with the long-standing Soviet tradition of supporting anti-colonial and anti-imperialist movements. Yes, this decision of ours will poison relations with the Arab world. Yes, it will enslave the native people of Palestine. But it can sway the American Jews to the side of the Soviet Union, and the American Jews will deliver the US to us." That was the true reasoning of Stalin and his men.

In those years, the strong sympathies of the American Jews towards the Soviet cause led to the Rosenberg Trial, and Senator McCarthy already felt it in the air. Stalin, as the Brits before him, did not care much about Palestine. He did not consider the British Empire an important enemy—after two world wars, England was ruined. He was not interested in oil. He thought, as did the Brits, of a contract with Jewry: to give the Jews what they want and to get their support in return.

It took him some time to understand his mistake. Israeli strongman David Ben-Gurion disabused potential friends of Moscow by stressing that the first and most important friend and master of Israel remained the American Jewish leadership. When the first Israeli ambassador, Golda Meir, arrived in Moscow, Stalin witnessed an incredible surge in Jewish solidarity. The Jewish wives of Kremlin commissars, from Mrs. Molotov to Mrs. Whatshisname, rushed in tears to Mrs. Meir as if to a long lost sister.

The Jews in Russia occupied too many important positions, and thousands of them crowded the streets in front of the Israeli embassy. Stalin hoped his support of Israel would help him captivate the minds of American Jews, but now he realised that, by means of Israel, the leaders of American Jews had captivated the minds of Russian Jews. Instead of getting his Fifth Column into New York, he had allowed Americans (via their Israeli ally) to activate their Fifth Column in Moscow. Stalin underestimated the hold Israel had on Jewish mind. He looked into this abyss and retreated as soon as possible.

VI

Two previous important partners of the Jewish state had supported it because they perceived Jewish influence in America as the joystick of the superpower control board. Their belief had been: give Jews what they want (Palestine), and they will give you what you want (America). For real or in perception, they came to grief. In a classic English story, *A Monkey Paw*, a magic tool fulfills the owner's wish but in such a horrible way that he has a reason to regret having wished it. The alliance with Jews had a similar effect. They got what they asked for: victory in war or the pro-Russian stand of American Jews, but they came to regret it.

Still the belief in Jewish power is the most common one among the elites of the world. That is why many countries send to Tel Aviv their best and most experienced ambassadors, usually on their way to or from the Washington Embassy. That is why, whenever a country wishes to beseech Washington, it sends an envoy to Tel Aviv. The Israelis pass the request to the right people in the US, and apparently, it works.

This belief is the most common one in the US as well. American politicians support Israel because they share the opinion of Lloyd George and Herzl. They also respect the condition demanded by heirs of Jacob Schiff and never, but never utter the dreadful words, 'Jewish power'. In the world free of taboos, a new Henry Miller won't shock his readers by referring to sex, but he will by referring to the Jews and their unseen might.

Is it only a perception? Perhaps. But the American traditional elites pay a real double price for it: they send their folk to fight the third war of the last hundred years for somebody else's perceived interests, and their positions at the top table are disappearing daily. This perception bleeds Iraq and Palestine, sends money to Israel, distorts the public discourse. Not in vain, Mark Twain used to say: a perception is almost as good as the real thing.

Notes

40. Palestine Papers, "Seeds of Conflict," compiled and annotated by Doreen Ingrams, John Murray: London, 1972, page 77.
41. Tom Segev, *One Palestine, Complete,* Henry Holt: New York, 2001, p. 36.
42. page 33.
43. Cambridge University Press, 1997.
44. page 302.
45. page 417.
46. PRO.CAB. 27/24, quoted by the Palestine Papers.
47. C20/3 quoted by Palestine Papers.

Orient Express

[This was written after the 9/11 attack and published a few days later.]

Like the Four Riders of the Apocalypse, the unknown kamikaze rode their giant crafts into the two visible symbols of American world domination, Wall Street and the Pentagon. They vanished in flames and smoke, and we do not yet know who they were. Theoretically, they could be practically anybody: American Nationalists, American Communists, American Fundamentalist Christians, American Anarchists, anybody who rejects the twin gods, Dollar and M-16, who hates the stock market and interventions overseas, who dreams of America for Americans, who does not want to support the drive for world domination. They could be Native Americans returning to Manhattan, or Afro-Americans who still have not received compensation for slavery.

They could be foreigners of practically any extraction, as Wall Street and the Pentagon ruined many lives of people all over the globe. Germans can remember the fiery holocaust of Dresden with its hundreds of thousands of innocent refugees incinerated by the US Air Force. The Japanese will not forget the nuclear holocaust of Hiroshima. The Arab world still reels under the creeping holocaust of Iraq and Palestine. Russians and East Europeans feel the shame of Belgrade. Latin Americans think of the Yankee invasions of Panama and Granada, of destroyed Nicaragua and defoliated Colombia. Asians count their dead—in the Vietnam war, in the bombings of bombings, in the Laos CIA operations—in millions. Even a pro-American Russian TV broadcaster could not refrain from saying, "now Americans begin to understand the feelings of Baghdad and Belgrade."

The Riders could be anybody who lost his house to the bank, who was squeezed from his work and made permanently unemployed, who was declared an *Untermensch* by the new *Herrenvolk*. They could be Russians, Malaysians, Mexicans, Indonesians, Pakistanis, Congolese, Brazilians, Vietnamese, for all their economies were destroyed by Wall Street and the Pentagon. They could be anybody, and they are everybody. Their identity is quite irrelevant as their message is more important than their personalities, and their message is read loud and clear in the choice of targets. I wonder whether the Fourth Rider was headed for Hollywood or for the NY Times building.

Their identity is quite irrelevant for another reason. The Jewish elite have already decided: it has to be Arabs. One would think that after Oklahoma, we should be less hasty with our conclusions. But my countrymen, Israeli politicians are impatient folk. The flames in Manhattan not yet died out and they have started on their political profit taking. Mr. Ehud Barak came 'live' on BBC, and said 'Arafat' within three minutes flat. On CNN, his twin Bibi Netanyahu affixed the blame to Arabs, Muslims, Palestinians. Shimon Peres, an old wizened wizard, spoke against suicide as a psychiatric adviser, reminding his audience of Palestinian attacks. He looked worried: it is hard to enslave people who are not afraid to die. This old killer of Kana even mentioned the Gospels. The accumulation of Israelis on the air approached saturation point. They insinuated and incited, pushing their shopping list into the chalk-white face of shell-shocked America: Plees, destroy Iran! And Iraq! And Libya, plees!

The first twenty-four hours of maximum exposure were utilised by the Jewish propaganda machine to its utmost. Not a single fact was yet known, but racist anti-Arab slurs became a commonplace. While we Jews quite reasonably object to any reference to the Jewishness of a bad guy, we really do not mind producing revolting racist drivel of our own. A noble-minded activist warned in al-Awda: "Making broad, all-inclusive statements and insinuations about 'Jews' completely marginalizes and discredits your organization." But how come the endless stream of 'broad, all-inclusive statements and insinuations' about 'the Arabs' did not 'completely marginalize and discredit' the Jewish organisations and media who practise it? Apparently, it is a Jewish right to decide who will be marginalized in America and who will not.

The connection was in the mind, as Israel is just a small-scale model of their new brave world of globalisation. There were no hard facts against Palestinians, but the Israelis and their agents in Western TV networks did their damnedest with the scenes of joy supposedly shot in East Jerusalem. That was a great distortion of the truth. Nobody celebrates the fiery death of innocent civilians, but people may rejoice at the collapse of a hated symbol. America celebrated its victory on V-day, not the deaths of Germans and Japanese. When Americans rejoiced at the 'precise hits' of their missiles at Baghdad 1991, they were celebrating their achievement, not enjoying the pleasing smell of burned human flesh.

The so-called 'Palestinian celebrations' are, therefore, an ugly brainwashing device, straight from the Nazi propaganda box. It recalls the previous Jewish invention, that of Palestinians sending their children to die for profit. Both lies are so inhuman, so outrageous, they speak mainly about their designers. I am sorry for the Palestinians, the most vilified folk on earth. I am even more sorry for the Americans who imbibe the poison of their Jewish-led media. They do not see that Israel's agents are trying to hitch a ride on dead Americans. Forget the Palestinians, there was a lot of élan all over the world.

In Agatha Christie's *Murder on the Orient Express*, her favourite detective M. Poireau encounters an unusual complication: all the passengers on board the train have a good reason to bump off the unpleasant old gentleman. My dear

American friends, your leaders placed your great country into the old gentleman's shoes.

Israelis used the event to the max. They killed twenty Palestinians including a nine-year-old girl, brought tanks into Jenin and Jericho, destroyed a few Goyish houses in Jerusalem. The reports were rather gleeful, in the style 'we told you', and the experts of Israeli TV concluded by one o'clock that the attack 'was good for the Jews'. "It is very good," said Bibi Netanyahu. Why? It would strengthen American support of Israel.

The kamikaze attack can do exactly that. America could enter a new cycle of violence in its troubled relations with the world. Revenge will follow revenge, until one of the sides will be obliterated by a nuclear blast. It appears president Bush prefers this course. He declared war on his and Israel's adversaries. Bush did not even understand that the war had been declared by the US many years ago, only now it started to come home. So many people are sick of America's ham-fisted approach that the countdown for the next attack has begun.

Alternatively, America could see this painful strike at her Wall Street and her Pentagon as the last call to repent. She should change her advisers, and build her relations with the world afresh, on equal footing. Probably she should rein in the domination-obsessed Jewish supremacist elites of Wall Street and the media, and part company with Israeli apartheid. She could become again the universally loved, rather parochial America of Walt Whitman and Thomas Edison, Henry Ford and Abe Lincoln.

Now it is President Bush's choice between the Old Testament drive for revenge and the New Testament spirit of love.

[Well, you know his choice, or the choice of his advisers. It was the attack on Afghanistan and the forthcoming war against Iraq.]

Last Sunny Days

[Based on a talk given in Trondheim, Norway.]

On a better day, I would use an occasion and chat with you to my heart's content, and what could be a better occasion than presentation of my book in the Norwegian translation. A talkative man from Jaffa, I would spin you endless yarns of ties that unite the Holy Land and the Nordic countries, from the Vikings to the Oslo negotiators. The Norsemen of old, your ancestors, Vikings or Varangs, as they were called in the Middle East, were hired by the Byzantine Emperors to serve the throne, and they would invariably make a pilgrimage to Jerusalem, Jorsala in their tongue, proceed to the River Jordan and afterwards sail to their new adventures. One of them, the Norse king Harald Hardrada, went to Jorsala-borg, but failed to take a dip in the waters of Jordan, and that is why he was slain at Stamford Bridge in an aborted attempt to take over England. St. Olav, your king and national saint, who is buried a few hundred yards away in the cathedral of Nidaros, is still venerated in Palestine, and a week ago I saw a Palestinian peasant woman praying at the medieval wax colour wall painting of St. Olav in the Bethlehem basilica. Maybe her prayers sustain Norway, while her home is saved by the efforts of Norse volunteers of the International Solidarity Movement.

On a better day, I would tell you the full story of my saintly ancestor Rabbi Jacobson who left our family house in Tiberias on the shores of the Sea of Galilee and sailed to Trondheim, this spiritual heart of the North, to lead the Jewish community of Norway, and of all my relations in Norway and Sweden, and of my pilgrimage to your land of wooden churches, fiery aquavit and deep fjords. But the days are not that good, and this yarn will have to wait.

Yesterday, I would tell you: the Holy Land suffers probably the worst times in centuries. It is being ruined, and its sons are being killed. Its villages are destroyed, while its peasants are languishing in the refugee camps of Jenin and Deheishe, or imprisoned in concentration camps of Ansar and Ketziyot. Hundreds of children have been shot by Israeli marksmen, thousands of trees uprooted, and springs ruined.

Maybe it would move you, and maybe not. Palestinians are being slain, you would say. What else is new? People kill each other everywhere, from Timor to Brazil to Bosnia to Rwanda. While feeling sorry and bla-bla-bla, why should we care about Palestine? And I shall be first to admit that until yesterday, this callous position made eminent sense. Only a small sect of dedicated men and women, members of pro-Palestinian groups, carried the torch in the desert. Now things changed, millions listen to the message, and as I speak to you today, my distinguished friend and teacher Noam Chomsky talks to multitudes in Gothenburg, just a few hundred miles to the south.

Why is yesterday so different from today? These beautiful days of autumn, when the leaves turn purple and gold over dark-blue waters of your lakes, and limpid air enhances white caps of your jagged peaks, could be the last good days we know for many years. A world war is in the making, a war that begins in Palestine. It is August 1914 all over again, the eve of the Great War. World War One began in the Balkans, in Bosnia. If you would say to a Frenchman in August 1914, you and your friends will die because of Bosnia, he would laugh at you. But in a few months after the Sarajevo assassination, the flower of French youth was slain at Verdun. It is 1914, it is 1939.

Now, as in 1939, again there is a strong will to re-shape the world, and speeches of George W. Bush vividly remind us of the speeches of the German chancellor. But who writes the speeches? Who pushes for the war? Is it monopolies, oil and weapon interests, as some people want us to think? The war-mongering speech of the Axis of Evil, directly taken from Austin Powers (Dr. Evil and his Axis) was composed by a Zionist speechwriter David Frum, previously a fighter against 'anti-Semitism'. Another Zionist, Wolfowitz is the man actually in charge of the US military. A leading Zionist thinker, Norman Podhoretz, calls for war, while the oh so liberal lawyer Alan Dershowitz promotes torture as the best way to learn the truth.

Let us examine the American plans carefully. Recently we've had a sneak preview of their campaign. The US plans to destroy Iraq, invade Syria, break Saudi Arabia into a few parts, separate the oil fields, pass them into the hands of Israel, and finish off with Egypt. The news was broken gently by a Jewish Lobby man, Laurent Murawiec, who works under the aegis of the Defence Policy Board Chairman Richard N. Perle. This hawk, a friend of Sharon, a devoted Zionist and a suspected Israeli mole, calls for seizure of the Arabian oil fields, transfer of Mecca and Medina unto Hashemite rule and confiscation of Saudi assets. He represents a voice of many American Jews. In the prestigious *Jewish World Review*,[48] a columnist Jonah Goldberg calls: "Baghdad must be destroyed . . . America must go to war with Iraq even if that risks innocent Iraqi—and American—lives." Professor David D. Perlmutter in the *LA Times*[49] is even more explicit: "I daydream—if only! If in 1948, 1956, 1967 or 1973 Israel had acted just a bit like the Third Reich, then today Jews, not sheiks, would have that Gulf oil." Endless abbreviations, think tanks, institutes connected to the powerful Jewish community in the US are interwoven into a dense spider-net around the Pentagon and the White House. And they are the moving force behind the new *Drang nach Osten* of President Bush.

Let us face the unpleasant reality: the Jewish elites of the US are pushing for the Armageddon, the Doomsday war, or in your Norse tradition, for Ragnarok, in order to establish the Jewish state at the top of the world. It is a plan of a megalomaniac, but these megalomaniacs are in control of the only superpower, as well as of their nuclear-powered Middle-Eastern bridgehead.

"Oh no, you say. We know Jews, a wonderful clever peaceful and pleasant folk. It should be some mistake." Let me remind you of a short story by the American writer and poet of the 19th century, Edgar Allan Poe, about the Germany of his days. He depicts Germans as placid and peaceful folk, much given to growing cabbage, playing the piano, constructing clocks, smoking pipes and talking philosophy. It is exactly the picture of Germans presented by Mark Twain in his travelogues. This image apparently corresponded to reality, and a German officer was a witness at my grandparents' wedding in the days of the German occupation of Minsk in 1916. Some 25 years later, my grandparents decided to flee the advancing German army, while their Jewish neighbours laughed at them: "You fell for the Bolshevik propaganda, there is no reason to run away, the Germans are wonderful peaceful folk and the best friends of the Jews." Still, my grandparents took flight and were saved from the cruel *Einsatzcommando*, from the Germans who did not care much about pipes and pianos.

People can change, and if peaceful Germans could become for a while a walking horror of the world, so can Jews. I do sincerely hope that as the Germans came back to their normal selves, so will the Jews, but I do not think it will happen by itself. There is an infection and it is spreading fast. It is caused by the inherent racism of the Jewish state. On my way to Ben-Gurion airport, I bought *Haaretz*, our main liberal newspaper. It contained a dispute between our chief of staff, Buki Ayalon and our previous Labour Prime Minister, Ehud Barak. Ayalon compared the Palestinians to a cancer growth, while the vice-chairman of Socialist International, Barak completely disagreed: they are rather a virus, he said. This racism spread over the Jewish communities like a forest fire. Provided the Jews are the prominent part of the American and to lesser degree European elites, they communicate the disease to the rest. Their newspapers and their film studios preach racism, hatred toward Muslims, Germans, French and toward everybody else, including the ordinary white working folk and the blacks of the United States.

In your Norse tradition, an evil cunning Loki cheated the gentle but blind Hoed and caused him to kill his brother, shining Balder, this Nordic pre-figuration of Christ. Now, Loki again tries to cause the war between the brothers. It is our duty and our right to refuse Loki's advice and to stop the Ragnarok.

It can't be done without attending to Palestine. For years, I would say: Palestine/Israel must be transformed into a democratic state, where Jews and Palestinians will live happily ever after, as equals. But the Democratic State wouldn't be a Jewish state, people would object. That is the best part of it, I would say. The Jewish state is as bad as the Aryan state, and whoever rejects the Aryan state, should reject the Jewish state, as well. Without the Jewish state, the

Jews of the US and other lands will return to their normal life, will forget the wet dreams of the world domination and become law-abiding citizens of their respective countries.

Until now, only our wonderful comrades, friends of Palestine, had supported this idea. But now it becomes necessary—not only for the sake of the Palestinians, these noble courageous and hard-working people, but for the sake of all of us, for the sake of world peace. There are Israelis who would like to live in peace with their Palestinian neighbours, in peace with churches and mosques, but we can not counteract the external forces supporting Sharon the Evil and Peres the Cunning. Good Israelis and their Palestinian allies can't win, unless their adversary's supply lines are cut, as in the Thor story.

The tale hath it, Thor the Mighty came to Utgard to boast his prowess. The gods of Utgard challenged him to drink up the Golden horn. He drank and drank, but the horn had remained forever full. It was no miracle: the horn was connected to a well. Only by severing the umbilical tie, could he meet the challenge and drink up the horn. If you, people of Europe, would block the spring of external support, we, Israelis and Palestinians, will be able to change the things on the ground and bring equality to Palestine and Israel.

The deconstruction of the Jewish state, its conversion into a state for all its citizens would become an important cardinal point in human development. Instead of being the pilot project of globalization, the Holy Land can become an ideal of integration. The invaders and the local folk will merge, as your ancestors the Normans did in East Anglia, Sicily and Normandy, as the children of Provencal Crusaders became Palestinians in the hilly villages of Sinjil and Gifna, while the Jews overseas will become again the blessing of their communities, like my sainted ancestor in your marvellous cathedral city.

Notes

48. "Debating War Against Iraq," by Jonah Goldberg, *Jewish World Review*, July 17, 2002. http://www.jewishworldreview.com/cols/jonah.html.
49. April 7, 2002.

PART V

A Yiddishe Medina

[This was written as President Bush proclaimed his Crusade of Revenge against the Third World.]

I

America prepares for a long war. It is called 'the war on terrorism', but the name has no meaning but 'a war on the enemy'. Noam Chomsky gave a witty definition, "terrorism is what they do to us." However, in the course of this war, thousands of our brothers by Adam and Eve will be strafed, napalmed and nuked. Boys and girls, unborn babes and old men will be brought to the altar of Vengeance and ritually slaughtered.

President Bush called his enterprise a 'crusade'. This title invokes in our memory the dour knights of Aquitaine and the pious Frankish warriors who took the Cross, and with the name of Our Lady on their lips, ventured into a long and hard pilgrimage. Reality was worse. The Crusade was a Western Jihad and it caused a lot of bloodshed. The Crusaders were wild and unruly. They sacked the most beautiful Christian city on earth, Constantinople, and they drenched in blood the holy ground of Jerusalem. A Crusader chronicler, Radulf of Caen, wrote of his comrades-at-arms: in the Syrian city of Maarra, "they impaled babies on spits, grilled and devoured them." They were rough folk, and still I would like to save the name of these killers and cannibals from being besmirched by association with Bush's Crusade. They sought glory, not revenge, this most un-Christian, even anti-Christian feeling.

The very essence of the Gospel is the rejection of revenge. That was the great difference between the Church and the Synagogue, the two sisters born two thousand years ago. This built-in difference is the inherent feature of the schism between the two faiths: while Christians are called to pray for their enemies, Jews are supposed to dream of vengeance.

II

The Old Biblical Judaism, Mother-faith of Jews and Christians, contained two different interpretations of 'Messiah'. Both can be found in the Old Testament.

In the schism between Christians and Jews, each new faith picked up and made predominant one of the interpretations. For Christians, Christ came to save, while for Jews, the Messiah comes to take revenge. This is explicated by the brilliant Israeli scholar, Prof. Israel Jacob Yuval of the Hebrew University in his new book, *Two Nations In Your Womb.*[50] 'Vengeful salvation', as Yuval called it, was derived by the Ashkenazi Jews from the old Pharisee sources and became the prevailing doctrine of the Synagogue.

When Dr. Israel Yuval published his perspicacious book on theology of vengeance in Judaism, it was accepted with great enthusiasm by his Israeli colleagues, but the American Jewish scholars hated it. Dr. Ezra Fleischer wrote a vehement critique, concluding it with the words: "*it would be better if such a book had not been published, but since it is published, it should be sentenced to oblivion.*"

Prof. Yuval quotes many ancient Jewish texts to support this point. "In the End of the days (when the Messiah comes) God will destroy, kill and exterminate all the nations but Israelites," according to the *Sefer Nitzahon Yashan*, written by a German Jew in Thirteenth Century. A liturgical poet Klonimus ben Judah had a vision of "God's hands full of Goyim's corpses."

Even more dreadful dreams of blood and destruction *precede* the first attacks on Jews in the end of the Eleventh Century. A hundred years before the Crusaders' onslaught on Jews, Rabbi Simon ben Yitzhak calls on God "to take His sword and slaughter the Goyim." In order to hasten their destruction, the Jewish sages of Europe adopted new horrible curses against Christians and Christ and introduced them into liturgy of Passover and Yom Kippur and even into daily prayer, in addition to the curses embedded there in the Second Century.

The Messiah of Vengeance has actually a different name in Christian theology. He is called the Antichrist. Christian theologians have tried to delve into the qualities of this apocalyptic figure. St. John of Damascus prophesied that the Antichrist will come to Jews and for Jews, against Christ and Christians. (John the Damascene was a friend of Islam and he interpreted the Muslim dogma of eternal Koran as a form of the Christian teaching of Logos.) The Church Fathers considered the Rise of the Antichrist as the rise and temporary triumph of Judaism. In the Tenth Century, St. Andrew the Byzantine prophesied that the kingdom of Israel will be restored and it will be the launching-pad of the Antichrist. Thus, Jewish and Christian theologians agree that their Messiahs are as opposed to each other as thesis and anti-thesis, or as Christ and Antichrist.

This proximity of Israel to the Apocalypse is felt by millions of devout Christians in the United States. They have been taught that the rise of the Antichrist is the stage before the Second Coming. But, being misled by their pastors, they draw a paradoxical conclusion and decide to side with the Antichrist. They forget the words, "the Son of Man will go as it has been decreed, but woe to that man who sides with the Antichrist."

Jews are not an Antichrist. But the idea of a Vengeful Messiah is a very dangerous one, and it should be confronted and argued against. It could be done by the tools of the Old, or the New Testament, or with general humanist concepts. Otherwise, this idea will poison our discourse.

III

It would be a mistake to attribute the vengefulness of the US to American Jewry. America is special, for its Jews and Gentiles are discursively united 'Judeo-Christians', or more precisely, 'Judeo-Americans'. Their mores have precious little of the spirit of Christ. As Karl Marx put it, "the practical domination of Jewish spirit over the Christian world has achieved in North America its unambiguous, complete expression."

Many American public figures, Jews and non-Jews alike, call for revenge. Said the former Secretary of State Lawrence Eagleburger, who heads the Jewish organisation for claims to Germany (at USD 300,000 per annum):

> There is only one way to begin to deal with people like this, and that is you have to kill some of them even if they are not immediately directly involved in this thing.[51]
>
> Said Steve Donleavy in the New York Post[52]:
>
> The response to this unimaginable 21st-century Pearl Harbor should be as simple as it is swift—kill the bastards. A gunshot between the eyes, blow them to smithereens, poison them if you have to. As for cities or countries that host these worms, bomb them into baseball courts.

In the *Washington Post*, Rich Lowry proposed: "If we flatten part of Damascus or Tehran or whatever it takes, that is part of the solution."[53]

The best quotable is Ann Coulter's, the preferred writer of the *World Jewish Review*:

> This is no time to be precious about locating the exact individuals directly involved in this particular terrorist attack . . . We should invade their countries, kill their leaders and convert them to Christianity (!?). We weren't punctilious about locating and punishing only Hitler and his top officers. We carpet-bombed German cities; we killed civilians. That's war. And this is war.

After writing these words, she was rightly sacked by her newspaper and taken aboard the neo-conservative Jewish magazine *Commentary*.

This vengeful spirit of the American press is an aberration in the Western discourse. If you sift the literature of the Christian and Muslim lands, you would discover that revenge appears rarely as the main subject of an important book. Nikolai Gogol wrote a Gothic short story called *The Terrible Revenge* and Prosper Mérimée wrote a novelette *Colomba* on a Corsican vendetta. *C'est tout.* Brits always considered revenge a very un-English trend, certainly not cricket. 'Vengeful' is a negative word in every Christian and Muslim culture. The Jewish culture, *au contraire*, is saturated with the idea of vengeance, as it draws straight from the Old Testament, without the redeeming filter of the New Testament or the Koran.

We Jews know it better than anybody. A brilliant American Jewish journalist, John Sack noted that in his *Eye for an Eye*, a chilling book about horrible revenge perpetrated by Jews on the German civilians after WWII. This book tells of tortures, 'extra-judicial killings', mass poisoning and other horrors. You are not likely to get this book, as the Jewish establishment succeeded in suppressing it and keeping it out of bookshops. Probably you can find another book on the same subject written by Michael Elkins, a veteran BBC correspondent in Jerusalem. It fared much better for it is a paean to revenge. Elkins glorifies and exalts even the dreadful attempt to massacre millions of Germans by poisoning waters of the Rein. It was published in 1996, as Elkins retired, but woe to the BBC that had a correspondent with such views, and woe to British people who were poisoned by Elkins, for this book is a successful attempt to poison minds.

Not surprisingly, Israel promoted vengeance into its daily policy. Its attacks on Palestinians were called *peulot tagmul*, the actions of vengeance. One of these actions was perpetrated by (the present Prime Minister) General Ariel Sharon on October 14, 1953, when he and his soldiers murdered some sixty peasants, women and children, in the village of Qibya. The invasion of Lebanon in 1982, with its 20,000 murdered Lebanese and Palestinians, Christians and Muslims, was an act of revenge for the attempted assassination of the Israeli ambassador in London. During the last Intifada, every act of Israeli terror was called 'retribution' or 'retaliation' by Israelis and by the American Jewish-owned media.

This Jewish infatuation with vengeance survived the hazardous crossing of the Atlantic. The American Jews created Hollywood, and Hollywood made vengeance its main subject. In a recent American re-make of *The Three Musketeers*, d'Artagnan is moved by the spirit of vengeance, though this motif is hardly present in the book or in the French movie. Actually, it is the bad guy, Mordred, son of Lady Winter, who nurses dreams of revenge. But for the new American movie, produced by a Jewish American, vengeance is a legitimate feeling. In a way, American cinema was an expression of the Jewish collective subconscious, and it was the main factor in the creation of the American psyche. From Hollywood, vengefulness flew all over the earth, and certainly helped to create the world we inhabit.

In other words, there was no need for a Jewish conspiracy. A grandson of a Trier Rabbi, who grew up in the Church, Karl Marx noticed in the 1840s (!) that America (with or even without a single ethnic Jew) had become a state with a 'Jewish' spirit, and had embraced the 'Jewish' ideology of greed and alienation. A Marx disciple, Werner Sombart, came to a similar conclusion about America's Jewish spirit, though in his opinion, America grew with Jews and was formed by Jews from its very first steps. The rather immature America could not withstand the impact of the Jewish mentality, and she became a Jewish State, the big sister of Israel.

This explains the successes of American Jews: it is just natural that in the 'Jewish' state, real Jews are more successful. This sudden rise to glory and riches should not be a cause for vertigo and self adulation—the other way around. In line with the reasoning of the great American philosopher, Immanuel Wallerstein, I say: material success in our days is a sign of moral failure. 'Success' and riches are not a sign of God's benevolence. Anyway, not of the God who blessed the poor. A man who succeeds in the robbers' gang fails in the eyes of God. Our world with its starving millions and over-prosperous minority is immoral and anti-Christian, as anti-Christian as the Judeo-American 'crusade'.

This explanation allows us to answer the question we posited previously: does America support Israel because of the Jewish lobby or because of the 'true interest of American corporations'? The putative answer is: the Jewish lobby is a superfluous body supportive of the Israeli right-wing, while America as a whole is a grander 'Jewish' state with interests outside the Middle East as well.

This presumption explains away a lot of queries. It explains the incredible 99% vote in support of Israel. It explains the Holocaust museums, Holocaust studies and Holocaust films. It explains the centrality of Jews in American life, as now America views world events from a traditional Jewish position, "Is it good for Jews?"

It explains the US walkout at Durban. G.W. Bush did not mind a quarrel with Europe and Japan and reneged on the Kyoto treaty. He did not give a damn about annoying Russia and China in his unilateral decision to drop the Strategic Arms Treaty. But here he heard His Master's Voice. The haughty rejection of Africa and Asia, the insulting dismissal of the Afro-American community, the rejection of the great struggle against racism were additional proofs that the US has become a sister state to Israel.

Recently, President Vladimir Putin tried to justify his onslaught on the Chechens in an interview with *Newsweek*.[54] He said the Chechen leaders "publicly called for the extermination of Jews," relegating critics of his war to the ranks of anti-Semites. Now, Chechnya has no Jews, and the Chechen leaders' opinion on Jews is irrelevant, if anti-Semitism is to preserve its original meaning of 'anti-Jewish prejudice or racism'. In this form it does not exist anymore, as we argued elsewhere,[55] but the word now has a new meaning. It has become the equivalent of 'anti-Americanism' of McCarthy's days, or of 'anti-Soviet' in Brezhnev's Soviet Union.

Americans tense and shriek whenever they feel their loyalty to Jews questioned. Whoever rejects the new American paradigm, in America or elsewhere, is an anti-Semite by definition. That is why good persons of Jewish origin—whether Noam Chomsky or Woody Allen, St. Paul or Karl Marx—are called 'anti-Semites'. They are usually rejected by the Jewish community, but their names are used to defend the structure they attacked.

An offence to the Jewish community is not considered a form of racism, as ordinary racism is tolerated with great ease, especially if it is directed towards Arabs (new enemies of Jews) or Blacks (old enemies of Jews). It is treated as a '*lese majesté*' [literally, 'injured majesty': an offense violating the dignity of a ruler as the representative of a sovereign power]; in the years of Jewish ascendancy in the Soviet Union (1917–1937), people were shot for an anti-Jewish remark. Manfred Stricker of Strasbourg campaigned to name the local university after Dr. Schweitzer, but the Jewish community preferred the name of a Jewish scholar with a loose connection to the city. As a result, Manfred Stricker was sentenced to six months in jail. Alexander Chancellor wrote in the *Guardian* (under a promising title, "It is not Black and White") of the assassinated Dutch right-winger: yes, he was an enemy of Islam, but he was good to Jews, and therefore, not a bad guy.

Speaking to students at Harvard, Emory and other Ivy League universities, I noticed they do not know the name 'Arnold Toynbee'. The greatest British philosopher of history of the Twentieth Century made an error: he spoke of the tragedy of the Palestinians. He also cited African slavery as a tragedy on a par with the Jewish holocaust. As a result, he was erased and disappeared from American consciousness. It is but impossible to find non-fiction by G. K. Chesterton in American or English bookshops. This brilliant essayist is relegated to almost non-existent 'Christian sections' of bookshops, and his rare reprints are sandwiched between *Bad Popes* and *Rabbi Jesus*.

This influence in public discourse explains the obedience of American (and European) intellectuals. In the Judeo-American state, the Jews form its 'Church', its ideological establishment. For an intellectual, it is better to be called a paedophile than an anti-Semite.

IV

Though the US has become a Judeo-Christian state, the question of Who Rules Whom in the *ménage á trois* of Jews, Israel and the US is not a simple one. The three *dramatis personae* form a triangle as mysterious as that of Bermuda and certainly no less perilous. Half a year ago, some dubious sources reported

Sharon saying at a cabinet meeting: "Do not worry about the US, it is under our control." The words were denied, but as the uprising in Palestine swiftly glides into a Joshua-style extermination campaign, while the US "supports the war against terrorism," the doubts grow.

The very existence of a corporate entity known as 'the Jewish People' (or, Jewry, or The Jews) is frequently denied. Some two hundred years ago Jewry existed as unambiguously as France or the Church. Our ancestors were members of this extra-territorial state, an authoritarian semi-criminal order, run by rich men and Rabbis. Its leadership, called Kahal (Hebrew for Community) made the important decisions, and ordinary Jews followed their directions. The leadership could dispose with life and property of Jews, just like any feudal ruler. There was no freedom of opinion within the walls of the ghetto. A rebellious Jew could be punished by death. Came Emancipation, and the power of the Kahal was broken from inside and outside. The Jews were set free and became citizens of their respective countries.

Nowadays, a new generation of Jews has emerged that does not know of Joseph. Years of apologetic brainwashing made them forget why our grandfathers wanted to break the iron walls of the Jewish community. The notion of Jewry has become a moot point. Are we, the descendents of Jews, citizens of our countries, or are we citizens of the Jewish People? Does 'Jewry' exist, in the same way any state exists, or is it just a figure of speech?

Here is a paradox: the Jewish leaders want Jewry to be a sort of Stealth jet, now you see it, now you don't. It is here to strafe, it is nowhere for flak. They say: "That's what Hitler said," or, "That was invented by the writers of the forgery, the *Protocols of the Elders of Zion*," and they forget to say that it is written into Israel's Declaration of Independence as well. Israel actually is described as 'the State of the Jewish People', and that is why it attracts disproportionate attention and influence as the visible (and territorially bound) part of Jewry. That is why an ambassadorial position in Tel Aviv is considered among the highest and most desirable for a career diplomat. The concept of 'the Jewish People' received a singular recognition in international law, when the Jewish People were declared in 1950 and in 1991 by modern Germany to be the residual heir of intestate Jews. The Israeli Criminal Law allows the state of Israel to judge and prosecute any person on the globe who acted against a person, health, life, property or dignity of a Jew, even if this Jew has no connection whatsoever with the state of Israel.

We, children of emancipated Jewish parents, are as surprised as anybody. Nothing prepared us for the miraculous recovery of Jewry. Just recently it was on its way out, indeed, proclaimed dead; and we had come to consider ourselves free men. Within our lifetime, things have changed drastically, and now we are being called upon to declare allegiance to this body, or suffer ostracism and humiliation, probably loss of livelihood, or worse. Jewry (please do not confuse this term with the millions of descendents of medieval Jews) has regained its place in world politics, and taken over the mind of the only superpower, the US.

Isaac Deutscher, a Jewish Marxist and a biographer of Trotsky, was among the first Jews to notice this phenomenon. He proposed in his essay, "Who is a Jew?" (published in the *Jewish Quarterly*, London 1966) to distinguish between 'Jews' and 'Jewry'. While Jews are individuals of various opinions and ways of life, Jewry is a quasi-national body with its own leadership and agenda. In his opinion, Jewry was on its way to disappearance, but from the ashes of World War Two 'the phoenix of Jewry has risen'. "I would have preferred Jews to survive and Jewry to perish," he wrote, but "the extermination of Jews gave a new lease on life to Jewry".

The self-appointed leadership of revived Jewry achieved the pinnacle of power in close liaison with super-rich Mammon-worshippers. They are intoxicated by their clout and by the lack of opposition. They support the war criminal Sharon, but they consider him too weak. They booed Paul Wolfowitz, the Jewish American super-hawk. Every Israeli politician knows and heeds: there are powerful Jews in America and elsewhere who want endless war in Palestine. They understand the salvation brought by the armies of Russia and America in World War Two as their personal victory over the Gentile world, as a sign of a new era of Jewry's world-wide supremacy, promised in Talmud and Cabbala teachings.

Isaac Deutscher ascribed the changes in Israel to their influence:

> A wealthy American Jew, a 'worldly businessman' among his gentile associates and friends in New York, Philadelphia or Detroit, is at heart proud to be a member of the Chosen People, and in Israel he exercises his influence in favour of religious obscurantism and reaction. He keeps alive the spirit of racial-talmudic exclusiveness and superiority. It feeds and inflames the antagonism towards the Arabs.[56]

It would be odd if this 'wealthy Jew' would influence only distant Israel. His influence is even stronger in his country, in the US, where he promotes the same idea "of racial-talmudic exclusiveness and superiority," in full harmony with the 'Jewish' spirit of America.

These rich men do not need Palestinian land. They are not going to migrate to Israel and work on its vineyards. They use Israel and its people as their dispensable tool in the world-wide game. They misunderstand the Gentiles' compassion as a sign of weakness. They misunderstand their friendliness as their submission. Like a cat with a mouse, they played with the Church of Nativity to check when Christendom is finally dead, if it will cease to respond. At the same time, they threaten the Mosques of Jerusalem and train American cruise missiles on Baghdad. Instead of Christianity and Judaism, they bring in a new faith: they supplant the Crucifixion by the Holocaust, and the Resurrection by the creation of the State of Israel. For them, Jewish control over the holy sites of Christendom and Islam is a visual proof of their dominance. Their destruction would be a sign of total victory. In a way, they are right: a society without its sacral values is doomed to extinction.

Many Jews and descendents of Jews feel threatened by the concept of Jewry. They usually object to 'generalities', to 'accusation of the whole people' or 'hate-mongering'. At first, I was taken aback by their response. Afterwards, I thought their reasoning is so good, it could be used by others as well. Pity to waste a good thing. For instance:

- How do you dare say the Americans nuked Hiroshima? I am an American, and I did not nuke Hiroshima.
- You say, "the English ruled India." What nonsense! I know hundreds of poor English workers who did not rule India.
- You call for the liberation of Algeria. This is anti-Frenchism! The real difference is not between the French and native Algerians, but between cultured people and Muslim fanatics.
- 'Russian imperialist policy'? This is a racist remark designed to cause hatred of Russians.

Probably you will admit this sounds silly. Policies are devised by the elites, carried out by the more-or-less willing majority, and the outsiders suffer the consequences. Jewry is not different from any other state or trans-national corporation. The Jewish leadership has policies, and is able to change them. Naturally, ordinary Jews can submit to or reject them.

V

This is not much like classified information, but you should not say it out loud. The Jewish establishment can tell Bush to say 'uncle' and he will. This is a *Polichinelle* secret, as the French say. The rest of the world, from the Far East to Northern Europe, knows it full well, and from time to time a reckless prime minister or a speaker of a parliament babbles about it. The US Congress always rises to the occasion and sends its strong protest to the babbling offender, like a henpecked husband who never would admit fear of his wife's anger in front of his beer buddies.

You can say the US is run by Africans, Wasps, Freemasons or Grey Aliens, and you will get no response. You may say the land is regulated by the Corporations, Standard Oil and Boeing, and nobody will object. But just try to say "the Jews run the US" and you will find yourself in serious trouble. Now, what is actually the position of the Jews in the US?

It can be described in many ways. They represent the Church (i.e., ideological apparatus) of the new Judeo-American faith. They are the Brahmin caste of America. They can be called even a very prominent, if not ruling ethnic minority. This turn of events is strange but not unique. Until recent times, England was run by a small caste of Eton graduates, as exclusivist as any Jew; they even married within their own group.

That is why Powell and Bush can't and won't give orders to Sharon. They have some free play, as long as the Jewish People are of two minds—before this unique entity has not decided what it wants. Now, apparently 'the Jews' (as opposed to 'Jews') are united by a common will, single purpose and a feeling of power. Intoxication by power and unity has caused this cautious people to drop masks, to cease pretence. The new openness provides us with an unprecedented insight into the soul of the Jews and their Mammonite supporters.

An authentic voice, Ron Grossman of the *Chicago Tribune*[57] writes:

> As a self-proclaimed humanist, I ought to recoil in horror from the thought of tanks rumbling through a city, anybody's city. My head should hang in sorrow at televised images of street fighting (rather, massacres—ISH) in Bethlehem and Ramallah. But here is a hint: Don't lecture or preach to us. Forget about appealing to our better selves.

Yes, forget about appealing to their better selves, for they have not got one. 'The better selves' were just a device, and now their real selves have emerged in all their brutal might.

VI

Let us turn this text into a movie script and alternate a few snapshots provided by the BBC from the field. In **Palestine,** UNRWA chief Peter Hansen said: "We are getting reports of pure horror. Helicopters are strafing civilian residential areas; systematic shelling by tanks has created hundreds of wounded; bull-dozers are razing refugee homes and food and medicine will soon run out." Dozens of dead bodies are lying in the streets of the Jenin refugee camp. The Church of Nativity is on fire, as in 614.

Meanwhile, tens of thousands of Jews turn up in **New York** to show support for Israel's massacre of Palestinians. 150,000 Jewish demonstrators take to the streets of **Paris** to express their solidarity with Israel. Waving Israeli flags and draped in the blue and white colours of **their** national banner (the tricolour is dropped and forgotten), protesters marched from the Place de la Republique to the Place de la Bastille in Paris, chanting in French and Hebrew and carrying signs that read: "Yesterday New York, today Jerusalem, tomorrow Paris."

In Israel, "no one can express the aspirations of most Israelis like the prime minister. This is not a war that was waged by Sharon, the 'warmonger', this is the war of all of us," writes Gideon Levy, a man of heart and conscience. "It will also be very difficult to blame Sharon for the consequences of the war, in light of the sweeping support he has been given by the majority of Israelis. Nearly 30,000 men were mobilized and they reported for duty as one man, making the refusal movement, with 21 refuseniks currently in jail, irrelevant.

"We didn't ask why, we just came," the reservists told the Prime Minister, expressing the 'together' syndrome that characterizes Israel at such times. Tens of thousands of men leave their homes, putting their normal life behind them, and set out to kill and be killed—and they don't even ask why? That is the behaviour of the herd," concludes Levy.

Levy is mistaken: it is the real strength of Jewry that comes through in this immense cohesiveness and unabashed ethnocentrism. For instance, a Mark Steyn [sic] writes in the *National Post:* "All civilized people can agree that **killing Jews** is wrong." (Not 'killing' is wrong, as then it would be wrong to kill Palestinians. Only 'killing Jews' is wrong. This approach is based on the Jewish reading of the Ten Commandments: "Thou shalt not murder a Jew," instead of the Christian "Thou shalt not murder."

Professor David D. Perlmutter writes in the *Los Angeles Times*:[58]

> I daydream—if only! If in 1948, 1956, 1967 or 1973 Israel had acted just a bit like the Third Reich, then today Israelis would shop, eat pizza, marry and celebrate the holy days unmolested. And of course Jews, not sheiks, would have that Gulf oil.

Such daydreamers should be carefully removed from the education system, for being unreconstructed Nazis. But have no fear! Judeo-Nazism is a winning ideology in the US.

Witty if snobbish Taki of the British weekly *Spectator* contributed the following anecdotal evidence of the new Jewish vehemence and single-mindedness:

> On Easter Sunday, during lunch, the richest woman in Israel, Irit Lando,[59] suddenly burst into my house and began to harangue my friends and family about Adam Shapiro. Despite the fact she's one of my wife's oldest friends and was invited to drop in after lunch, I was extremely annoyed. I reminded Irit that my house was not Israeli occupied territory; that it was Easter; and knowing how I feel about the plight of the Palestinians, she should change the subject. Which she did, turning on the press, instead, and how they gave publicity to that godawful traitor Adam Shapiro.

As a few mavericks of Jewish origin like Adam Shapiro are increasingly marginalized, the Jews *en masse* rally to support Sharon and Israel. The US officials have no choice but to take the hint. American Gentiles figured it out a long time ago: if you want to make a career in politics or the media, you have to support the Jews wholeheartedly. Otherwise you will find yourself thrown to the dogs. If a man has found his way to the higher echelons of American power, then he has learned the ropes and knows the limits of his power.

VII

Eric Alterman of the *Nation* published a list of American pundits unreservedly supportive of Israel. It is an exciting read:

> COLUMNISTS AND COMMENTATORS WHO CAN BE COUNTED UPON TO SUPPORT ISRAEL REFLEXIVELY AND WITHOUT QUALIFICATION:
>
> George Will, the *Washington Post, Newsweek* and *ABC News*; William Safire, the *New York Times*; A.M. Rosenthal, the *New York Daily News*, formerly Executive Editor of and later columnist for the *New York Times*; Charles Krauthammer, the *Washington Post*, PBS, *Time*, and the *Weekly Standard*, formerly of the *New Republic*; Michael Kelly, the *Washington Post*, the *Atlantic Monthly, National Journal*, and MSNBC.com, formerly of the *New Republic* and the *New Yorker*; Lally Weymouth, the *Washington Post* and *Newsweek*; Martin Peretz, the *New Republic*; Daniel Pipes, the *New York Post*; Andrea Peyser, the *New York Post*; Dick Morris, the *New York Post*; Lawrence Kaplan, the *New Republic*; William Bennett, CNN; William Kristol, the *Washington Post*, the *Weekly Standard, Fox News*, formerly of *ABC News*; Robert Kagan, the *Washington Post* and the *Weekly Standard*; Mortimer Zuckerman, *US News and World Report* (Zuckerman is also Chairman of the Conference of Presidents of Major American Jewish Organizations); David Gelertner, the *Weekly Standard*; John Podhoretz, the *New York Post* and the *Weekly Standard*; Mona Charen, the *Washington Times*; Morton Kondracke, *Roll Call, Fox News*, formerly of the McLaughlin Group, the *New Republic* and PBS; Fred Barnes, the *Weekly Standard, Fox News*, formerly of the *New Republic*, the McLaughlin Group, and the *Baltimore Sun*; Sid Zion, the *New York Post*, formerly of the *New York Daily News*; Yossi Klein Halevi, the *New Republic*; Norman Podhoretz, *Commentary*; Jonah Goldberg, *National Review* and CNN; Laura Ingram, CNN, formerly of MSNBC and *CBS News*; Jeff Jacoby, the *Boston Globe*; Rich Lowry, *National Review*; Andrew Sullivan, the *New Republic*; Seth Lipsky, the *Wall Street Journal* and the *New York Sun*, formerly of the *Jewish Forward*; Irving Kristol,

the *Public Interest*, the *National Interest* and the *Wall Street Journal* Editorial Page; Chris Matthews, MSNBC; Allan Keyes, MSNBC, WorldNetDaily.com; Brit Hume, *Fox News*; John Leo, *US News and World Report*; Robert Bartley, the *Wall Street Journal* Editorial Page; John Fund, the *Wall Street Journal, Opinion Journal*, formerly of the *Wall Street Journal* Editorial Page; Peggy Noonan, the *Wall Street Journal* Editorial Page; Ben Wattenberg, the *Washington Times*, PBS; Tony Snow, *Washington Times* and *Fox News*; Lawrence Kudlow, *National Review* and CNBC; Alan Dershowitz, *Boston Herald* and *Washington Times*; David Horowitz, Frontpage.com; Jacob Heilbrun, the *Los Angeles Times*; Thomas Sowell, *Washington Times*; Frank Gaffney, Jr., *Washington Times*; Emmett Tyrell, *American Spectator* and *New York Sun*; Cal Thomas, *Washington Times*; Oliver North, *Washington Times* and *Fox News*, formerly of MSNBC; Michael Ledeen, *Jewish World Review*; William F. Buckley, *National Review*; Bill O'Reilly, *Fox News*; Paul Greenberg, *Arkansas Democrat-Gazette*; L. Brent Bozell, *Washington Times*; Todd Lindberg, *Washington Times*; Michael Barone, *US News and World Report* and The McLaughlin Group; Ann Coulter, *Human Events*; Linda Chavez, Creators Syndicate; Cathy Young, *Reason magazine*; Uri Dan, *New York Post*; Dr. Laura Schlessinger; morality maven Rush Limbaugh, radio host.

"What is perhaps most interesting is the long list of non-Jews who support Israel reflexively and without qualification," wrote Professor Kevin MacDonald of California State University.[60] "Unconditional support for Israel is a critical litmus test of acceptability by the major media in the U.S. Prospective pundits "earn their stripes" by showing their devotion to Israel (and, presumably other Jewish issues). It seems difficult to explain the huge tilt toward Israel in the absence of some enormous selective factor as the result of individual attitudes. And there is the obvious suggestion that although the Jews on this list must be seen as ethnic actors, the non-Jews are certainly making an excellent career move in taking the positions they do. This litmus test for prospective opinion makers is further supported by the fact that Joe Sobran was fired from the *National Review* because he had the temerity to suppose that the US foreign policy should not be dictated by what's best for Israel.

The careerists were chosen for their ability to disregard the interests of the American people. A good indicator of elite composition and behaviour can be found in the student-admission figures of the Ivy League universities. The share of the traditional elites of the US, the WASPs, has shrunk from 85% to 35%, while the Jews' share (2% of the population) has reached 40%. In other words, a non-Jew's chance of finding a place among the elite has decreased significantly.

Thus, after many years of selection process, pro-Jewish forces have risen to positions of power and influence in the US. All this said, America was almost doomed to become a Neo-Jewish state by virtue of its ideology. Anthony Judge wrote, "There is an extraordinary parallel between the unusual exclusivist perception of America as 'God's own country', and of Israel as a gift from God to the 'Chosen People'. Why have these perceptions justified encroachment on the lands of others, the displacement and death of the indigenous populations, their restrictions to 'reservations', and the development of a strategic framework for the expansion of 'western civilization' into the spaces of other cultures?"

The Fathers Pilgrims, the founders of America, called themselves a New Israel. However, Satan played a cruel game with their WASP descendants. He promised to make them new Jews, and he made his promise good. They became a minor partner in the Judeo-Mammonite alliance, doomed to swear their allegiance each day.

VIII

Still, Professor MacDonald is mistaken in oversimplifying the reasons for the Gentile support for the Jews. Apart from Bush and Rumsfeld, apart from the careerists, there are good non-Jews who support the Jews, just as there are maverick Jews and 'non-Jewish Jews', by definition of Isaac Deutscher. This is due to the contradictory nature of the centrifugal and centripetal tendencies within the Jewish community. By their individual responses to encounters with the non-Jews, the Jews can be classified as Rim Jews or Core Jews. Rim Jews try to leave the community by marrying out, by adopting Christianity, Communism or other faiths, by seeking communion with God. Core Jews proclaim the primacy of the community in permanent warfare against the Goyim. In the millennia-old tug-of-war, Christendom tries to undo the Core, while Jewry tries to undo the Rim.

That is why there are two kinds of 'philo-Semites'. One of them, the good Gentiles, look to a new spiritual home. They are influenced by the positive parts of the Bible, by 'love thy neighbour'. They like the spirit of community, of belonging, of the tradition that Jews exude. They like a light touch of 'outsider' that attracts poetic natures. There are many people, who want to break the tiresome strangling ties of their immediate surroundings. James Joyce, the Irish writer, saw the Jews as a way out of the bloody feud with Brits. Marina Tsvetaeva, the Russian poetess, felt herself an outsider in her steady middle-class family, and wrote, "In this most Christian world, all poets are Jews." The charming female characters of Woody Allen's early comedies are attracted to this eternal foreigner, the Jew.

It is not a coincidence that such people usually meet with marginal Jews on the outer rim of the Jewish community. The Jew of Joyce was the Italian Jewish writer Italo Svevo; the Jew of Tsvetaeva was the Russian Communist spy Sergey

Ephron. The Jew of Diane Keaton and Mia Farrow was this amusing outsider, Woody Allen. As the rim of the Jewish community is quite large, there always is intermingling with the better sort of Gentile mavericks.

The second set of allies consists of the hard businessmen who appreciate the practical side of Jewish ideology. They like the idea of the Mob, the pursuit of money, the disregard of morals and of social consequences thereof, of others' property and very life. People who see everybody as an enemy and life as eternal warfare, notice that in Jewish ideology, no stranger is a 'neighbour'. That is why the cruellest rulers, princes and kings were those who took Jewish advisers and ministers. They learned from them how to disregard their subjects. Such people as Nero and Pedro the Cruel, Conrad Black and Margaret Thatcher, the Mafia Godfathers and Third World dictators loved the Core (as opposed to Rim) Jews.

Thus, good people have their Jews, and bad people have their Jews. There is a problem: the Jews of good people are the outsiders, who hardly qualify as Jews, while the Jews of bad people are the powerful Jewish leaders. And the Jewish fraternity is a structurally hierarchical body, strongly influenced by its authoritarian leadership. Unwillingly, the good Jews were used by the bad Jews. Albert Einstein rejected the Jewish community, disapproved of Zionism, never went to a synagogue and was a charming man. But his achievements were used by bad Jews to promote their own concept.

It happened because not too many people dare to understand: the Jews are neither a people, nor a religion, nor a race. They are a quasi-religious organisation; a likeness of the Catholic Church bundled together with the International Monetary Fund like browser and mailer are bundled in the Windows. One can find all sorts of Catholics, but decisions are made in Rome. One can find all sorts of Jews, but the decisions are made on Wall Street.

While fighting against the Core, it is important to support the Rim. That was the traditional approach of the Christian Church: fight Jewry for the soul of Jews. A Jewish Zealot, 'Mad' Goldhagen, claimed in his books that the Church was 'anti-Semitic' and its policies led to the Jewish holocaust. Nothing could be more wrong: the Church wished to correct the mind, not to kill the body. Indeed, the true interests of Jews and the Jews are at loggerheads.

The Jewish elites know that people should be given a choice, and they try to ensure that it will be the wrong choice. That is why the Mammonite Jews support the Zionist Zealots. They want us, Jews, to make our choice between these two evils, the Zealots and Mammonites. But there is 'the third philosophy' as well. Its adepts believe in the great fraternity of mankind, and they reject both the Zealots' hate and the Pharisees' drive for the world domination. They can adhere to different political and religious schools, be on the left or on the right of the political map, believe in Christ or Allah, Lenin or Chomsky, the New Age or Buddha, Art or Love. They are the remnant of Israel, proclaimed by St. Paul.

In their merging with mankind, the words of Christ will be fulfilled: a corn that dies, lives. A corn that lives, dies.

The story of the Death and the Resurrection has this mystic meaning: do not be afraid of death and disappearance, as it is the way to life. The Jews who died as Jews remained alive. After the curtain descended on the Jewish community in Spain, St. Teresa of Avila and St. John of God died as Jews and remained alive forever. The names of exiles who went to Amsterdam and Morocco are gone and forgotten: they remained alive as Jews, then died forever. It was repeated in 1917 in Russia: that those who remained Jews died forever; those who embraced the revolution live forever.

IX

Just before 9/11, a group of US congressmen visited Palestine, and one of them made headlines. It was Congresswoman Shelley Berkley (a Democrat from Nevada) who said to the Palestinian Minister Saeb Erakat: "This is our country; we won the war. If the Palestinians do not like living under Jewish rule, I would not prevent them from leaving."

Who are the Hon. Shelley Berkley's 'we'? She certainly did not mean 'we the Americans', or 'we the Nevadans' who sent her to Washington. Nevada did not wage a war in the Middle East, to the best of my knowledge. Some naïve person would probably reply 'Israel', and even accuse her of 'dual loyalty'. Strict mentors would censure her for betraying the trust of her electorate by switching her allegiance to a foreign country. But it would be a dishonest misinterpretation. Miss Berkley never switched allegiance. Together with many other members of Congress and the Senate, she has a single loyalty, which is to the Jewish cause.

Miss Berkley makes sense. If Nevadans and other Americans do not mind living under heavy Jewish influence, why should the Palestinians mind it? Americans apparently do not mind that their wealth is managed by big investment bankers, under the umbrella of Mr. Greenspan's Federal Reserve. Jesus saves, but Moses invests. Jewish influence does not stop where the buck stops. The ideals of Americans are formed by Hollywood with its cult of greed and success. Their thoughts are supplied by the Jewish pundits in the universities and media. For comfort, they take the *New York Times* chicken soup. Their history has shrunk down to Holocaust studies. Their books are written by Bellow and Malamud. Americans do not mind that their politics are in the hands of people whose single devotion is to the Jewish cause.

If they do not mind, why do I, an Israeli Jew, mind it, instead of feeling pride for this great achievement of my brethren the American Jews? After all, it is no mean feat to take over the only superpower without a single shot being fired. This is not a rhetorical question, it has an answer, and it is not 'self-hatred'. I feel perfectly comfortable with myself, and with the majority of Jews I meet. Separately, we are nice and cuddly. Well, as nice as any. But together, we form a formidable and repulsive social machine, hell-bent on power grasping and greed. I like 'the Jews' as much as the great American Henry Thoreau loved the American Empire, as Voltaire loved his Catholic Church, as Orwell loved Stalin's Party.

Jewry has become the adversary of Jews in Israel: Israelis who would like to live in peace with their Palestinian neighbours, in peace with churches and mosques, can not counteract the raw muscle of the American Jewish leadership. Good Israelis and their Palestinian allies can't win, unless this power is contained. In a Nordic story, the hero-god Thor came to Utgard to prove his power. The gods of Utgard challenged him to drink from a horn. He tried and failed: The horn was connected to a well. Only by severing the connection, could he meet the challenge. If you, my readers overseas, will block the sea of the Jewish support abroad, we, Israelis and Palestinians, will be able to change things on the ground. The supporters of the Jewish state in your midst should be contained, for your and our sake.

X

A few months ago, my travels took me to the Amazon basin, to the Peruvian jungle deeply cut by Rio del Madre de Dios. In this remote location, small rivulets meander for miles among endless forests, navigable just by small pirogues. After a long sailing from Puerto Maldonado, my native guide brought me to the Lost World of many-coloured parrots and of friendly monkeys that sat on my shoulder. On a narrow path, I noticed a huge tree. It was bigger than all the other trees of the jungle. Its huge roots were spread across many yards. It is the telegraph-tree, my guide replied to my query. He tapped on the trunk of the monster tree and the sound boomed throughout the jungle. The giant was hollow.

I looked at it closely and noticed a strange feature I had missed before: some seven yards above the ground, another trunk, a partly digested palm tree, protruded from the embracing, smooth bark. The telegraph-tree was a monstrous parasite, a growth on a palm tree. The parasite had no trunk of its own, but it enveloped the tree and grew on it, eventually blocking it and digesting its life juices. The tree rotted inside its shell, and the hollow trunk climbed to new heights, creating a perfect drum for the local Indians.

It was a living image of the United States of America, this huge and hollow trunk, towering above the forest of nations, but dead inside. The American Empire has entered its period of decline. The dollar is still the world currency, the American army is still the formidable war machine, the stock market still runs into trillions, but the great state of the West is a spiritual nonentity. Political life in the US has entered the twilight reminiscent of the last days of the Merovingian kings. For an outsider, it is hard to comprehend that this nation of 275 million could not find better leaders than the two nincompoops Bush and/or Gore. Both appear to be weak of mind, lacking in basic knowledge, and totally devoid of political will. Probably an average city could field better men than these two.

General political decline is accompanied by weakness of mind. America of the mass media and public life is silly. There are no important new books, comparable with the pre-war American output. The US TV is an insult to human intelligence. Museums are full of rusty junk and videotapes purporting to be American art. The Judeo-Mammonite takeover has eliminated the living forces of America, and directed them into consumption.

XI

The 'Jewish' spirit of America, denounced by Marx, was glorified and exalted by a Jewish American journalist Phillip Weiss[61]:

> No one is allowed to speak up about something we all quietly know: Jews changed America. The civil rights movement reflects Jewish values of justice. Feminism is a reflection of liberal Jewish matriarchal values. Ever-more-powerful Jews in the media have ushered in the information age. Psychologically attuned Jews and Hollywood Jews changed the language of popular culture—Seinfeld, Weinstein. And the new emphasis on educational achievement throughout our society reflects the Jewish love of learning. I have not even gotten to finance or the law . . . These trends have made America a fairer and more creative place. Jews have fostered the separation of church and state. The greatly diminished influence of church on public mores wouldn't have happened without secularized Jews gaining cultural power. And no one ever talks about it. The most important change in establishment culture in the last 25 years, and it goes unspoken.

This smug self-adoration of Weiss calls for some sobriety. These changes can be seen in a less felicitous light. Jews changed America during the last 25–30 years, says Weiss. These were golden years for American Jews, as their share of power and influence grew. But these years were rather bad for un-Chosen Americans. A British weekly, the *Economist*, an ardent supporter of the neo-liberalism, reported[62] recently:

> The gap between the poor and the rich is rising. In America, in the last twenty years, average income of the richest fifth of population [rose]

> from 9 to 15 times [the] income of the poorest fifth. In 1999, British income inequality reached its widest level in 40 years.

The growth of Jewish influence was accompanied by divergence: the rich became richer, the poor became poorer, and the middle class lost. It should have been expected, as traditionally the prosperity of the Jewish community runs counter to the interests of common folk. The Bible provided us with an archetypal story of Joseph and his brothers, who prospered by enslaving ordinary Egyptians to the Pharaoh. The Jewish community stood by the king and against the ordinary folk in Spain in the days of Don Pedro the Cruel, in Poland and the Ukraine of the 17th century. Not in vain were Jewish neighbourhoods located next to royal palaces everywhere in Europe.

The 'ever-more-powerful Jews in the media' were engaged in their usual drivel: glorifying Israel, bemoaning the Jewish Holocaust, supporting every nasty case from mass murder in Iraq to the blocking of the Blacks' advancement in the US. Under the Jews, Hollywood made American cinema even more violent, moralistic, repulsive, and philistine. There is a good Jewish guy in the movies, Woody Allen, but he is not in Hollywood and he is anyway considered an anti-Semite. In the law, the advent of the Jew did not make America a more just society, but a more litigious one. 'A Jewish lawyer' has come to stay as the bogeyman for scaring kids at night. 'Separation of church and society' can be considered to be its forced de-Christianisation and de-spiritualization.

XII

The US has become a Jewish state in more ways than one. It has the same security checks, the same holocaust museums, the same poverty for many and riches for a few as Israel. The similarity is felt by its friend and foe alike. David Quinn[63] wrote in the *Sunday Times*, that the feel of Irish intellectuals' rejection of American policies is "so strong, so palpable, so irrational (!?), that it reminded me of nothing so much as anti-Semitism." Quinn continued:

> Americans are like the Jews in having become the scapegoats of choice for half the planet. The Jews were accused of controlling the world's finances; so is the United States. The Jews were accused of promoting decadence through their control of culture and the arts. So is the United States. The Jews were accused of putting their power to a range of nefarious uses. So is the United States.
>
> Given America's power and wealth, and the strength of its Jewish lobby, in the Middle East it has been simplicity itself to mix anti-American with age-old anti-Semitism to produce a truly poisonous brew. Tens of

> millions of people have imbibed this concoction and are now filled with a hatred of America as strong as that of many Germans in the Weimar Republic.
>
> Osama bin Laden and his followers have followed their hatred to its logical conclusion, just as Hitler did: If America really is to blame for the world's problems, then it, and its people, must be eradicated.

This article is important, as it displays the subconscious of an adept of Judeo-Americanism. Quinn appeals to Jews and Neo-Jews: support America as America is a Jewish state that carries out Jewish policies and causes normal anti-Jewish response. Quinn considers Jews and America to be identical, and he uses the many clichés of Neo-Jewish propaganda.

One of the clichés is that the rejection of Jewish/American policies is 'irrational' for there is a tenet of faith: "Thou shalt not try and understand why thy policies cause rejection." Elie Wiesel, the prophet of holocaustism, recites at every occasion: 'totally irrational . . . no explanation . . . no reason, just pure hate of everybody toward Jews', and Rabbi Tony Bayfield repeats it with usual Jewish vehemence[64]:

> I am seething with rage at anyone who dares suggest that, in any way, such acts (attack on Pentagon, etc.) are even explicable, let alone justifiable.

Without knowing Rabbi Bayfield personally, I would venture a wild guess. If you mention Deir Yassin to him, or the genocide in Iraq, he will seethe with rage: How can one compare! He will find these mass murders justifiable, certainly explicable. But whenever Jews suffer, it can not be explained and understood but by some mystic means.

Quinn, as any Neo-Jewish apologist, denies the undeniable. For him, America does not control world finances, **she is accused** of it. Probably, America is only **accused of** occupying a large part of North America. In Quinn's mind, she lives in a poor house, in a little *schtetl*. I have no idea of David Quinn's origin, but nobody can be more Jewish than he.

For Quinn, every enemy of Jewish supremacy/American domination is a new Hitler who wants to wipe out all Jews/Americans. Nasser was a Hitler when he nationalized the Suez; Arafat was a Hitler and Beirut was his bunker. Soviet Russia was the same as Nazi Germany from the moment Moscow completed its part in vanquishing Hitler. Osama bin Laden, or "tens of millions of people in the Middle East" became a new Hitler. The idea behind this comparison is that these "tens of millions" of Muslims should be dealt with as Hitler and his "many Germans in the Weimar Republic."

Judeo-American discourse inherited this demonisation idea from its Jewish predecessor. Introduction of fury, hatred and vengefulness into a discussion of the adversary is a potent traditional Jewish ideological weapon. It is never turned on inside the community, but used outside of it. Demonisation and fury causes general nastiness and bias in discourse and eventually destroys society. Rabbi Shmuel Boteach, formerly the Chabad Rabbi at Oxford University, presented this Jewish approach in his aptly named piece, *A Time to Hate*:[65]

> The proper response to the cowardly brutes who perpetrated the horrific attacks against America is to hate them with every fibre of our being and purge ourselves of any morsel of sympathy which might seek to understand their motives. Hatred is a valid emotion . . . Contrary to Christianity, which advocates turning the other cheek to belligerence and loving the wicked, Judaism obligates us to despise and resist the wicked at all costs. For us to extend forgiveness and compassion to [sinners] in the name of religion is not just insidious, it is an act of mocking G-d, who has mercy for all, yet demands justice for the innocent. The only response to Hitler is utter contempt and violent hatred. The only way to react to incorrigible evil is to wage an incessant war against it until it is utterly eradicated from the earth. I maintain that any culture that does not hate Hitler and his ilk is a non-compassionate society. Indeed, to show kindness to the murderer is to violate the victim yet again. Thus, in the interest of justice, the appropriate response to the evil person is to hate him with every fibre of our being and to hope they find no rest, neither in this world nor in the next.

XIII

In the struggle of ideas, there is a formidable weapon of mass destruction: demonisation of the opponent. Theologically it is called the 'Manichean' heresy. There is no better systemic weapon if you intend to destroy society. One should not divide people unto Sons of Light and Sons of Darkness.

Jews usually are quite tolerant of ideas produced within the community. The founder of Zionism, Theodor Hertzl was anything but a pious Jew. Religious Jews greatly disliked him. Still, when a Rabbi was asked to say something good about him, he found good words: Theodor Hertzl never spoke on mundane subjects in a synagogue, never entered a toilet while wearing phylacteries, he never studied the Talmud on Christmas Eve. The truth is that Hertzl never visited a synagogue, never wore phylacteries, never studied the Talmud, full stop. In a similar vein, Jews were quite tolerant of Leon Trotsky the Communist, and of Yair Stern the Nazi supporter, for they knew every idea has its positive elements. Nowadays, the leader of Left Opposition Yossi Sarid was a friend of the assassinated Judeo-Nazi minister Zeevi and touchingly eulogised him.

But to the outside world, Jews usually offered the idea of the eternally blessed vs. the eternally damned, of seething rage, of anger and vengeance. In order to restore the balance of mind, this Jewish internal tolerance should be universalised, and Jewish external intolerance rejected.

Judeo-American thought keeps producing intolerance for external consumption. Ronald Reagan called Russia 'the Evil Empire'. Bush called Saddam Hussein 'Hitler'. Barbara Amiel, wife and guiding light of the media magnate Lord Black, remarked that now, Israel and the Jews are presented as an Evil Empire.

Wrong, Ms. Amiel: there are no Evil Empires, only unchecked ones.

Soviet Russia was not an Evil Empire, nor was Communism embodied in Stalin and the Gulag. Sholokhov, Block, Pasternak, Esenin, Mayakovsky and Deineka embraced the Revolution and expressed its ideas in art. It was a land of the great and partly successful experiment in equality and brotherhood of Man, of a brave attempt to defeat the spirit of Greed. Communists and their supporters tried to liberate labour, to bring the Kingdom of Heaven upon earth, to remove poverty and free the human spirit. Communism brought forth the social democracy of Europe.

Germany was not an Evil Empire, nor was the spirit of organic traditionalism embodied in Hitler and Auschwitz. The Traditionalists tried to establish an alternative paradigm based on Wagner, Nietzsche and Hegel, to go to the roots and traditions of the folk. Not in vain, the best writers and thinkers of Europe from Knut Hamsun to Louis Ferdinand Celine to Ezra Pound to William Butler Yeats to Heidegger saw a positive element in the Traditionalist organic approach. If Russia and Germany had not been demonised, it is quite possible we would not have seen them coming to such extremes.

We have to restore the balance of mind and discourse lost in the aftermath of World War Two, due to the too-complete victory of the bourgeois 'Judeo-American' thought. While condemning excesses and war crimes, we should regain the kingdom of the spirit from Mayakovsky to Pound. There are no evil men, we are created in the image of God, and all ideas are needed to produce new thought.

The two great protagonists of the 1930s and 1940s committed many atrocities, but whoever is without sin, let him throw the first stone. After Dresden and Hiroshima, and the Deir Yassin and Jenin massacres, there are not many takers. They should be de-demonised, as their demonisation creates a dangerous imbalance of ideas.

We should not demonise their opponents, either. America is not an Evil Empire. It can and should be brought to its senses. The American spirit of entrepreneurship, invention, self-reliance, unbridled freedom and democracy should be kept as all-human valuable assets.

The Jewish People are not an Evil Empire. Good organisers and ambassadors, stubborn and devout, easily carried away, high-strung, first-class thinkers and brave soldiers, light travellers, compassionate and cheerful; Jews are needed for the prosperity of mankind.

But every one of these approaches can destroy the world if left unchecked.

The Soviets killed and exiled millions in their drive to demolish the Old Order. They ruined old churches, uprooted peasants and supported uniformity as much as their American antagonists. The Nazis unleashed the most horrible war on the world and killed millions of Slavs and Jews. Now, the Judeo-American forces have been unhinged by the completeness of their victories in 1945 and in 1991. They understand it as a licence to drive the world to perdition. Their programme of globalisation would eliminate all beauty and specific quality of the world, kill the spirit, undermine art, wipe out spirit, destroy nature, undo social achievements, divide mankind into Masters and Slaves. Wherever they go, old cafés and restaurants disappear and Starbucks and McDonalds take over. Workers lose their working places, museums are filled with trash, art is replaced by TV. Still, they should be contained, not destroyed.

Usually we discuss war as the conflict of state interests. But the never-ending World War Two was the war of ideas, as well. It was wrong and unneeded, as various ideas should coexist in eternal struggle, as Yin and Yang, or feminine and masculine forces. The Judeo-American idea will emasculate the world if left to run unchecked. This emasculation is strongly felt in the US, where men do not dare to be men anymore. They can be sued if they look at a girl, and sued if they do not look at a girl. In *Beowulf*, the great Anglo-Saxon epic poem, a cruel queen kills every man who dares to look at her. Little did they know that the spirit of the cruel queen will rule supreme in the world.

The Judeo-American idea has a strong attachment to biological life, but rejects spirit. It is not for nothing that no great pieces of art, no great new ideas appear under its rule. On the other hand, the purely masculine tendencies of its opponents were also dangerous for the survival of the human race.

All three adversaries of the last Century had a common feature: they rejected Christ and the Holy Virgin, the base of our spirituality. None of the great leaders of WWII ever turned to God. Americans are and Communists were, scared to mention Christ in order not to be ridiculed or rebuked by Jews. The Nazis were strongly anti-Christian, and dabbled in the occult. This spirit is the fourth element missing for the restoration of the balance.

Thus, we should look for a synthesis of the four tendencies: the organic native love of nature, local roots and tradition, social communal justice for all mankind, love of life and entrepreneurship; and spirituality. They would present the new meaning of the Cross, and bring mankind to its unity in spirit, while preserving its beautiful variety.

XIV

Many scholars of the Rise of the Jews encounter a difficulty. Their Darwinist instincts called them to presume some better qualities of the Jews that led them to succeed. MacDonald came to the conclusion that Jews possess a higher intelligence, the result of eugenics and careful breeding. I felt myself proud while reading his work, until I looked around at real Jews, my neighbours. His concept did not survive encounter with reality. If it is not higher intelligence, what then?

The Darwinists' error lies in their inability to see success as a function of society. In traditional Gentile societies, a model of success was provided by a poet, a saint, an artist, a brave warrior, a good worker or peasant, a man who made life better for others. For Homeric Greeks, good sportsmen, seafarers, poets, musicians and dancers were the models for success as we can learn from the wonderful utopia of the Feacians. These idyllic people, like the jolly Oxford student of old, despise a trader and a businessman, and prefer a good yachtsman.

According to Jews, there are two different concepts of success: one, success within the Jewish community, achieved by studying the Talmud; another, success in the Big World of Jews and Gentiles. This success is measured by the ruthless amassing of money and power.

From the Jewish point of view, Jews were always successful, as they always had both sorts of success. But until recently, the Jewish external success was not considered a success by Gentiles at all. There were always Gentiles who shared their view, but be they Richard III or Harpagon, they were considered monsters rather than models of success. In the Nineteenth Century, the critical mass of monsters was achieved and thus the Mammonite world was born. By actively participating in discourse (media + universities), Jewish thinkers and ideologists promoted the Mammonite idea of success and made it the standard one in Western society. Modern Harpagon and Richard, be they Iacocca or Soros, are generally approved of in the new society formed by the Mammonite discourse-masters. The Western world became Jewish, as Marx put it, and it adopted the Jewish idea of success. In plain words, Jews did not 'become successful', rather, their normal behaviour became a norm of success.

If the discourse of the US were transferred into Afro-American hands, it is possible that good sportsmen and musicians would come to be considered successful, while lawyers and bankers would be considered failures. That would be better for the future of mankind than the present adoration of money and power.

XV

Even the material success of Jews is not achieved by a miracle. A tentative explanation was offered by two Israeli directors and producers, Menachem Golan and Yoram Globus. People of meagre talents whose cinematographic achievements remain strictly in the B-class, they made a fortune in Hollywood and produced many awful films until they suffered a setback. Their key to success lay in vertical networking. Golan and Globus bought cinemas all over England and the UK, and there they screened the movies of their choice. They invariably (well, almost) chose awful movies, as they had no taste, talent or ability. They said: If you own a chain of cinemas, you do not have to worry about the quality of your movies. Globalisation and creation of networks is the way to avoid competition by merit. Instead of opening a better café, it is easier to buy every café and turn it into a Starbucks. People will have to come to your café.

The second reason for Jewish success is in our mutual psychological compatibility. Adversaries usually describe it as Jewish 'freemasonry', almost a conspiracy. But it is quite natural for Jews to like similar things, like Englishmen like bacon and eggs. Still it creates a problem for human development. In Prague of the 1920s, there were two equally good but very different writers, an alienated and abstract Jew, Franz Kafka and an earthly Czech Communist, Jaroslaw Hasek. Both are good, both are necessary for the development of mankind, but the genius of Kafka is more palatable for Jews. As there are many more Jewish professors of literature and newspaper editors than the Czech ones, it is but natural that Kafka is universally known and recognised, while Hasek's name remains in Bohemia. More writers imitate Kafka than so much as consider Hasek. As a result, mankind, not only America, turns more and more 'Jewish'. As writers know, they must write in a way palatable to the Jewish editors and professors. Otherwise they can expect only a parochial success. Thus, without any conspiracy, normal human Jewish tendencies influence the spirit of mankind by eliminating its beautiful variety.

Now, these problems can be solved. While some amount of private initiative is good, networking should be banned. One may own a bookshop or a cinema or a café. But an attempt to buy or establish control over a second one should attract criminal prosecution.

An Inuit who was hit by a steam train while visiting the continent, tells a Northern joke. He survived the accident, but since then, he destroys every kettle he sees. They should be eradicated while small, he says. After seeing the monopolisation, we should follow the advice of the wise Inuit. It is better for us to have a hundred different cafés than a hundred Starbucks.

Man's income should be capped by a double-average industrial wage, and above that amount, taxes should exceed one hundred percent. Managerial privileges should be capped severely as well. Media and discourse in general should be freed. In the area of human thought, the Brahmanite tendency of Jews should be made visible and confronted. The Brahman is not an enemy, but his traditional tendency to dominate should be counteracted by better visibility and accountability.

A joint communion of spirit proclaiming our unity should be established. It implies rejection of interest and racial discrimination. St. Ambrose, in his comments on Deut. 23:19, wrote: "From him exact usury whom it would not be a crime to kill. Where there is a right of war, there also is a right of usury."[66] People who share communion with their brothers and sisters in spirit do not demand usury. But, if the communion is gone, usury, unlimited exploitation and slavery come in. Slavery was introduced by Calvinists and Jews in North America, while it was unknown in the lands where the communion united the people in one Church.

In his witty *Catch-22*, Joseph Heller has a General ask his chaplain in disbelief: "Do enlisted men pray to the same god as we do?" This is the idea of the world without a shared communion. It is not without reason that the Talmud forbids a Jew to drink wine with a Gentile, as sharing wine is a communion. As the purpose of Jewish Law was to maintain low-intensity warfare of Jews against Gentiles, a Jew was also forbidden to make an interest-free loan to a Gentile. By sharing communion, society will overcome this difficulty.

With this, the Rise of the Jews will be transformed into a Rise of Man.

The long saga of the Jewish people is headed for an unknown end. It began with rejection of communality, and it ends with the same question asked again. If Zionism and its elder brother Mammonitis were to win world-wide, it would remove variety, mercy and spirit. If the spirit of communality wins, the prophecies of old will become true. We shall say: We be of one blood, the Palestinian people, descendents of Abraham, of the Israelites, of the Apostles, the rightful dwellers of Palestine, and their close kin and kith, the wandering Jewish folk, who came back like the Prodigal Son to the land of his fathers. The exiled sons of Palestinian villages, of Kakun and Suba, will return and they will rebuild the ruined cities, never again to be uprooted (Amos 9:15). In the Holy Land, the two branches of one people, the Jews and the Palestinians will unite, intermarry and create a new folk—like the Normans did in East Anglia, Sicily and Normandy—never again to disturb the peace of the world.

Notes

50. Publisher-Alma/Am Oved: Tel Aviv, 2000, ISBN 965-13-1428-1.
51. CNN, 9/11/01.
52. 9/12/01.
53. Rich Lowry, *National Review* editor, to Howard Kurtz (*Washington Post*, 9/13/01).
54. 2.7.01.
55. The Third Dove.
56. "The Israeli-Arab War, June 1967," *New Left Review*, 23.6.67.
57. http://www.chicagotribune.com/news/opinion/perspective/chi-0204070422apr07.s.
58. April 7, 2002.

59. I normalised the spelling of her name. Taki the snob had to spell quite an ordinary Jewish name 'Landoi' (var. Landau) in the French way.
60. In private communication to the author.
61. *New York Observer*, by Philip Weiss, Jan. 22, 2001.
62. June 16, 2001.
63. "Blaming America," Irish edition, *Sunday Times*.
64. *Guardian*, Sept. 15, 2001.
65. http://www.arutzsheva.org.
66. The quote supplied by David Pidcock.

The Elders of Zion and the Masters of Discourse

The troublesome concept of the Hidden Hand or the Elders of Zion is superfluous and unnecessary.

"The latest controversy to involve the Arab World concerns a TV program, *A Rider without a Horse*, that started airing on several Arab satellite channels on Wednesday, Nov. 5, the first day of the holy month of Ramadan. The source of the controversy is that the program is partly based on *The Protocols of the Elders of Zion*, the old forgery originating in Tsarist Russia," writes Qais S. Saleh, a business consultant from Ramallah on the excellent website, CounterPunch.[67] Expectedly, Saleh condemns the broadcast and warns the Palestinians and Arabs to stay away from the bad old wolf of anti-Semitism, or, as he put it, "the trend of importation of anti-Semitic bigotry."

Saleh's view coincides with that of Michael Hoffman, on whose site the *Protocols* can be found. Hoffman thinks Arabs have no need to import anti-Semitic arguments from the old and far-away sources, provided they have a fresh round-the-clock local source: actual behaviour of the Jewish state and its Jewish citizens. It is much more convincing than old tales.

However, the *Protocols* are still with us and still entertain minds. Recently, the leading Italian novelist and thinker Umberto Eco contributed his opinion on the subject to the *Guardian*.[68] Eco "explains" the popular feelings towards the Jews: "They . . . engaged in trade and lent money—hence the resentment towards them as "intellectuals." In my limited knowledge, it is not the intellectuals who lend money, but bankers and loan sharks, while true intellectuals find their behaviour repulsive. Probably Eco has a different definition of 'intellectual' up his sleeve. "The ill-famed *Protocols of the Learned Elders of Zion* were a rehash of serialised fictional material, and prove their own unreliability, since it is hardly credible that 'the baddies' would reveal their fell purposes so blatantly," concludes Eco.

One can forgive a business consultant from Ramallah, but Umberto Eco could notice that his definition would fit some other books, for instance, *Gargantua* and *Pantagruel*, an even older forgery, pretending to be a real chronicle of the Giants family, and built on 'serialised fictional material'. *Don Quixote, Pickwick's Club, 1984* of Orwell—all these books "pretend" to describe real events to the same extent. They are 'forgeries', as they are ascribed to somebody else: *Don Quixote* to Sid Ahmed Benengeli,[69] and *Gargantua* to Maitre Alcofribas Nasier.[70]

The Protocols of the Elders of Zion are best described as 'pseudo-epigrapha', rather than 'fake'. They belong to the same category as Thomas Friedman's "Letter of President Clinton to Mubarak." After all, pseudo-epigraphic genre is an old and venerable one. It is even better to consider the *Protocols* 'a political pamphlet'.

In this essay, we shall attempt to find out why the *Protocols* refuse to lie down and die. We shall stay clear from the usual question, "who wrote it." Its real author remains unknown, and it is difficult to imagine this person, for the *Protocols* are a literary palimpsest. In the days of yore, a scribe would write his composition on a piece of old parchment, previously removing an older text. The erasure was rarely total, and a reader was treated to an integrated version of the *Golden Ass* and *Fioretti* of St. Francis. In the *Protocols*, there are layers of old and even older stories, and it precludes a meaningful quest for the ultimate creator. Every text should be treated on its own merits, disregarding the question of authorship. Although, Jorge Luis Borges wrote that the author is an important part of a text. Indeed, if we would know the *Protocols* contain a real blueprint of some Jewish elites, we would have our answer ready in minutes. But *Protocols* were published in the end of the 19th-beginning of the 20th century "as found"—as apocrypha. They became a great bestseller and still stay there, though in some countries (notably the Soviet Union), mere possession of the text was punishable by death.

The Anonymous author of the *Protocols* describes a master-plan for vast restructuring of society, creation of a new oligarchy and subjugation of millions. The final product is not too different from the one described in a contemporary piece of writing, *The Iron Heel* by Jack London, the great radical from Oakland, California. However, London expected a harsh crack-down, while Anonym's way to subjugation leads through Machiavellian manipulations and mind control a la Orwell's *1984*. (Orwell's homage to the *Protocols* is even more striking as it is rarely noticed.)

"The difficulty of the *Protocols* is in an uncanny dissonance between its uncouth language and deep social and religious thought. It is a rude parody-like rendering of a satanic, subtle and well-thought out plan," wrote the Nobel Prize winning novelist Alexander Solzhenitsyn[71] in his (written in 1966 and published in 2001) analysis of the *Protocols*:

> *The Protocols* . . . show a blueprint of a social system. Its design is well above abilities of an ordinary mind, including that of its publisher. It is a dynamic process of two stages, of destabilization, increasing freedom and liberalism, which is terminated in social cataclysm, and on the second stage, new hierarchical restructuring of society takes place. It is

> more complicated than a nuclear bomb. It could be a stolen and distorted plan designed by a mind of genius. Its putrid style of an anti-Semitic grubby brochure [intentionally] obscures the great strength of thought and insight.

Solzhenitsyn is aware of the faults of the *Protocols*: "Its style is that of a filthy leaflet, the powerful line of thought is broken and fragmented, mixed up with ill-smelling incantations and psychological blunders. The system described is not necessarily connected with the Jews; it could be purely Masonic or whatever; while its strongly anti-Semitic current is not an organic part of the design."

Solzhenitsyn makes a textual experiment, removes the words 'Jews', 'Goyim' and 'conspiracy' and finds many disturbing ideas. He concludes: "The text demonstrates impressive foresight on the two systems of society, the Western and the Soviet one. While a powerful thinker could possibly predict the development of the West in 1901, how could he grasp the Soviet future?"

Solzhenitsyn braved the Soviet regime, dared to write and publish the mammoth *Archipelago Gulag*, an indictment of the Soviet repression, but even he stalled and did not publish his research on the *Protocols*. He asked that it be published after his death only, and it was printed against his will in a very small number of copies in 2001. Let us follow Solzhenitsyn's line of thought and gaze into the crystal ball of the *Protocols*, while temporarily discounting its "Jewish line" and paying heed to the idea of creating a new system, not necessarily a Jewish-dominated one. The master-plan begins with the reshaping of the human mind:

> People's minds should be diverted (away from contemplation) towards industry and trade, and then they will have no time to think. The people will be consumed by the pursuit of gain. It will be a vain pursuit, for we shall put industry on a speculative basis: what is withdrawn from the land by industry will slip through the hands of workers and industrialists and pass into the hands of financiers.
>
> The intensified struggle for survival and superiority, accompanied by crises and shocks will create cold and heartless communities with strong aversion towards religion. Their only guide is gain that is Mammon, which they will erect into a veritable cult.

Foresight of Anonym is amazing: in the days of the *Protocols*' publication, Man was still the measure of things, and a full eighty years would pass until Milton Friedman and the Chicago School would proclaim Market and Profit as the only guiding light.

The tool for enslavement of minds is the media, writes Anonym. "There is a great force that creates the movement of thought in the people, and that is the media. It is in the media that the triumph of freedom of speech finds its incarnation. Through the Press we have gained the power to influence minds while remaining unobserved. We shall erase from the memory of men the historical facts we do not want them to know, and leave only those we wish [to have them remember]."

Years were to pass after the time of the publication of the *Protocols* until a small group of people, the media lords, who control our discourse while remaining unobserved, would arise. The open discussion of the media barons, Berlusconi and Black, Maxwell and Sulzberger, Gusinsky and Zuckerman is banned from the media they own, while their cooperative affinity remains impressive. Freedom of discourse survives wherever independent (from media barons) media still exists. Hundred years ago, this force was much weaker than it is now; it is amazing that Anonym recognised its potential.

A century before the rise of the World Bank and the International Monetary Fund, the *Protocols* noticed that the foreign loans are the best tools to rob countries of their wealth. "While the loans were internal, money remained in the land, but with externalisation of loans, all nations pay tribute of their subjects to the oligarchy." Indeed, the bigger loans poor countries get, the poorer they become.

Concentration of capital in the hands of financiers, concentration of media in few hands, extra-judicial killings of unyielding leaders, and the stock market with its derivatives, suck out wealth. It accumulates in the hands of the priesthood of Mammon, gain (or "market forces") as the only measure of successful strategy. Yes, the interest to the *Protocols* does not disappear because the described plan of creating oligarchic (not necessarily Jewish) rule is being implemented in real time and it is called the New World Order.

Sometimes, the *Protocols* are described as an extreme-right-wing anti-utopian piece of writing. However, it spans both left and right-wing discourse. A right-wing writer would bless the strengthening of Law and Order, but the following prediction of Anonym could be written today by a leftist libertarian, say, Noam Chomsky, witnessing the present transition to the New World Order: "The race of armaments and the increase of a police force will bring forth society where there are only the masses of the proletariat, a few millionaires, police and soldiers."

However, the deepest thought of Anonym remains in the spiritual sphere:

> Freedom might be harmless and have its place in the State economy without injury to the well-being of the people if it rested upon the foundation of faith in God, upon the Brotherhood of humanity. This is the reason why it is indispensable for us to undermine all faith, to tear

out of the people's mind the very principle of God and the Spirit, and to put in its place arithmetical calculations and material needs.

Anonym connects Faith and the idea of the Brotherhood of humanity. The undermining of Faith ruins the Brotherhood. Freedom, instead of a desirable and beautiful state of mind, turns into a destructive drive when unhinged from the Faith. Instead of Faith, the Enemy offers the pursuit of Mammon.

While reading in today's (16.11.02) *International Herald Tribune* philippics against gay priests and nuns, one notes the following lines in the *Protocols*: "We have taken care to discredit the Christian priesthood and ruin their mission which might still hinder our plans. Day by day, their influence on the people is falling lower. Collapse of Christianity is nigh."

We witness implementation of this plan: religion is removed from consideration, neo-liberalism or Mammon worship takes its place, while with disestablishment of socialism, this brave attempt of a non-faith-based brotherhood collapses, leaving an ideological vacuum.

This observation caused some reviewers to exclaim, "The true designer of the Master-plan is our old foe, the Prince of the World, whose ultimate aim is the elimination of the Divine Presence and ruination of Man." True, but the Prince of the World can't act directly. He needs free agents that choose to accept his plan. These chief agents and possible allies, according to the pamphlet, are financial capitalists and Masters of Discourse, 'the Mind'.

They promote to the highest positions "politicians who, in case of disobedience to our instructions, must face criminal charges or disappear. We shall arrange elections in favour of candidates with some dark, undiscovered stain in their past. They will be our trustworthy agents out of fear of revelations." For us, contemporaries of Watergate and Lewinsky, it sounds familiar.

The shift from Stage One (liberalism and freedom) to Stage Two (tyranny) took place in our lifetime. If in 1968 the *New York Times* promoted the Freedom Riders, in 2002 it supports the Patriot Act. An important American lawyer, Alan Dershowitz of Harvard made a U-turn from Human rights to the Right to Torture. This U-turn was predicted by the *Protocols*, as the purpose beyond the struggle against the old elites.

"The aristocracy enjoyed the labour of the workers, and it was interested in seeing that the workers were well fed, healthy, and strong. The people have annihilated the aristocracy, and have fallen into the grips of merciless money-grinding scoundrels."

In less emotional terms, the new bourgeoisie removed the old elites with the support of people, while promising freedom and objecting to their privilege. After its victory, it took the privilege for itself, and turned out to be as bad (or worse) as the feudal lord. Marx referred to this complaint of aristocracy in one of the numerous additions to the *Communist Manifesto*, and considered it futile if partly justified. However, he did not live to witness a similar process which took place in the last days of the Soviet Union. The rising new bourgeoisie took control over the discourse and convinced the people to fight the privilege of Nomenclature for the sake of equality and freedom. After their victory, it assumed and multiplied the privilege, and rejected equality and freedom.

The *Protocols* predict the rise of the New Bourgeoisie, globalist Mammon-worshippers who are inherently hostile to Old Elites, to spirit, to religion, and to the ordinary people. For a long while, they were the engine of the left, democracy-seeking movements, until their purpose was completed, and then they made the U-turn towards oligarchy.

This U-turn can be quantified by the inheritance and land tax rate in England: while the financial bourgeoisie and Masters of Discourse fought against the old ruling classes, the rates were high and eventually dismantled their power base. After their victory, the rate decreased allowing consolidation of the new ruling classes. It is possible that the Old Order had had some advantages. It is almost certain that a transition from the Old Order could be different if the people understood the intentions of the enemy. But history can't be reversed, and it is futile to dream of return of the good lords and benevolent Party bosses.

Thus, the *Protocols* (purified of references to the Jews and conspiracies) are useful as they describe a blueprint of the New World Order, and help its adversaries to form a defensive strategy against the designs of the Enemy. But the references to the Jews constitute a large and important part of the text.

Notes

67. *A Horseless Rider, The Protocols Of The Elders Of Zion* & *Imported Bigotry*, by Qais S. Saleh, CounterPunch, November 13, 2002 http://www.counterpunch.com/saleh1112.html. See more on http://abcnews.go.com/sections/world/DailyNews/egypt021121_TV.html.
68. http://books.guardian.co.uk/review/story/0,12084,775668,00. html, "The poisonous Protocols" by Umberto Eco.
69. *Cide Hamete Benengeli*, in Cervantes' spelling.
70. Nom de plume of François Rabelais.
71. Alexander Solzhenitsyn, Evrei v SSSR i v budushei Rossii, 2001 (in Russian).

The Jews and the Protocols

The *Protocols* identify the moving force of the New World Order as a powerful group of extremely chauvinistic, manipulative and domination-obsessed Jewish leaders. The leaders, according to the *Protocols*, despise ordinary community members; they utilise and support anti-Semitism as the means to keep their 'lesser brethren', innocent ordinary folk of Jewish origin, in thrall to their rule. The leaders are described as pathological goy haters, bent on destroying culture and traditions of other nations while preserving their own. Their goal is to create world government and rule the homogenised and globalised world.

Their aims and intentions are stated in an extremely contrarian and obnoxious way. Solzhenitsyn concluded that no sane person would deliver his favourite ideas in such a self-demeaning and self-defeating way. "We extract gold from their blood and tears," "our power is based on workers' hunger," "revolutionaries are our human tools," "brutish minds of Goyim," are, in his opinion, words ascribed to the Jews by their enemies. A Jew would rather put such ideas in an oblique way, he felt.

It is not a water-tight argument. Some people speak in an oblique way; others prefer a direct one. An Armenian from the Azeri capital, Baku told me in long gone 1988, "The Azeris are our cattle. Without our Armenian mind their country would collapse in a course of days, as they are silly donkeys." (A few months later, an explosion of native violence expelled the clever Armenians from Azerbaijan, and since then the Azeris manage their own land quite all right.)

David Ben-Gurion, the first ruler of the Jewish state, coined an equally arrogant maxim: "Who cares what Goyim say? What matters is what the Jews do!" This sentence is an almost direct quote from the *Protocols*.

The *Protocols* ascribe to the Elders a saying, "Each Jewish victim is worth in the sight of God a thousand goyim." This line, a pinnacle of arrogance, is not a vain invention of an anti-Semite. Two ministers of Sharon's government, Uri Landau and Ivet Lieberman demanded to kill one thousand Palestinian goyim for each Jewish victim. A Jewish extremist at a demo for the Jewish Temple Mount (18.11.02) called each Jew to kill one thousand Palestinian goyim. Apparently, some ideas of the *Protocols* are not foreign to some Jews.

The late Israeli scholar Israel Shahak and an American Jewish writer Norton Mezvinsky present in their book, *Jewish Fundamentalism in Israel*[72] a plethora of sayings by Jewish Rabbis that wouldn't be out of place in the *Protocols*.

"The difference between a Jewish soul and souls of non-Jews is greater and deeper than the difference between a human soul and the souls of cattle" (p. ix). Shahak and Mezvinsky proved that the rage of the Jewish chauvinists does not differentiate between Palestinians, Arabs and Goyim in general. In other words, whatever happened to Palestinians could happen to any Gentile community standing in the way of the Jews.

Indeed, if the *Protocols* had no relation to reality, they probably wouldn't be as popular as they are. The Jews are sufficiently powerful to dream of domination, and some do. Apparently some Jewish ideas found their way into the text. Other thoughts are ascribed to the Jews on the basis of *qui bono* [who benefits].

The least acceptable idea of the *Protocols* is the presumption of an extremely ancient conspiracy of the Jews aiming to take over the world. The extreme philo-Semitic view denies the Jews their ability to act together and presents them as separate individuals united by prayer only. This view is not accepted by the Jews, and it does not agree with the common sense.

Solzhenitsyn does not believe in the existence of the Elders of Zion, though "the togetherness and coordination of Jewish activity for the sake of their advancement caused many writers (beginning from Cicero) to imagine there is a single commanding centre for directing their attacks. Without such a world centre, without conspiring, the Jews understand each other and are able to coordinate their actions."

The Jews are perfectly able to coordinate their actions, but I doubt that human beings, Jews or English, Russians or Chinese are able to form long-standing plans spanning centuries and continents. Nobody was able to prove such a plot exists. Usually, 'anti-Semites' (the people who doubt or deny inherent benevolence of the Jews to Gentile society) argue for its authenticity as Henry Ford did. The car king said:[73] "The only statement I care to make about the *Protocols* is that they fit in with what is going on." Indeed they do, exclaims Victor Marsden, the English translator of the *Protocols*.

However, it is not proof of a Jewish plot. We can reach similar results rejecting the conspiracy line altogether, by applying the concept of self-interest to the real Jewish community as it was aptly described by Shahak-Mezvinsky. We shall prove that **the troublesome concept of the Hidden Hand or the Elders of Zion is superfluous and unnecessary.**

The traditional Jewish community had a structure of the 'upturned pyramid'. In the words of Zionist theoreticians, it contained many persons of wealth, learning and management, and very few workers. It appears an odd thing, until one understands that the Zionists artificially view the Jews in divorce of the society they live in. The Jewish 'upturned pyramid' couldn't exist without a real down-turned pyramid of Gentile low classes. The Jews compete with the native elites of the Gentile society for the right to exploit the Gentile worker and peasant. The *modus operandi* of the two competitors differs.

Although native elites shared some values with their lower classes and usually provided for some upward mobility, the Jewish community had its own structure and values.

Economically it stood for capitalist or quasi-capitalist exploitation of the natives, while ideologically the community declared loyalty to its leaders, rejection of common humanity with the natives, extreme ethnocentrism and feelings of racial and religious superiority towards the natives. It was a marginal community which formed no bonds of marriage and friendship with the natives. As a marginal community, it was free of long-standing considerations the native elites had had.

For instance, the Jewish community of 17th century Ukraine had been a collective tax-farmer and leaseholder, extracting from the natives SIX times more taxes and dues per person than a gentile landlord did, wrote a prominent Jewish Ukrainian historian, Saul Borovoy in a book recently published in Jerusalem. The Jewish communities of Maghreb supported the colonial power against their gentile neighbours, etc. Their traditions forbade normal relations with the natives.

Let us presume that such a community acts on its egoistic interests. Forget conspiracy; forget the Elders of Zion, learned or otherwise. The community's only aim is to promote its own well-being. For a marginal group it means to make the social gap between its members and the native population as broad as possible, while minimising the backlash potential.

The group would naturally, for its own self-interest, support every movement against native elites, whether initiated by the King (as the Jews did before the French Revolution) or by the rebelling low classes. It would not be done for the Jewish love of democracy or rebellious nature, but for the improvement of their own positions. An ideal situation would be created by massacre or expulsion of the native elites, as the group members would be able to appropriate their positions. Indeed, it happened in Soviet Russia of Cheka and Soviet Hungary of Bela Kun in the aftermath of World War One. Massacre and exile of the native elites made the positions of power and influence available to the competing Jews.

Self-interest explains the Jewish involvement with the dreaded Cheka, the Soviet security services. Until 1937, the Jews occupied the top echelon of the KGB predecessor body, while millions of Russians lost their life or liberty. Objectively, these executioners made jobs and houses available for their fellow Jews. After the massacre and exile of Russian elites, the Jews were ready for equality, as a son of a Rabbi could easily compete with a son of a Russian worker or peasant, though he wouldn't be able to compete with a son of a Russian noble.

In a similar way, the Jews in Israel granted limited equality to the Palestinians in 1966, after confiscation of 90% of native lands and expulsion of

90% of the natives. Now, the settlers promise to extend equality to the rest of Palestinians, after they expel the majority of them elsewhere. In light of the great Jewish support for Israel, there is no reason to presume that the Jewish *modus operandi* in Palestine is intrinsically different from the Jewish intentions abroad.

Solzhenitsyn writes:

> Executed [during the revolution] army officers were Russians, the noblemen, priests, monks, deputies were Russians . . . In 1920s, the pre-revolutionary engineers and scientists were exiled or killed. They were Russians, while their place was taken by Jews. The best Russian Psychiatric institute in Moscow, its Russian members were arrested or exiled, while their place was taken by the Jews. Important Jewish doctors blocked the advancement of Russian medical scientists . . . The best intellectual and artistic elites of Russian people were killed, while the Jews grew and flourished in these (deadly for Russians) years.

The new Jewish elite did not fully identify with Russia but carried out a separate policy. It had a fateful effect in 1991, when over 50% of the Jews (as opposed to 13% of the Russians) supported the pro-Western *coup* of President Yeltsin. In 1995, 81% of the Jews voted for pro-Western parties, and only 3% for the Communists (as opposed to 46% of Russians), according to the publication by the Jewish sociologist Dr. Ryvkina in her book, *Jews in Post-Soviet Russia* (1996).

In ever-expanding America, the Jews did not have to kill or remove the native elites; they became its important part, controlling discourse and wielding considerable financial clout. They still do not identify with the goyish America: every year, they force the Congress and the Administration to send five billion dollars to their Israeli offshoot and now they are trying to let America fight their war in Iraq. They do discriminate against other Americans; otherwise 60% of the leading positions in the media would not become Jewish.[74]

Jews of France do not identify with France, either. "Their identification with Israel is so strong, it overshadows their ties to the country they live in," writes Daniel Ben Simon in *Haaretz*. This dual loyalty was made very clear to me by a Jewish doctor in Nice. "If the choice is between Israel and France, there's no question I feel closer to Israel," he said, without a moment's hesitation. He was born and bred in France; he went to medical school in France; his patients are French; he speaks French with his wife and children. But in the depths of his heart, he feels a greater affinity with the Jewish state.

In Palestine, the Jews have no compassion for the natives. They travel by segregated roads, study in segregated schools, while a Jew consumes ten times more water resources than a goy, and has an income seven times higher. Thus, the Jewish separateness remains a fact of life for many Jewish communities.

For their own well-being the Jews have to obscure their unique position, wealth and power by the following means:

- Holocaust discourse helps to fight envy.
- In a mono-ethnic society, the Jews as the only foreign body do stick out and attract attention, while in multicultural society they are hardly visible. For this purpose, the Jews support immigration from non-European countries, as their presence would remove the stamp of Jewish exclusiveness.
- The Political Correctness is another device forbidding the discussion of Jewish influence.
- Fight against Christianity and the Church makes sense for a non-Christian community: if the Church would be strong, the Christians would prefer their own, Christian elite.
- Globalisation is a natural development for the people spread all over the globe, if they attach but little importance to the local ways.
- Impoverishment of the natives is but another side of growing wealth of the Jewish community.

Summing it up, a big share (though not all) of the ideas ascribed to the Jews by the *Protocols* are indeed the ideas useful or necessary for the Jewish communal well-being, without any need for great hatred towards Gentiles and/or the guidance of mythic Elders of Zion. That is the reason for the *Protocols*' long life. Paradoxically, without Israeli apartheid these facts would remain invisible for the host communities.

Notes

72. Pluto Press, 1999.
73. In an interview published in the *New York World*, February 17th, 1921.
74. The data provided by Kevin MacDonald of California University.

Love Labours Lost

[A response to Seumas Milne's article in the *Guardian*: "Slur of Anti-Semitism Used to Defend Repression."[75]]

I

In civilised New York, a girl eager to brush-off an insistent admirer does not have to be rude. She slips him a phone number to call, and there a recorded message informs him, "The person you are calling does not wish to remain in contact with you. If you want to listen to a sad poem, press ONE, if you want to cling to unrealistic dream of reunion, press TWO, if you want to have counselling and advice, press THREE."

The important article by the *Guardian* editor Mr. Seumas Milne is a rejected lover's complaint. Apparently, he can't overcome his rejection by the Daughter of Zion. He laments the glorious days of their alliance: "Since the French revolution, the fates of the Jewish people and the Left have been closely intertwined. From the time of Marx, Jews played a central role across all shades of the left." Mr. Milne and the Left are in need of some advice and counselling (press THREE).

Everything that has a beginning, Mr. Milne, has an end as well. Before the French Revolution, the Jewish people supported despotism against the aristocracy, and the Magna Carta was signed by King John despite their opposition. After Napoleon, the Jewish people had had a long alliance with the Left. It was long, but not everlasting. This alliance was severed in the aftermath of the failed 1968 revolution. Since that time the Jewish People have built a new alliance, with Globalisation forces. One saw the new alliance in action when it supported the victory of Margaret Thatcher, the shift to the Right of Labour under Lord Levy's protégé Tony Blair, and in the US, the programme of Globalisation and World War Three ('clash of civilisation').

Give it a thought, Mr. Milne: if the Daughter of Zion could ally herself with the Left, why could she not change her partners? Should she be considered a permanently beneficial force, next to God Almighty? Jewish leadership benefited from the union with the Left while it was an aspiring force, struggling with the traditional upper classes. After their aspirations were satisfied, they had no more interest in such an ally.

For thirty years this major and obvious fact of the Jewish people's re-alignment was not sufficiently discussed by the Left. Like a ditched boyfriend, the Left hoped to re-forge the union of old. One ground for this hope was advanced sentimentally by Mr. Milne: "The Left's appeal to social justice and universal rights created a natural bond with a people long persecuted and excluded by the Christian European establishment."

Why should one describe as a 'natural bond' rather than a 'marriage of convenience' this relationship with the rich Jewish bankers and newspaper owners who had supported the Left? It was quite an unnatural bond, formed against the obvious class interests of the involved sides, and its collapse was inevitable. The Left accepted the help of rich Jews, disregarding their motives. It paid a heavy price: alienation from the working classes who had had a long and painful history of Jew-Gentile relations, alienation from the Church, and the uncompromising hostility of the upper classes. The Jews used the energy of the Left until it ran out, and then ditched it. Now, the Left can dial a phone number in New York and listen to the pre-recorded message.

II

Mr. Milne objects to Jews calling the Left 'anti-Semitic'. He thinks the Left does not deserve it. But it is mainly a point of definition. In the eyes of Mr. Milne, "anti-Semitism is an anti-Jewish racism," and its use, "a slur." In the Jewish eyes, 'anti-Semitism' is a policy counteracting the policy of the Jewish people. Thus, until 1968 the Right was 'anti-Semitic' by definition, as "the fates of the Jewish people and the Left have been closely intertwined." After 1968, as time moved on, the anti-globalisation Left (and Right), and environmentalist groups have become 'anti-Semitic' by definition. In 1953 McCarthy's Committee for anti-American activities was 'anti-Semitic', but in 2002 'anti-American' means 'anti-Semitic', according to *Commentary*, the main ideological Jewish American magazine.

In Russia of the 1990s, which I covered for the daily *Haaretz*, any movement against 'market forces', for socialism or for the preservation of the Soviet Union was considered 'anti-Semitic'. Anti-globalisation is 'anti-Semitic' as is objection to Zionist policies. Thus, the anti-Semitic labelling is not a slur but a definition of every policy at deviance with the present ideas of the Jewish People.

If you are NOT called an anti-Semite you should immediately reconsider your writing, Mr. Milne. But if you ARE called an anti-Semite it does not mean too much: even Wolfowitz, the Jewish Zionist bigot hawk and supporter of Sharon, was booed as an anti-Semite by more fervent American Jews. Even Ariel Sharon, the mass murderer of Sabra and Shatila, of Qibya and Jenin, was relegated to the ranks of the 'anti-Semite lefties' by the bloody-minded supporters of Benjamin Netanyahu.

That is why there is no reason to incessantly apologise for offending sensibilities. The Left can accept the offered definition and to reply with a shrug while being called 'anti-Semitic', as it would certainly respond to accusations of 'anti-British' or 'anti-aristocratic' behaviour. The Jews are not *Les Misérables* any more; since the 1960s, they occupy (in the US and Europe) a position similar to that of the Brahmins in India. The Left should try to undo their supremacy, while preserving and using their talents and abilities.

Even more important, it should overcome its rejected-lover syndrome and reassess its positions vis-à-vis the Jews in the light of Marxist teachings. Karl Marx (certainly not a biological Jew-hater) rejected his ties with the Jews and called for the emancipation of the world from Jews. Later, the Left chose to forget these words of Marx, but they can be brought back.

Mr. Milne writes, "Jews remain disproportionately active in progressive political movements—including Palestinian solidarity groups—throughout the world." There is a big difference between Marx and many politically active Jews. Marx and Trotsky were descendents of Jews who embraced the cause of the working people and rejected that of the Jews. Certainly there are descendents of Jews who emulate their behaviour, for instance in the al-Awdah movement. But there are other Jews who act as Jewish emissaries "in the progressive political movements—including Palestinian solidarity groups." Their contribution is but damage limitation. The war in Palestine caused these emissaries to reveal their hidden agenda and gave the Left a chance to reassert its cause.

The Left, free of its emotional entanglement with the Jewish people, should offer the Jews the same deal it offered after the French Revolution; namely, equality everywhere, including Palestine. Equality, not privilege. The Left's fight against the aristocracy and other traditional ruling classes was not for Jewish privilege.

Mr. Milne writes, "A two-state settlement (in the Middle East) is now the only possible way to secure peace in the foreseeable future." *Au contraire*, it is an impossible and unjust way, and it will never take place. The condition of equality means deconstruction of the exclusivist Jewish State and its transformation into a state of all its citizens, like other states. That is the way to peace, to justice and to a new rise of the Left in Europe and the world.

Notes

75. This slur of anti-semitism is used to defend repression.
    "Ending Israel's occupation will benefit Jews and Muslims in Europe," Seumas Milne [Thursday May 9, 2002] *The Guardian*:

    > Since the French revolution, the fates of the Jewish people and the left have been closely intertwined. The left's appeal to social justice and universal rights created a natural bond with a people long persecuted and excluded by the Christian

European establishment. From the time of Marx, Jews played a central role across all shades of the left. They were heavily represented among the leaders of the Russian revolution—hence Hitler's denunciation of communism as a "Judaeo-Bolshevik conspiracy"—and the left-led underground resistance to the Nazis. It was the Red Army which liberated the Auschwitz death camp. In Britain, it was the left which fought to defend the Jewish East End of London from fascists in the 1930s. In the Arab world, Jews were crucial to the building of political parties of the left. And despite the changed class balance of many Jewish communities, Jews remain disproportionately active in progressive political movements—including Palestinian solidarity groups—throughout the world. But now the left stands accused of anti-semitism because of its opposition to Israel's military occupation and continuing dispossession of the Palestinians. As the Palestinian intifada and Israeli repression rage on, rightwing commentators and religious leaders have claimed the left is guilty of "anti-Jewish prejudice," double standards towards Israel and even aping the anti-semitic "blood libels" of the Middle Ages with the ferocity of its charges of Israeli massacres. Britain's chief rabbi, Jonathan Sacks, has widened the attack to the media and equated any questioning of Israel's legitimacy with "calling into question the Jewish people's right to exist collectively." In the US, the denunciation of the left over Israel has been extended to include the whole mainstream European political system. A two-state settlement is now the only possible way to secure peace in the forseeable future.

On the Move

I

In the early autumn, when the pomegranates ripen, I embark for the ruins of the destroyed Palestinian village of Saffurie. The native city of Mary's mother, it still guards the Crusader church of St. Anne. This old village was an important city some two thousand years ago, when, under name of the Sepphoris, it refused to join the Jewish Zealots, and remained loyal to the Empire. It provided a comfortable home to the man who reinvented Judaism after its collapse, Rabbi Judah the Prince, and for many Christian sages and Roman nobles. It survived all vagaries of time, until in 1948 it was stormed by the Israeli army and destroyed. Its villagers became refugees and went to refugee camps or to nearby Nazareth.

The groves of the dead village remain hidden in the valleys, bringing full, off-round, heavy and bursting pomegranates each year, but there is nobody left to pick the fruit. People from the Jewish settlement built next to the ruins are indifferent to the fate of pomegranates and of the peasants who planted them. In this kingdom of desolation amid bountiful red-fruit-laden trees, there is also a carefully laid Roman floor mosaic sometimes called the Mona Lisa of Galilee. Its thousands of small stones of various shades form a proud elongated face with a straight nose, high hairdo and full lips and frame it with acanthus leaves.

This mosaic always reminds me of our beautiful world, this delightful mosaic of small towns, green meadows, civilized urban areas, castles and cottages, rivers and streams, churches and mosques. Each piece of the mosaic is fine, precious and perfect. I have seen lots of them and I love them all: the rocky, low-lying islands in the lucid and transparent Baltic where yellow-haired kids wave from the pier to passing ships; La France Profonde of Conque, a tiny hamlet in the Massif Central on the old pilgrim road to St. Jacques, where a narrow chatty river skirts the hill, the slated roofs, and streets paved a thousand years ago; domes of Russian churches in the high grass on Oka River, where girls in flowery shawls listen to a melody; pretty voices of Suzhou girls reverberate in the temple courtyard among canals criss-crossing South China; baroque houses of Trinidad tobacco factories and the proud bearing of Cubans dancing in its streets; the superb bodies of tattooed Masai around a bonfire in the Serengeti savannah. This world is lovely and its folks are very good.

This beautiful and intricate set-up is threatened by the forthcoming hostilities, as this Third World War is not only against the Third World. This war started even before the first bomb fell on the rocky ground of Afghanistan. A million new refugees are on the road, creating great commotion and unsettling Asia. Without a doubt, sooner or later the refugee wave will hit Europe. Hundreds of thousands of refugees already are on the move towards Europe, Russia and the relatively stable countries on the rim. One can understand them: as the US promised to use nuclear weapons against their homes, the defenceless population has no choice but to flee the target areas. No border controls will be able to withstand their hectic push. Pakistan will be first, but not last. As the US and Britain plan to turn their Crusade into a long war 'against terror', there will be more and more refugees, until, eventually, the fragile social fabric of Europe will crumble and collapse. Europe will be overrun, as was the Roman Empire in its day, and it will face a stark choice: establish a system of apartheid and discrimination, or lose its identity.

Will Europe be an incidental victim of American fury, like an innocent bystander in a Western shoot-out? It appears to me that Europe is one of the real targets of the forthcoming offensive. It is not what the ordinary people of the United States wish, but they are not being asked. The new ruling elites of the US and their partners and agents overseas have put the destruction of the prosperous, independent and cohesive Europe on their list. This desire has a practical short-term reason: Europe is a competitor to America; it is too independent and has established its own monetary unit that can displace the dollar. Europe supports a more evenly-balanced policy in Palestine. Europe is too egalitarian: in New York, I saw a lift boy, an immigrant from devastated Panama, who actually lives in the elevator. You would not find such things in Europe, as Europe is not yet Mammonized.

II

The new ruling elites do not care much for Christ or Muhammad, it is true, but they have a lot of religious feeling towards another old Deity, Mammon. This ancient god of greed was much loved by the Pharisees, some two millennia back, as we learn from the Gospel. Jesus told them: you can not serve both God and Mammon. But the Pharisees sneered at him, because they loved money.[76] This faith was pushed aside by the following development. Love of Mammon became known as Avarice, one of the Mortal Sins; it was condemned by Christian and Muslim societies alike.

But it did not disappear completely. Two thousand years later, a grandson of the Trier Rabbi, Karl Marx, came to a revolutionary conclusion: the faith of Mammon, this 'week-day religion of Jews', in his words, became the real religion of the American elites. Marx approvingly quoted a Colonel Hamilton: "Mammon is Yankee's idol; they worship it not only with their lips, but with all strength of their body and soul. In their eyes, the earth is but a stock exchange, and they are convinced that they do not have other purpose on earth but to become richer than their neighbours." Marx concluded, "The practical domination of the Jewish spirit over the Christian world has achieved in North America its unambiguous, complete expression."

This victorious Jewish spirit, for Marx, was based on "greed and egoism, its confession was business, it's god—Money."[77] These words, as other ideas of Karl Marx, were known but their deep spiritual meaning was not understood in full—for a good reason. Until our days, the religious features of the creed of Greed were not expressed, and one could imagine the possibility of a capitalist who thinks of his own interest and promotes the common good, as did Adam Smith.

Things changed with the advent of 'neo-liberalism'. Lectures of Milton Friedman manifested the 'outing' of Mammonites, adepts of the new/old faith. They differ from ordinary greedy folks, as they elevate Greed to the level of the jealous God that does not suffer other gods. The traditional wealthy men would not have dreamed of destroying their society. They cared about their land and community. They wanted to be the first among their own kind. They still considered themselves 'shepherds of men'. It is true that shepherds also eat sheep, but they would not sell the whole lot to the butcher just because the price is right.

The Mammonites see such consideration as a betrayal of Mammon. As Robert McChesney wrote in his Introduction to Noam Chomsky's *Profit over People*,[78] "They demand a religious faith in the infallibility of the unregulated market," in other words, a faith of egoism and greed unlimited. They are devoid of compassion to the people they live amongst, they do not see the local people as 'their own kind'. If they could eliminate local folk and supplant them with poor immigrants to optimise their profits, they would do it, as their brothers did in Palestine.

The Mammonites do not give a damn for the people of America, but use them as their tool to achieve world domination. Their ideal picture of the world is archaic, or futuristic: they dream of a world of slaves and masters. In order to achieve it, the Mammonites strive to destroy the cohesion of social and national units.

As long as people stay on their land, speak their tongue, live among their own kith and kin, drink water of their rivers, worship in their churches and mosques, they can not be enslaved. But if their lands are flooded by masses of refugees, their social structure will collapse. They will lose their great advantage, the feeling of belonging together, the feeling of brotherhood, and they will become an easy prey for Mammonites.

III

Afghanis are wonderful folk, sturdy, independent, self-reliant. They are formed by their mountains, and like all highlanders, they are quite stubborn and conservative. Fear of American bombs would push them into the lowlands of Holland and into the cities of France, and they will unwillingly but irreversibly change the land they enter. This process has been going on for quite a while. As the global policies of the Mammonites deplete the poor countries of the Third world, pump out natural resources and incomes, support the nasty quisling rulers and destroy their nature, more and more people are forced to join the stream of refugees to Europe and the US.

This threat is already felt in Europe. Oriana Fallaci, a well-known Italian journalist, published in the leading Milanese newspaper, *Corriere della Sera*,[79] an article bewailing the fate of Europe overrun by 'Muslim hordes'. She viewed immigrants as a courtier of Romulus in Ravenna, considered the Germanic warriors. Oriana says that "Somali Muslims defaced and shitted on and outraged for three months the main square of my city," that some "children of Allah" urinated on the walls of the Cathedral, that they had mattresses inside the tent "to sleep and fuck on" and poisoned the square with the smell and smoke of their cooking. Oriana goes on to say that Florence, "once the capital of art and culture and beauty" is "wounded and humiliated" by "arrogant Albanians, Sudanese, Bengalese, Tunisians, Algerians, Pakistanis and Nigerians" who "sell drugs" and pimp whores. She calls for the support of an American-led Crusade and contends, "If America falls, then Europe will fall . . . instead of church bells, there will be the muezzins, instead of miniskirts, chadors, instead of cognac, camel's milk."

Before condemning her style, let us attend the faults of her logic. Ms. Fallaci, an experienced and not too young journalist sees in America a possible protection, rather than the source of her, and Florence's, trouble. She should be worried by victory, not by fall of America. If America succeeds in her Afghan war, Oriana's nightmare can become a reality.

She does not want to notice that the refugees and immigrants are arriving in Italy because their lands were devastated by the US and its allies. She would not be seeing Albanians if NATO had not ravaged the Balkans. She would not be seeing Sudanese, if Clinton had not bombed the Sudan. She would not see Somalis, if Somaliland had not been ruined by Italian colonization and American intervention. Neither she, nor America would see a Palestinian immigrant if the peasants of Saffurie could still be tending their pomegranate groves.

Nobody, but nobody would leave his own land with its unique nature, lifestyle, friends and relatives, holy places and fathers' graves for the dubious pleasure of camping by the walls of an Italian Cathedral. Like ducklings have their imprinting, men are born to love their native land. Young Telemachus compares his lean and rocky island with the broad meadows and rich fields of Lacedaemon, and says to his host, "We have no meadow land at all, and my island rises rock-like from the sea. Yet its goat-pastures are more lovely in my sight than your fields for grazing horses."[80] People immigrate when their lands are ruined. The Irish would not have left the green fields of Erin for Chicago, if the English government had not starved them out. My own Russians would not have come to occupy Palestine if Russia had not been ruined by the pro-American forces of Yeltsin and Chubais.

For host folk, an immigration wave is a nuisance at best, a disaster at worst. It is not their fault; it is the question of numbers. Carlos Castaneda joined an Indian tribe and learned a lot of their ways. I am sure the tribe learned something from Carlos Castaneda. Now imagine that a thousand wonderful guys and gals from Yale and Berkeley join the Indian tribe. The tribe would disappear; it would not be able to keep its ways. While a single émigré is always welcome and adds colour to a society, mass immigration is no better than invasion.

Whether immigrants come as invaders and conquerors, or as refugees, the receiving society gets a shock. If they are smart, they push local people away from interesting and important social positions and create their own subculture. If they are violent, they can take over the land by other means. If they are humble and timid, they will bring down the price of labour. That is why in normal circumstances immigrants are not popular.

A good man and my friend, Miguel Martinez, who brought Oriana's article to the attention of the English-reading audience, was justly horrified by her racism. He is right; Ms. Fallaci speaks as a racist, as does Ann Coulter, this American scourge of 'swarthy men'. But he failed to see some truth in her words. A man whose garden was overrun by buffaloes does not notice the hunter who rushes the herds his way and then blames the innocent animals. He is mistaken: the blame rests with the hunter—but that does not mean the buffaloes did not ruin the garden. Mass immigration is painful for immigrant and host alike.

But it is not painful for the Mammonites. They actually like immigration, as it lowers the price of labour. A leading Mammonite magazine is the British weekly, the *Economist*. Their leader called a few weeks ago, before the 'new Pearl Harbour' for an increased intake of immigrants from the Third World. The most dynamic, best qualified people from Africa, Asia and South America could be useful for Britain, Europe and the US, wrote the *Economist*. They would push down the salaries of European workers and increase profits for entrepreneurs. As a side profit, the outflow of the dynamic element weakens the donor societies and makes them an easy prey for hostile takeover. It is an improved version of slave trade, as what could be better than willing slaves competing to board a slave ship. Naturally, the pre-condition for such an intake was not articulated in the leader: the countries of the Third World must be devastated and ruined.

Mammonites need immigrants for their own sake, as well. A cohesive and healthy society rejects men of greed instinctively, as greed is a socially destructive drive. In a healthy society, Mammonites would remain pariahs. Immigration destroys cohesiveness of the host society. Mammonites do not like their society being cohesive; they prefer it thinnish and liquescent, thus easier to drink up. That is why Mammonites support immigration. Immigrants conceive them as their natural allies and fail to comprehend that the Mammonites like them as vampires like fresh blood. Because of this lack of understanding, immigrants support with their votes the Mammonite power of Tony Blair and the New York Democrats. It is the Mammonites, who should be on the receiving end of Oriana's diatribes, not the innocent immigrants on the streets and squares of Europe.

IV

A Mammonite senator for California, Diane Feinstein, imports more and more poor Mexicans into her state. They give her the vote, stay out of politics for many years, agree to work for less and undermine organised labour. Ordinary Californians live worse, but she does not care. Some people consider her a Zionist by virtue of her support for Israel.

However, it would be a mistake to call her a Zionist. Historically, Zionists felt that man needs roots. They considered the easy mobility of Jews to be a symptom of deficiency. They wanted to provide the rootless Jews with roots in the Holy Land. Mammonites do not understand who needs roots. They want to uproot everybody. Zionists felt the Mammonite way of life was wrong. Mammonites of all backgrounds adopted the way of life discarded by Zionists.

The Zionists were wrong as they did not understand that without Palestinians they can not achieve their goal of striking roots in the soil of Palestine. They were wrong, as a person of Jewish origin can strike his root anywhere, not only in Palestine. A Jew can become an American, English, Russian as well as Palestinian. It calls for identification with his countrymen, for supreme concern with his land. Every land is a Promised Land to the man who loves it. People who force America to send away billions of dollars to Israel instead of providing for America's poor are not loyal to America. But they are not loyal to Israel, either. They admire Israel as the model of their world.

Many good men dislike Zionism, for it caused this massive destruction of the lovely land of Palestine and uprooted Palestinians. But Zionism is a local disease. Its big brother, Mammonitis, is a world-wide plague that wants to turn the world into a 'Big Israel' with shopping malls and destroyed villages, settlements for the chosen few, and many-many refugees as a source of cheap labour. Zionists ruined the nature of Palestine, Mammonites ruin the world environment. Zionists uprooted Palestinians, Mammonites uproot all.

Zionists fight Christ. In modern Israel, St. Paul and St. Peter would be jailed for teaching the Gospel. Mammonites fight every faith, every conviction, Christ and Muhammad, Nationalism and Communism. The enemies of Zionism hope

Mammonites will rein in the Zionists, as the too independent policy of Zionists can become an obstacle to the world-embracing plans of Mammonites. But I tell you, God tolerates the excesses of Zionists so you will notice the plans of Mammonites.

V

This is not the cry of a dyed-in-the-wool Leftie. We can live with some people of wealth; we can survive some amount of privilege. Both the Left and the Right are good and needed by society, just as the left leg and the right leg are needed for standing up. Imagine a springtime meadow in the Jerusalem mountains, a magic carpet of flowers, that calls you to recline on it. If masses swamp it, there will be no flowers left. If it is fenced away, none will enjoy it. These two tendencies: access and preservation, are the paradigms of the Left and the Right. Their correct combination allows many people to enjoy the meadow.

The Right is the conservative force, preserving the power of the traditional elites. They save the landscape, protect nature, uphold tradition. The Left is the moving force of society, the guarantee of its liveliness, of capacity for change, of social mobility. A society without its Left would rot; a society without its Right would collapse. The Left provides movement, the Right guarantees stability. But Mammonites create for their purposes a pseudo-Left and a pseudo-Right, and deploy the errors of the real Left and Right.

One of the faults of the European 'real' Right was its lack of compassion and racist tendency. Their knee-jerk reflex was correct: immigrants destabilize the society. But it is not because immigrants are lesser men, as racists say. Immigrants can be wonderful folk, and still be trouble. The Dutch moved to Indonesia, and plagued the land for quite a while by their presence. They ruined Indonesia heavily. Indonesians went to Holland and troubled it back. English plagued America in the heavy way: they exterminated the natives. Colonial process often leads to mutual plaguing: Brits despoiled Ireland and were troubled by the Irish.

Racism is wrong, as it claims that some groups of men are inherently better or worse than others. Everybody is wonderful: Zulu and British, Russian and Chechen, Palestinian and French, Pakistani and Turk, while on home ground. On others' land, these good people become a nuisance. In the days of European imperialism and colonial expansion, racist theories were necessary to justify the one-sided flow of men. Without racism, one could not exterminate natives, take their property, ban their industries, create huge landholdings, and deprive people of basic human rights. But now racism is not needed anymore. As the colonial adventure of Europe is over, the morally wrong and scientifically mistaken theory of racial superiority can be laid to rest.

The real Left should promote the interests of working classes, which means it must object to mass immigration. But, under Mammonite influence, the liberal Left supports immigration for the reason of compassion. Mammonites, normally devoid of compassion, utilise this humanitarian reasoning for their own purposes. It gives them an additional profit: European and American working people are being alienated from the Left. For workers, the dangerous nature of immigration is obvious. Immigrants live in close quarters with the local workers and suffer from their competition for work places. Thus, they are forced to embrace the racist Extreme Right.

There is a good way out of the impasse, a way that is good for everybody but Mammonites. Stop immigration and open a money-transfer line to the Third World. Africa and Sweden should have the same income. Tax money should flow to the Indians of the Amazon and to the peasants of Afghanistan. Not many Pakistanis would immigrate to Britain, if they had the same (or almost the same) income back home. The European Commission is proof of this: though the Swedes still earn more than the Portuguese, Greeks and Italians, the difference is not that big, and these lands are peaceful, so there is very little inter-communal immigration into Sweden or Germany. In the matter of compassion, true Christian compassion tells you to let people live at home, under their vines and their fig trees, as good as they would live in your land. You would not have very cheap cleaners, but you will live in a cleaner and better land. That would be just, as for hundreds of years Europe and the US pumped wealth out of the South and the East.

The immigrant's lot is a sad one. After all, immigration is exile, this saddest state of man. Ovid bewailed it on the Moldavian shore, and prince Genji decried in Suma. My Palestinian friend Musa brought his elderly father from the village of Aboud to his new home in Vermont, and the old man began to build terraces, as on the slopes of the Samarian hills. We are so much a part of the landscape, part and parcel with mountains and valleys. Now, when in the US there are attacks on immigrants, probably many of them think of their homes they were forced to leave.

Although I think that immigration should be stopped and supplanted by transfer of funds to the poorer lands until incomes level, immigrants who have already come over, have probably come to stay. They can become locals: Germans in Germany, French in France, Americans in America, Palestinians in Palestine. The ancestors of European and American people also migrated and adapted to new ways. Germanic tribes of Franks overran Romanised Celtic Gaul, and together with its old population they formed the modern French. Descendents of European Crusaders still live in the Palestinian village Sinjil that preserves the glorious name of the Provençal commander Raymond de St. Gilles, but they have become Palestinians in every way and are being besieged by Israelis like everyone else. Likewise, the Georgians were brought eight hundred years ago to the Jerusalemite village of Malcha by the orders of Queen Tamar. They became Palestinian, and shared the fate of other Palestinians when they were expelled from their houses by Zionist invaders in 1948.

Human beings are adaptable, and if the immigrants love their new land, they can become locals. I know it: a native of Siberia, I choose to become a Palestinian.

VI

WWIII is a war against variety *per se*, initiated by the adepts of Greed. They do not like the delightful mosaic of races and cultures; they would rather homogenise the world. They have a practical reason: it is easier to sell goods to homogenised mankind. They have a moral reason: they do not want people to enjoy this beauty for free, so it has to be destroyed. They have a religious reason: the Mammon worshippers feel this jolly plurality is a sacrilege against their jealous god. Beautiful things of old belong in a museum, where they can charge an entrance fee, after the village is destroyed.

In a beautiful adolescent movie, *The Never-Ending Story*, the many-coloured world of Fantasy disappears into Nowhere. The same thing happens to our marvellous world. Old and unique places are being erased and supplanted by shopping malls and scorched land. The Left and the Right should join forces against the Nowhere that threatens our very existence.

The positive role of immigrants already settled in Europe is discussed in the following essay.

Notes

76. Lk 16, 13–14.
77. *Deutch-Franzosische Jahrbucher*, 1844.
78. Chomsky, *Profit Over People*, Seven Stories Press, 1999, page 8.
79. English translation: "Leading Italian Daily Spews Racist Hatred," by Miguel Martinez http://www.kelebekler.com Italian original Saturday 29 September 2001, "Corriere della Sera."
80. Odyssey IV.

The Sparrow and the Beetle

I

Around 1923, a Russian poet Carney Chukovsky wrote a delightful short tale for children, "Tarakan the Giant Beetle," an all-time favourite nursery rhyme for Russian kids. It is a story of the Animal Kingdom intimidated by Tarakan. The Beetle threatened to devour the disobedient animals, and the awed Lions and Tigers were holed up in their lairs. True, a beetle has no fangs or horns, but menacing Tarakan would brandish his great long mustache, and no beast would dare to challenge the small monster, until a little Sparrow flew in and ate up the Beetle, to everyone's relief. Despite his threats, Tarakan was just an insect.

This nursery rhyme came to my mind as the great nations of Europe, "whose step once shook the earth, who endeavoured revolutions of great magnitude, populated new continents, conceived and inspired faiths and religions," tremble in fear like schoolchildren in front of their strict teacher. Once, England ruled the waves, English Tommies climbed the Khyber pass, marched into Cairo and stormed the Atlantic Wall. A Prime Minister of England could decide the fate of millions. Now, he can't apologise fast enough for a *faux-pas* of his wife, who dared to doubt the divine right of Jews to murder Palestinian children as they see fit.

The French were not afraid to get rid of their king and aristocracy, to disestablish their Church, to conquer Africa and move out of Algeria. But their selfless adoration of the Jews was put in doubt, and they lost their confidence. The Germans created the best music, philosophy and science, and Germany was the first welfare state in human history. Now they go into a collective toxic shock whenever the word 'Jew' is pronounced. Europeans agreed to become 'younger brothers of Jews', and follow the line ordered by New York and Tel Aviv.

The fate of Americans is not better. Proud to the point of arrogance, they assumed the White Man's Destiny will lead them from conquest to conquest. They took over the great landmass of North America, forcibly opened the doors of Japan, and won two world wars, just to find themselves strangers in their own house. Now, instead of their own history, they study the Holocaust; instead of promoting their own interests, they fight mercenary wars for Israel. They work harder and harder to supply the goods to their new elite. They judge the world by one criterion, 'whether it is good for Jews'.

Fear of the Jews has become ridiculous and disproportionate. We Jews have no horns and fangs, we should be treated like any group of people our size and cultural output: say, Welsh or Slovak. It is a cause of embarrassment for everybody concerned, not least to ordinary folks of Jewish origin. It is the right time for the fearless Sparrow to come in and deflate the overblown Tarakan, and to save the Lions and the Tigers, as well as the little white Lamb of the Holy Land. Well, the Sparrow is here, and I have seen it.

II

Marseille is a dynamic neat Mediterranean city facing one of the best harbours in the world, well protected by its two forts. The hometown of the French Revolution and of the French national anthem, it was sung by Pagnol, but not everybody in Marseille is called Marius; not everybody drinks Pastis. The City's hero is called Zidane, a Franco-Arab football player of renown. In the Medina, the colourful Oriental Quarter of the City, throngs of relaxed and joyful Franco-Arabs, natives of France, second and third generation of Algerians, Tunisians and Moroccans create an exciting mixture of Maghreb and Provence. They are free people, restful and fearless. I was guided there by Rabha Attaf, a large jovial smiling and chatty woman in a colourful long and spacious dress, born in France but keeping ties with the other shore of the Mediterranean. Rabha was chairing a conference for equality of Jew and Gentile in the Holy Land.

It was a great relief to meet jolly Rabha and her friends, children of immigrants and natives of Provence. They cared for Palestine and did not care for the seal of kosher approval by the crypto-Zionists. Such approval is not coming cheaply: the Jews for Two States allow activists a meagre defence against anti-Semitic labelling and extract recognition of the exclusionary racist Jewish state in exchange.

A crypto-Zionist I met in Marseille gave me the most ingenious argument against universal suffrage. "Israel is a racist state," she said. "Why do you want the Palestinians to become citizens of the racist state?" It was almost as good as Zeno's proof that Achilles would never overtake a tortoise.

In the city of the Golden Gate, beautiful San Francisco, I met the second generation of immigrants who achieved prosperity, but saved their hearts and desire to help. They do not embrace the Judeo-American faith, they remain immune to the Mammonite malady, and they are not easily intimidated by the slur of anti-Semitism. Together with the brave Afro-Americans, immigrants retain the true American values lost by many docile WASPs.

Immigrants from the Muslim world usually are described as 'Muslims' or 'Arabs', though many of them belong to Eastern Christian Churches, Orthodox, Maronite or Nestorian. They have found a new home in Europe, and became a part of the old continent's new mosaic. They even object to continuing immigration as much as anybody. Innocent of the WWII guilt, Semitic by race (if it exists) and language, free of hate or fear of Jews, certain in their religious beliefs, they are probably the only people (excluding Israeli dissidents) who are not afraid to take on the Judeo-Zionist establishment. They smile at the slur of 'anti-Semitism' as the Sparrow probably smiled at Tarakan's menacing mustachio.

These days, the immigrants have received their baptism of fire in Germany, the European stronghold of Zionist influence. The Syrian-born German MP, Jamal Karsli, called on Germany to stop selling weapons to Israel because, among other things, its armed forces employ Nazi methods. Immediately his own Green party ditched him. A lesser man would learn the might of the Giant Beetle and retire, but this Asian Sparrow joined the Free Democratic Party (FDP) and broke another taboo by openly speaking in an interview about the strong influence of the Zionist lobby over the German media.

The Zionist minders of Germany launched a ferocious attack on the brave man. Karsli was forced to resign from his new party and, at a very crucial moment for the Palestinians, most of the potential German supporters of a just peace in the Middle East became almost completely neutralized, wrote Shraga Elam, an Israeli dissident living in Germany. Many courageous Israeli dissidents, including Dr. Ilan Pappe of Haifa University and Gideon Spiro of the Israeli Campaign for Mordechai Vanunu, supported Karsli.

Shraga Elam writes: "In the present atmosphere in Germany many people are afraid to utter loudly what they think and to express their legitimate critique against Israeli war crimes. Because of this, a growing number of people feel that only the right-wing radicals are courageous enough to declare publicly the widespread disapproval of Israeli politics."

His analysis practically coincides with that of Dr. Kevin MacDonald, a California State University Professor, who wrote: "In Germany, a critical discussion of Jewish policies . . . is virtually impossible. Whether conservative or liberal, a contemporary German intellectual who says anything outside a narrowly defined spectrum of codified pieties about Jews runs the risk of professional and social suicide. Discussions of the work of Jewish intellectuals have come to dominate German intellectual life to the almost complete exclusion of non-Jewish Germans. Scholars have lost all sense of normal standards of intellectual criticism and have come to identify more or less completely with the Jewish victims of Nazism. Jewish writers like Kafka are seen as intellectual giants who are above criticism. Even minor Jewish writers are elevated to the highest levels of the literary canon while Germans like Thomas Mann are discussed mainly because they held views on Jews that have become unacceptable in polite society. Indeed, it is not too far fetched to suppose that German culture as the culture of Germans has disappeared entirely, replaced by the culture of the Holocaust."[81]

It seems even obedient Germans got tired of it. Just a few days after the brave interview of Jamal Karsli, the Germans flocked to buy a controversial novel, *Death of a Critic* by Martin Walser. The main character in the book, a creative writer, kills a vehement Jewish critic (like in Bulgakov's *Master and*

Margarita). The leading German newspaper, *Frankfurter Allgemeine Zeitung* called the novel 'anti-Semitic,' but it was sold out on its first day of publication in Germany. A few years ago, Walser caused the rage of the Zionist lobby in Germany saying the WWII tragedy was used as a "moral cudgel" to hammer home "German disgrace for current-day purposes."

Apparently, Europe and America need immigrants from the Islamic world as the jungle needs the fearless Sparrow. That is a great irony of history, as immigrants were considered natural and obedient allies of anti-nationalist forces. Now these allies have parted their ways.

III

Immigration from the Islamic world was an important tool of the neo-liberal, globalist, Mammonite policy. While good people helped refugees, the Mammonites encouraged immigration as a means to lower native workers' salaries, to extract more profit by using cheap foreign labour and to undermine homogeneity of the society. The new rich outsiders supported immigration in order to displace traditional elites and occupy their place. European nationalists had a valid reason to object to the immigration from Dar al-Islam, as they perceived it a threat to their society's traditional way of life.

But the Mammonites stepped on their own petard. The immigrants had settled, moved socially upwards and discovered the unwritten taboos of the Western society. They noticed that the Mammonites obstruct their social integration and full participation in the public discourse. "Could it be that Arab-Americans can't write?" exclaimed the gifted Ahmed Amr from Seattle as he noticed the Jewish owners and editors of newspapers openly discriminate against immigrants from the East. The immigrants noticed that the persecutors of Palestinians are their real adversaries, and they have had no hate or fear of Jews. It caused the rift between the immigrants and their former supporters. From Marseille to Berlin, from San Francisco to Rome, a new constellation took place, as the Mammonites dropped the Politically correct and started to attack the immigrants.

A top Jewish official, Stephen Steinlight, Director of National Affairs at the American Jewish Committee,[82] frankly called on the Jews "to disregard our own Politically Correct gods, and to risk upsetting old and new friends and allies." Unless the Jews contain the immigrants, said Steinlight, "Jewish political power will diminish." "Our present privilege, success and power do not inure us from the effect of historical processes. We have an enormous stake in the outcome of the process, and we cannot contemplate the loss of power with complacency." In order to protect their privilege, Jews should discourage non-Jewish immigration and undermine the meagre influence of the immigrants, as "the non-European immigrants harbour no feelings of guilt and see the Jews only as the most privileged and powerful of white Americans." The white Americans are docile and obedient, but the immigrants from the Muslim world, whether Muslims or Orthodox Christians, do not accept the Jewish privilege as a norm.

Steinlight expressed hatred to Latinos, "who unseated our best congressmen," but utmost hostility of this spokesman of Jewry is aimed at Muslims and Eastern Christians, immigrants and converts alike, who threaten "our disproportionate political power." He proposed to use "the Jewish power disproportionally concentrated in Hollywood, TV and news industry" in order to "divide and conquer" various communities of Americans.

Steinlight draws a self-portrait of an American Judeo-Nazi: "I was taught that Israel is my true homeland. More tacitly and subconsciously I was taught the superiority of my people to the gentiles. We were taught to view non-Jews as untrustworthy outsiders, while the primary division in the world was between 'us' and 'them.' "

The policy of "divide and conquer" was executed in Europe through publication and promotion of the racist writings by Oriana Falacci. Take her article, substitute 'Jews' for 'Muslims', publish it and you will find yourself in jail doing five years for a hate crime. Put 'Muslims' back and laugh all the way to the bank. Muslims for Falacci are "scoundrels with a turban or kaffiah."

The mass murderer of Sabra and Shatila, Qibie and Jenin is "the tragic and Shakespearean figure Sharon." Well, Shakespeare has such figures, but usually they have no names, just 'Second Murderer'.

Oriana regrets that "nobody can keep a Mustafa or a Mohammed from enrolling in a University (something I hope will change)." Indeed, let them wash dishes, as in her beloved Israel.

She blasphemes Jesus Christ, and refers to "a Jew without whom the priests would all be unemployed" (probably Judas?).

Her narration of history is as perverted as that of the present. She writes: "I find it shameful that almost all of the Left forgets the contribution made by the Jews to the fight against fascism." One could add, "but the present fascist Right of Italy did not forget the contribution made by the Jews to the cause of fascism." Indeed, many Italian Jews ardently supported Italian fascism from its very beginning. Three out of five Martyrs of Fascism were Jews, and there were Jewish ministers in the governments of Mussolini. Zionist leaders, including Sharon's mentor Jabotinsky, adored Italian fascists, and now, the neo-fascist party of Italy is a good friend of Sharon and of the state of Israel.

The enlightened Jews, yesterday's fighters against racism, now support this Judeo-Nazi line. A liberal Jewish professor forwarded to me her article with an introduction saying, "What Oriana Fallaci is saying about the Islamic leaders is eye-opening. This is a real prophetic call addressed to the West. If we do not realize where the danger comes from, it will be over with us." Yes, it is indeed eye-opening. It should open eyes on the new idea promoted by the Masters of Discourse: "You may be a racist to anybody, as long as you are OK to Jews."

This concept was spelt out by Alexander Chancellor in the *Guardian*[83] in his eulogy of the assassinated Dutch right-wing leader Pim Fortuyn aptly called "Not Black and White." The late saint "was never suspected of anti-Semitism. Islam was his great enemy and he supported Israel in its war against Palestinians." It makes this enemy of immigrants a good guy even for the liberal *Guardian*. I hope the Guardian will provide us with portraits of other saints, as well. What about Jack the Ripper? He was never suspected of anti-Semitism, either.

Nor was Mussolini, neither was Franco. As Albert Lindemann[84] convincingly demonstrated, Adolf Hitler was unique in his rejection of Jews. Other fascists, most notably Mussolini, tried to persuade Hitler to desist of his struggle with Jews, as they did. Judeo-Nazism proposed by Steinlight, preached by Oriana Falacci, exemplified by Ariel Sharon, accepted by the *Guardian*, is the winning proposition, the one the Masters of the Discourse are trying now on our world. Not in vain, an Israeli government delegation participated in deliberations of the European extreme Right in Brussels.

It is a complicated and decisive moment in the history of European and American Nationalist forces. A generation ago, they were pushed to fight Communism, and in the end both antagonists found themselves almost extinct. Now the same forces bent on 'divide et impera' try to set them up and against the immigrants from the Muslim world, in order to preserve "unprecedented power and privilege of American Jewry." The Mammonites have powerful tools: media and universities, a political system and business. It is a moment when the enemies of yesteryear, leaders of Nationalists and immigrants should meet and work out a common strategy, for the general well-being and against privilege.

"The Prince of the World could pervert any idea of the Lord; but the Lord can turn every Satan's idea into a wonderful thing."[85]

[This is an ashamed apology of Islam and Muslims. I live in the Dar al-Islam, the Islamic World, and feel daily its wonderful humanity and tolerance.]

Notes

81. Kevin MacDonald, Preface to Second edition of the *Culture of Critique*.
82. http://www.cis.org/articles/2001/back1301.html.
83. 18 May 2002, *Guardian Weekly*.
84. Albert Lindemann, *Esau's Tears*, 1997.
85. "Apocalypse Now," see on www.israelshamir.net.

Part VI

Maidens and Warriors

I

It is not much fun to be a Muslim in the West today. Not even to be taken for one. I felt it in my own skin while flying into the US. A Mediterranean man with mustachio complete, I was asked by the US customs officer whether I read the Koran a lot. A piece of chewing gum wrapping paper with a comic strip on it has been mistaken by this officer for an instruction to pray on board the plane, call *Allahu Akbar* and attack the crew.

"You are up to no good," he concluded. I was taken aback. Our Palestinian brothers and we Israelis are facially quite similar; I am often taken for a Palestinian by both sides, but I did not expect US immigration to copycat the Israeli Border Police.

Should I say plainly, "I am not a Muslim"? It did not seem fair. In occupied Denmark of 1940, the Germans ordered the Jews to wear the yellow Star of David, and according to the folktale, the king of the Danes wore such a star as a sign of his solidarity with his Jewish subjects. Would I fail this test of common humanity and proclaim my non-Muslim kosher origin? It would feel like the sacrificing of a Muslim in my stead. I tried to compromise:

"I do not read the Koran a lot," said I.

The officer, one Gomez, a big dark man, did not relent. "But you read Koran?"

"Occasionally," I tried again.

This cowardly response was the beginning of my undoing. I was searched and verbally abused; every piece of my luggage was checked and double-checked.

The personal affront did not matter. In 1812, a French soldier on the streets of occupied Moscow turned back Pierre Bezuchov, a Russian nobleman in Tolstoy's *War and Peace*. "The soldier had stopped my immortal soul," thought Bezuchov, and laughed. St. Francis of Assisi found even more joy at being refused entry to a monastery one cold and rainy night. A turn at being humiliated is good for the soul, he explained to his sidekick St. Bernard.

It was more upsetting to see Islam as the accused in the Judeo-American culture. In the US newspapers and on the Internet, theological debates are back in vogue with a vengeance after an eight-hundred-year lull, and are as subtle as ever. Even good friends of Muslims began to hesitate as the powerful brainwashing machine started to produce its hateful output. Islam is accused of being the faith of Jihad, the permanent war with infidels, of intolerance and cruelty, of providing the theological basis of terrorism. The allegations do not stop at politics.

The semi-literate Crusaders of the Twelfth Century accused the Muslims of having orgies in front of their divinity, Baphomet (probably corrupted from the name of the Prophet). The latest frontal attack on American public opinion of Islam has amusing sexual overtones, too. An appeal to bomb the hell out of Afghanistan, Iraq, Syria, and Palestine usually contains a weighty disapproval of the Prophet's sexual mores and of the alleged Muslim ill-treatment of their womenfolk.

II

The Prophet's love of his youngest wife, Aisha, causes much consternation in America; almost fifty years after the US Supreme Court removed the ban on that ode to underage love, Vladimir Nabokov's *Lolita*. For the prudish accusers it does not matter that Muhammad, peace be upon him, was in love with the girl, as she was with him. They know better what is good for everybody. If the Prophet had chosen a boy of Aisha's age, one feels that fear of homophobia would soften the blows. But the Prophet was a man of orthodox tastes.

A modest Talmudic scholar from Jaffa, I would rise to his defence in the name of our Jewish tradition. Far from being a sinner, Muhammad (peace be upon him) acted according to the letter and the spirit of our holy faith. Biblical Jacob fell in love with Rachel when she was only seven, and brought forth from her a line of saints including Mary, mother of Christ.

The Talmud stipulates the permitted age of marriage for girls at "three years and one day." This gives us a dialogue worthy of Boccaccio that took place in Sepphoris of Galilee. A Roman princess Justine, daughter of Emperor Septimius Severus, son of Anthony asked Rabbi Judah the Prince, the greatest spiritual and legal authority of Jews in the post-Biblical period, the permitted age for marriage and cohabitation.

"Three years and one day," replied the Rabbi.

"What is the age for childbearing?" persisted the Princess.

"Nine years,"[86] he replied.

"I was married at six, and gave birth at seven," she reflected with great regret, "so I wasted in vain three excellent years of my young life."

Muhammad's wife, Aisha, wasted *six* years of her young life, as she was wed at nine. Thus, the Prophet demonstrated great prudence, and is in full accord with our Jewish teachings. Our holy Rabbis permitted very early marriage, but they were not absolutely sure that three-year-old girls are sufficiently ripe. They taught: proselytes and paedophiles delay the Coming of the Messiah and of the Kingdom of Heaven.

"Who are the paedophiles in this context?" asked the Talmud. They have to be persons of legitimate but objectionable behaviour, and therefore, not the sodomites (as they deserve death by stoning) nor masturbators (they merit a watery grave). It is those who marry girls before the nubile age of nine. Thus, the Prophet is above suspicion, according to our Jewish law.

He had a few wives, continue the accusers. Well, Jewish law permits us to have as many wives as we can get. Nowadays a Muslim has to limit himself to four wives in this world, but we Jews have no such constrictions.

The presumed barbarous Muslim custom of veiling women and keeping them away from a stranger's lusty eye annoys today's accusers. An avid reader of the *Washington Post* would assume that the US attacked Afghans just to bomb the veil away. As the first fruit of American victory in Afghanistan, CNN presented the sale of smut in smitten Kabul.

Here again, our Jewish law firmly stands on the side of the Talibs. A Talmudic sage, Rabbi Isaac taught: "If one gazes at the little finger of a woman, it is as if he gazed at her you-know-what!" (Do not confuse it with the You-Know-Who of Harry Potter.)

Rabbi Hisda wistfully noted: "A woman's leg is also quite an incitement."

Rabbi Sheshet improved on him, reminding that "a woman's hair is a sexual incitement." That is why pious Jewish women don the wig. And that master of oneupmanship, Samuel, upstaged him saying, "A woman's voice is a sexual incitement, as quoth the Holy Writ: 'sweet is thy voice.' " The conclusion of the debate was the rule *kvod bat ha-melech pnima*, meaning "a good Jewish woman should stay indoors," which is the Taliban's idea, or close enough.

III

Enemies of Islam would not dare to attack our Jewish faith, though all the features of Islam they profess to dislike can be found in Judaism. This goes beyond sexual matters. Jihad is but an Arab translation of the Jewish concept of *Milhemet Mitzva*, the Commanded (or Preordained) War. These concepts differ in this: in *jihad*, one is not allowed to kill civilians, but in *milhemet mitzvah*, one is commanded to do so. Look up in your Pentateuch and you will find it there, without an effort. The Messenger, peace be upon him, softened this Message.

If you think Islam is intolerant, let me quote you the story written by "the perfect sage and excellent doctor of medicine, R. Samuel Sholem, in Constantinople, capital of the great King, our ruler, mighty Sultan Suleiman" about Rabbi Gaon Isaac Campanton (d. 1463), the chief rabbi of the Castilian community, the most enlightened Jewish community of all times. He writes:

> The great Rabbi, the honorable R. Isaac Campanton burned Rabbi Samuel Sarsa at the stake. Once, Rabbis gathered to announce a marriage contract. They read "such and such a year since the Creation of the world," and this Sarsa fellow placed his hand on his beard and alluded to the world's existence since time immemorial. The Rabbi Campanton rose to his feet and exclaimed, "Why isn't the bush consumed?[87] Let the bush burn!" They sentenced him to death by burning because he denied the Creation of the World to be 5000 years ago, and burned him at the stake.

If you believe Islam is the reason for Muslim terrorism, probably Judaism is the reason for Jewish terrorism. Until now, Muslims succeeded in assassinating only one Israeli minister. When Jews dealt in private (as opposed to state) terror, my saintly ancestors assassinated two Russian tsars and a whole row of government ministers, officials, ambassadors and statesmen of Britain, Germany, Sweden, Russia and Arab countries. At the present time, the records of terror established by Jews are not beaten, and as a proud Jew I reject the futile efforts to pass this crowning achievement to Muslims or to anybody else.

In America, Jews can't do wrong, and whoever thinks otherwise, is branded an anti-Semite or self-hating Jew. By proving the Jewish origin of the alleged faults of Islam, we therefore proved that the Islam-bashers are anti-Semites and probably hidden Holocaust deniers. Whoever doubts this may look up the *Washington Post* of November 27, 2001. The editorial by the ex-CIA chief, James Woolsey, is accompanied by a much-retouched hysterical close-up picture of the bestial and demonic Semite, dark-skinned, full-lipped, cruel, and savage. *Der Sturmer*, the Nazi newspaper, would have loved it. The contents of the article are also eminently suitable for *Der Sturmer*. Woolsey, in an Orwellian-named article, *Objective: Democracy*, calls to "take out Iraqi air defences and hit Iraqi ground forces" as "we did to Afghanistan."

The great Russian playwright, Anton (*The Seagull*) Chekhov, established a law for stage settings: if there is a gun hanging on the wall in the First Act, it will fire in the Third Act. Life imitates theatre, or, as Shakespeare put it, this world is but a stage. The gun of anti-Semitism fired as expected, but it shot at the real Semites, the Arabs. Paradoxically, among new anti-Semites there are many persons with Jewish names, or known by their sympathy to Jews. How can this be?

It brings us back to the adage of our sages about paedophiles and proselytes. The Jewish faith is extremely suspicious of proselytes. They are like scabs on the head of Israel, taught Rabbi Helbo, and modern practice supports his learned opinion. Judaism is too complicated to receive in mature age. People born and raised as religious Jews have become used to being the Chosen folk and take it easy, but neophytes go dizzy at the thought.

This is not strange. The true English aristocrat, Tony Benn, supports the rights of ordinary folk, while freshly created parvenu Conrad Black promotes the oppression of Europeans and Muslims alike in his numerous newspapers. Some of the worst racists in Hebron, a frontline of Israeli apartheid, are actually proselytes who took some risky Biblical ideas literally. Witness the converted American Gentile Nazi who took the name of Eli Hazeev ('the Wolf') and was slain by Palestinian guerrillas, or this scourge of cyberspace, Dr. Andrew Mathis who converted and began to defend his version of Judaism on various Internet localities. Some new-Jews are un-aware that Judaism is a thoroughly interpreted/commented religion in which NO WORD of the Bible may (safely) be supposed to mean what it seems to say.

IV

A reader sent me a disturbing letter:

> My sister who converted to Judaism years ago (although we're WASPs) has gone over the edge. Last night when I asked her to interrupt her niggerization of Arabs long enough to cite just one example anytime in history when Israel did something—anything wrong (pointing out that peace cannot possibly be attained when one party thinks itself totally OK, and thinks the other party is completely at fault), the best she could come up with was "collateral" damage, i.e., the unintentional bombing of civilians when a "legitimate" target was the intent. My sister is quite active in the Jewish community in St. Louis, and perhaps in a position to do a fair amount of damage to whatever chances remain for world peace.

Yes, Rabbi Helbo had good reason for his suspicion. Real Jews know they live in the real world, and leave their fantasies for the Sabbath. They remain humble, study the Talmud and do not try to find a modern equivalent of Amalek or the Red Heifer, to retake the Holy Land by force or by stealth, nor to preach hatred of Gentiles. They knew: these concepts should be left untouched, like hidden files in the Windows filing system. They are there for historical reasons and one should not meddle with them. Neophytes lack the ability to make suitable distinctions.

It is not a question of race: neophytes, whether of Jewish or Gentile extraction, are equally blind to reason. That is why the ferocious Neo-Cons of America, Gentile Israel-firsters like Jeanne Kirkpatrick and secular 'red-diaper'

Jews like the infamous Norm Podhoretz, her mentor from *Commentary*, relentlessly call for the destruction of the Islamic world and poison the minds of Americans.

Islam is a form of Christianity particularly close to the Jews. While the Eastern Orthodox Church was influenced by Greek culture, and the Catholics partook of the Roman world, Islam returned the ideas of Christianity to the Semitic milieu. The Prophet, peace be upon him, upheld the Jewish concepts of strict monotheism, of fear of graven images, of protectiveness towards women, and integrated them with the universal message of Christ and his apostles. The cowardly enemies of Islam besmirch it, as they fear and envy its unbroken spirit, the valour of its warriors and the chastity of its maidens.

Notes

86. Twelve in some manuscripts.
87. Alluding to the verse in Exodous 3:3.

Poisoning Wells

[This essay deals with a new phenomenon, an active participation of organised Jewry in racist anti-immigrant propaganda. This is a part of the discussion about the new alliance of the Jews and the Right, and an urgent need for a more creative and careful approach to the Extreme Right forces.]

I

A spectre haunts the West, a spectre that was not seen around for quite a while. Exorcized long ago, it was imprisoned in the dark lab like a deadly virus, biding its time. Now, as Israel stoops to commit more crimes, its supporters broke the seals and removed the magic pentagram.

For over a millennium, we Jews were connected in the European popular mind with well-poisoning, to the great chagrin of our ancestors. Now, the fantasies of the past become true, as some dark minds turn tales of old into today's reality.

Abba Kovner, a Jewish socialist leader, had tried to poison the sources of the Rhine. He had dreamed of exterminating millions of Germans, children, women, men. He had received the virulent potion from a man who became afterwards the President of Israel, and who never regretted nor denied it. His last-minute cowardice (or a miracle?) saved the heart of Europe. (You can read about it—no remorse—in his *Life* lovingly depicted by an Israeli historian Dina Porat, or in an interview given by his assistant to *The Observer* in March 1998.[88])

It happened half a century ago, but now, a new poison flushes through the Zionist tentacles into the wells of Europe and North America. In the Canadian daily, *National Post* (August 27, 2002), published by Israel Asper, a great friend of my country, Daniel Pipes and Lars Hedegaard published an article with an alluring title, "Muslim extremism: Denmark's had enough."

Judging by its contents, Canada had scrapped its 'hate laws' that expressly forbid promoting hatred of ethnic and religious communities. Pipes-Hedegaard tandem writes:

> Predominantly Muslim immigrants constitute 5% of the population but consume upwards of 40% of the welfare spending . . . Muslims are only 4% of Denmark's 5.4 million people but make up a majority of the

country's convicted rapists, an especially combustible issue given that practically all the female victims are non-Muslim.

"They steal our money and rape our daughters"—this concept was successfully applied in the past, notably by Adolf Hitler in his *Mein Kampf*, against the Jews. Now, it is promoted by the mighty Jewish propaganda machine, this globe-embracing conglomerate of media moguls, obedient journalists and deferential university professors. Hitler or Stalin never had had such a network at their disposal. The hate potion is prepared by professor Lewis, multiplied by Pipes the journalist, published by Israel Asper, the owner of almost all Canadian media, and of our *Jerusalem Post*. It flows to Conrad Black in England, and to Mort Zuckerman in the US, and to innumerable media owners and editors all over the world.

This mighty machine rolled out the Ku Klux Klan scaremongering image of a crouching dark-skinned rapist, lusting the white skin and golden hair of Aryan maidens of Denmark. Imported from the great KKK-worshipping silent movie by Griffith, *The Nation Is Born*, the racist image opens a new film of *Men in Black II*: big Negro with big knife, big teeth and big prick attacks an innocent White woman in the park. The film was produced by the creator of *Schindler's List*, the sad story of persecuted Jews.

Still, there is a difference between Pipes, Zuckerman, Asper, Black and the ordinary racists of old. The German dictator and the Klan Wizard were sincere men who truly and wholeheartedly hated Jews. Pipes and his kin have no feeling of special hate towards Blacks or Muslims. For them, there is no difference between a Muslim or a Christian. They churn their hate potion for others, in preparation for the great assault on the Holy Land.

II

While the propaganda mills produce their output of hate, their potential victims still argue among themselves. Steven Salaita, a nice young American-born Palestinian student from Oklahoma, writes[89] in the YellowTimes.org: "For the first time in my life, I was disgusted to receive messages in support of the Palestinian people." Why? Because they were sent by "right-wing ideologues" as "a number of far-right racists, David Duke foremost among them, now invoke Israel's behaviour as a 'proof' of inherent Jewish depravity."

It is fairer to convey the main argument of these "right-wing ideologues" as follows:

1. There is a great proximity between the behaviour of Jews in Palestine and behaviour of the Jews elsewhere.

2. The horrors committed by Jews in Palestine and supported by Jews of the Diaspora prove the presence of a troublesome component of the Jewish policies, practice and ideology elsewhere.
3. The Jews represent a destructive (for others), dangerous and repulsive ideology and theology, and should be contained and counteracted.
4. Ideally, people of Jewish origin should be brought to see the light and leave their erroneous path; they should become "non-Jews."

Although the key point (3) is an unpleasant (for many Jews) notion, it is a non-racist age-long discourse. It is not a right-wing discourse either, as this opinion was shared by Karl Marx and Leon Trotsky, Theodor Herzl and Boruchov, St. Paul and Martin Luther. Zionists were foremost rejecting the 'goodness of Jewry'. A leading French socialist, PJ Proudhon, perceived the Jews as supporters of the modern bureaucratic, centralised state. Marx called to free mankind from Jews, and to de-Judaise Jews.

If Salaita wants to find a total rejection of the Jews as ideology, he does not have to go to David Duke. He could look up a book called *The Jewish Question: Marxist Interpretation*, by Abram Leon, a young follower of Trotsky, who perished in the walls of Auschwitz. Leon (I am grateful to Noam Chomsky who introduced me to this author) called the Jews 'people-class', historically attuned to usury and exploitation of others. A man of Jewish origin always could leave 'the Jews' and join mankind, wrote Leon.

Salaita notes that "extremist websites post articles critical of Israel from respectable publications, many with Jewish authors" and concludes, "the organizations' hatred of Jews is so strong that they are willing to employ Jewish voices in order to promote their agenda. Their naïveté is as striking as their stupidity." It is an unexpected and unwarranted reasoning. Rather, the websites employ voices of people of Jewish origin who reject the Jewish approach, and thus they prove their non-racist basis.

Salaita rejects the remote possibility of linkage between the Jewish behaviour in Palestine and the Jewish behaviour elsewhere. The apartheid established by Jews in Israel is not connected to the policies, ideology and practice of the Jews elsewhere, in his opinion. Well, this doubtful point of view is highly comfortable for the Jews in America. They can support Sharon and retain their angel wings. Maybe it is young Salaita who is naïve in his desire to disengage the war in Palestine and the confrontation elsewhere?

The article of Pipes we discussed earlier is just the latest proof of futility of this desire. The war for Palestine became a global war, the World War Three, and in this war, the organised Jewry is strictly on the side of the bad guys. Now they employ the evil weapon of racist hate, trying to rouse the Europeans against the Blacks and Muslims everywhere, from Alabama to Chechnya, from Copenhagen to Kabul. They should be confronted and defeated, as otherwise they will poison the wells of the mind. We should not allow our adversary to enforce the Black vs. White, or Christian vs. Muslim chasm. Instead of discussing David Duke's anti-Semitism, we should discuss the anti-Gentilism, hatred of a goy, so evident in the Jewish-owned media. If we succeed, the Jewish communities abroad will pay more attention to their own well-being, and let Palestine cool off.

Our war is NOT a total war. Despite childish remarks of Salaita, no sword of ethnic cleansing, no threat of physical annihilation hangs over Jewish heads, since Christians and Muslims always wished to bring their Jewish brothers to the light, out of their dark separatism. The enemies of Christ should be shown the error of their ways, not be hurt; that was the traditional approach of the Church. Even after a horrible holocaust of Palestinian Christians made by Jewish hands in 614, the Christian rulers retained brotherly Christian love to the misled Jews and did not punish them.

That was the Muslim approach as well. Despite much confrontation and trouble, "the Qaynuqa and the Nadir Jewish tribes cooperated with the Prophet Muhammad, and so did the Jews of Khaybar, after he took the oasis in 628 (he married the daughter of one of the chiefs of Nadir)," a reader from Virginia reminds me. Later, Jews collaborated happily with the conquering Arab armies in Syria, North Africa, and Spain, knowing the Arabs would give them greater toleration and protection than their previous rulers.

The Jews and non-Jews would be able to live together happily, after the Jewish supremacy trend would be vanquished. However, until it is achieved, we, the friends of Palestine, should seek understanding and cooperation with all possible allies, black, white, red, green or rainbow, as blessed are the seekers of peace.

Notes

88. March 27, 1998—"Survivor reveals 1945 plan to kill 6 million Germans," Douglas Davis, Jewish Telegraphic Agency:

> LONDON—Israel's first president supported a Jewish group's plans to murder Germans immediately after World War II, according to the man who led the avengers. Details of the plan, which included poisoning bread at a bakery, were unveiled by Lithuanian-born Joseph Harmatz, 73, in an interview published recently in the British newspaper, the *Observer*. Harmatz, who lost two brothers in the Holocaust, led an organization—Din, or Judgment—made up of survivors of the Vilna Ghetto. Their objective: the deaths of 6 million Germans as vengeance for the Jews who died in the Holocaust. The idea for the organization apparently came from the poet, Abba Kovner—a leader of the Lithuanian partisans who is credited with describing Jews as "being led like lambs to the slaughter."

89. http://www.yellowtimes.org/article.php?sid=610.

Phantom of Terror

[In Kuala Lumpur, a futuristic and lush tropical city of hospitable Malays, the Foreign Ministers of the Islamic States convened the Conference on Terror. I attended it as an observer. The following is A Talk I Never Gave at the Conference.]

"My wife has been raped by a Martian." This was a favourite and frequent headline in the 1950s, when the journalists had to deal with UFO stories. Over the years, the veracity of the opinion-makers has not changed, but their malice has grown considerably. Millions of newspaper copies, billions of TV frames and zillions of words postulate Islamic Terror as the latest scourge of mankind. It is not strange, Your Excellencies, that your defensive reflexes have taken precedence over your common sense, and you try to renounce, justify, or explain Islamic Terror—by the persecution of Palestinians in the Apartheid State of Israel, or by the US siege of Iraq and colonisation of Saudi Arabia. You give some pretty good reasons, but one can find good reasons even for Martians' raping housewives.

In the fervour of explanations, you forgot to ask yourselves the first question a scientist asks: does it exist? Is there such a phenomenon, 'Islamic Terror'? Yes, there is a lot of spin, and the media takes it for granted. But say-so does not suffice as proof of existence. In the Eighteenth Century, the good people of Salem in New England carried out a crusade against witches. Whoever doubted the very fact of female alliance with Devil was surely marginalised or presented as a Satan's stooge. For centuries, there was a spin about Jews consuming Christian children's blood at Passover. Hundreds of books and articles were published on the subject; England still has a child saint supposedly martyred by bloodthirsty Jews.

But now we disregard this silly spin. It is the right time to do the same with the latest Witch Hunt, the newest Blood Libel, the so-called Islamic Terror.

In my opinion, it exists in the same way and to the same extent as the Jewish Conspiracy and the Yellow Peril. There is a scattering of a few disjointed and unconnected guerrilla movements in the world: the Basque ETA and the South Lebanese Hezbollah, the Corsicans and the Mindanao in the South Philippines, the Irish IRA and the Columbians, the Tamil Tigers in Sri Lanka, UNITA in Angola and HAMAS in Palestine. There is no reason to select a few of them on the spurious ground of some religious affiliation and ascribe 'Islamic Terror Network' to them.

The people of South Lebanon, Northern Ireland, South Philippines, Corsica, the Basque country, and Palestine have their legitimate grievances, but connection of those grievances to their religion is just a question of colouring. In the same vein, the war between Iran and Iraq could have been (but should not have been) described as a war between Sunni and Shiite Islam, because we know the religious factor was not an important one in the decisions of Saddam Hussein and the Iranian leaders.

Practically nowhere can one find an Islamic terror organisation *per se*, fighting for the establishment of an Islamic State, on par with the Jewish State. Before the collapse of Communism, the Palestinians preferred a left-wing ideology to fight their oppressors. Among Palestinian militant leaders, a place of honour was held by a Christian, George Habash. HAMAS of Palestine grew as the only movement expressly permitted by the Zionist Apartheid state, while the non-religious FATAH was suppressed. Thus, the feelings of the oppressed Palestinians were channelled by the Jews into this quasi-religious movement.

The Hezbollah fighters of Lebanon fought against Israeli and American occupation, not for Islamic rule. They are similar to the Irish Republicans, not famous for their Islamic beliefs. Chechens continued their two-hundred-year war against Russian rule, building temporary alliances with America, Germany and Turkey. Their biggest alleged crime, the exploding of Moscow high-rise apartment blocks, is now frequently ascribed to 'rogue elements within the intelligence community', to 'supporters of President Putin', or even to 'prominent Israeli citizens'. A media mogul, Dr. Boris Berezovsky spoke on this subject quite openly after his exile from Russia.

Can we identify 'Muslim terrorists' by their methods? Surely not. The IRA was bombing Birmingham pubs well before Hamas discovered Tel Aviv cafés. The Tamil Tigers, a non-Muslim militant organisation, trained by the Israeli Mossad,[90] are the world leaders in suicide bombings. There was no case at all for assuming the existence of Islamic Terror until 9/11, when President Bush proclaimed its existence and introduced the World Wide Muslim Conspiracy 'al Qaeeda'.

The perpetrators of 9/11 are still unknown to us. The instant recovery of a hijacker's passport, intact on the scene of the jet crash should be counted among the most spectacular miracles of all times, well ahead of Daniel's trip into the fiery furnace. The old Babylonian furnace surely had not built up to the temperature of burning jet-fuel. Arab-language flying manuals in the trunk of a car, inaudible videotapes and other conveniently recovered exhibits make of the Moscow trials of 1937 a shining example of justice uncorrupted. The Afghani prisoners of war have been kept away from prying eyes, in the limbo of Guantanamo Bay, lest they disclose the greatest secret of all: their innocence.

On the other hand, there is accumulating evidence of an Israeli Connection. Warning messages on the Israeli network ODIGO were sent to Israelis in

Manhattan, in real time, when the planes left their airfields. In all airports utilised by hijackers, one Israeli company ICTS[91] attended to security. It was alleged that Jewish financial companies had sold futures of insurance companies, as if they knew of the impending disaster. A big Israeli company Zim reneged at considerable cost on its lease in the World Trade Center.

Israel utilized the 9/11 events to its full capacity: the ongoing massacre in the Palestinian cities is being described as 'the war on terror'. The Muslim neighbours of Israel were terrorised into passivity by the American rage. Destruction of Afghanistan raised the threshold of the world sensitivity to horror, and made possible the April invasion of Palestinian cities. Probably this is not enough for a 'guilty' verdict, but the same is true about al-Qaeeda's alleged involvement.

There is no Islamic terror, but there is an Israeli-American terror of Dar al-Islam. You have not sinned; but you are sinned against. Thus, when the US President and his media pose the question, "what do you do about 'Islamic terror?', I suggest, Your Excellencies, a good Jewish reply, 'What terror?'

Notes

90. According to Ostrovsky's *Way of Deception*.
91. http://www.icts-int.com/, see also http://afrocubaweb.com/news/israelispying.htm.

Bali Halloween

[The concept of 'Islamic Terror' is further deconstructed in the following piece.]

There were no previous demands; no terrorist group took responsibility for the Bali bombing, making it an act of unnecessary carnage. President Bush 'assumed' the Bali explosion was connected to al-Qaeeda and demanded to scan Indonesia for Muslims. It is our luck he never heard of Atlantis, otherwise he would assume the continent was sent to the bottom of the sea by the omnipresent Muslim terrorists. However, important new information came to us from London, and it allows us to peer through darkness surrounding the explosion.

Last week, one of the most powerful figures of our day, a colourful Russian billionaire and media lord, Boris Berezovsky, the man who enthroned Vladimir Putin and later parted ways with the Russian President, gave an exhaustive interview[92] to *Zavtra*, the main Russian opposition weekly, in his London exile. Although it is an exciting read for Russia-watchers, it provides a clue to the Bali mystery.

Three years ago, Russia was shaken by massive explosions. Whole apartment blocks in Moscow and other cities were stuffed up by extremely powerful explosive RDX (also called Hexogen in Russia and Germany) and were blown up by terrorists, causing a huge death toll. It was immediately presumed the Chechen terrorists were behind the acts, and they served as *casus belli* [an act to justify conflict] for the Chechnya War. The Russian people were thoroughly horrified, and supported the bloody military campaign. Grozny city was bombed and strafed, Chechnya invaded and thousands lost their lives; while two major changes occurred in Moscow. One, the war of vengeance guaranteed the election of Vladimir Putin to the post of President and secured positions of pro-American forces in the ex-USSR. Second, Russia was turned against the Muslim world, after one thousand years of peaceful coexistence, and became a strategic partner for the US-led and Israel-orchestrated War on Terror.

In his interview last week, Berezovsky claims there were two teams working to assure the election of Putin. While he personally led one of the teams acting via his TV channel, the second team chose a violent path. Berezovsky quotes the words of the Russian Parliament speaker, Gennady Seleznyov, who informed the Parliament on 13.09.99 about a horrible explosion in a small Russian city of Volgodonsk. It was the best documented piece of prophecy in recent history, as Volgodonsk was bombed only three days LATER, on 16.09.99.

In the London interview, Berezovsky was asked how he explains this incredible botch-up of the perpetrators. "These security services are not as professional as they want us to think," he said. "They are not united, either. Within the security services, there are many groups serving various power structures. One of them botched up its job, or failed its tie-in with another group. They reported the explosion before it was done, and it revealed the truth."

In a Muslim neighborhood in Ryazan, watchful residents discovered bags with RDX in the basement of their tenement block and called up the police. Police removed the bags, but claimed it was just sugar planted by the security services in order to check people's vigilance. Berezovsky states it was real RDX with real explosive devices.

In Moscow, journalists connect 'the second team' to a strongman of Russian politics, the man behind a vast privatisation campaign that made him and his cronies immensely rich, and other Russians—immensely poor. A great friend of Israel, he supported a pro-Israeli turn in Russian politics.

Revelations of Boris Berezovsky came in real time, while the bodies of Australian tourists were being counted in Bali. Is it a sheer coincidence that our Prime Minister, Ariel Sharon, began his glorious career by exploding fifty homes of Palestinians on the heads of their inhabitants in Qibie, in far-away 1953? Is it a sheer coincidence that the perpetrator of these explosions, from Moscow 2000 to New York 2001 and to Bali 2002, used the same technique to horrify people and cause them to support Israeli and American plans? Is it a sheer coincidence that the Zionist-infested media covered up the obvious faults in the official versions, starting with the unique 'prophecy' of Gennady Seleznyev, and continuing with the ODIGO internet warnings to a few Israelis in Manhattan on 9/11?

One thing is certain: the 'Islamic' tag speedily attached to the Bali explosion by Bush and Sharon is a revolting blood libel against one billion Muslims. There is no 'Islamic' terror but in the eyes of the beholder. The 'Catholic' IRA was bombing Birmingham pubs well before Hamas discovered Tel Aviv cafés. The Tamil Tigers, 'Hindu' militant organisation trained by the Israeli Mossad, are world leaders in suicide bombings. French OAS terrorists bombed Algerians and their French adversaries as well. The biggest terrorist act in Palestine was and remains the explosion of the King David Hotel by a Jew, Prime Minister Menachem Begin. Apparently, people who object to every reference to 'Jewish' crimes, terror or genocide, do not hesitate to turn Islam into the bogeyman of this Halloween.

Notes

92. http://zavtra.ru/cgi//veil//data/zavtra/02/464/21.html.

Sultan and Shaitan

I

The Sultan is good, only his viziers are given to evil counsel. This thought comforted many an unhappy subject throughout human history. Unhappy as we are, we comforted ourselves with vain hopes of a positive American intervention in Palestine, and we are still clinging to the myth of the US as a severe but honest ruler. Even though Deir Yassin Day became Deir Yassin-a-Day, our hopes did not abate. "A real test of the Bush presidency," wrote Robert Fisk in the *Independent*. "No time to waste," seconded Helena Cobban of the *Christian Science Monitor*. But the visit of the US Secretary of State provided no respite for the Palestinians, nor even a lull in the Israeli onslaught. Brilliant Norman Finkelstein reminded us:

> The problem with the Bush administration, we are repeatedly told, is that it has been insufficiently engaged with the Middle East, a diplomatic void Colin Powell's mission is supposed to fill. But who gave the green light for Israel to commit the massacres? Who supplied the F-16s and Apache helicopters to Israel? Who vetoed the Security Council resolutions calling for international monitors to supervise the reduction of violence? And who just blocked the proposal of the United Nation's top human rights official, Mary Robinson, to merely send a fact-finding team to the Palestinian territories? Consider this scenario. A and B stand accused of murder. The evidence shows that A provided B with the murder weapon, A gave B the "all-clear" signal, and A prevented onlookers from answering the victim's screams. Would the verdict be that A was insufficiently engaged or that A was every bit as guilty as B of murder?

He is right. It is time to stop daydreaming about the good sultan. If a mental block forbids you to doubt his good intentions, you may think he is a captive of evil eunuchs, as so many rulers were. From regret and sorrow, we should move into action. After all, the US policies in the Middle East aren't weather that everybody complains about, but can do nothing about. But can we do something about it, if demonstrations and protests are of no avail?

The answer is "yes," and not by Jihad, or Crusade. Robert Jensen[93] of the University of Texas wrote: "I helped kill a Palestinian today. If you pay taxes to the U.S. government, so did you." He implied that the US taxpayers' money goes into rearming Israel and killing Palestinians. Let Jensen be comforted. The US taxpayer is innocent. The liability is broader: the slaughter is paid for by us, the five billion people on earth living outside of the US.

Every day we transfer five billion dollars to the US in order to keep this great country's leaders in the style they are accustomed to, and also to kill as many Palestinians as they find fit. A buck a day, from each of us, Europeans and Africans, Chinese and Japanese, Russians and Arabs. These mind-boggling numbers were published by the British weekly, the *Economist*. We do this because since 1972 the US has assumed the right to print as many dollars as it likes, and we have subscribed to the fiction that the greenback, a small sheet of paper, is an equivalent of our labour and of worldly goods.

As a matter of fact, the US dollar has no cover. It is a cheque written by a bankrupt wastrel, good for framing and hanging on a wall. Since the Americans issue as many dollars as they need, it is not amazing there is one superpower and all the rest of us are in its debt. It is not a secret: brave Fidel Castro tells it at every conference, thus assuring endless hostility from the US.

The US financial wizards, Greenspan et al, are playing an old confidence trick on us called 'pyramid'. Such games have been played in many countries, notably in Albania and Russia, by local tricksters. Usually they end with a catastrophic crash. The Judeo-American con-game differs by virtue of its size. It is global. Otherwise, it is the same pyramid. Ninety per cent of all financial transactions are speculative transactions, writes Noam Chomsky. The pyramid is supported by a massive propaganda brainwash to encourage consumption and expansion. The ordinary people of the US and its allies get no fun out of it: in England, child poverty has grown threefold since Margaret Thatcher came to power. In the US, there are millions of homeless children. The Americans, Brits, Germans are deeply indebted, as are the countries of the Third World.

The US dollar has succeeded in replacing the gold, because it offered an attractive fixed-interest rate. The interest rate has become a honey trap for mankind; it has caused the burden of debt, impoverished states and persons, and created the ugly aberration of globalisation. Not in vain, Sam Bronfman the Bootlegger, the founder of the powerful Bronfman dynasty and father of the World Jewish Congress Chairman, when asked what the most important human invention is, replied without hesitation: "interest rate."[94]

That was the second Fall of Man. Adam was tempted by the apple, we were tempted by the fixed-rate interest on the dollar, the modern equivalent of old-fashioned usury. In the old days, the 'anti-Semitic' Church condemned usury as the exclusively Jewish occupation, but now it is free for all. Everybody is a partner, in the words of Heller's *Catch-22* character, Milo Minderbinder. Yet, there is a catch, Catch-22. You can not take your winnings and go away to enjoy them. You have to stay in the game.

The US dollar is not 'money' anymore; it is a license, like a Microsoft license, or a patent by a pharmaceutical company. Whenever the US rulers decide, they can freeze the assets of a rebel country. Iran had its assets frozen, as had Libya and Iraq; surely the Saudis will suffer the same fate the moment they object to American policies. Here is a good riddle for Bilbo Baggins: what is overpriced, unsafe, green and greatly desired by fools?

II

In the last days of the war in South East Asia, I travelled by a slow junk boat down the Mekong River, in the company of fellow-journalists, adventurers, local peasants, pigs and chickens. The boat was frequently stopped, searched and taxed by warring parties, but it made its unhurried progress from the old royal capital of Luang Prabang towards Vientiane. In a sleepy village of twenty huts and three elephants, where we stayed overnight, I wandered into a Chinese shop. In front of me, a dark and dour Pathet Lao guerrilla in rubber tyre Ho Chi Minh sandals and AK assault rifle on his back completed his modest shopping and paid for it with some funny money. I recognized its colourful pattern: it was the Pathet Lao currency. As the soldier went away, I took out a few Pathet Lao bills I got as change on the boat and asked the shopkeeper for a pack of cigarettes. The Chinese did not move. "But I have seen you accept this money," I protested. He replied with wise words worthy of Lao-Tzu, "Only from people with a gun."

The US dollar is still accepted by the world community out of fear, and that is why the US military budget grows every year. That is why the hermit kingdom of North Korea, and Iran and Iraq became The Axis of Evil: they do not accept the dollar. But fear is a bad adviser. The collapse of the pyramid is imminent. The meltdown began in August 2001, as the *Economist* advised its readers on August 25, 2001, and, but for timely intervention of persons unknown on September 11, 2001, the US dollar would now be of value to numismatists only. But World War III can only delay the completion of the process.

Sheer prudence and enlightened self-interest have caused the wise rulers to move out of the dollar sphere. The European countries launched the Euro, the Japanese Yen rose sharply. But their attempt to substitute paper for paper while maintaining the interest rate is necessarily flawed. In a revolutionary proposal, Dr. Mahathir, the Prime Minister of prosperous Malaysia, proposes to return to gold and silver, more specifically to the idea of the golden 'Islamic' Dinar, the zero-interest rate reserve currency of the world. His great idea to undo the 'dollar and loans' double-hold deserves to be compared with the reform of Solon, the legendary Sage of Athens, who cancelled debts, defeated the Oligarchy, and returned land and freedom to the people. If implemented, it would put an end to the suffering of Palestinians and to the suffering of the Third World in general. The US dollar would fall as fast as in 1929, and with it, the US support for Israel and your debts.

This should not be seen as an attack on America. Ordinary Americans would regain their homes from the banks' clutches, as mortgages would disappear. The burden of debt would fall off the backs of people. True, Marc Rich and George Soros will have to apply to the welfare office, together with many ardent supporters of Israel. But that would hardly be a misfortune: they will be too busy to make mischief if they have to earn their living.

That is the answer to the question, how can we help Palestinians? Ask the leaders of your countries to take the right and prudent step of moving their funds and capital out of the US banks and out of the US dollar. It would be more efficient than Jihad and Crusade, more humane and final than suicide bombing.

I liked the idea of Dr. Mahathir. The golden Dinar would usher us into a new world, a world of zero interest-rate; a world without usury would help to reconcile society. Marx would enjoy the irony of history: that the Jewish onslaught in Palestine can be stopped only by rejecting partnership in a dollar-denominated usury.

III

Religious considerations can not be removed from our practical decisions. The 'Islamic' Dinar would complete the system of performance-connected banking. It is called nowadays 'Islamic banking', but it was practiced by very Catholic Venice for centuries before the advent of usury. On this point, as on many others, Dar al-Islam and Christendom do not differ. The Church banned fixed interest rates until John Calvin's fateful folly, and the great religious reformer, Prophet Muhammad, reinforced the prohibition.[95]

Jewish Law forbade Jews to charge interest to their 'brothers' (other Jews), but required that it be charged to 'strangers' (non-Jews). St. Ambrose understood the implications of this approach when he wrote:

> From him demand usury, whom you desire to harm. From him exact usury, whom it would not be a crime to kill. Where there is a right of war, there also is a right of usury.[96]

That is why the Jews will have peace in Palestine and elsewhere when they accept the maxim of Thomas Aquinas, "there are no strangers," and consider non-Jews, the Palestinians and others, as their brothers and neighbours.

Notes

93. *Houston Chronicle*, http://www.chron.com/cs/CDA/story.hts/editorial/outlook/1351792.
94. *Haaretz*, 20.11.98, Musaf p. 36.
95. sura 2, 275–280.
96. The quote supplied by David Pidcock.

Take the Money and Run

Travel opens up the vistas of your mind. It is wonderful to roam our beautiful Earth, from France to Norway, from China to Russia, from Africa to Latin America, enjoying its variety and hospitality, and the profession of a reporter gives you a chance to see the world. But eventually one pays attention to an interesting coincidence. It could happen to you in Marseille, as you walk by the inner harbour, or in Brittany, in the fisherman's city of Oriente, in Guatemala or Nicaragua, in Milan, this capital of Italian fashion, in Naples or in Shanghai, in the Russian White Sea port of Archangel—or in the middle of China, in Berlin and Hamburg, in the passes of Hindukush, in Tokyo and Baghdad, Manila or Havana. Suddenly you notice that all these exotic and diverse places have one thing in common—they were bombed by Brits and Yankees. These guys sure get around. Today we bomb Afghanistan, tomorrow—the rest, or whatever they sing in the Air Force.

The reasons vary. They had bombed China because the stubborn Chinese did not want to buy their opium; Columbia, because they were selling drugs; the Russians and Vietnamese, for being Commies; the Cambodians, for being there; the Germans and French, for offending Jews; Iraqis, for hard cash; and the Sudanese, by mistake.

Now, we've got a sneak preview of their next campaign, courtesy of the *Washington Post.*[97] The men in charge of the US, and I mean real *mensch*, not this nincompoop in the White House, conspire to erase Iraq, to continue with Saudi Arabia and finish off with Egypt. The news was broken gently by a strategist with a wholesome all-American name 'Murawiec', smuggled into the Pentagon by one of the *mensch* in charge, Defence Policy Board Chairman Richard N. Perle. This Jewish hawk, a friend of Sharon, a devoted Zionist, should be considered the real author of the blueprint calling for seizure of the Arabian oil fields, transfer of Mecca and Medina unto Jordanian rule, and confiscation of Saudi assets.

The Saudis have feigned amazement, while the US columnists[98] tried to play down the story and have a good laugh. It surely has its comic value. Glib assessments, "Wars have been the principal output of the Arab world" sound particularly rich when coming from a proponent of the Judeo-American cult, probably the most violent and war-prone since Genghis Khan. Murawiec's rhetorical question, "What has the Arab world produced?" reminded me of a thieving banker, Flatto-Sharon, who had escaped the French police to Israel, bribed voters, got elected into the Parliament and then had the temerity to ask Yitzhak

Rabin in his beginners' Hebrew: "What did you do for the state of Israel?" ("*Ma ata asita bishvil hamedina*?"). It remained as one of the best Israeli jokes.

But I was neither amazed nor amused. The desire to plunder and kill Arabs is frequently vented in the Jewish circles, but recently it has run into snags. The Palestinian property had been looted years ago, their lands and houses taken over and resold. Although killing Palestinians may be pleasing to the god of vengeance, it is not a very profitable exercise. Squeezing out the remainder of anything profitable goes too slowly for the impatient folks accustomed to NASDAQ growth.

Iraq seems to be an appealing target for mass murder, and in the prestigious *Jewish World Review*,[99] a Jewish American columnist Jonah Goldberg writes: "Baghdad must be destroyed . . . America should go to war with Iraq even if that risks innocent Iraqi—and American—lives." Although life or death of a Goy is surely no objection, there is no money in bombing Iraq, either.

The riches of the Arabian Peninsula hoodwink the Jews, being tantalisingly within the reach of Israel Defense Forces Merkaba tanks. This temptation was well expressed by Jewish American Professor David D. Perlmutter in the *LA Times*:[100] "I daydream—if only! If in 1948, 1956, 1967 or 1973 Israel had acted just a bit like the Third Reich, then today Jews, not sheiks, would have that Gulf oil." One would think that Saudi crude goes to the US, why should an American professor mind it? But your average American Jew values his Jewish-ness well above his American-ness. Witty Joe Sobran noted, "It was once considered 'anti-Semitic' to impute 'dual loyalty' to [American] Jews. This is now passé. Dual loyalty nothing! Dual loyalty would be an improvement!" in comparison with their single-minded devotion to their own national interests.

In order to turn Perlmutter's daydream into reality, normally quite diverse Jewish voices of Right united with shades of Left. Although Richard Perle is as right-wing as they make it, Justin Raimondo took note of "ex-leftist David Horowitz, who demands all-out war on the Arab world, and Stephen Schwartz, ex-Trotskyite, who became a major theoretician of the Riyadh-as-'kernel of evil' school." Even anti-Zionist Trotskyite Lenni Brenner, whose brilliant pen and cheerful style I admire, decided to join the US warriors, and called to launch a feminist crusade against Saudi Arabia.

The Jewish-owned media amplified these opinions. A Jewish journalist, Miss Slavin, reported in *USA Today*,[101] published by the top Jewish leader, Mort Zuckerman, that a Jewish analyst Max Singer [a founder of the conservative Hudson Institute, who never had been to Saudi Arabia but frequents Israel], suggested to Pentagon officials to dismantle the Kingdom. Value of Mr. Singer's opinion is next to nil, but it has received good media coverage, while many more important opinions have been denied. There was no article by an Arab-American calling to dismantle Israel, just for the balance. It appears the organised Jews firmly planted Saudis in the cross-hairs of their formidable weapon, the mass media.

This leaves us with a difficult query: why do some American forces, and the American Jews among them, want to destroy Saudi Arabia, the faithful ally of the US and a very moderate power in a regional context? And another one: what can be done about it?

Notes

97. "Briefing Depicted Saudis as Enemies, Ultimatum Urged To Pentagon Board," by Thomas E. Ricks, *Washington Post* Staff Writer, Tuesday, August 6, 2002, Page A01.
98. "The PowerPoint That Rocked the Pentagon, The LaRouchie defector who's advising the defense establishment on Saudi Arabia," by Jack Shafer; and "Going after the Saudis: Big Oil joins up with the neocons and a LaRouche 'defector'," by Justin Raimondo August 9, 2002. http://www.antiwar.com/justin/justincol.html.
99. "Debating War Against Iraq," by Jonah Goldberg, *Jewish World Review*, July 17, 2002. http://www.jewishworldreview.com/cols/jonah.html.
100. April 7, 2002.
101. Anti-Saudi arguments get heard Friday, Aug 9, 2002 Barbara Slavin, *USA Today*.

Why and How

Optimists argue it is just a threat, a psychological warfare, a pressure applied to the kingdom. The reasons for such pressure could be explained by the need of American oil companies to threaten the Saudis into obedience and extend their contracts. Alternatively, the US military needs to use Saudi air bases for attack on Iraq, and the Arabs are not sufficiently obsequious.

But I am not sure it is an empty threat. We live in the shadow of ongoing meltdown of the dollar and the American-based financial pyramid.[102] It began in August 2001, caused 9/11 as the means to slow the meltdown, and goes on, gathering speed as an avalanche snowball. Saudis have too much dollar reserve. Elimination ('freezing') of their dollar assets would slow the meltdown, as vast trillions of dollars will vanish from the marketplace. While injection of money causes inflation, its evaporation will cause deflationary, upward pressure on the dollar. In other words, for Wall Street, it makes sense to freeze Saudi assets, as they froze the assets of Iran and Iraq.

Saudi rulers probably have time to counteract it, if they use the advice of Woody Allen: "Take the money and run." They should shift their holdings out of the collapsing dollar zone, into Euro, Yen or gold. The great idea of golden 'Islamic dinar' promoted by the wise Prime Minister of Malaysia, Dr. Mahathir should be activated immediately. The Saudis could learn much from Dr. Mahathir who succeeded to turn his strife-torn poverty-stricken country, living off palm oil and natural rubber, into the prosperous land of national accord and stable economy. The Malaysians squared the circle: their immigrant communities are fully integrated, have equal rights, and still do not endanger the indigenous Malay group. They develop high tech industries and provide welfare to needy people. There is no discrimination and no poor or needy people in Malaysia. They do not depend on the US, do not provide their land for the US bases, do not invest in the US, and still remain on friendly terms with Washington. Following the Malaysian way, the Kingdom will reduce its vulnerability.

Alas, it would not diminish the Jewish appetite for Arab oil, nor the organised Jewish hostility toward ar-Riyadh. Saudi rulers are uncomfortably conscious of the threat, but they misinterpreted its context. They accepted as a real coin, the fake three-dollar bill of 'peace-seeking Israel'. That is why Prince Abdullah tried to entice Israel with his peace plan. That is why the Kingdom's support of the Palestinian cause is symbolic. Saudi rulers have been told by their

American advisers that Israel would not push for Saudi destruction if Saudis would behave, that is, stay away from the Palestinian problem.

Now, the Saudis have to pay heed to unpleasant reality. Israel is not just a small Middle Eastern country anymore, but a forward element of the new aggressive international force, Jewish supremacists. They have too many good reasons to undo Saudi Arabia.

- This prosperous and well-armed country must be brought down to its knees before Israel will make its most important step, seizure and destruction of the beautiful Umayyad Mosques in Jerusalem.
- Saudis have too much money, too much oil and too few friends. This combination brought Kuwait down, but the US bombed Iraq to restore the Emir of Kuwait. Washington is not going to repeat this feat when the Saudi oil fields pass into Israeli hands.
- The Viagra of Saudi money would invigorate the flabby Dow Jones.

There is an additional reason. The Jewish conscience has been poisoned by sweet dreams of revenge for the defeats of times long gone. Mainstream Jewish scholars of the 19th and 20th centuries betrayed their audience, and, instead of describing real Jewish history, created an idealised and distorted picture of a past of old grievances, undeserved wrong-doing and revengeful dreams. Their readers swallowed the fabricated stories and grew up as unrestrained nationalists. Modern Jews are victims of nationalist propaganda. They are misled and disoriented, induced with desire to rectify the mythic wrong.

The Jewish state was established to undo the perceived results of the Roman victory of AD 70. And now a new idea floats in the air—to undo the perceived results of Prophet Muhammad's victory over the Jewish tribes[103] and to bring the peninsula under Jewish rule. Together with the desire to undo the victory of Christianity, this archaic spirit will inevitably cause more turmoil in the world.

This spirit reminded me of Sweeney Todd, the Demon Barber in a late 1970s horror musical comedy. Sweeney Todd "has served the dark and vengeful god, and trod the path few did trod"; namely, turned his customers into savoury pie filling in order to exact revenge on the Judge who wronged him.

The Saudis should act before it is too late. They should

- Re-think their relationship with the Palestinians, and treat them as their outward defence rather than as poor relatives. Without Palestinians, Saudi Arabia would be taken over tomorrow.
- There should be more effort and money spent on public discourse in the US and Europe, as Edward Said constantly reminded the Arabs.

- We should confront the archaic tendency among Jews and promote a different spirit, a spirit of understanding and brotherhood. Though it is not taught in Jewish schools, the Prophet Muhammad won his battles not only by the sword, but by attracting like-minded Jews to the banner of Islam as well. Early converts, the Jews for Allah and His Messenger, fought under the green banner of Islam on every battlefield from Yarmuk to Cairo.

There are many good Jews, in Israel and in the US alike, and there is no reason for a confrontation between the descendents of Abraham. But the restless spirit of Sweeney Todd should be exorcised.

Notes

102. Sultan and Shaitan.
103. Kainuka, Kuraiza and Haibar tribes of Arabia in AD 627.

PART VII

The Third Dove

I

In the movie based on the mammoth tale by Jean Auel, *Clan of Cave Bear*, there is a glimpse of the sex life of the Palaeolithic people who roamed the earth some 35,000 years ago. Apparently, whenever a Neanderthal wished to have fun, he didn't need to bring flowers or arrange dinner for two. He would make a certain sign with his hand and the chosen girl would immediately, without further ado, submit to his desire.

The sign to submit is still with us. Whenever people discuss the things done in the name of Jews by, say, Sharon or Abe Foxman, the moment the discussion starts to get out of hand, one of the leaders of the community chants the magic word 'anti-Semitism', and, as if under a spell, we immediately bend over. It is amazing that grown men and women who have never personally experienced any prejudice in their life still respond to this spell like the girl, Ayla, in Auel's novel.

The machine of the official Jewish establishment and its Israeli offshoot nauseates many Jews. The Israeli government commits war crimes on a day-to-day basis. It is run by a certified mass-murderer. Medieval-style sieges of cities, summary executions and assassinations are now routine. Bombing, strafing and shelling of civilians are no longer anything to get worked up about. Many Jews see it, and are ready to say so in a cosy '*entre-nous*' environment. They read news from Israel with resignation and disgust, like an English Victorian squire learning of the new exploits of his wild brother in a far away colony.

The American Jewish establishment is not better than Israel's leadership. It provides unconditional support to Israeli and other Jewish criminals, from Sharon to Gusinsky, the Russian media lord. Abe Foxman, the head of ADL, files compromising materials, bugs phone calls and intrudes on the privacy of many Americans. The whining voice of Elie Wiesel and his colleagues traffic in schmaltzy self-righteousness. Conrad Black and others of his ilk take morally unsustainable positions, supporting freaks such as the Chilean torturer, Augusto Pinochet, and Henry Kissinger, the destroyer of Cambodia.

But the moment a word of objection exits our lips, we see the sign of Ayla and bend over. If nobody says it, we whisper it to ourselves: "Sh-sh-sh! It will cause anti-Semitism!" We can not help ourselves, it is too deeply engrained. Like a spoilt child, we take any criticism as a sign of hate. We dared to rebel against kings, but we do not dare to fight our self-proclaimed and self-imposed leadership, as "it will cause A-S."

II

Abe Foxman, besieged for taking a $100,000 check from the Marc Rich Foundation, gave the sign of Ayla in the *New York Times* (March 21), proclaiming, "anti-Semitism is a disease, and we have seen a big eruption of that disease in New York." There were no takers. Rabbi Lapin of *Toward Tradition* called him "a guy who's not in close touch with reality" and a "dealer of the Anti-Semitism Manufacture." He noted that the ADL gets paid (by contributors) according to how much anti-Semitism it finds.[104]

The *Guardian* [March 28, 2001], to prove its pluralism, published an op-ed by a Simon Sebag Montefiore, who declared that "the most energetic media-campaigners against Israel are, in private, virulent anti-Semites." He pictures the British journalists and public figures as "dogs besetting the bear." For 'dog' read 'Lord Gilmour'; for 'bear', Conrad Black.

He specifically objects to the "most wicked implication that Israel is replicating German behaviour: this approaches Holocaust denial in its iniquity." Well, it is a question of standards. Years ago, an Israeli writer noted that the Jews measure their actions by the Nazi stick, and invariably find themselves "a good and benevolent occupier." Maybe even this "generous" standard has been set aside. Yes, the Nazi chapter in Poland was much worse than the thirty-four year Israeli military rule in the occupied territories. But the Nazi occupation of France was probably milder for the French than the Israeli occupation is for Palestinians, and mercifully it was much shorter. Daily life under the Vichy government was certainly better than life in the 'autonomous' Gaza strip.

Montefiore calms the Brits as his "aim is not to launch witch-hunts, just to warn decent people" of the abyss ahead. Another purpose of this op-ed, which was probably sponsored by Black, is to frighten British Jews silly into supporting General Sharon.

This game is not for the right wing only. An Israeli liberal, Amnon Rubinstein, called his compatriots to fight the danger of anti-Semitism. This plague, in his opinion, was manifested by Greece bringing to court a Jewish stock market swindler, a local Milken or Rich. For Rubinstein, a Jew must be immune to persecution, and all Jews must support every Jewish rascal. The Israeli peace activist, Uri Avnery of Gush Shalom, called Arabs to fight anti-Semitism, as "anti-Semitism brought one million Russian Jews to Israel."

He could say anti-Semitism brought half-a-million Chinese guest workers to Israel, as well.

III

In order to deliver peace to your souls, I will give my personal testimony. An aging baby-boomer, I have travelled the world, lived among Russians and Palestinians, Germans and Swedes, the English and the Japanese, Indians and Africans, and I can tell you, on the basis of my experience, anti-Semitism no longer exists. As a Jew, you can walk freely in any city of men; you will be safe everywhere, if you come as a friend. The prejudice against Jews has vanished. You can find a Jew-hater, but there are many more people who hate the Poles or the Irish or have a beef against the WASPs. You are much more likely to encounter an Arab-hater or those who hate blacks or Asians.

I have met many people who have been branded with the scarlet letter of anti-Semite. These so-called anti-Semites object to the policies of the organised Jewish community, of the unholy alliance of Sharon and Abe Foxman, Gusinsky and Rich, Conrad Black and William Safire. I concur with them wholeheartedly, as it is not a question of prejudice.

The professional anti-Semitism fighters know this very well. Their true purpose is not to fight anti-Semitism but to frighten ordinary Jews into submission. That is why the pillars of the community write them generous checks and report every insult, magnifying it by a factor of ten. The Holocaust Industry is but a branch of the Anti-Semitism Manufacture, a two-pronged weapon: it pumps money from Gentiles and forces Jews into obedience to the leaders of the community.

In 1991, when Iraqi Scuds landed in Israel, and the gas-warfare alarm sounded, a dozen Israelis suffocated in their gas masks and died. There was no poisonous gas outside, just the fresh and fragrant air of the Judean hills, but they would not breathe it. They thought they would die the moment they took their masks off. Instead, they suffocated in their masks. This is the paradigm of modern Jewish existence in the shadow of fear.

When Noah released the first dove from the ark, it had to return. The second dove, however, brought back an olive branch. The third dove did not come back. He found the deluge was over, and saw no reason to come back to the stifling air of the Ark. I am your third dove. You may take off your masks. The air outside is perfectly good. The deluge has subsided. Step outside to greet the human race, your brothers and sisters.

Jews and Gentiles, we have the same enemies and the same friends. The enemies are those who push us back into a goy-hating ghetto; for a Jew-hater is but a mirror image of a goy-hater. A few generations separate us from the stifling world of traditional Jewish community life. Those who pine for it can take a trip to Brooklyn.

IV

Yossi Klein Halevi, an Israeli-American journalist, wrote about his childhood:[105]

> We lived on the border of Borough Park. Beyond our Brooklyn enclave, were Italians, Puerto Ricans, and Scandinavians. They evoked no curiosity in us, only fear. We saw them all as members of the same ethnic group: Jew-haters. *Goyim* we called them, a Hebrew word that literally means 'the nations' but that we understood to mean the enemy. We lived in a sealed Jewish world . . . had it been possible, we would have surrounded Borough park with a moat . . . Borough Park's interests were limited to its own borders, and leapt over the Christian neighbourhoods to embrace other Jewish enclaves—as if the only civilized parts of the world were Jewish, the rest being inhabited by rabid creatures capable at any moment of unprovoked violence. 'The world' existed only insofar as it affected Jews. The Jews and 'the world' could never coexist; at best we would endure each other from a distance. Some of our religious laws seemed meant not to bring us closer to God but to separate us from the goyim, and I accepted that estrangement as self-evident.

Bear in mind, he was writing of modern New York with its large Jewish population, not of some medieval town. It is not strange that Halevi, brainwashed in his youth, became an activist of the goy-hating Nazi group, Meyer Kahane's Jewish Defence League. He moved on, but even now, this correspondent for the *New Republic* in Israel supports settlers, who behave "as if the only civilized parts of Palestine were Jewish, the rest being inhabited by rabid creatures capable at any moment of unprovoked violence." A few generations ago, all the Jews lived in such enclaves, subservient to the Jewish elite of wealth and learning. The rule of the elite was based on patronage and on our fathers' fear of anti-Semitism. The Jewish aristocracy has adapted to new conditions and continues to reinforce this fear in order to control us.

V

The 'mutual support' of the Jewish community is immoral. If an Irishman or an Italian steals, he goes to jail and his parish priest might send him a Christmas pie.

If an influential Jew steals, be it Vladimir Gusinsky or Marc Rich, the Jewish community demands his impunity. If the Jewish state commits war crimes, the Jewish community supports it without reservation. This is abnormal behaviour for an ethnic community, a shameful remnant of our habit of dealing with the outside world as if we were members of a medieval guild.

Let us help one another to overcome the impulse to bend over. A man should be able to voice objections to the homicidal policies of his leadership without being called a traitor. That was the position of Mark Twain, who fought the US intervention in the Philippines. That was the position of Thoreau during the war over Texas. These were the positions of Alexander Solzhenitsyn, Thomas Mann, and Bertolt Brecht. It should be easy for Jews to emulate these men, as the self-styled Jewish leadership has no real power over Jews; it can only resort to scare tactics.

The pursuit of the bogeyman of anti-Semitism leads away from the real problem. During WWII, the brilliant Russian Jewish writer, Iliya Ehrenburg, in a moment of rage, called out (on the pages of *Pravda*) to his countrymen to "kill the German vermin." Marshal Joseph Stalin rebuked him: "The Nazis come and go, but the German people remain forever." German propaganda made a killing out of the hate-speech of Ilya Ehrenburg, trying to obscure the fact that the problem was not the anti-German remark of the Jewish writer, but the German war crimes. In the same vein, the problem today is not the mythic anti-Semitism, but the Israeli war crimes—and US complicity in those crimes.

Anti-Semitism is a weapon of the scoundrel, said Lenin in the 1920s, echoing the maxim of Samuel Johnson. This sentence, as so many Biblical verses, has retained its validity in a changed context: scoundrels still use anti-Semitism as a weapon, but now most of these scoundrels are Jewish.

Notes

104. http://www.vny.com/cf/News/upidetail.cfm?QID=172359.
105. *Memoirs Of A Jewish Extremist*, Little, Brown and Co. 1995.

Chosen and Choosing

[This Letter to a British Friend was addressed to a BBC journalist, Miss Deborah Maccoby, and published in early 2002. It deals with the feeling of Jews who were offended by my reference to Jews in a less-than-complimentary sense.]

In an article of mine,[106] I described a British Jewish scholar Dr. Hiyam Maccoby, a 'Jewish nationalist'. His daughter, Miss Deborah Maccoby, of London, a correspondent and a friend, rose to the challenge and objected to "the completely distorted picture of Dr. Maccoby." She wrote:

> He cannot be described as a right-wing Jewish nationalist. In the 1970s, he was one of the signatories of a letter to the *Times* advocating a federal solution to the Israel/Palestinian problem. He is now a supporter of the two-state solution. His views are very close to those of Amos Oz, who is hardly a right-wing Jewish nationalist.

It is nice to know that the important British Jewish scholar, Dr. Maccoby, does not belong to the right-wing of Jewish nationalism. Or is it? He would like the Gentiles of Palestine to have their separate state, permanently disarmed, broken into a few separate pieces, its borders permanently guarded by the Jewish state next door, its newspapers and TV programmes censored by the Jews, its holy places under Jewish control. He would not return the properties confiscated from the Gentiles in 1948 and 1967, probably not even the lands confiscated last year. In other words, Dr. Maccoby stands for the creation of a ghetto for Goyim spread over small slivers (often and appropriately called Bantustans) of their land.

Let us translate his position into British realities. What would you call a man who supports the creation of a separate Jewish state in [the London suburb of] Golders Green, the transfer of all British Jews into this state, the confiscation of all Jewish properties outside of Golders Green, and, of course, the disenfranchisement of the Jews in Britain? Would he qualify as a right-winger? Oh yes. As a member of the lunatic fringe? Absolutely. As a mad Nazi? Probably. He would surely be well to the right of any British party, even to the right of the National Party and the National Front. But in Jewish politics, such a man would not even be a right winger, only a 'moderate'.

Unwittingly, you touched on the core problem of the Jewish community in England (and that of the US). If the opinions I described above are 'moderate' for the community, the community needs a psychoanalyst. Probably a programme of de-Nazification would do even better, because, as you correctly say, these opinions are considered moderate among Jews. As I do not wish to hurt your filial feelings, I'll tell you that my own mother considers your father's opinions as left-wing and defeatist. She would have the Gentiles expelled or killed. Like many Israeli Jews, she is dreaming and hoping for a Jewish Hitler.

Apparently, the Jewish community nurtures dark thoughts. I do not know whether these thoughts are induced by the conflict in Palestine or whether the conflict in Palestine just made these thoughts visible. If the desire for Palestine unhinges their minds, Jews should forget Palestine and save their souls. Let my right hand forget me, if I forget Jerusalem, said R. Judah ha-Levy, but it is better for you to lose one hand than for your whole body to go to hell, replied the Gospel.

If the conflict in Palestine just made these thoughts apparent, British society should limit the influence of the sick community until it heals. It is an illusion or self-deception to presume that Jewish opinions on Palestine/Israel do not influence their vision of the world. The prominence and influence of the sick Jewish community in your country is a major source of trouble in our troubled world. The elevation to Peer of the Realm of that man-eating ogre (the Pillar of the Tories, Conrad Black, friend of Pinochet, Sharon and Thatcher, husband of Barbara Amiel, the owner of the Telegraph and numerous other newspapers) is proof of the influence and infectious nature of the malady.

And what of Labour? Another freshly minted Lord, Michael Levy a.k.a. Viscount Reading, a friend of Sharon, is the grey eminence behind the New Labour leader, the Prime Minister of Great Britain and US envoy plenipotentiary, Tony Blair. A fervent Zionist, Levy was the man who made Tony Blair the Prime Minister of England. He found youthful Tony, managed his election campaign and brought him to power. (Levy learned a lot from Bronfman, who was instrumental in bringing Clinton into the White House.) Blair made Levy his special envoy to the Middle East, but the Foreign Secretary, Robin Cook blocked Levy's attempts to re-Zionize British policy. He even refused to give the freshly knighted Michael Levy a room with a secretary in the Foreign Office. It was short-sighted of Cook, who had annoyed Israelis on previous occasions as well. After Blair's re-election, Cook got the boot, and Levy was elevated.

You can see the consequences of this at work, in the BBC. The intrepid Robert Fisk of *The Independent* reported on August 4, 2001:

> BBC officials have banned their staff from referring to Israel's policy of murdering its guerrilla opponents as "assassination." BBC reporters have been told that in future they are to use Israel's own euphemism for the murders, calling them "targeted killings."

Robert Fisk concluded that this was due to "Israel's diplomatic pressure." Probably that is how it looks from Beirut, but if Fisk checked the story with London he would find another source of influence: the British Jewish community and its prominent members in both major parties.

We have a perfect witness of the racism inherent in the Jewish community in the well-known feminist writer and a good person Andrea Dworkin, who wrote:

> I realized only as a middle-aged adult that I was raised to have prejudice against Arabs and that the prejudice wasn't trivial. I was taught that Arabs were irredeemably evil. Over the years, I learned about Israeli torture of Palestinian prisoners; I knew Jewish journalists who purposefully suppressed the information so as not to "hurt" the Jewish state. My [liberal] opinions put me into constant friction with the Jewish community, including my family, many friends, and many Jewish feminists. I don't believe that American Jews raised as I was, are free of this prejudice. We were taught it as children and it has helped the Israeli government justify in our eyes what they have done to the Palestinians. We've been blinded, not just by our need for Israel or our loyalty to Jews but by a deep and real prejudice against Palestinians that amounts to race-hate.

This race-hate produces the horrible fruits of genocidal war. Dave Edwards wrote last week in ZNet:

> We live in a world where Tony Blair can insist that "nothing can justify the killing of civilians," even as B52s are doing just that in Afghanistan. Never has the deep, unconscious racism of Western society been more apparent. And at the heart of this belief, in turn, I fear, lies a truly lethal conceit: that our men, women and children really are more valuable, more precious, more fully human, than their men, women and children.

Do you recognise the source of this lethal conceit? Could it be the idea of chosenness, rejected by Christ but upheld by our Jewish community? Does it remind you of the maxim, "the life of a hundred Gentiles is not worth one Jewish toenail"? It was proclaimed by Rabbi Yaakov Perrin, on Feb. 27, 1994 and quoted by the *New York Times* on Feb. 28, 1994. It was repeated by Rabbi Yitzhak Ginzburg, one of the leading Cabbalists, and implemented by the reprisal tactics of Ariel Sharon.

Do you think the increased influence of the Jewish community is purely coincidental with this outburst of racism, with the bombing of Afghanistan, with the continuing destruction of Iraq, and with Israel's full-scale Nazi treatment of Palestinians?

Look at another coincidence. The Jewish state has the biggest gap in the developed world between the richest ten per cent and the middle classes. Bank managers earn ten thousand dollars a month, after taxes; Jewish office and industrial workers earn up to about $1,250 a month; native Gentiles earn about 1200 dollars a year. Do you think the increased influence of the Jewish community is purely coincidental with the steep rise of the social gap in England and in the US, the next two states on the ladder?

You do not have to feel accused because I am not accusing you. We do not choose where to be born. You could have been born into the family of a Prussian Junker, a steadfast supporter of the Third Reich. I could have been born to the family of cannibals who ate Captain Cook.

Still, the children of Junkers and cannibals whose eyes have been opened to alternative moralities have a choice: to stick to the family and community tradition or to reject the evil ways of their fathers and embrace humanity. We are not Chosen, we are choosing. That was the message of Jesus misunderstood by your respected father.

Notes

106. Yuletide controversy.

Deconstruction of Jewishness

[A French Professor NN responded to the article in *La Presse* of Montreal.[107] Quotes in italics are excerpts from the Professor's letter. He asked that it not be made public.]

Dear Mr Shamir, Please excuse my harshness, I write with no intention to hurt or offend you.

Dear Professor, it is a pleasure to read your letter. It is said: "The rebuke of a wise man is better than a fool's flattery." It is also said, "Rebuke a wise man and he will love you," In this spirit I read your words and reply to them.

When I discovered through [*the*] *"togethernet" discussion group that you were a Russian Jew I was flabbergasted. How was it possible that in the same discussion group a Russian Jew and a relative of an SS officer could share the same attitude toward modern Israel?*

The descendant of an SS officer does not frighten me. Fathers ate unripe grapes, etc. My uncle Daniel was the chief NKVD (State Security) officer in Vilna after the war, and according to Lithuanians, he was responsible for many deaths and deportations. They pronounce his name with the same horror as a Jew would name Eichmann, but I remember him as a kind and well-educated (Diploma in Architecture from the University of Bruxelles) man. I like his son and his grandchildren. My first love was a Russian girl, daughter of one of Stalin's forced-labour camp commanders. Ariel Sharon was my own commanding officer. My army buddy shot unarmed prisoners while I watched. No doubt, the Nazis were bad, but I think one should not demonise them to such extent as to exclude their children from discourse.

I wonder if the Nazis had not bothered with Jews, would we feel the same about them if they had mistreated, say, Byelorussians, Poles, and Lithuanians? I am not sure. John Sack wrote about a Jewish NKVD man accused of mass executions. His extradition was demanded by the Poles, but Israel replied with one word, 'chutzpah'. For me, Jews and non-Jews are quite the same: all of us are children of Adam. That is why I am unable to feel differently about a Jew-killer and a Jewish killer.

On top of it you compare the policies of the people in power in your country to the policies of the Nazis. So what's the fuss? You too speak from a position shared by Nazi ideologues and Nazi activists.

My position is quite the opposite one. German Nazis believed in the superiority of their race, and Jewish supremacists believe in their superiority. I deny any superiority of race, faith, nation, etc. Although the argument between Nazis and Jews was an argument about who is the Chosen one, I reject both. If I reject the Bourbon claim to the throne, does it make me a Bonaparte supporter?

Your credibility is null.

'Credibility' is not a neutral term. Credibility is granted by the Masters of Discourse: pro-government professors, the *New York Times* and their equivalent elsewhere. There is a whole machinery that grants credibility. Naturally I have no such 'credibility', nor do I seek it. I fight against the Masters of Discourse for the freedom of discourse.

One has to toe the line if one wants to be 'credible'. I stopped being 'credible' while I was reporting from Moscow, in 1990. My colleagues, Western correspondents in Moscow, wrote about growing anti-Semitism, forthcoming pogroms and *Pamyat.* I found that the dreadful *Pamyat* had maybe ten members; there was no anti-Semitism, no pogroms but a lot of hot air produced by Israeli Intelligence. I lost credibility, as every Western publication ran full features on Russian anti-Semitism and the approaching pogroms. As a matter of fact, there were no pogroms or persecution. Russia was (and is) governed by Jewish Prime Ministers, and Israel became the model of behaviour for Russians and Russia, judging by the Chechen war.

I was ready to give you the credit of ignorance that you did not know that one of the participants in your discussion group was a notorious anti-Semite.

This would not scare me, for two reasons. One could object to the 'Biological anti-Semites' from whom some particularly noxious anti-Jewish and anti-Gentile discourse has emanated, but they are gone and extinct. In modern discourse, 'anti-Semites' are people who doubt eternal benevolence of the Jewish People to their Gentile neighbours. They do not hate Jews *per se.* Should we shun Dostoyevsky and T.S. Elliott, Andre Gide and Jean Genet, Toynbee and Gumilev? They are often described as 'notorious anti-Semites', but their rejection of the Jewish spirit (or, if you wish, 'Jewish values') was not a question of 'prejudice'. Jews and anti-Semites agree about the prominent role of Jews in modern history. They note it with an opposite sign, + or –, but the value is high. One can reach a liveable compromise: the Jewish idea should be balanced by other systems of values, as lack of balance is a source of the present tragic state of world affairs.

The second reason is more important. The Zionists' success was built on their love affair with anti-Semites. Jacques Soustelle of OAS, Lord Balfour of the Declaration, Pat Robertson of the Christian Majority do not like Jews, and are fond of Israel. Notorious anti-Semites befriended Zionists and vice versa. This union created a monstrous offspring, the evangelical friends of Israel who wish for Armageddon. It is our task to break the Zionists' charm.

You think we Jews should cease to exist as an independent nation.

We have to make a decision. The Jews of old did not pretend to be anything but Jews; some modern Jews want to keep their duality. However, one can not eat a cake and have it forever. As long as there is a Jewish state, it is urgent to sort out our priorities. In my opinion, a French Jew is still French, a Russian Jew is still a Russian. We could complete the interrupted job of Emancipation and integrate with our respective societies. Jewish origin should be as important as an Irish one, and that is not much (Pace, my friends). The alternative is too awful to contemplate.

You say, our only salvation is to be subdued, dominated, downtrodden, dispersed.

No, no, no! Our only salvation is in equality. Give up this dualistic approach; it is possible to live as equals, not only nor necessarily as the dominated and the domineering.

The Hebrew Bible is a human product by many different authors. How can you have such little regard for all those people who cogitated, grappled with various problems of existence and handed them down for posterity? The fact that Jews survived all those centuries of active and most virulent persecution in Europe and Islamic countries should give you an idea of the power of your own tradition in furthering survival and overcoming obstacles.

You fuse four distinct questions into one, but I shall unravel them. I love the Bible, as every Hebrew speaker does. It is a complicated book, and it is not a subject to deal with lightly. Sometimes I wonder whether the world without the Old Testament would be a better world. But I would miss The Song of Songs, Hosea, Amos, Job. Rabbi Akiba said that the Song of Songs was written on a full-moon night, when the Temple stood high. The Bible contains wonderful poetry as well as dangerous poison. This poison was counteracted by the New Testament, by the Koran, etc. Whoever drinks it straight is liable to commit many crimes, including genocide. In the Second Century, Marcion would throw it away, declaring the god of the Jews to be Satan. In the Twentieth Century, Marxists likewise wanted to dispose of the Bible. I would say that the Old Testament should be treated as a fine, sharp sword: with infinite care.

Now, our Jewish religion is something else. It is not based on the Hebrew Bible, but on the Mishna and the Talmud. That is vastly entertaining literature as well. I personally enjoy it. But I am aware of its moral faults. It came into being as a reaction to Christianity, from circa 100 AD onwards. It has run its course and is almost extinct now. It makes little sense to argue for or against it.

The perseverance of Jews is something else, again. Your approach is based on your misunderstanding of the Jewish past. Yes, we like to say that we were persecuted and humiliated. But do not take these words on their face value. Do not forget: Jews were and are a part of the privileged classes. The medieval Jew was as privileged as a nobleman, and certainly richer than the average nobleman. That is why every baptised Jew became a nobleman. It was not thought a good idea for a Jew to give up his Jewishness and to join the downtrodden.

Abram Leon, a young Jewish Marxist who perished in Auschwitz, (you probably know his book, as it was published in French with Maxim Rodinson's introduction) proved that a Polish nobleman who wished to be a loan shark, was forced to become a Jew, while a Jew who preferred to join the landed gentry became a Christian. It was not an obvious choice for practical reasons, well outside of religious arguments.

Jewish-ness is not a religion-based phenomenon. In Spain, crypto-Jews lived as Christians for 400 years, but preserved their separateness and occupation niche. Nowadays, the majority of Jews in Israel and elsewhere are not religious at all. Jewish-ness is about separateness and privilege.

The story of the French aristocracy could be told as a story of 'active and virulent persecution' as well. So many of them were beheaded in 1793. So many of them died for France on the battlefields of Crecy and Poitiers. Still, the story of the nobility is not only the story of suffering: there was a lot of privilege as well. Although the noblemen have lost their privileges, the Jews have not given up theirs.

Israelis are not reading properly their own religious tradition.

Dear Professor, it is possible. It is also possible that you kindly try to re-interpret the Jewish religious tradition in your own humanistic way. I remember how years ago Hanan Porath, the charismatic leader of Mafdal, told me there are no *gerim* (strangers to be treated as neighbours) nowadays. By some legal trick, all good provisions of the Bible appear to relate to Jews only in the minds of the real Jews, my contemporaries. Can it be different? Yes, but then it will be Christianity or Islam. Judaism is based on the two-tier approach of ingroup-outgroup. It is a Way, but it is too destructive for the world.

Sometimes I think the Jewish way of life won some two hundred years ago, when the other parts of Western society decided to turn bourgeois: to behave like Jews. The Jewish way is quite tempting: it means disregard of the Common Good of the community you live in. You would say this is not a big invention; it is done by every crook or criminal. The difference is in moral stability, in positive reinforcement of internal morals. A crook does not offer a way of life, as his lack of morals brings his collapse. The Jewish Way allows us to act as crooks while keeping the high moral ground.

Your intervention at McGill in Canada confirmed my intuition that in spite of your brilliance you are a Jew who has lost his way, lost the light of his own tradition, left to grapple in the dark. Your intervention at McGill made me finally react and decide to write to you. You are destroying and tearing down what the previous generation of Israeli leaders has tried to build. McGill is symptomatic of your work of deconstruction. The great British historian Arnold Toynbee whom I still admire for the brilliance of his insight on many topics, had nevertheless an unfortunate anti-Semitic or anti-Israeli streak. He branded Judaism as "fossilization" and questioned the very existence of the State of Israel. On January 31, 1961 the McGill University organized a public debate between Toynbee and Yaacov Herzog, the Israeli ambassador to Canada on the essence of the Jewish history and the "moral character" of the State of Israel. Now Toynbee is symptomatic of what you would like to achieve: to make Anglo-Americans abandon their commitment to Israel, and stop supporting it financially and militarily. I am afraid this is going to happen. The winds of change are blowing. I am not surprised that you went to McGill. You are too clever to have missed this historic connection.

Dear Professor, you are too kind. The main character of *Tales of Ise*, a 9th century Japanese poem, compared his peasant love with a pine tree. He wanted to say she is as uncouth as a tree. But she loved pine trees and was pleased by his comparison. Though I am about to make the same error, I am so fond of Toynbee that I'll just repeat: dear Professor, you are too kind.

Yes, the Anglo-American entente with the Jews should be terminated. These two paradigms register a resonance that can bring our world to its premature end. A cat is a lovable creature, unless it is tiger-sized. The Anglo-Americans entered the deal that brought them prosperity, but now they have to pay for it dearly. This prosperity was achieved by the financial pyramid of the overpriced dollar, and by speculative capital.

Ninety per cent of all transactions in the US are speculative transactions. It was supported by a massive propaganda war to encourage consuming and expansion. In order to cover the pyramid, Anglo-Americans intimidate the world with their weapons of mass destruction. Ordinary people of the UK and the US get no fun out of it: in England, child poverty has grown threefold since Margaret Thatcher came to power. In the US, there are millions of homeless children. Many American Jews push for the destruction of Abraham's homeland, Iraq. That is the result of the entente.

Arnold Toynbee could not have expected in 1961 that a few years later, 'the fossil' would come to life, too much alive. He never saw the movie, *The Alien*, where a frozen fossil turns out to be a source of danger. His contemporary Jewish thinkers also thought that Jewry was on its way to disappearance. That was a precondition of emancipation, after all. But it just did not happen.

In my opinion, it should happen, for it would be good for the descendants of Jews and for the world in general. A descendant of Spanish crypto-Jews, Jacques Derrida, brought to France the idea of Deconstruction. Now it is the time to bring Deconstruction home and deconstruct Jewish-ness.

Notes

107. Professor NN responded to the article in *La Presse*, an important newspaper of Quebec, Canada.

Binoculars of Ms. Klein

[Response to an article[108] by Naomi Klein in *Globe and Mail* on Globalisation and anti-Semitism.]

Binoculars are a handy thing, usually used to enlarge small distant objects. But one may turn them the other way around and turn a close and threatening object into a small and distant one. This procedure, usually reserved for kids, was applied by Naomi Klein, the best-selling author of *No Logo*, in her letter to the Canadian daily, *Globe and Mail.*[109] Under her magic pen, the most powerful group of people in North America, owners of almost all Canadian and the US media and of a sizeable chunk of real estate, was turned into a handful of fearful Jews hiding for their lives in a remote synagogue. It takes time to understand that she writes about people living today, not about some medieval event.

Ms. Klein writes: "Most Jews are so frightened that they are now willing to do anything to defend Israeli policies." The second half is right. We know that most Jews are willing to do anything to defend and support and promote ethnic cleansing in Palestine. They are willing and doing it all the time. They booed down Paul Wolfowitz, the most bloodthirsty member of the Neo-Liberal pack for not being sufficiently bloodthirsty. In your average synagogue, they consider Sharon a bit too kind-hearted for his job, a closet Leftie. But fear does not enter this equation: nowadays the Jews have nothing to fear. They say and do what they want, without looking back. The Jewish tradition forbids mistreating a Goy, as long as such mistreatment has the possibility of misfiring and endangering a Jew. Apparently, now the Jews do not feel themselves threatened at all.

A few days ago, I went to a Jewish solidarity gathering in Brighton Beach near New York. The Jews cheered Yvet Lieberman, an Israeli minister who left Sharon's government protesting Sharon's liberal approach. They spent a lot of money and put up screens and satellite links to proclaim their feelings unequivocally. One does not have to go to a public gathering: open any Jewish newspaper, from the Israeli *Haaretz* to the *American Jewish Week*, and a stream of unadulterated hatred will hit you square in the face.

It is not news: ten years ago, Danni Rubinstein, a liberal Israeli journalist, complained that the American Jews invariably support the most extreme nationalist forces in Israel. American Jews are not alone: the Jews of England and Russia are braying for the Goyiish blood, as well. A skilful apologist, Ms. Klein prefers to explain away this criminal and culpable encouragement for mass murder, by their fear. She would make a fine defence lawyer in Nuremberg. Indeed, who is not fearful? As Dr. Nolte wrote, the Nazi atrocities were caused by their fear of Russian Communism. Communist atrocities were caused by their fear of imperialist aggression, etc. In other words, fear is not a defence. If they are afraid they can consult a shrink, not support genocide.

Ms. Klein builds a syllogism: Jews support Sharon because they are afraid, let us therefore fight anti-Semitism, and the problem will be solved. Alas, her conclusion is as weak as her premise that Sharon does not use Jewish fear; he mobilizes Jewish chauvinism, including that of Ms. Klein. In her book, *No Logo*, she tells us that her activism began with defence of the rich Jews who were underrepresented at the board of their companies. It ended with the defence of Sharon's supporters. Now, most of the Jews speak with one voice, from 'left' Naomi Klein to 'right' Barbara Amiel. For them, there is no Left nor Right; just the Jewish ethnic interests.

Ms. Klein gets a lot of mileage out of some damaged synagogues. We have not heard a word of protest from her and her friends about the siege of the Nativity Church in Bethlehem, or destruction of the ancient Green Mosque in Nablous. Not a word! I can imagine what would happen if a synagogue would be besieged and its occupants starved and shot as in Bethlehem. Klein would like us to care about synagogues. Synagogues are used to collect money for Sharon's offensive. Netanyahu and other monsters habitually speak in synagogues to their devotees. Should there be peace to synagogues and war to churches and mosques? Synagogues are not neutral, and Ms Klein admits it: "At my neighbourhood synagogue," she writes, "the sign on the door says, "Support Israel . . . Now more than ever."

Now—after the massacre of Jenin, after the attack on Bethlehem, after mass destruction of Ramallah and Hebron, they wish to support Israel more than ever. Without their support, Sharon would never commit his atrocities. Without their support, Israel would shrink to its natural size. In my opinion, these people should not be protected, as some wee little innocent group of religious believers. These powerful and influential men should be treated with extreme prejudice.

There is no danger of racist attacks on peaceful Jews, and it is good. The present level of intermarriage and social connections excludes such a possibility. Even Jean-Mari Le Pen has a Jewish son-in-law, Samuel Marechal and a very close Jewish friend, Jean-Claude Martinez, both prominent members of Front National. But the Jewish extra-territorial state, this extension of Israel overseas, should be pointed out as a perpetrator of atrocities.

Notes

108. globeandmail.com, Wednesday, April 24, 2002 *Toronto Globe and Mail*: "Old hates fuelled by fear," by Naomi Klein:

> On Sunday night, I turned on my television and I saw triumphant Jean-Marie Le Pen celebrating his newfound status as the second-most popular political leader in France. When hundreds of globalization activists began flocking to Ramallah to act as "human shields" between Israeli tanks and Palestinians, the theory that has been developing outside trade summits was put into concrete action. But when I saw Mr. Le Pen beaming on TV, arms raised in triumph, some of my enthusiasm drained away. There is no connection whatsoever between French fascism and the "free Palestine" marchers in Washington (indeed, the only people Mr. Le Pen's supporters seem to dislike more than Jews are Arabs). And yet, I couldn't help thinking about all the recent events I've been to where anti-Muslim violence was rightly condemned, Ariel Sharon deservedly blasted, but no mention was made of attacks on Jewish synagogues, cemeteries and community centres. Or about the fact that every time I log onto activist news sites such as Indymedia.org, which practise "open publishing," I'm confronted with a string of Jewish conspiracy theories about 9-11 and excerpts from the *Protocols of the Elders of Zion*. The hatred of Jews is a potent political tool in the hands of the right in Europe and in Israel. For Mr. Le Pen, anti-Semitism is a windfall, helping spike his support from 10 per cent to 17 per cent in a week.

109. globeandmail.com, Wednesday, April 24, 2002.

A Strange Case of Jared Israel

The Masters of the Discourse would not be what they are unless they were cunning. Many people arrive at the conclusion that they are being misled by the media, experts and politicians. But what is the true reality? The Masters provide a huge choice of traps and misleading explanations of reality, partly true, partly false. Only careful reading allows us to notice the hidden trap.

The website Emperor's Clothes has all the qualities to pass for an opposition. They object to the present policies of the Bush administration. They can disapprove of Israeli high-handedness. They show very well some of the lies permeating the media and politics in the US. And only sometimes their words express their true agenda. A reader's letter alerted me to one of the traps.

A recent exchange of remarks http://emperors-clothes.com/letters/joan.htm between Jared Israel, one of the Emperor's Clothes' most active voices, and a reader provides us with a unique opportunity to see through the fake opposition. A reader asks Jared Israel, does he not see a connection between the war axe grinding of Bush administration and the Jewish lobby.

And the fake opposition voice immediately denies it: "I know many Jewish people and I can tell you that, regarding Israel, they are mostly convinced that the aftermath of 9/11 has made things much worse for that country. Most US Jews do *not* want war with Iraq."

> If you believe that, one day you will buy the Brooklyn Bridge. Most US Jews THAT MATTER push for the Doomsday. Among them are Richard Perle, the chairman of the Pentagon's Defence Policy Board, an ex-employee of the Israeli weapon manufacturer Soltam, and the great supporter of the war; Paul Wolfowitz, Deputy Defence Secretary and a leading Zionist; Douglas Feith, a representative of an 'Israeli Armaments Manufacturer'; Dov Zakheim, Under Secretary of Defence; Edward Luttwak, of the National Security Study Group of the Department of Defence at the Pentagon; Lewis Libby, Vice President Dick Cheney's Chief of Staff and a lawyer for the thief Marc Rich; Robert Satloff, the U.S. National Security Council Advisor, and the executive director of the Israeli lobby's "think tank," Washington Institute for Near East Policy; Elliott Abrams, National Security Council Advisor; and many, many others. For sure, there should be some Jews against the war, but they keep quiet.

It is not classified information, spread by obscure sites: an honest Jewish voice, Philip Weiss, admits in the *New York Observer*:[110] "Holy or Unholy, Jews and the Right in an Alliance" and they push for War. "What about the natural proclivity of Jews to be liberals?" asks Weiss, and replies:

> Liberals have yielded authority in the debate. The refusal of liberal American Jews to make an independent stand has left the American left helpless. American liberalism has always drawn strength from Jews. Liberal Jews often have private conversations about the Middle East in which they acknowledge the absence of leadership in the Israeli government and the desperation of the Palestinians, but they generally do not wish this to become a public conversation with other American citizens.

Intra-Jewish discourse became coarsely racist, and the Jewish Press published an attack on "The Plague of Jewish-Arab Marriages," concludes Weiss.

So much for the first lie of Jared Israel. But he does not stop here. He has to dissuade his readers that it is Israel and the US Jews who push for war. In a stupefying piece of disinformation, [Jared] Israel writes: "There is *nothing* worse for Israel than war in the Middle East. Israel is a tiny country with very hard-to-defend borders, surrounded by Muslim-dominated countries with about 50 times Israel's population . . . The worst thing for Israel is a war in Iraq because it can only fan the flames of Muslim fanaticism, which will then be directed at Israel. The U.S. and England attack; Israel pays."

Well, Israel is surrounded by 'Muslim-dominated countries', but this 'tiny country' with the third nuclear potential in the world is fully supported by the 'Jew-dominated country', which happens to be the world's only superpower. Though Jared Israel thinks the war against Iraq is the worst thing for Israel, probably he has in mind some other Israel, as all senior politicians of the Jewish state, its prime-ministers and ministers for defence, its spokesmen, official and unofficial, publicly and privately, call for war. An ex-Mossad agent Victor Ostrovsky[111] asked his superiors why they were trying to cause a war between the US and Iraq. The reply was that Israel does not have the manpower and aircraft carriers to do the job.

The first utterance from Ehud Barak and Bibi Netanyahu on 9/11 were their demand to destroy Iraq (followed by Iran and Libya). Ariel Sharon pushes for war relentlessly and even now went to Moscow in order to persuade President Putin to support the war.

Yes, the war is against the true interests of Jews living in Israel. But we have no voice: our politicians are fully integrated in the Judeo-American establishment, they get their financial support from the American Jews, they dance to their fiddle. Our true interests can emerge only if and when the American Jews will lose their commanding heights in the American discourse.

The third lie of Jared Israel is even more brazen: "The U.S. and England attack; Israel pays." What nonsense! Israel NEVER pays. Whatever happens, the Israeli Army's redeployment or violent attack on Palestinians, the settlements in the occupied territories or the murder of children, everything is paid for by the people of the United States and Europe. They paid for Israeli withdrawal from Lebanon and from a part of the Golan heights. They pay now for food for the starved Palestinians, they will pay for any 'peace settlement' Israel would agree to sign. When the Israeli 'peace camp' promotes an idea of some compensation for the Palestinian refugees, they never offer to pay for the stolen lands and houses they live in. It is always one condition: "all will be paid for by the world community." The bill of Israel is not paid by the US Jews, either: they are not that silly. The US Jews pay their politicians or threaten them into political oblivion, unless they pay with the money of American goyim. If political considerations cause them to desist, they force the Goyim of Germany or Switzerland to foot the bill.

How can a reader become aware of the hidden agenda of a liar with a straight face? There are telltale signs. He throws 'Nazi' at everybody, from brothers Dulles to yours truly. He needlessly invokes the Jewish holocaust. And whenever pushed he immediately refers to 'conspiracy theories'. Jared Israel writes to his reader: "If you see an Israeli plot in Fleischer being Jewish, why not see an Israeli plot in *my* being Jewish as well?" Well, that is what they said when all the luminaries of the Jewish America AND of the state of Israel, from Foxman to Barak, begged Bill Clinton to pardon their crony Marc Rich. The clear-thinking Jewish American writer, Norman Finkelstein, remarked: "If the leading Jews act together, should we shut our eyes in despair and cry: oh no, it can not be, otherwise we shall be condemned as 'conspiracy-theorists'?" In plain words, yes, Mr. Jared Israel, you are a part of the Judeo-Zionist plot. You provide the Jewish instigators of the war with much needed camouflage.

It is very good that the Emperor's Clothes website objects to the war. It is good that they do not support the war effort of the Jewish Lobby. But it is not worth one penny if they do not speak against the real instigators of the war. It is not the nincompoop in the White House nor the Pentagon, but the US Jewish establishment, *the Jews that matter*, that push for the war, with the connivance of silent liberals. Our only hope was expressed by the brilliant Canadian Jewish philosopher Michael Neumann: "Sooner or later, the great white men of America will wake up to their true interests, and get themselves a new set of speechwriters and pundits. The Jews will go out of style."

Notes

110. http://www.observer.com/pages/frontpage4.asp#.
111. "The Other Side of Deception: A Rogue Agent Exposes the Mossad's Secret Agenda," 1995.

Human Shield

[A reply to Rabbi Michael Lerner, who objected[112] to the 'Zionism is Racism' resolution.]

I

Dear Rabbi Lerner,

I read your letter with growing unease. It is very good that you speak against Jewish racism. It is commendable that you condemn human rights abuses in Palestine. I sympathise with your position, and regret you are threatened by some Jewish punks.

By speaking against the deeds of people you consider your own, you gained high moral ground held by dissidents of many lands and countries, next to Thomas Mann and Bertolt Brecht, next to Solzhenitsyn and Bukovsky, next to the brave French who rejected the war in Algeria and the good Americans who travelled to Hanoi during the Vietnam war. You became one of those who preferred the cause of humanity to the jingoist spirit. You are an example for many Jews of conscience. In brief, you and the Tikkun are doing a wonderful job.

II

But for God's sake, do not squander your moral capital so prodigally! Do not cause people to doubt your sincerity. Your enemies will consider you a Trojan horse in the besieged camp of harmony seekers. They will say your words against Israeli excesses were but a tactical move, as on the first occasion you stood at the side of Israel and brought disarray into our ranks.

Nowadays, some very good men and women from overseas come to Beit Jalla near Bethlehem to serve as human shields against possible Israeli bombardment. We applaud them for upholding the spirit of humanity and saving lives. Do not turn yourself into a human shield to protect Israeli racism from a UN resolution. It will bring a just ridicule.

Maybe the time will come when your defence of the people of Israel will become necessary, when you will be called to act as a human shield against real weapons of destruction. But we are very far away from that moment.

Our forefather and our example, Abraham pleaded mercy for Sodom when God wished to destroy it. If Abraham would plead against condemnation of Sodom in the UN, probably God would not even consult him before the day of wrath.

Consider Joe Slovo, the great South African of Jewish origin. He was a friend of all South Africans, and as a member of the ANC (their equivalent of PLO) he was instrumental in causing reconciliation on the ruins of apartheid. Would he be able to do so if he would speak against the UN condemnation of apartheid? As a matter of fact, he supported guerrilla warfare ('terrorist actions') of the oppressed against the oppressors. But you began to stall rather too early, on the positions of the South African Progressive Party.

Consider your American hero, John Brown. He joined forces with the Blacks and fought for their (and everybody's) liberty. In our terms, he would take an AK machinegun and stand on the barricades of Jenin and Beit Jalla, or rather, do an armed sortie into Tel Aviv. And actually there was an American of Jewish origin who supported John Brown, as Lenni Brenner reported.

On this scale, we are just moderate salon abolitionists or bleeding liberals. We still have not wholeheartedly embraced the idea of a single common destiny of people of Palestine, and, actually, of the people of the world.

You know the Jewish saying, "He acts as Zimri and demands the reward of Pinchas." It is *chutzpah* to act as a liberal Confederate and to demand the reward of John Brown.

III

The motion of condemning Israeli politics as racist is a just and a moderate one, although your reasoning is too faulty even to argue with. You repeat the old Zionist propaganda rehashing it with modern terms. Still, it remains the same call of Jewish exclusivity and uniqueness. On a historical level, your reasoning is unacceptable.

'Rectification of 1800 years of history' is a silly idea. It would allow the druids of Wales to expel the majority of Englishmen from the British Isles 'back' to the forests of Saxony, dunes of Denmark, and Normandy beaches for an eternal holiday season. More to the point, it surely would allow the Native Americans to claim and possess your lovely house with its beautiful view over San Francisco Bay. Leave such grand scale rectifications to the day when His feet will stand on the Mount of Olives.

The idea of unique Jewish suffering is just another form of the false Chosenness claim. All people of the Earth suffered a lot, and many of them continue to suffer. It justifies nothing.

The Huguenots of France suffered the Night of St. Bartholomew, but it does not justify the apartheid in South Africa they helped to establish.

The Germans suffered the iniquity of Versailles and Dresden, but it does not justify the Nazi mass murders.

The Hutus of Rwanda and Burundi suffered under the yoke of the Tutsi, but it does not justify the genocide.

IV

Israel, Zionism and Jewish chauvinism should be dealt with by humankind on a priority basis, without fear of a double standard. It is not because of Palestinian suffering only. It is because of the great influence of Jews in the US, Europe and Russia. The descendents of Jews occupy important positions in their societies, and their opinions have more of an impact on the world's fate than opinions held by Hutus or Khmer. This is reality. As more people of power become poisoned by the ideas of exclusivity, they move the world on the path of globalization, nature destruction, social Darwinism, and into a bleak future of Masters and Slaves.

Your place as a Rabbi is on the front line of the war for the Jewish souls. Help them to reach the Tikkun, the mystic correction of the soul, by thorough exorcism of the haughty spirit of Chosen-ness. Consider the old fashioned verse, *Hosech shivto sone bno*, "There is no correction without some chastisement." The planned condemnation of Jewish racism is but a mild chastisement, and it should be accepted with love.

[Rabbi Lerner consistently tried to hold a Meretz-like position of accepting the Israeli discourse and arguing against the occupation. That is why I responded to him again in the end of 2002.]

Notes

112. Rabbi Lerner, the publisher of *Tikkun* magazine, wrote:

> "Say 'No' To The 'Zionism Is Racism' Lynch Mob"
> by Rabbi Michael Lerner, Editor, *Tikkun*
>
> Nothing could be more destructive to the struggle against racism than to attempt to divert it into a struggle against Israeli policies today, policies with which I disagree. I am horrified that some misguided friends of the Palestinians will use this moment to misdirect the conference against racism into a futile propaganda battle against Israeli policy.

Here are several reasons why this is a big mistake:
There is nothing racist about affirmative action to rectify histories of past oppression. Israel is the first state to be created as an act of international affirmative action in light of:

a. A history of world-wide discrimination, oppression, and genocide against the Jewish people that went on for1800 years.
b. The forceful dispossession of the Jewish people from their land by Roman and later by Islamic forces.
c. The long history of apartheid against Jews in Islamic countries, culminating in assaults and pogroms—which, though never as intense as those in Europe, were as intense and oppressive as the treatment of Africans by the white population of South Africa during apartheid.
d. The illegitimate and racist actions by Palestinians seeking to prevent Jews from immigrating to Palestine when the Jews were the refugees climbing out of the crematoria and gas chambers of Europe or fleeing from racist mobs in Islamic countries.

Child Murders and Rabbi Lerner

Rabbi Michael Lerner published a letter containing an attempt to attach collective guilt for a single crime to the whole Palestinian people, and to shift the blame for the bloodshed to the victims. The Metzer murder, a revolting crime committed by a deranged individual, is (mis)presented by Michael Lerner as an act of Arafat's (and Palestinian national) policy. Moreover, it is described as a "Palestinian act of terror." It is an unacceptable lie. If we were to refer to yesterday's murder of two Palestinian toddlers in Khan Yunes as 'Jewish child-murders', or even to Marc Rich's deeds as 'Jewish fraud', Rabbi Lerner would certainly call it 'anti-Semitism'. That is why his letter should be condemned as an incitement to hate.

The deranged criminal from Metzer acted alone, and his action was met with horror by Palestinians and Jews alike. If and when he will be apprehended he will certainly be punished. On the other hand, the murderers of the Palestinian children in Khan Yunes remain at large; they are protected and their crimes condoned by the Jewish state. When a Palestinian girl child was murdered by a Jewish fanatic near Nablous, the witness for defence, Rabbi Yitzhak Ginzburg, claimed a Jew may kill a Goy with impunity. It appears his opinion won the day: practically none of the Jews who murdered three hundred innocent children in Palestine have been brought to justice. Hilmi Shusha, a Palestinian child from Husan, was murdered by a settler Naum Korman in full view of the entire village, but the Jewish judge Ruth Orr has sentenced Nahum Korman, the child murderer, to six months of public service in an old folks house.

Friends of Palestine won't stoop as low as the late Prime Minister Golda Meir, who proclaimed "I can't forgive the Palestinians that they force us to kill their children." We won't lie like the late Prime Minister David Ben-Gurion who tried to attach blame for the Deir Yassin Massacre to 'Arab irregulars', and for Sharon's massacre in Qibie to the relatives of 'Arab terror victims'. We won't try the line of Madeline Albright who thought the murder of Iraqi children was worth its while. Instead, we call to bring to the International Criminal Court every Jewish murderer of Palestinian children.

Rabbi Lerner should pay heed to a recent letter to *Haaretz* newspaper by Dr. Miriam Reik, who wrote:

> Killing kids gets to be routine.
>
> Israel is, in many ways, unique. It is the only country in the world in which a child, throwing a stone, is considered to have committed a capital

Nablous Kids

crime, and a soldier can kill him with a bullet with impunity—no questions asked.

Haaretz reported the death in this fashion yesterday of Mohammed ali Zeiz, a 15-year-old, without comment. It is the only country in the world in which the occupying army does not hold its fire when an innocent child is on the scene, much less rush to protect him.

Ibrahim al-Madani, 12 years old, died in this way yesterday, as reported by *Haaretz*, without comment. We all know of dozens of such incidents, which led Amnesty International to characterize the current conflict as one in which the lives of children are treated with "utter disregard," a charge met with cynical protestations of innocence by the IDF.

> However, it is also a sad comment on the general deterioration of standards in Israel, that *Haaretz* can report such incidents, time and again, without editorial comment. Anything, I suppose, can become routine.
>
> —Miriam M. Reik, Ph.D.

Rabbi Lerner writes: "There is never any moral equivalence between one act of murder and another." He is absolutely right. That is why, while mourning the dead of Khan Yunes and Metzer, we observe the vast difference between a one-man-crime and an act of the Jewish state-condoned and sponsored child murder.

Part VIII

Ode to Cynthia

[This was written in summer 2002, when American primaries showed again the awful might of the Jewish election machine in interlinked destinies of America and Palestine. It was written to express support for Cynthia McKinney, a congresswoman from Atlanta. Its follow-up, Blacks and Jews, was written for this edition.]

Things must be bad indeed if a woman steps forward to the line of fire. Nature arranged that a woman does not court danger unless her land and her folks are in real trouble. But when she does, she teaches men a lesson of manly behaviour.

When France was fading away, a shepherd girl Joan of Arc took a heavy sword and led the flower of French nobles to assault the walls of Orleans. When cities of Republican Spain were strafed by the Nazi Luftwaffe, it was a woman, Dolores Ibarruri, La Pasionaria, who said to her people: it is better to die tall, than to live on your knees. In 1990, when Mikhail Gorbachev led his country to disaster and disintegration, a year before the wealth of Russia was embezzled in a privatisation spree, only one person dared to raise her voice against the dictator in the parliament. She was the indomitable Sashie Umalatov, an MP from the Chechen Mountains.

Now it is the turn of the US to feel the chilly wind of eternity on its face. It came from an unexpected direction. People of America became hostage in the hands of a few men with too many dollars in their pockets and endless greed in their hearts. For millennia, the difference of income, education, and standard of living was not so vast in one land. The wealth of the nation could provide every American with a superb education, perfect medical care, happy childhood, secure old age, guaranteed home, and free time to open one's mind to new thoughts and old friends. America could be on its way to the Golden Age of universal happiness and wisdom.

Instead, a small group of men squeeze the nation in order to add another billion to their coffers. They would surely destroy the US by their limitless greed. The devotees of Mammon, they are totally devoid of compassion for the people they live amongst. They do not see the local people as 'their own kind'. If they want to show compassion, they send money to Israel. Out of the five dollars the American taxpayer gives for aid, four dollars lands in the coffers of the Jewish state. They appear unstoppable, as the politicians are scared of them and docilely raise their hands and sign the pledge promising to send more money to Israeli generals. Support of Israel is not a foreign policy. It is the covenant of the Mammonites, and you sign it with blood. With Palestinian blood.

But one woman refused to sign the pledge. One woman, Cynthia McKinney, a member of Congress from Georgia, dared to refuse. Four hundred congressmen signed it; they preferred their own personal advancement to the good of the country. Ancestors of Cynthia were slaves in her native Georgia. But she is one of a very few free persons in the US Congress. As we Israelis were used to saying about our Golda Meir, she is the only man over there. McKinney is a black woman, but she is the whitest man of them all, they would say before the Politically Correct era. She knew the billions of Israeli aid are needed for the poor people of the United States, for her own Afro-American community. She wanted to uphold the sovereignty of the people and Congress of the United States, in face of encroaching servility to the Jewish Lobby.

She is not alone. Another wonderful Afro-American congresswoman, Barbara Lee, cast the only vote against the slaughter in Afghanistan; John Conyers, Jessie Jackson, Jr., and Maxine Waters supported the cause of Palestine on different occasions. Ron Paul of Texas voted against the all-house resolution, sending an obsequious greeting to General Sharon. Nick Rahall, John Sununu, David Bonior did not bend.

Cynthia was just as outspoken about the evil she saw. Said McKinney:[113]

> There are many Members of Congress who want to be free. I am one of them. I wanted to be free to vote according to my conscience, but I had been told that if I didn't sign a pledge supporting the military superiority of Israel, no support would come my way. And sure enough, I didn't sign the pledge and no support came my way. I suffered silently year in and year out, because I refused to sign that pledge. And then, like a slave that found a way to buy his freedom . . . I went to work . . . I wanted to be free . . . Free to cast the votes in the United States Congress as I saw fit and not as I was dictated to.

Now she stands for re-election, and her chances are dim, as the frightful AIPAC, the spearhead of the organised Jewish community, targeted her. They do not want to see independent and free congressmen on Capitol Hill. Their immense financial might, network of connections in the media and universities are used to smother every free voice. They succeeded in unseating Earl Hilliard, another Black Congressman, who did not bow to Sharon, and now they also plan to do Cynthia in. If they succeed, the cause of freedom will suffer a huge setback. If she succeeds, the myth of Jewish omnipotence will evaporate, and America will look towards better days, as support or rejection of segregated Israel speaks volumes about the true agenda of a candidate.

Cynthia is not 'against Jews', as there are many very good folks of Jewish origin. While the organised Jewish community implements a disgusting policy, in domestic and foreign affairs alike, there are wonderful outsiders, 'the remnant of Israel'. Rejected by the community and rejecting it, they stand for integration in Palestine and in the US. Some of them have supported Cynthia's campaign; another outsider manages her campaign. Through them, "you will be blessed by all people," the Lord's promise to Abraham is made true.

I am not sure whether Rabbi Michael Lerner, the editor of *Tikkun*, a "Progressive Jewish monthly" from California, will be equally blessed. Rabbi Lerner has spoken in support of Cynthia McKinney, but demanded in return to "call for Israel to be given either membership in NATO or a mutual defence pact with the U.S." Such a support defeats its purpose. As if the military and political US backing of the racist Jewish state were not sufficient, Lerner wants to establish it in law. Cynthia openly spoke against hegemony of the Zionist Lobby, against the Israel connection. Lerner offers to achieve the purpose of the Zionist lobby under pretence of fighting it. This sophisticated cunning is not unusual for crypto-Zionists, acting as deep penetration agents outside their milieu, and Lerner already has performed a similar task for the Zionists during the Durban Conference.[114] Next time, he will fight heroin addiction by demanding that the drug to be sold in every shop. Cynthia and other congressmen should accept his offer of help for what it is worth, but reject his demand of political payoff to Zionists.

Cynthia's is not a divisive voice of Blacks vs. Whites, or Democrats vs. Republicans, or Left against Right. She speaks for the people of the US against foreign interests. She is the congresswoman who dared to remind us of the *USS Liberty* seamen, butchered by Israeli heavy machine guns and missiles. She reminded her audience of the last stand of Faris Ode, the brave Palestinian kid who faced the Israeli tank with a stone and was murdered. She stands against corporate greed. She stands for the nature deemed expendable by the Greedies.

This woman with a name from the love lyrics of Propertius, the delicate Greek poet, who called himself 'a pale knight in thrall of my angry Cynthia', is an all-American figure, brought forth by the spirit of America. The great country does not want to die. In such moments, the land calls for its sons and daughters to step forward to the line of fire. Cynthia heard the call. Support of Cynthia is the ultimate test of love for America, of belief in America's future in the family of nations, as an equal and friendly nation, not as an enforcer of the creed of Greed.

It is paramount to rally around her, as the French nobles rallied around Joan of Arc. Whether you are a descendant of African slaves or Muslim immigrants, a son of the Confederacy or a Daughter of the American Revolution, a freedom-loving Jew or a born-again Christian—it is the time to unite for Cynthia and for America.

Notes

113. Speech at the ADC Chapter in San Francisco on May 22, 2001.
114. See the Human Shield on www.israelshamir.net.

War and Peace

The two-party system of the US is dead. It has lost the trust of the people; fewer and fewer voters care to cast their ballots, as the choice they offer is always a wrong one. The last bell of the two-party system sounded with the defeat of Congresswoman Cynthia[115] McKinney, a member from Georgia, in the Democratic primaries.

She was ambushed in the Democratic Party primaries, when her enemies brought in thousands of Republican voters to vote against Cynthia. Have the Republicans seen the light? Alexander Cockburn of Counterpoint had another explanation: "Torrents of American Jewish money showered her opponent. Buckets of sewage were poured over McKinney's head in the [Jewish-managed and edited] *Washington Post* and the *Atlanta Constitution*."

"Cynthia was not the first Afro-American victim of the Jewish Lobby": Earl Hilliard, first elected black congressperson in Alabama since the Reconstruction, was defeated by "a torrent of money from out-of-state American Jewish organizations," writes Cockburn, for "calling for some even-handedness in the Middle East."

Cockburn's conclusion was denied by Stephen Zunes,[116] who stressed it is the pro-War forces that defeated Cynthia. "Thousands of conservative Republicans voted in the Democratic primary for the sole purpose of defeating one of Congress' most outspoken defenders of civil rights, labour and the environment and one of its most vocal critics of President George W. Bush. These Republicans were particularly incensed at McKinney's criticism of President Bush's 'war on terrorism'. Majette's top contributors include a sizable number of major Republican donors and very few names commonly associated with a Jewish ethnicity," wrote Zunes in the adequately named article, "Don't Blame the Jews for Cynthia McKinney's Defeat."

Brilliant Edward Herman[117] rejected Zunes' conclusion by connecting McKinney's defeat with that of Hilliard, another Black congressman who dared to oppose the Jewish Lobby. "The unique factor in both elections was the [Jewish] anger at these blacks for daring to oppose [their] policy. [Jewish Lobby's] intrusions into the Alabama and Georgia elections and successful removal of Hilliard and McKinney are arguably a form of disenfranchisement of black voters, by money power rather than legal tricks or coercion, and should be strenuously opposed."

In this political whodunit we have a luxury of choice between two potential culprits, the Jewish Lobby and the War Party. Let us look at the names. The crossover of Republican voters was organised by John Podhoretz, David Horowitz and Jonah Goldberg of William F. Buckley's *National Review* magazine. They inspired Newt Gingrich, the Ex-House Speaker and right hand of Richard Perle of the 'National Defense Advisory Council', aka the Wolfowitz cabal. Gingrich, a Georgia man, did the hatchet job. They got away with it due to the Democratic Party's connivance. The Governor Roy Barnes, a Democrat, was closely connected with Gingrich.

Our choice was that of a drunken driver, who sees everything double. The Jewish Lobby is the War Party, the closely-knit gang of Jewish supremacists and their Gentile neo-con allies. In 1990, Joe Sobran listed the commentators who constantly defend Israel: Podhoretz, Rosenthal, Dershowitz, Martin Peretz, George Will, Mortimer Zuckerman, Morton Kondracke, Jeane Kirkpatrick, Kenneth Adelman, Amos Perlmutter, Eric Breindal, Cal Thomas, Max Lerner, Ben Wattenberg, Charles Krauthammer, William Safire, Fred Barnes ... Now all of them have emerged as advocates of the War Party.

Bill White[118] followed the fates of the people on Sobran's list: "Not only are those names still with us, but they are in power, having snuck in under the curtain of the Bush administration. America is no longer concerned about Israeli infiltration of the government—instead, the American government has become a colonial outpost of the Zionist terror-state. Norman Podhoretz, of course, is still the war-mongering imperialist swine he always was. David Frum is now writing the speeches that George the Second is using to take us into war. [He penned the Axis of Evil speech.] Alan Dershowitz is now, in the words of CBS, 'tell[ing] Correspondent Mike Wallace that torture is inevitable' [and promoting racism]."

Thus, both Republicans and Democrats appear to be infiltrated. With Gore as President, the War on Iraq might start even sooner. The place of the two old parties is taken now by two new parties, the Party of Peace and the War Party.

The Party of Peace wants to keep America out of foreign adventures, revitalise the economy and improve the life of an ordinary American. A spokesman for peace, the writer Gore Vidal, called to uphold the values of the Republic and to reject the Imperial ambitions.

The War Party wants to turn the US into a fighting machine for alien interests, to destroy Iraq, seize Saudi Arabia, reshape the Middle East and turn Israel into the new centre of the world. The Jewish Lobby became the moving force of the War Party. It is not a sincere Jewish worry about their coreligionists in the Middle East.

God knows, there are enough Jews in the Peace party as well. Noam Chomsky, Howard Zinn and many others upheld peace and rejected World War Three. But organised Jewry ('the Jews' as opposed to 'Jews') chose the war hoping to make the

Jewish state the most powerful force in world politics. They demanded a fealty oath from any politician, and a promise to obey the instructions of the Jewish Lobby, not only about the marginal [for Americans] question of Palestine, but also about the central question of power in the US. Cynthia refused it.

Cynthia McKinney became a target of the Jewish Lobby/War Party, as she was loyal, stubborn, honest and kind. Loyal, she considered her loyalty was due to her voters, the people of Georgia. Stubborn, Cynthia won't pledge blind support to Israel. Honest, she won't take money from her voters' pockets and send it to Tel Aviv. Kind woman, she won't send Georgian boys to their death in the river valleys of Iraq and deserts of Arabia in the looming World War Three. For an Afro-American, it makes no sense to imperil his country in war for the sake of a state whose symbol is a barbed wire fence around the native ghetto. It makes no sense for other candidates, as well, unless they are hell-bent to get to power, or just bent.

Her mistake was to rely upon the Democrats. It would be better if she would have run as an Independent. Both "old parties" were made irrelevant by reliance on one force, the single-minded media network of Israel's supporters. They should be counteracted by a new force, pro-peace, rejecting imperialism and based on a new vision. Mercifully, people are increasingly tired of the two-party system trap. It is time to change patterns, to form new alliances, and to reject the old rivalries and hatred, first and foremost, the interracial strife.

Notes

115. See my "Ode to Cynthia."
116. Stephen Zunes's "Don't Blame the Jews for Cynthia McKinney's Defeat" (Aug. 26).
117. "A Reply to Stephen Zunes on the Jews and Cynthia McKinney's Defeat," by Edward S. Herman, CommonDreams.org., Tuesday, August 27, 2002.
118. "The Purge of Joe Sobran And The Axis Of Evil: How Letting The Neo-Cons Gain Control Has Brought The Nation To The Brink Of War," by Bill White, www.overthrow.com.

Divide and Rule

I

The Congresswoman Cynthia McKinney, a member from Georgia, was derailed by the Jewish Lobby, as she did not want to pledge blind support to the Jewish state. The blind support of Israel is a modern fealty oath, a promise given by a politician to obey the instructions of the Jewish Lobby, not only about the marginal [for Americans] question of Palestine, but about the central question of power in the US. This power could not be sustained without some Black support.

A top Jewish official, Stephen Steinlight, Director of National Affairs at the American Jewish Committee,[119] frankly called the Jews to maintain "our present privilege, success and political power" by undermining the meagre influence of Blacks, Latinos and other non-whites, as "they harbour no feelings of guilt and see the Jews only as the most privileged and powerful of white Americans." He proposed to use "the Jewish power disproportionately concentrated in Hollywood, TV and news industry" in order to "divide and conquer" various communities of Americans.

II

This drive to "divide and conquer" was the motive of the long "special relationship" between the Blacks and the Jews. It began in the 1950s and 60s, when the American Jews were the most important and powerful friends of the Blacks. Two-thirds of Freedom Riders, the young men from the North, who came down South to wake the Blacks up, were Jews.[120] It sounds like a fairy tale; for nowadays, the policies of the Jewish community are anything but egalitarian, but before 1968, Jewish activists inspired the Blacks of the South to fight for their civil rights, and brought unrest to the campuses. They were supported by very unlikely allies, by the crème of the Jewish community, New York bankers and newspaper owners.

It was an unexpected alliance, for in the past, the Jews have been prominent slave-traders. In the West Indies, the slave trade was in Jewish hands since the Sixteenth century. The Jews in the US utilised their connections in the West Indies and brought the Black slaves to the plantations of the South. An important Jewish leader, Rabbi Isaac Mayer Wise, opposed Lincoln and supported the right "to buy and sell black savages."[121] It is often said that the Jewish tradition stands for human dignity and equality, but Maimonides, the greatest Jewish religious authority, denied humanity of Blacks and approved of slavery.[122]

The Jewish support of the Blacks' rights could be conceived as a tactical move designed to promote the Jewish interests by using the Blacks' anger and energy. In these days, the Jews were still a separate social body, outside of the traditional elites, 'pariah elite' in the words of witty Lenni Brenner. Facing the assault of the Blacks led by Jewish activists, the old elites were forced to open the doors to the Jews. With integration of the Jewish elite into the new elite of America, the Jewish activism collapsed. The revolution of '68 was betrayed. Previously liberal Jewish newspapers like the *New York Times* began to preach a new agenda: the bracing mix of neo-liberalism and Jewish supremacy. The activists disappeared, went into business, opened furniture shops, or were marginalized, as if they were satisfied to establish 'meritocracy', the foundation stone of the New World Order.

The Black foot-soldiers of the revolution remained without their partners—even worse: they were attacked by yesterday's allies. Martin Luther King was assassinated when his movement for equality and integration of the Blacks went too far; as far as wealthy Jewish suburbs. When the Blacks started to move into the privileged areas in the North, King was killed and the civil rights movement was rolled back. The suburbs remained Jewish and the Blacks remained in their ghetto, I was told by a prominent Jewish American participant of the events.

The Jewish volte-face began in 1967, according to Lenni Brenner,[123] when the predominantly Jewish teachers and lawyers of New York went into action to stop Black children from receiving proper education and competing for jobs: "Them niggers can't even keep their cotton pickin' hands off our graft," as he put it.

III

An outsider would imagine that we Jews are professional double-dealers; that we preached the rights of the Blacks but planned just to use them and promote our own agenda. But I am not an outsider, and this sort of duplicity can not be imagined outside of fiction. The young Jewish activists of pre-'68 America were sincere people, but their success was partly due to support of their parents, of Jewish banking and media elite. When the elite made a full turn around, the revolutionaries were lost, as soldiers forgotten by their commanders far beyond enemy lines. It was a deep personal tragedy for many of them. A small remainder of the Jewish progressive forces survived the shift, but it was not reinforced by younger members of the community. After 1968, the young and dynamic Jews were sent by their parents to Israel, hitherto a far-away place of little importance.

It is often said that the great and impressive victory of Israeli forces in the Six Day War of 1967 caused this turn to Zionism. But this claim (stated by Norman Finkelstein and others) does not survive critical examination. In 1956, Israel achieved no less of a spectacular victory, but the American Jews were not interested. In 1968, they turned to Israel for a very different reason: Zionism was promoted as an alternative cause for the young Jewish activists to keep them off the revolutionary course.

The betrayal of the equality cause by the Jewish elite was a rational step. Revolution is similar to a marriage: people enter it for different reasons. Whenever the traditional elites lose, it is the big time for the next-in-line. Betrayal (Thermidor, in terms of French Revolution) is a normal bourgeois response to successful revolution going too far. The Jewish elite did not care about Blacks, about equality or about flower-power, but just used it to undermine the traditional structure of the society.

Incidentally, this U-turn derailed the old anti-Semitism, as it had strong right-wing roots. Anti-Semites used to view Jews as crypto-Communists, but after 1970, even Genghis Khan would not have believed it. The left-wing contained too many pre-'68 Jews and did not understand why it was ditched by the previously friendly Jewish community. Only now, as the generation changed, lamentations have been replaced by anger.[124]

"The fortunes of the American Jewish population changed from humble beginnings to the present position of wealth, power and influence," wrote Anton Baumgarten[125] and asked: "What were the turning points of this development? When and how did the Jewish bourgeoisie gain entrance into the largely anti-Semitic Establishment and, especially, into its holy of holies, the big finance capital, Wall Street? What role if any did the 'civil rights movement' of the '60s, with the *New York Times* as its mouthpiece, have in promoting not only the rights of black people but of Jewish bankers as well ("the cunning of history")?"

The U-turn became evident soon, as the Jews fought affirmative action, besmirched independent Black activists and suborned others. In 1978, National Security Adviser Zbigniew Brzezinsky compiled a secret confidential memo NSC-46, calling to fight the Black movement in the US as the Afro-Americans naturally oppose the Jewish supremacists. This call was heard, and the armed gangs of the Jewish community, the Jewish Defence League, targeted, assassinated and framed the Black leaders, McKinney told her supporters. The FBI connived with the Jewish Defense League as it still does: though this terrorist gang is outlawed, it freely operates in the United States and in Israel.

The most promising black diplomat Andy Young was dismissed from service and his career was terminated when he dared to show some independence of spirit. He was followed by others, all the way to Cynthia, as the Jewish minders kept the blacks under their control. It is not strange that the positions of the Afro-Americans went downhill, while the positions of American Jews, their former allies, constantly improved.

IV

Last year I visited Atlanta, Cynthia McKinney's home town. It is a modern soulless megalopolis of high rise office buildings and the usual suburban spread of rather segregated neighbourhoods. No spirit of Scarlet O'Hara or her black companion haunted the place. I was a guest of Emory University, supposedly the best in the state. I came to preach the idea of integration of Jews and Palestinians in the Holy Land. The Jewish students' organisation objected to integration and called for a boycott. They offered to pay all expenses, just cancel the lecture and kill my message. In the end, the lecture went on, but I still haven't received even my travel expenses back from Emory.

In Atlanta, I saw the true beneficiary of the great struggle for Blacks' liberation. After bussing and fights with KKK, and after many Black casualties, the Jewish students now constitute forty per cent of the elite Emory, while the Blacks, the plurality of Atlanta, retain a statutory 10% presence. The Jewish students do not come to the university from integrated schools their fathers and uncles demanded: they go to superb private segregated schools.

The blacks do not compete with the Jews in the universities, as they are preferred tenants of privately-managed and profit-making jails. While the percent of Jewish students increased, "the number of black men in jail has grown five-fold," reported the *New York Times*,[126] and there are "more black men behind bars than are enrolled in colleges." Twenty years ago, there were one hundred fifty thousand black prisoners and half a million black students. Now eight hundred thousand blacks are in jail and only six hundred thousand are enrolled in colleges or universities.

The Blacks began to understand that they've got a raw deal. The Black Commentator[127] summed up the feelings of many Afro-Americans:

"The electoral defeat of Rep. Cynthia McKinney signals the end of any "special relationship" between African Americans and mainstream organized American Jewry. The final break has been a long time in the making; the relentless attacks on affirmative action mounted by mainstream Jewish groups beginning in the Seventies sundered Black-Jewish connections. But when the relationship is truly over, both parties will know it.

"Jewish American mainstream organizations have fallen under the sway of racist right-wingers in both Israel and the United States. They have acted in concert with the Christian and corporate Hard Right to undermine Black political cohesion and independence. They promote the careers of Black surrogates to thwart the genuine aspirations of the people. This is the conduct of an enemy.

These organizations have acted with cruel, gratuitous arrogance. They brag and strut, revelling in their power to intervene in the politics of the Black community. They have lied and smeared and, yes, conspired to foist their own candidates upon Black people. On the Jewish Left, the near-silence is appalling. To us, that signifies either cowardice or capitulation to the racists of the congregation."

These words wouldn't mean much: the Black-Jewish 'special relationship' was declared[128] dead long ago, but the rumours of its death were premature. However, now the Jewish leadership, in a new sharp turn of policies, decided to support a racist agenda. I wrote about this shift in Poisoning Wells:[129]

"They steal our money and rape our daughters"—this concept is promoted by the Jewish propaganda network, this globe-embracing conglomerate of media moguls, obedient journalists and deferential university professors. Hitler or Stalin never had such a network at their disposal. The mighty machine rolled out the Ku Klux Klan scaremongering image of a crouching dark-skinned rapist, lusting after the white skin and golden hair of Aryan maidens of Denmark. Imported from the great KKK-worshipping silent movie by Griffith, *Birth of a Nation*, the racist image opens a new film of *Men in Black II*: big Negro with big knife and big teeth attacks a White woman in the park. The film was produced by Stephen Spielberg, the creator of *Schindler's List*."

V

The Afro-Americans should think of a new mode of action, look for new allies and prove their ability to act independently. The debacle of Cynthia shows that two officially established parties offer no way out. They take the blacks for granted. Mercifully, people are increasingly tired of the two-party system trap. It is time to change patterns, to form new alliances, and to reject the old rivalries and hatred.

The people of the South: blacks, whites, Native Americans and immigrants have to live together and decide the future of the South. Much of the inter-communal hostility was imported from New York for 'Divide and Rule' purposes.[130] The most extreme groups, from the KKK to the Black Panthers, had connections in the same circles.

A few days ago, the *New York Times*[131] made an unusual promotion campaign for a racist Rev. Matt Hale, "America's scariest hatemonger." Francis Boyle, the well-known lawyer and a friend of Palestine, responded to this write-up: "Hale was nothing more than a small time Central Illinois bigot and racist until Dershowitz came along, and deliberately gave Hale tens of millions of dollars of free publicity in the world's news media in order to promote his violent racial hatred against Blacks, Jews, Asians and now Latinos and Native Americans. The [Jewish] Anti-Defamation League also supported Hale."

The people of the South should understand who promoted the divisions of the past and reject it. Confrontational approach leads nowhere, and it is good that there is readiness to proceed from disunity to cooperation. The legacy of slavery does not have to mean an eternal confrontation. The Russian peasants were freed from their serfdom in 1861, almost simultaneously with the Blacks' liberation. However, now a descendant of a Russian serf feels no animosity toward the descendant of a Russian squire, and vice versa.

The War Party media and opinion-making bodies stand in the way of peaceful coexistence, as they actively demonise all parts of the Southern population. They present the white folks as white supremacists, racists, and a lynching mob. They present blacks as criminals, lazy, and layabouts. They present immigrants as nasty Usama fanatics. However in Atlanta, the local folks who cherish the heritage of Confederacy understood their true interests, and actively supported McKinney.

Memory of the Confederacy does not have to divide; it could be uniting glue, as there were many blacks and Native Americans in the defeated army as well. It is not a secret that so-called whites and blacks of the South are often brothers or cousins. This division could become as irrelevant as the division of Yaman and Kais among the Arabs. The Civil War ruined the South for many years; it brought no happiness to blacks or local whites. Its memories kept the South divided, while the power eluded the people. However, the Southerners of all shades of skin can live together in mutual respect, rejecting the Divide and Rule goading.

Notes

119. http://www.cis.org/articles/2001/back1301.html.
120. "Arthur Liebman, Jews and the Left," quoted by Lenni Brenner, *Jews in America Today*, p. 227.
121. Hertzberg, Jews in America.
122. You will not find these words of Maimonides in the English translation, as they were suppressed by the American Jewish publishers, but remained intact in the Hebrew version. Noted by Israel Shahak in his *3000 Years of Jewish Religion*.
123. Lenni Brenner, *the Jews in America*, Saki Books: London.
124. See "Love's Labours Lost," on www.israelshamir.net.
125. Left.ru magazine.
126. "Study Finds Big Increase in Black Men as Inmates, by Fox Butterfield, *New York Times*, August 28, 2002.
127. http://www.blackcommentator.com/10_letter_to_readers.html.
128. *Broken Alliance: The Turbulent Times Between Blacks And Jews In America*, by Jonathan Kaufmann, Charles Scribner's Sons, 1988.
129. See www.israelshamir.net.
130. See "Divide and Rule." www.israelshamir.net.
131. Nicholas D. Kristof, *New York Times*, August 30, 2002.

Conclusion

Private Peace Treaty

The most recent massacre in the Holy Land, this time of fourteen men, women and children near Gaza, was described by our Prime Minister, General Sharon, as "a necessary and successful operation." He also promised more of the same, and there is no reason to doubt his word. There is no reason to doubt the reprisals, promised by the relatives of the murdered folks, either. This war will go on forever, and an anonymous IDF colonel advised the *New York Times* correspondent amidst ruins of Nablous that "we are in the middle of Hundred Year War." Thank you for the good news!

An ancient Greek farmer, the main character of the funniest comedy by Aristophanes, Acharnians, found himself in a similar predicament. His country was run by a General Lamachus, an early version of General Sharon, hell-bent on waging wars of domination. Tired of endless struggle, ruined economy, war drums instead of music, funerals instead of weddings, the farmer-hero Dicaeopolis strikes a separate peace treaty with the Spartans.

It makes a world of difference. On one end of the stage, the General asks for more swords, on the other end, the Farmer calls out for more sausages. I want a new system of air-to-air missiles, bellows the general. Bring me more wine and blondes, yells the Farmer. In the apotheosis, Dicaeopolis chairs a great feast, while beaten up Lamachus heavily slumps down.

This solution, offered in 425 BC, is still valid. I signed a separate peace treaty with all my neighbours in the Middle East. As for me, Syrian children may come and swim in the Sea of Galilee, and children of Palestine are welcome to the amusement parks of Tel Aviv, while I shall sip Lebanese *arak* at Bardaouni in Ramallah. The refugees of Gaza may come back to the fields they owned before 1948, and deal directly with the few old Polish Jews who "privatised" the lands.

Keep me out of it. In Israel, there are no more lands belonging to all of us. Every strip of land, every drop of water was carefully privatised. Now, let the happy new owners pay for whatever they need, including new defence systems, the army expenses, fences and other useful devices. Maybe when they see the bill they'll rather opt for a new soft armchair and a separate peace.

This vast undoing of collective property and dismantling of remnants of socialism should be completed. It is the right time to bring more hard-nosed neo-liberalism into daily use. While an increasing number of unemployed

Israelis have taken to stealing food from public hospitals, the Army still gets what it wants anytime it asks. This socialist easy-going approach should be stopped. If generals want a new aircraft, let them chip in and buy one, on the free market, without government subsidies. Sharon can barter his sheep for the bright new state-of-art toys from McDonnell Douglas. And if it would not suffice, I can offer him the advice of my wise late grandmother: if you have no money, do not buy arms.

The same advice could be given to our American friends and allies. They calculated that the war in Iraq will cost 800 billion dollars. In my opinion, until the people of America see at least double this amount in ready cash produced up front by Richard Perle and other Zionist warmonger agents of influence, they should not bestir themselves. And do not take personal cheques!

Even better advice: join A Separate Peace, and if Sharon calls upon you, reply to him as I do:

"General, if you want war, please wage it personally. And do not call us, we shall call you."

Acknowledgements

This book was written thanks to the efforts of many people. I am indebted to Noam Chomsky and Norman Finkelstein, Michael Neumann and Edward Herman, Marc Ellis and Edward Said for their support, advice and encouragement.

Albert Lindemann, Kevin MacDonald, William Dalrymple, the late Israel Shahak and Leon Gumilev provided me with their important historical perspective. My dear friends and combatants, Hans Olav Brendberg and Knut Bergem of Norway; Miguel Martinez, Susanne Scheidt and Roberto Gianmarco of Italy; Paul Badde of Germany; Marcel Charbonnier, Maria Poumier, Xavier Lavaud, Brigitte Faoder, Christian Chantegrel; Istvan Lovas of Hungary; Anton Baumgarten of Russia; Bob Green, Jeff Blankfort, Alison Weir, Miriam Reik, Eugenie Trone, John Williams, Rima Anabtawi, Ahmad Amr, and Jennifer Loewenstein in the US gave me much needed feed-back, translated my essays and occasionally corrected my follies.

Israeli scholars Paul Wexler and Israel Jacob Yuval provided me with a shining example of intellectual daring. I am grateful to Father Atallah Hanna of the Orthodox church and Father Raed of the Catholic church for their spiritual guidance.

The manuscript was edited by Sophie Johnson in Australia, to whom I owe a great debt of gratitude. I would like to thank many people, but in the present political climate their names must remain locked in my memory.

The ideas behind the book were formed in reckless discussions with Alice Shamir, my partner, friend and spiritual light. My son Yohanan put some of these ideas into action by his stand at the Church of the Nativity.

My Palestinian and Israeli friends, city folk and peasants were the main reason for this book being written. The ultimate source of inspiration was the unique land of Palestine and its holy protectors.

—Israel Adam Shamir

About the Author

A Jewish folk tale relates of a mute child who has never said a word despite the efforts of many doctors. Once, at a ripe age of ten, he dropped his spoon and cried out, "The soup is too salty!" His parents asked him in amazement why he kept silence for years, and the child replied, "Until now, everything was all right."

That is the story of Israel Shamir's sudden appearance in the English-language media. This leading Russian-Israeli intellectual, writer, translator and journalist, was well known to his Russian readers, thanks to his books, *The Pine and the Olive* and *Travels in Japan*, and to his translations of Joyce, Homer and Agnon into his native Russian. He did not write in English until January 2001, when Israeli attacks on Palestinians forced him to give up literature and turn to politics. His articles appeared on the Internet, were placed on many sites, reprinted by numerous newspapers and magazines, and translated into many languages. By using the Internet, Shamir proved that a word of freedom can overcome any censorship.

A native of Novosibirsk, Siberia, grandson of a professor of mathematics and descendant of a Rabbi from Tiberias, Palestine, Shamir studied at the prestigious School of the Academy of Sciences, and read Math and Law at Novosibirsk University. In 1969, he moved to Israel, served as a paratrooper in the army and fought in the 1973 war. After the military service, he resumed his study of Law at Hebrew University of Jerusalem, but abandoned the legal profession in pursuit of a career as a journalist and writer. He got his first taste of journalism with Israel Radio, and later went freelance. His varied assignments included covering Vietnam, Laos and Cambodia in the last stages of the war in South East Asia. In 1975, Shamir joined the BBC and moved to London. In 1977–79 he wrote for the Israeli daily *Maariv* and other papers from Japan. While in Tokyo, he wrote *Travels with My Son*, his first book, and translated a number of Japanese classics.

After returning to Israel in 1980, Shamir wrote for the Israeli daily newspaper *Haaretz* and *Al Hamishmar* and worked in the Knesset as the spokesman for the Israel Socialist Party (Mapam). He translated the works of S.Y. Agnon, the only Hebrew Nobel Prize winning writer, from the original Hebrew to Russian. His work was published and reprinted many times in both Israel and in Russia. He also translated selected chapters of Joyce's *Ulysses*, which were well received by publishers in Moscow, Tel Aviv, New York and Austin, Texas. Another of his translations, the *Israeli-Arab Wars* by President Herzog, was published in

London. His most popular work, *The Pine and the Olive*, the story of Palestine/Israel, was published in 1988. Its cover carried a painting by the Ramallah painter, Nabil Anani.

As the first Palestinian Intifada began, Shamir had left Israel for Russia, where he covered the eventful years 1989–1993. While in Moscow, he reported for *Haaretz*, but was sacked for publishing an article calling for the return of the Palestinian refugees and rebuilding of their ruined villages. He wrote for various Russian newspapers and magazines, including the daily *Pravda* and *Zavtra* weekly. In 1993, he returned to Israel and settled in Jaffa. He wrote for Russian newspapers both in Israel and Russia and contributed to various literary magazines. During this period, Shamir also worked on a new translation of the *Odyssey*, which was published in 2000 in St. Petersburg, Russia. His next big project was translating a Hebrew medieval Talmudic manuscript into Russian.

In response to the second Palestinian Intifada, Shamir has abandoned his literary occupation and resumed his work as a journalist. In the midst of the endless talk of a "Two State Solution," Shamir, along with Edward Said, has become a leading champion of the 'One Man, One Vote, One State' solution in all of Palestine/Israel. His most recent essays have been circulating widely on the Internet and are now posted on many prominent media sites. With every new article, Shamir is establishing himself as a journalist whose work speaks to the aspirations of both the Israelis and the Palestinians. Shamir (50) lives in Jaffa, he is the father of two sons.

Index

IF YOU LIKED THIS BOOK, YOU WON'T WANT TO MISS OTHER TITLES BY DANDELION BOOKS

Available Now And Always Through www.dandelionbooks.net And Affiliated Websites!!

TOLL-FREE ORDERS—1-800-861-7899 (U.S. & CANADA)

Non-Fiction

Stranger than Fiction: An Independent Investigation Of The True Culprits Behind 9-11, by Albert D. Pastore, Ph.D... Twelve months of careful study, painstaking research, detailed analysis, source verification and logical deduction went into the writing of this book. In addition to the stories are approximately 300 detailed footnotes Pastore: "Only by sifting through huge amounts of news data on a daily basis was I able to catch many of these rare 'diamonds in the rough' and organize them into a coherent pattern and logical argument." (ISBN 1-893302-47-4)

Unshackled: A Survivor's Story of Mind Control, by Kathleen Sullivan... A non-fictional account of Kathleen Sullivan's experiences as part of a criminal network that includes Intelligence personnel, military personnel, doctors and mental health professionals contracted by the military and the CIA, criminal cult leaders and members, pedophiles, pornographers, drug dealers and Nazis. "I believe my story needs to be told so that more people will understand how 'Manchurian Candidate' style mind-control techniques can create alter-states in the minds of unwitting victims, causing them to perform deeds that are normally repugnant." (ISBN 1-893302-35-0)

Ahead Of The Parade: A Who's Who Of Treason and High Crimes—Exclusive Details Of Fraud And Corruption Of The Monopoly Press, The Banks, The Bench And The Bar, And The Secret Political Police, by Sherman H. Skolnick... One of America's foremost investigative reporters, speaks out on some of America's current crises. Included in this blockbuster book are the following articles: Big City Newspapers & the Mob, The Sucker Traps, Dirty Tricks of Finance and Brokerage, The Secret History of Airplane Sabotage, Wal-Mart and the Red Chinese Secret Police, The Chandra Levy Affair, The Japanese Mafia in the United States, The Secrets of Timothy McVeigh, and much more. (ISBN 1-893302-32-6)

Another Day In The Empire: Life in Neoconservative America, by Kurt Nimmo... A collection of articles by one of Counterpunch's most popular columnists. Included in this collection are: The Son of COINTELPRO; Clueless at the State Department; Bush Senior: Hating Saddam, Selling Him Weapons; Corporate Media: Selling Dubya's Oil War; Iraq and the Vision of the Velociraptors: The Bleeding Edge of Islam; Condoleezza Rice at the Waldorf Astoria; Predators, Snipers and the Posse Comitatus Act, and many others. (ISBN 1-893302-75-X)

Palestine & The Middle East: Passion, Power & Politics, by Jaffer Ali... The Palestinian struggle is actually a human one that transcends Palestine... There is no longer a place for Zionism in the 20th century... Democracy in the Middle East is not safe for US interests as long as there is an atmosphere of hostility... Suicide bombings are acts of desperation and mean that a people have been pushed to the brink... failure to understand why they happen will make certain they will continue. Jaffer Ali is a Palestinian-American business man who has been writing on politics and business for over 25 years. (ISBN 1-893302-45-8)

America, Awake! We Must Take Back Our Country, by Norman D. Livergood... This book is intended as a wake-up call for Americans, as Paul Revere awakened the Lexington patriots to the British attack on April 18, 1775, and as Thomas Paine's *Common Sense* roused apathetic American colonists to recognize and struggle against British oppression. Our current situation is similar to that which American patriots faced in the 1770s: a country ruled by "foreign" and "domestic" plutocratic powers and a divided citizenry uncertain of their vital interests. (ISBN 1-893302-27-X)

"Evil Fire Made to Burn"—A True Account of the World's Greatest Cover-Up, by Dan Eden [Gary Vey]... In the spirited Indiana Jones tradition, Gary Vey, editor of an internet underground website, viewzone.com, finds himself transported from a sleepy New England suburb to a waking nightmare in the barren Alaskan tundra, the unpredictable vortices of Yemen and ultimately the wilderness of the Australian Outback. Eden accidentally stumbles into what turns out to be the most startling revelation of his life. Besieged by his newly-discovered destiny as prophesied translator of ancient texts, he learns he holds the key for unlocking secrets that have the power to change the course of history. From that point on, Eden becomes one of the most wanted—and haunted—persons on the planet. (ISBN 1-893302-41-5)

The Perennial Tradition: Overview Of The Secret Heritage, The Single Stream Of Initiatory Teaching Flowing Through All The Great Schools Of Mysticism, by Norman D. Livergood... Like America, Awake, this book is another wake-up call. "It was written to assist readers to awaken to the Higher Spiritual World." In addition to providing a history of the Western tradition of the Perennial Tradition, Livergood also describes the process that serious students use to actually *realize*—bring to manifestation—their Higher Consciousness. "Unless we become aware of this higher state, we face the prospect of a basically useless physical existence and a future life—following physical death—of unpleasant, perhaps anguished reformation of our essence." (ISBN 1-893302-48-2)

The Awakening of An American: How America Broke My Heart, by Meria Heller, with a Foreword by Catherine Austin Fitts... A collection of choice interviews from Meria Heller's world-famous www.meria.net rapidly growing radio network that reaches millions of people daily. Dr. Arun Gandhi, Greg Palast, Vincent Bugliosi, Mark Elsis, William Rivers Pitt, Mark Rechtenwald, Nancy Oden & Bob Fertik, Howard Winant, Linda Starr, Dave Chandler, Bev Conover, John Nichols, Robert McChesney, Norman Solomon, Stan Goff and Mark Crispin Miller. (ISBN 1-893302-39-3)

America's Nightmare: The Presidency of George Bush II, by John Stanton & Wayne Madsen... Media & Language, War & Weapons, Internal Affairs and a variety of other issues pointing out the US "crisis without precedent" that was wrought by the US Presidential election of 2000 followed by 9/11. "Stanton & Madsen will challenge many of the things you've been told by CNN and Fox news. This book is dangerous." (ISBN 1-893302-29-6)

America's Autopsy Report, by John Kaminski... The false fabric of history is unraveling beneath an avalanche of pathological lies to justify endless war and Orwellian new laws that revoke the rights of Americans. While TV and newspapers glorify the dangerous ideas of perverted billionaires, the Internet has pulsated with outrage and provided a new and real forum for freedom among concerned people all over the world who are opposed to the mass murder and criminal exploitation of the defenseless victims of multinational corporate totalitarianism. John Kaminski's passionate essays give voice to those hopes and fears of humane people that are ignored by the big business shysters who rule the major media. (ISBN 1-893302-42-3)

Seeds Of Fire: China And The Story Behind The Attack On America, by Gordon Thomas... The inside story about China that no one can afford to ignore. Using his unsurpassed contacts in Israel, Washington, London and Europe, Gordon Thomas, internationally acclaimed best-selling author and investigative reporter for over a quarter-century, reveals information about China's intentions to use the current crisis to launch itself as a super-power and become America's new major enemy... "*This has been kept out of the news agenda because it does not suit certain business interests to have that truth emerge... Every patriotic American should buy and read this book... it is simply revelatory.*" (Ray Flynn, Former U.S. Ambassador to the Vatican) (ISBN 1-893302-54-7)

Shaking The Foundations: Coming Of Age In The Postmodern Era, by John H. Brand, D. Min., J.D.... Scientific discoveries in the Twentieth Century require the restructuring of our understanding of the nature of Nature and of human beings. In simple language the author explains how significant implications of quantum mechanics, astronomy, biology and brain physiology form the foundation for new perspectives to comprehend the meaning of our lives. (ISBN 1-893302-25-3)

Rebuilding The Foundations: Forging A New And Just America, by John H. Brand, D. Min., J.D.... Should we expect a learned scholar to warn us about our dangerous reptilian brains that are the real cause of today's evils? Although Brand is not without hope for rescuing America, he warns us to act fast–and now. Evil men intent on imposing their political, economic, and religious self-serving goals on America are not far from achieving their goal of mastery." (ISBN 1-893302-33-4)

Democracy Under Siege: The Jesuits' Attempt To Destroy the Popular Government Of The United States; The True Story of Abraham Lincoln's Death; Banned For Over 100 Years, This Information Now Revealed For The First Time! by C.T. Wilcox... U.S. President Lincoln was the triumphant embodiment of the New Concept of Popular Government. Was John Wilkes Booth a Jesuit patsy, hired to do the dirty work for the Roman Catholic church—whose plan, a well-kept secret until now—was to overthrow the American Government? (ISBN 1-893302-31-8)

The Last Atlantis Book You'll Ever Have To Read! by Gene D. Matlock... More than 25,000 books, plus countless other articles have been written about a fabled confederation of city-states known as Atlantis. If it really did exist, where was it located? Does anyone have valid evidence of its existence—artifacts and other remnants? According to historian, archaeologist, educator and linguist Gene D. Matlock, both questions can easily be answered. (ISBN 1-893302-20-2)

The Courage To Be Who I Am, by Mary-Margareht Rose... This book is rich with teachings and anecdotes delivered with humor and humanness, by a woman who followed her heart and learned to listen to her inner voice; in the process, transforming every obstacle into an opportunity to test her courage to manifest her true identity. (ISBN 1-893302-13-X)

The Making Of A Master: Tracking Your Self-Worth, by Jeanette O'Donnal... A simple tracking method for self-improvement that takes the mystery out of defining your goals, making a road map and tracking your progress. A book rich with nuggets of wisdom couched in anecdotes and instructive dialogues. (ISBN 1-893302-36-9)

The Clear and Simple Way: The Angel Lessons, by Judith Parsons... a book about heart, with heart. Parsons, known throughout the world for her spiritual workshops and seminars, shows us how to transform our lives into infinite "presents"—"gifts" and moment-by-moment experiences—of peace, joy and self-fulfillment. (ISBN 1-893302-43-1)

Cancer Doctor: The Biography Josef Issels, M.D., Who Brought Hope To The World With His Revolutionary Cancer Treatment, by Gordon Thomas... Dr. Josef Issels treated more than 12,000 cancer patients who had been written off as "incurable" by other doctors. He claimed no miracle cures, but the success record of his revolutionary "whole person treatment" was extraordinary... the story of his struggle against the medical establishment which put Dr. Issels in prison, charged with fraud and manslaughter. (ISBN 1-893302-18-0)

Fiction

Ticket to Paradise, by Yvonne Ridley... Judith Tempest, a British reporter, is searching for the Truth. But when it starts to spill out in her brilliant front page reportage of Middle East suicide bombing in retaliation for Israeli tanks mowing down innocent Palestinian women and children, both "Tempest" and "Truth" start to spell "Trouble"—with a capital "T", joke her friends and colleagues. A non-stop mystery thriller that tears along at a reckless pace of passion, betrayal, adventure and espionage. (ISBN 1-893302-77-6)

The Alley of Wishes, by Laurel Johnson... Despite the ravages of WWI on Paris and on the young American farm boy, Beck Sanow, and despite the abusive relationship that the chanteuse Cerise endures, the two share a bond that is unbreakable by time, war, loss of memory, loss of life and loss of youth. Beck and Cerise are both good people beset by constant tragedy. Yet it is tragedy that brings them together, and it is unconditional love that keeps them together. (ISBN 1-893302-46-6)

Freedom: Letting Go Of Anxiety And Fear Of The Unknown, by Jim Britt... Jeremy Carter, a fireman from Missouri who is in New York City for the day, decides to take a tour of the Trade Center, only to watch in shock, the attack on its twin towers from a block away. Afterward as he gazes at the pit of rubble and talks with many of the survivors, Jeremy starts to explore the inner depths of his soul, to ask questions he'd never asked before. This dialogue helps him learn who he is and what it takes to overcome the fear, anger, grief and anxiety this kind of tragedy brings. (ISBN 1-893302-74-1)

The Prince Must Die, by Gower Leconfield... breaks all taboos for mystery thrillers. After the "powers that be" suppressed the manuscripts of three major British writers, Dandelion Books breaks through with a thriller involving a plot to assassinate Prince Charles. *The Prince Must Die* brings to life a Britain of today that is on the edge with race riots, neo-Nazis, hard right backlash and neo-punk nihilists. Riveting entertainment... you won't be able to put it down. (ISBN 1-893302-72-5)

Waaaay Out There! Diggertown, Oklahoma, by Tuklo Nashoba... Adventures of constable Clint Mankiller and his deputy, Chad GhostWolf; Jim Bob and Bubba Johnson, Grandfather GhostWolf, Cassie Snodgrass, Doc Jones, Judge Jenkins and the rest of the Diggertown, Oklahoma bunch in the first of a series of Big Foot-Sasquatch tall tales peppered with lots of good belly laughs and just as much fun. (ISBN 1-893302-44-X)

Synchronicity Gates: An Anthology Of Stories And Poetry About People Transformed In Extraordinary Reality Beyond Experience, by Stephen Vernarelli... An inventive compilation of short stories that take the reader beyond mere science, fiction, or fantasy. Vernarelli introduces the reader to a new perception of reality; he imagines the best and makes it real. (ISBN 1-893302-38-5)

Daniela, by Stephen Weeks... A gripping epic novel of sexual obsession and betrayal as Nazi Prague falls. The harboring of deadly secrets and triumph of an enduring love against the hardest of times. Nikolei is a Polish/Ukrainian Jew who finds himself fighting among the Germans then turning against them to save Prague in 1945. Nikolei manages to hide himself among the Germans with a woman working as a prostitute. (ISBN 1-893302-37-7)

Unfinished Business, by Elizabeth Lucas Taylor... Lindsay Mayer knows something is amiss when her husband, Griffin, a college professor, starts spending too much time at his office and out-of-town. Shortly after the ugly truth surfaces, Griffin disappears altogether. Lindsay is shattered. Life without Griffin is life without life... One of the sexiest books you'll ever read! (ISBN 1-893302-68-7)

The Woman With Qualities, by Sarah Daniels... South Florida isn't exactly the Promised Land that forty-nine-year-old newly widowed Keri Anders had in mind when she transplanted herself here from the northeast... A tough action-packed novel that is far more than a love story. (ISBN 1-893302-11-3)

Weapon In Heaven, by David Bulley... Eddy Licklighter is in a fight with God for his very own soul. You can't mess around half-assed when fighting with God. You've got to go at it whole-hearted. Eddy loses his wife and baby girl in a fire. Bulley's protagonist is a contemporary version of the Old Testament character of Job. Licklighter wants nothing from God except His presence so he can kill him off. The humor, warmth, pathos and ultimate redemption of Licklighter will make you hold your sides with laughter at the same time you shed common tears for his "God-awful" dilemma. (ISBN 1-893302-28-8)

Adventure Capital, by John Rushing... South Florida adventure, crime and violence in a fiction story based on a true life experience. A book you will not want to put down until you reach the last page. (ISBN 1-893302-08-3)

A Mother's Journey: To Release Sorrow And Reap Joy, by Sharon Kay... A poignant account of Norah Ann Mason's life journey as a wife, mother and single parent. This book will have a powerful impact on anyone, female or male, who has experienced parental abuse, family separations, financial struggles and a desperate need to find the magic in life that others talk about that just doesn't seem to be there for them. (ISBN 1-893302-52-0)

Return To Masada, by Robert G. Makin... In a gripping account of the famous Battle of Masada, Robert G. Makin skillfully recaptures the blood and gore as well as the spiritual essence of this historic struggle for freedom and independence. (ISBN 1-893302-10-5)

Time Out Of Mind, by Solara Vayanian... Atlantis had become a snake pit of intrigue teeming with factious groups vying for power and control. An unforgettable drama that tells of the breakdown of the priesthood, the hidden scientific experiments in genetic engineering which produced "things"—part human and part animal—and other atrocities; the infiltration by the dark lords of Orion; and the implantation of the human body with a device to fuel the Orion wars. (ISBN 1-893302-21-0)

The Thirteenth Disciple: The Life Of Mary Magdalene, by Gordon Thomas... The closest of Jesus' followers, the name of Mary Magdalene conjures images of a woman both passionate and devoted, both sinner and saint. The first full-length biography for 13 centuries. (ISBN 1-893302-17-2)

ALL DANDELION BOOKS ARE AVAILABLE THROUGH WWW.DANDELIONBOOKS.NET... ALWAYS.

Printed in the United Kingdom
by Lightning Source UK Ltd.
103482UKS00001B/53